Lincoln Looks West
From the Mississippi to the Pacific

Edited by Richard W. Etulain

Southern Illinois University Press
Carbondale and Edwardsville

13 12 11 10   4 3 2 1

Library of Congress Cataloging-in-Publication Data
Lincoln looks West : from the Mississippi to the Pacific
/ edited by Richard W. Etulain.
    p. cm.
Includes bibliographical references and index.
ISBN-13: 978-0-8093-2961-8 (cloth : alk. paper)
ISBN-10: 0-8093-2961-1 (cloth : alk. paper)
ISBN-13: 978-0-8093-8558-4 (ebook)
ISBN-10: 0-8093-8558-9 (ebook)
1. Lincoln, Abraham, 1809–1865. 2. West (U.S.)—
Politics and government—19th century. 3. United
States—Territorial expansion—History—19th
century. 4. Slavery—United States—Extension to
the territories. I. Etulain, Richard W.
E457.2.L8335 2010
978'.02—dc22   2009021082

Printed on recycled paper. ♻
The paper used in this publication meets the minimum
requirements of American National Standard for Information Sciences—Permanence of Paper for Printed
Library Materials, ANSI Z39.48-1992. ∞

To Adam Scofield Partch,
a young Lincoln of the West

Contents

Preface ix

Abraham Lincoln and the Trans-Mississippi
American West: An Introductory Overview 1

1. Lincoln and the Mexican War: An Argument by Analogy 68
   Mark E. Neely Jr.

2. Lincoln, the West, and the Antislavery Politics of the 1850s 90
   Michael S. Green

3. Lincoln, the Thirteenth Amendment, and
   the Admission of Nevada 113
   Earl S. Pomeroy

4. Lincoln and the Territorial Patronage:
   The Ascendancy of the Radicals in the West 121
   Vincent G. Tegeder

5. Lincoln's New Mexico Patronage: Saving the
   Far Southwest for the Union 134
   Deren Earl Kellogg

6. The Tribe of Abraham: Lincoln and the Washington Territory 153
   Robert W. Johannsen

7. Dr. Anson G. Henry (1804–65): Lincoln's Junkyard Dog 174
   Paul M. Zall

8. The Mormon Connection: Lincoln, the Saints,
   and the Crisis of Equality 189
   Larry Schweikart

9. Lincoln and the Indians 210
    David A. Nichols

Lincoln and the American West:
    A Bibliographical Essay and a Bibliography 233

Contributors 251

Acknowledgments 253

Index 255

Preface

This volume attempts what no other book has done. Among the more than fifteen thousand books written about Abraham Lincoln, none has sketched out the full dimensions of his important connections with the trans-Mississippi American West. A few scholars have focused on one Lincoln link with the West, and a limited number of books present an episode or two of the story, but no one has traced the whole outline.

This book introduces readers to the two decades of Lincoln's major involvements with the West. The first essay provides an introductory overview of Lincoln's connections with the region beyond the Mississippi. In the first stage of his career, Lincoln defined himself as a "Man of the West" and adopted a plan of government-supported internal improvements that would be of central importance to his later dealings with the West. In the second stage, from roughly 1847 to 1861, Lincoln was forced to handle the controversial issues around slavery as a legislator and candidate, and as a result he accepted the Wilmot Proviso principle of no expansion of slavery into the western territories. In the third and most complex stage, Lincoln attempted both to deal with slavery in the West and to utilize the central government to develop the region economically. Lincoln's western patronage appointments and his political friendships were of major significance, helping to organize large sections of the West into federal territories and to establish the Republican Party in the region. Lincoln was also involved in Indian policy issues and conflicts, military decisions, and Reconstruction programs vitally important to the West.

The extensive introductory overview has two purposes: First, to provide readers with a compact story of Lincoln's ties to the West, from his first reactions to western issues in the 1840s until his final connections in early 1865. Second, to furnish brief introductions to all the topics expanded upon in the following essays.

These nine topical essays expand and deepen the discussions of Lincoln's western links introduced in the overview and furnish different, even alternative viewpoints on those subjects. The opening essay by Mark E. Neely Jr. provocatively argues for a less negative interpretation of Lincoln's opposition to the Mexican War. Then follows a newly written essay by Michael S. Green, expertly summarizing Lincoln's reactions to western issues of the 1850s. The next four selections—by Earl S. Pomeroy, Vincent G. Tegeder, Deren Earl Kellogg, and Robert W. Johannsen—deal with Lincoln's patronage appointments in the West, his most notable connection with the region. In another essay especially prepared for this collection, Paul M. Zall supplies an entertaining portrait of Anson G. Henry, Lincoln's close friend and political doctor in the Pacific Northwest. Larry Schweikart's essay summarizes Lincoln's dealings with the Mormons in Illinois and Utah. In the last of the topical essays, David A. Nichols, the author of the only book-length study of Lincoln and Indians, presents his findings in a thought-provoking essay.

These specific essays were chosen to provide discussions of most of Lincoln's major connections with the West. Those important links include Lincoln's opposition to the Mexican-American War and the extension of slavery into western territories, his political patronage decisions, his friendships in the West, and his attitudes toward and treatment of Mormons and Native Americans. Nearly half of the selections treat Lincoln's western political actions because those notable decisions were, by far, his most significant and time-consuming dealings with the West. Unfortunately, no first-rate, stand-alone essays on Lincoln's presidential support for a transcontinental railroad, a homestead act, and land-grant colleges are available.

Following the topical essays is a bibliographical essay and bibliography providing an overview of significant books and essays that deal with Lincoln and the American West. This discussion furnishes the fullest historiographical coverage now available on this important but largely overlooked subject of Lincoln's career.

A few words of explanation are necessary about the expansive West treated here. American historians often disagree about a definition of "the West." Some think of it as all of the United States from the Mississippi to the Pacific, others consider it the region west of the 100th meridian, and still others argue it is the area from the North Dakota to Texas range of states up to the eastern boundaries of the Pacific Coast states. Here the first, the largest, West is treated. Taking into consideration this expansive region allows for a fuller glimpse of Lincoln's numerous political, economic, and social dealings with the entire trans-Mississippi West.

As the volume editor, I hope that this collection, through the introduction, reprinted and newly written essays, and the bibliographical overview, will encourage new research and publication on Abraham Lincoln and the American West. The published materials gathered here, as well as primary documents in important Lincoln collections, in collections of his political friends and appointees, and in western regional and governmental archives, provide abundant sources for a fresh crop of essays and books on Lincoln and the West.

I am indebted to several friends and scholars for aid and encouragement in the preparation of this book. Several years ago, my colleague Ferenc (Frank) Szasz at the University of New Mexico challenged me to bring together my lifelong interest in Abraham Lincoln and my research specialty, the American West. More recently, my good friend G. Thomas Edwards provided a critical reading of one section of the introduction, helping to improve its arguments. I'm also grateful to Mike Green and Paul Zall for preparing new essays for this collection. I wish, too, to thank Sylvia Frank Rodrigue for contacting me about publishing this book with the Southern Illinois University Press. In all ways, she is a model for other editors. Finally, the book is dedicated to my young grandson, Adam Scofield Partch, already a fan of "Mr. Lincoln" and even now developing Lincoln-like qualities.

Lincoln Looks West

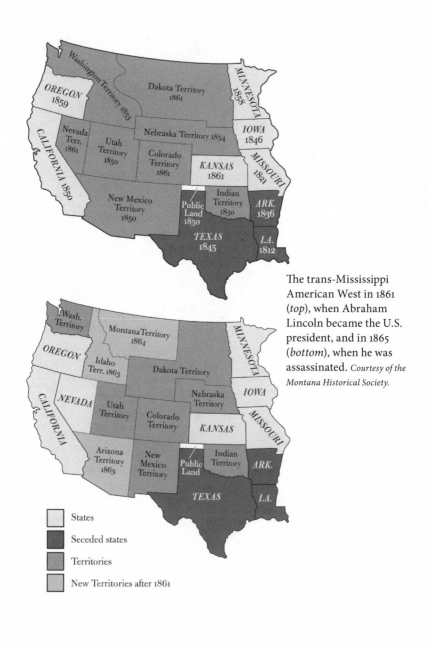

The trans-Mississippi American West in 1861 (*top*), when Abraham Lincoln became the U.S. president, and in 1865 (*bottom*), when he was assassinated. *Courtesy of the Montana Historical Society.*

States

Seceded states

Territories

New Territories after 1861

Abraham Lincoln and the Trans-Mississippi American West: An Introductory Overview

On the last day of his life, Abraham Lincoln was thinking about the American West. When Schuyler Colfax, Speaker of the House, visited the president in the White House on the morning of Good Friday, 14 April 1865, Lincoln requested Colfax to carry a message to miners in California. "Tell the miners," Lincoln directed, that he would "promote their interests to the utmost of . . . [his] ability; because their prosperity is the prosperity of the nation. And we shall prove in a very few years that we are indeed the Treasury of the world." He also told Colfax he was going "to try to attract" returning veterans to work in the western mines and point immigrants "from overcrowded Europe" "to the gold and silver that waits for them in the West." Colfax remembered too that Lincoln enthusiastically told him, "How I would rejoice to make that trip! . . . I can only envy you its pleasures."[1]

The same fateful Friday, as the president and his wife, Mary, took their accustomed afternoon carriage ride, Lincoln revealed to her his hope of their visiting California. They might even move to the West Coast—and not return to Illinois—because future opportunities promised much for their two sons on the West Coast.[2]

Before the Lincolns set out on their tragic trip to Ford's Theatre that evening, Lincoln dealt with patronage matters touching on the West. During his presidency, these time-consuming duties had eaten up more of his attention than any of his other connections with the region. On this day, he dealt with a commission for a judge and signed another commission naming a territorial governor, both in Nebraska, and appointed two territorial officials in Idaho. Also squeezed in were brief chats with California journalist Noah Brooks, William Pitt Kellogg of Nebraska, and the new senator from Nevada, William M. Stewart. Then Colfax returned for a few minutes of additional conversation about his trip to California. Lincoln seemed reluctant to let him go, perhaps thinking again vicariously about a trip to the West Coast. Finally, the Lincolns entered their carriage, and the president headed for his rendezvous with destiny.[3]

These brief encounters on Lincoln's final full day reflected his growing interests in the West from the 1840s onward. From the political controversies swirling around the annexation of Oregon and the Mexican-American War in the mid- and late 1840s, through the 1850s, and into his presidential administration from 1861 to 1865, Lincoln dealt with major issues involving the trans-Mississippi West. Historians have, understandably, focused on Lincoln's notable roles in several other endeavors: as a Whig and then a Republican leader who opposed the expansion of slavery in his prepresidential years; and as a military and political leader who fought the South in an all-encompassing civil war and managed to keep the federal ship afloat in the most vicious of domestic storms during his presidency. Those important roles and events obscure that Lincoln also became involved with the West—in national affairs as well as personally.[4]

Lincoln's connections with the trans-Mississippi West moved through three stages. From his early twenties into his mid-to-late thirties, he gradually defined himself as a "western man" and formulated a Whig political-economic credo that called for government support of internal improvements such as roads, canals, and railroads. But a second stage of Lincoln's links with the West began when he entered Congress in 1847. There he faced new issues, mainly slavery and its possible expansion, and began to subscribe to the Wilmot Proviso and its call for no extension of slavery into western territories. This emphasis dominated Lincoln's political career until he entered the White House in 1861.

In the third and most complex stage of Lincoln's ties to the West, he worked with several sets of issues. He supported congressional legislation that shaped the fate of the West through the creation of a transcontinental railroad, a homestead act, the Department of Agriculture, and land grants for agricultural education. Most complex of all, Lincoln dealt with literally hundreds of ambitious friends and others who were eventually appointed to positions of political leadership in western territories and states. As time allowed, he also turned his attention to slavery issues, military decisions, Indians policies, and Reconstruction efforts impinging on the West. In the four years of his presidency, Abraham Lincoln was intimately linked to the American West.[5]

Lincoln's earliest connections with the West surfaced in several ways. Although Lincoln was born in Kentucky and resided most of his life in the North, he was, like many other political leaders of Illinois (and sometimes also those of Ohio, Indiana, and Kentucky). considered a "western" man. Not until the mid-1840s, after the opening of the Oregon Trail, Texas's annexation, the Mormon exodus westward, the Mexican-American War, and the California Gold Rush, did many Americans begin to think of the territory beyond the Mississippi as different from an earlier West that included Lincoln's Illinois. By the time Lincoln entered the White House, states situated on or west of the Mississippi—that is, Minnesota, Iowa, Missouri, (even) Louisiana, Kansas, Texas, Arkansas, California, and Oregon—were considered part of "the West."

In Lincoln's time, labeling a person "a Westerner" or "Western man" carried ambivalent meanings. As American Studies scholar Henry Nash Smith demonstrated more than a half century ago in his classic book *Virgin Land: The American West as Symbol and Myth,* the West could represent bold, new, courageous opinions and actions and the American future. Conversely, a westerner might symbolize an uncouth, illiterate, and undesirable sociocultural wilderness. Natty Bumppo, the fictional hero of James Fenimore Cooper's Leatherstocking Tales, for example, could epitomize a fresh new frontier, but he might be depicted, too, as a wilderness barbarian who belched at dinner. These complex attitudes about and reactions to the West helped shape reactions to Lincoln and his depiction as a westerner. Lincoln, too, thought of himself as a Man of the West.[6]

Early, superficial reactions to Lincoln as a westerner were sometimes decidedly negative. Critics often commented on his backwoods appearance and his uncultured manner of speaking. When Lincoln first came to New Salem, Illinois, after leaving his family home, one viewer, noting his "homespun" clothing, "bushy hair," and "lank and tall" stature, concluded that Lincoln displayed "a rather Singular grotesque appearance." Another thought of him "as ruff a specimen of humanity as could be found." Some of these dissenting opinions about Lincoln's western appearance and qualities continued throughout his career. The negative voices were particularly shrill in 1860–61. "Lincoln is a third-rate western lawyer . . . who cannot speak good grammar, and who, to raise the wind delivers his hackneyed, illiterate compositions. . . . He is a stiff-necked, cold-blooded man . . . homely . . . uncouth," a journalist in Manchester, New Hampshire, wrote. Even more critical were southern newspapers: Lincoln is "an illiterate partisan without talents, without education" (*Richmond Enquirer*, 21 May 1860), and even more viciously, "a horrid looking wretch . . . a cross between the nutmeg dealer, the horse-swapper, and the night man. . . . He is a lank-sided Yankee of the unlovliest and of the dirtiest complexion" (*Charleston Mercury*).[7]

But others found much in Lincoln's western background to praise. They saluted his plainness, lack of pretension, and obvious connection with common people. While Lincoln was serving in Congress from 1847 to 1849, a journalist in Washington revealingly described the Illinois legislator's visits to the venerable New Englander Daniel Webster. At the august solon's home, "the Western congressman's humorous illustrations of the events of the day . . . [gave] great delight to 'the solid men of Boston' assembled around the festive board."[8] This reporter, as well as others, delighted in portraying the home-spun westerner entertaining the eastern elite with his vernacular ways.

But it was in 1860, during Lincoln's successful run for the Republican nomination, that popular images of Lincoln as a "Man of the West" became particularly widespread. At the raucous Republican nominating convention in Illinois in May, an event of reverberating symbolism occurred. Lincoln's cousin, John Hanks, and a colleague trotted into the assembly with a banner on which were emblazoned the words: "ABRAHAM LINCOLN. The Rail Candidate for President in 1860." With the banner came two fence rails Hanks claimed Lincoln had split. In attendance at the convention, Lincoln even laughingly admitted he might have mauled them. The crowd broke out in a cheer, and the "Railsplitter" candidate was born.[9]

From that day forward, Lincoln became the railsplitter candidate and then the railsplitter president. Republican newspapermen made much of the frontier image. "The nomination of Lincoln is demanded not only by the great West but by the people of all sections," the *Ohio Statesman* editorialized on 30 May 1860. Horace Greeley, the noted editor of the *New York Tribune*, expanded further than others on the meaning of Lincoln as a westerner in the fall of 1860: "That he splits rails is itself nothing; that a man who at twenty was splitting rails for a living is at fifty the chosen head of the greatest and most intelligent part in the land, soon to be head also of the Nation—this is much, is everything."[10] For these commentators, a western man had succeeded to the White House and promised a truly democratic administration based on his own frontier experiences and virtues.

Occasionally Lincoln even played on his western background. Sometimes he defined his "western" identity in terms of his occupational and class backgrounds. In his first run for public office in spring 1832, Lincoln told voters, "I was born and have remained in the most humble walks of life. I have no wealthy or popular relations to recommend me." Nearly thirty years later, he related to a Connecticut audience that he was "not ashamed to confess that twenty-five years ago I was a hired laborer, mauling rails, at work on a flat-boat—just what might happen to any poor man's son!" Lincoln sometimes burnished his western, rustic image. On his way to the second Lincoln-Douglas debate in Freeport on 27 August 1858, he rode in a "horse-drawn Conestoga wagon, seated alongside an escort of 'old-fashioned farmers.'" For the debate itself, he dressed down in plain, if not worn, coat and trousers and coarse boots, setting him off from the "richly" dressed Stephen A. Douglas. Quite possibly Lincoln might have agreed with the description of himself by Isaac N. Arnold, longtime Illinois politician and close friend of the sixteenth president. In the 1880s, Arnold wrote of Lincoln: "He lived simply, comfortably, and respectably, with neither expensive tastes nor habits. His wants were few and simple." On occasion, Arnold continued, the Lincolns invited a few guests to their home and gave them "a cordial, hearty, western welcome. . . ." By the time Lincoln entered the presidency, then, he was known and described as the railsplitting, western president, an image that his fellow Republicans and Lincoln himself accepted if not fostered.[11]

Early on, Lincoln began to embrace political and economic ideas that later shaped his stances vis-à-vis the American West. The most significant of these surfaced while Lincoln was still in his midtwenties in Illinois. When he launched his political career as a candidate for the state legislature in 1832, he already was committed to what became the Whig Party's position on internal improvements.[12] In the 15 March 1832 issue of the *Sangamo Journal*, Lincoln wrote: "Time and experience have verified to a demonstration, the public utility of internal improvements. That the poorest and most thinly populated countries would be greatly benefitted by the opening of good roads, and in the clearing of navigable streams within their limits, is what no person will deny." He added: "There cannot justly be any objection to having rail roads and canals, any more than to other good things, provided they cost nothing."[13] Obviously, if money were available for these internal improvements, and Lincoln had a plan to raise the funds, Illinois should move ahead with them.

In advocating increased government support for expansion of transportation networks in his state, Abraham Lincoln proved himself heir to the ideas of Alexander Hamilton, John Quincy Adams, and Henry Clay. Like most Whigs then and in the next two decades, Lincoln also supported banks, protective tariffs, and funding for educational measures. Although popular images of Lincoln often represent him as a homespun, railsplitting champion of common people, his political allegiances were not with the Jacksonian Democrats but with the Whigs and their championing of government aid for economic development.[14]

To understand Lincoln's major links to the American West, one must recognize his Whig—and later Republican—advocacy of government support for economic expansion. In the 1840s and 1850s, Lincoln gradually adopted several of his ambitious designs for governmental-economic partnership in his home state and then transferred them to his plans for the West. This partnership was the central facet of the first stage of Lincoln's connections with that region. These ideas, once joined to his growing concern about slavery and his view of the West as the future of the United States, provided the major components of Lincoln's plans for the United States beyond the Mississippi.

The merger of these ideas began in the 1840s. But Lincoln was not always in the vanguard of them. Indeed, in the two major western controversies, those surrounding Oregon and the Mexican-American War, Lincoln seemed much less involved than many other Americans, including his longtime rival from Illinois, Stephen A. Douglas. Dreams of expansion and western opportunity and the heat of political party clashes help explain some of the major competitions for office throughout the1840s, but Lincoln was slow to jump into these dogfights.

At first Lincoln remained removed from discussions of Oregon, but then he became much more involved with that debate from the late 1840s onward. Even as things began to heat up after Oregon Fever struck the Mississippi Valley and hundreds and then thousands headed up the trail to Oregon during the mid-1840s, Lincoln kept quiet about Oregon, as he did about nearly all things beyond the Mississippi. When other Whigs called for settlement of the Oregon Question and the establishment of a northern boundary with Canada as the perfect answer for the "Texas Humbug" brewing in the Southwest, Lincoln did not join in the conversations. Some Illinois newspapers urged Lincoln to speak out on Oregon, especially after it became clear that he would be a candidate for Congress in the mid-1840s. The *Springfield Register* queried Lincoln, asking whether he was "for 54 4[o], or for 'compromising' away our Oregon territory to England." "This, the People ought know," the newspaper added, "before they vote next August. No shiffling, Mr. Lincoln? Come out, square!"[15] But Lincoln didn't say much; nothing about Oregon appears in Lincoln's papers until July 1846.[16]

Meanwhile Lincoln's future political competitor from Illinois, Douglas, was deep in the debate over Oregon. As biographer Robert Johannsen points out, Douglas and many fellow Democrats, unlike Lincoln and large numbers of Whigs, "espoused the new and controversial issues of national expansion."[17] When Douglas entered the U.S. House of Representatives in December 1843, enthusiasm for territorial expansion had reached a new pitch of intensity. Texas had broken from Mexico in the Texas Revolution of 1836 and expressed a desire for annexation to the United States. And the rumors of agricultural riches in Oregon sparked a new wave of covetousness for that far-off Eden. When Democrat James K. Polk won the election of 1844 over Whig Henry Clay on a platform of annexing Texas and "reoccupying" Oregon, Stephen Douglas took that political mandate to the floor of Congress. For Douglas, Texas and Oregon "were like man and wife: when separated, the welfare and happiness of both were seriously injured; but when once united, they must be kept together forever."[18] As he pushed for the organizing of Nebraska as a territory, Douglas also began to support the idea of a transcontinental railroad to the Pacific. He also spoke out for legislation to establish a territory in Oregon and to provide 160 acres of land for bona fide settlers. Before the idea was coined, Stephen Douglas preached America's Manifest Destiny, evangelizing for westward expansion, adding his own glosses to expansionist scriptures. And he sermonized on these ideas well before Abraham Lincoln.

Similarly, Lincoln said little about Texas before the Mexican-American War broke out in 1846. On 6 June 1844, the *Sangamo Journal* vaguely reported that Lincoln, along with others at a general meeting held at the Illinois State House, considered Texas annexation, in "the terms agreed upon by [President] John Tyler," to be "altogether inexpedient"[19] More than a year later, in October 1845, after the Texas annexation measure had passed Congress, Lincoln admitted to an abolitionist friend he was "never much interested in the Texas question." Although he considered "annexation an evil" and would have opposed it, he was not convinced that Texas in or outside the Union would make much difference in the expansion of slavery. Lincoln continued that he "never could very clearly see how the annexation would augment the evil of slavery," and thus the Texas question did little to excite his political participation.[20]

But Lincoln's lack of involvement in the Oregon and Texas questions dramatically changed after his election to Congress in 1846. A year later on his route from Springfield to Washington, D.C., Lincoln stopped in Lexington, Kentucky, to visit his wife's relatives. While there he heard his political mentor Henry Clay harpoon President James K. Polk for bringing about the Mexican-American War. Undoubtedly, hearing Clay's attack on Polk set Lincoln to thinking about what he might say when he took his seat in Congress.

Once Lincoln arrived in Washington, he moved quickly to the center of controversies surrounding the Mexican-American War. On 22 December 1847, less than three weeks after taking his seat as an unknown freshman congressman from out west, Lincoln introduced what became called "the Spot Resolutions" in the House of Representatives. It was one of Lincoln's most important presentations—and among the most controversial of his career. It also did more to link Lincoln with western issues than any of his previous actions.

From the opening sentence of his Spot Resolutions, Lincoln questioned President Polk's contention that Mexico had "invaded *our territory*, and shed the blood of our fellow *citizens* on *our own soil*." Instead, Lincoln characterized the imbroglio as the president's making, "Mr. Polk's War." Like a debater addressing his opponent, Lincoln "respectfully requested" that Polk show "the spot" where U.S. citizens (rather than "*armed* officers and *soldiers*") lost their lives and demonstrate whether that spot was on Mexican, Texan, or U.S. soil.[21] Three weeks later, on 12 January, in a much longer and decidedly more militant speech, Lincoln hammered the Democrat Polk, accusing him of not telling the "*whole truth*." "I can not be silent," Lincoln told his listeners, because what the president argues is "sheerest deception." He next challenged Polk to answer the questions he had raised, "fully, fairly, and candidly . . . as [George] Washington would answer." Finally, Lincoln characterized Polk as a "bewildered, confounded, and miserably perplexed man." Perhaps, Lincoln stated in closing his speech, Polk's conscience would be more upright and moral than the "mental perplexity" he displayed.[22]

Lincoln's strong—even harsh—words upset Illinois Democrats, his law partner William Herndon, and not a few biographers and historians in the century and a half since he made his maiden speeches in Congress. Not surprisingly, the "locos," as Lincoln called his Democratic opponents, attacked him as unpatriotic, if not intensely treasonous, in his assaults on President Polk. The *Peoria (Ill.) Press* hammered Lincoln as the "miserable man of 'spots,'" following a "traitorous course in Congress."[23] Other critics derisively referred to him as "spotty Lincoln." Herndon also strongly dissented from his law partner's position on the Mexican-American War. He told Lincoln so, suggesting that he was alienating Illinois Whigs and possibly committing political suicide by his outspoken criticisms of Polk and the Democrats.[24]

Memoirists and popular historians writing after Lincoln's death and into the 1920s followed Herndon's interpretation of Lincoln's "spotty" behavior in Congress. These writers concluded that Lincoln's outspoken views on the Mexican-American War caused Stephen T. Logan, Lincoln's law partner, to lose in the Illinois Seventh District congressional contest in 1848. The negative conclusions about Lincoln's congressional actions received extensive coverage in Albert J. Beveridge's influential multivolume biography of Lincoln's prepresidential years, *Abraham Lincoln, 1809–1858* (1928). But more recent scholarship, especially key essays by Gabor S. Boritt and Mark E. Neely Jr., indicates that most other western Whigs shared Lincoln's harsh view of Polk and opposed the war and that Illinois Whig newspapers, by and large, refrained from criticizing him. Moreover, returning Whig veterans did not abandon their party despite its negative view of the war.[25] But in the dozen years immediately following Lincoln's antiwar comments, his position came under attack from his opponents, especially from Stephen Douglas, who repeatedly portrayed Lincoln as an unpatriotic American a decade later in the Lincoln-Douglas debates of 1858. Lincoln tried carefully to distinguish between his criticism of Polk and the war and his votes in support of the troops, but those distinctions were lost on his critics.

In the mid-to-late 1840s, the intense debate on Oregon's territorial status signaled the rising political brouhaha about slavery and its possible expansion. Lincoln gradually became involved in the controversy. In midsummer of 1846, a treaty with Great Britain settled the boundary question between the United States and Canada, making the Oregon Country (essentially the current states of Washington, Oregon, and Idaho) American territory. A few weeks later as Congress debated what might happen with territory taken from Mexico in the war then raging, David Wilmot, a Democratic legislator from Pennsylvania, introduced an amendment (later dubbed the Wilmot Proviso) to a legislative bill under consideration, calling for the disallowing of slavery in any area gained from the war. Although the Wilmot Proviso failed to pass, it became the rallying cry for many northern Whigs and eventually of the Republican Party in the late 1850s. The no-extension-of-slavery principle also became the most important link in the second stage of Lincoln's connections with the West.

Concurrently, proslavery advocates were calling for the expansion of slavery into the new areas, especially those below latitude 36°30′, the line established in the Missouri Compromise of 1820. Still others urged the adoption of the Ordinance of 1787 outlawing slavery in new territories. Meanwhile the Treaty of Guadalupe Hidalgo in 1848 had ended the Mexican-American War and ceded huge sections of Mexican territory to the United States.

These conflicting attitudes toward slavery and its expansion engulfed Lincoln during the consideration of the Oregon territorial bill in the summer of 1848. The decisions concerning Oregon, as Lincoln understood, also had implications for the areas of California and New Mexico. So as Lincoln and his fellow legislators debated Oregon's future, they kept their eyes on the larger questions of slavery and its possible expansion into the newly acquired territories.

Generally, Lincoln supported legislation granting Oregon territorial status. His shifting positions on those decisions also reveal much about his growing comprehension of the slavery issue and its impact on western expansion. When a Senate bill extending the Missouri Compromise to the Pacific was introduced in the House, Lincoln and the majority voted against the extension. Probably Lincoln voted nay because that extension would have allowed for the possible introduction of slavery into the Mexican cession. On 12 August 1848, the House of Representatives considered legislation organizing Oregon as a territory, a bill that included the antislavery clause from the Northwest Ordinance of 1787. Lincoln voted for that measure, and in a fractious, all-night meeting the next day, the Senate accepted the House bill giving Oregon territorial status.[26]

Lincoln's votes on Oregon seem unclear, but he did consistently support the essence of the Wilmot Proviso, keeping slavery out of the new territories. He claimed later, with a good deal of political exaggeration, that he voted for the Proviso at least forty times. Within the next half dozen years, as the slavery issue heated up and the new Kansas-Nebraska war of ideas erupted in 1854, Lincoln become increasingly recognized as a Wilmot Proviso advocate, as a supporter of no extension of slavery into the western territories.[27] That remained his stance into his presidency.

After the first session of the Thirtieth Congress concluded on 14 August 1848, Lincoln campaigned for the Whig presidential candidate Zachary Taylor and then returned for the second session beginning the following December. In those speeches and in the next congressional session lasting until March 1849, Lincoln became immersed in controversies impinging on the West, particularly decisions about new territories taken from Mexico at the end of the Mexican-American War, and, even more important, the crucial issue of the possible expansion of slavery into the western territories. He continued to speak for the no-extension principle and, after planning to introduce a bill in the House calling for the end of slavery in the District of Columbia, decided against submitting the legislation when his support melted away. Like most other congressmen, Lincoln seemed to drift and failed to act on measures addressing the territories taken at the end of the Mexican-American War.

Once out of Congress, Lincoln returned to Springfield. He wrote letters recommending his friend Dr. Anson G. Henry for positions in the new territory of Minnesota and also supported the plan of his fellow Whig congressman from Illinois, Edward D. Baker, who thought of moving to California to establish the Whig Party in that booming territory. Most of all, Lincoln got caught up in a controversy over the position of commissioner of the General Land Office, which, to Lincoln's great disappointment, went to Illinois lawyer Justin Butterfield rather than to himself.[28]

Five months after Lincoln left Washington, he received a telegram that might have markedly changed his career and forged even stronger links to the American West. Secretary of State John M. Clayton telegraphed Lincoln in August 1849 offering him the position of secretary of the new territory of Oregon. After Lincoln quickly rejected this offer—he had nominated his close acquaintance and Illinois journalist Simeon Francis for the office—a second message came one month later in early September. This time Secretary of Interior Thomas Ewing proffered the governorship of Oregon, at an annual salary of $3,000.[29]

Lincoln may have seriously considered the Oregon governorship. The wagon trains setting off each summer for Oregon and California had caught Lincoln's attention. Perhaps a seat in the Senate, which Lincoln coveted in Illinois, might come more quickly in Oregon's move into statehood. Lincoln's law partners John Todd Stuart and William Herndon were convinced that he pondered the move to Oregon. After Lincoln's death, Stuart recalled that Lincoln "finally made up his mind that he would accept the place if [his wife] Mary would consent to go."[30] Some of Lincoln's political friends warned him, however, that Oregonians had consistently voted for Democrats in local elections, so what political opportunities would a Whig have there? After some delay, Lincoln also rejected the position as Oregon's territorial governor. What might have happened to Lincoln's career—and to

West Coast politics—had he taken the governorship and moved to Oregon in 1849–50?[31]

Lincoln was without a political position, having lost out in the battle for commissioner of the land office and having turned down the positions in Oregon. He was to write later that he "was losing interest in politics" in these months and the following years of uncertainty.[32] But he remained active, even if in a less public way. He rallied support for Whig candidates, gave eulogies for Zachary Taylor and Henry Clay, and seemed to relish hammering on Stephen Douglas and other Democrats. Subscribing to the *Congressional Globe* and the leading Whig newspaper, the *National Intelligencer*, he kept his watchful eyes on the state and national political scenes.[33]

But other demands pulled at Lincoln. Needing to rebuild his family finances, he expanded his legal work, taking more cases and increasingly working with railroads and other firms. Tragedy added to Lincoln's load when his second son, Edward (Eddie), suddenly sickened and died on 1 February 1850. Mary Lincoln, sinking into black despair, had difficulty recovering from the death of her son. She was soon pregnant, however, and gave birth to William Wallace (Willie) the following December.

Meanwhile in Washington, Congress was wrestling with several issues inherited from the U.S. victory in the Mexican-American War and the emerging slave controversies that increasingly divided Americans in the next decade. Several of the conflicts were inextricably linked to the trans-Mississippi West. Should Congress enact the Wilmot Proviso forbidding slavery in the lands secured from Mexico in 1848? Would California enter the Union as a free state? What would happen to the New Mexico and Utah areas? And what of slavery? Would the slave trade be abolished in the District of Columbia and a stronger Fugitive Slave Law enacted? These controversies eventuated in the Compromise of 1850, and they elicited the memorable speeches of the great senatorial triumvirate—Henry Clay, John C. Calhoun, and Daniel Webster—that appeared consistently in the publications Lincoln read. So did news of the speeches and political stances of Lincoln's nemesis from Illinois, Stephen A. Douglas, who did more than any politician to bring forward the agreed-upon measures of the Compromise of 1850.

Nor could Lincoln have missed the "On to Oregon" and "Ho for California" cries that rang across the prairies of Illinois. Douglas, with his eye on the West and as chair of the House Committee and then the Senate Committee on Territories, was already a cheerleader for western expansion.

He was propounding measures for development of the trans-Mississippi West well before the dramatic events of 1854. But Lincoln had not caught that fire; he needed something to spark his western dreams and to show him how slavery issues and the West were bound up together. That needed inspiration came in the drama of the Kansas-Nebraska conflagration, which ignited in 1854.

Lincoln's attitudes about the West clearly moved in new directions, into a second stage, in the 1850s. Up to the beginning of his two years in Congress, Lincoln as a Whig looked at the trans-Mississippi region much as he had toward Illinois, a place wanting government-sponsored internal improvements. But the rising controversies surrounding slavery forced him in a new direction, even if slowly and sometimes reluctantly.[34]

Historians and biographers frequently misstate that Lincoln retired from politics from 1849 to 1854. He remained active in Whig politics in Illinois, criticizing the speeches of Douglas; he also served as an elector for the Winfield Scott presidential ticket in 1852 and was named a national Whig committeeman. In delivering a eulogy for Henry Clay in July 1852, Lincoln touched on his own positions. The Missouri Compromise (1820), the Nullification Crisis (1833), and the Compromise of 1850 were legislative testaments of Clay's notable achievements in domestic diplomacy. Most recently, Clay's role as "freedom's champion" shone forth in "the late slavery question, as connected with the newly acquired territory, involving and endangering the stability of the Union." Was there not in Lincoln's praise for Clay the negotiator a preview of his own mediating stance between the radical abolitionists who wished to destroy all vestiges of slavery despite its constitutional protection and the proslavery advocates who wished to open new territories in the West for the expansion of the "peculiar institution"?[35]

The new political fires exploded in 1854. When Stephen Douglas introduced, directed, and pushed the Kansas-Nebraska Act through Congress by May 1854, he lit a firestorm that eventually led to the outbreak of the Civil War seven years later. In the three-year period from 1854 to 1856, Lincoln moved to the front of the anti-Nebraska men and then on to the Republican Party. If the Illinois Whig was more an onlooker than a participant in 1854, he had become a leader in a newly formed political party two years later, so much so that he was prominently named among the vice presidential candidates in the first Republican run for the White House in 1856.

In 1854 Lincoln was quiet about the Kansas-Nebraska legislation for nearly three months after it passed Congress. But during those weeks he obviously had been thinking and researching the controversial bill as anti-Nebraska groups sprang up all over the North. In the late summer and early fall, he helped lead Illinois opponents of Douglas and the Kansas-Nebraska Act in a series of hard-hitting speeches all over the state.

The most significant of these presentations—and one of Lincoln's most powerful speeches—occurred in Peoria on 16 October. Significantly, two years earlier Lincoln also spoke in Peoria but on internal improvements. Now he moved in an important new direction in this long speech, which he evidently had given a few days earlier in Springfield. The three-hour oration, wrote Lincoln biographer Albert J. Beveridge, was his "first great speech."[36]

Granted, Lincoln was running for election to the Illinois legislature, a seat he won in 1854 but gave up to compete for the U.S. Senate the next year. But much more than campaign puffery, the Peoria speech was a powerful synthesis of Lincoln's developing position on slavery and its expansion into western territories. He also revealed a good deal about his attitudes toward race and his emerging moral stance against slavery.[37]

The Peoria peroration prefigured Lincoln's views on the most-pondered issues of the mid-1850s, especially those at the center of his debates with Douglas in 1858. Early on, he pointed to the "*lullaby*" arguments that Douglas and others made in asserting that slavery would not, by nature, expand into Kansas and Nebraska. He admitted, more than most persons of anti-slavery sentiments, that he held no prejudice against southerners for owning slaves; he would not know what to do himself if he lived in a slave state. But he could and did attack the specious argument that if one could take hogs from the South into Nebraska, why not slaves. That might be logical, Lincoln quickly added, "if there is no difference between hogs and negroes," but the Negro was a man and thus a part of the Jeffersonian credo in the Declaration of Independence, "all men are created equal." "Let no one be deceived," Lincoln continued. "The spirit of seventy-six and the spirit of Nebraska, are utter antagonists; and the former is being rapidly displaced by the latter." Finally, Lincoln made what he considered a clear distinction between Douglas's and his views concerning slavery: Douglas seemed blind to the moral implications of slavery, but "the great mass of manhood," Lincoln pointed out, took "a totally different view"; they "consider slavery a great moral wrong."[38] He was not willing, however, to sacrifice the Union to benefit the full rights of Negroes. Their full political and civil rights were not part of Lincoln's argument, as they would not be a decade later.

Lincoln's fears that the precedent-breaking and unwise Kansas-Nebraska decision would lead to violent disagreement were quickly realized in eastern Kansas, four hundred miles to the west of Lincoln's Springfield. In a March 1855 election, greatly influenced by invading "Border Ruffians" from Missouri, a proslavery legislature was elected at Lecompton. When opponents pushing for a Free State Kansas organized an illegal legislature at Topeka, clashes followed from November 1855 to a tragic highpoint in May 1856. Missouri renegades engineered a sack of antislavery Lawrence, and three days later John Brown's small group attacked and massacred citizens at Pottawatomie Creek in Kansas. Fierce guerilla warfare followed throughout 1856. In September 1857, a constitutional convention, called by the proslavery, rigged legislature, met in Lecompton and drew up a document calling for the introduction of slavery. Although new territorial elections selected an antislavery legislature, proslavery citizens dominated the constitutional proceedings. Once the proslavery document was sent to Washington, the James Buchanan administration accepted the constitution, but it failed to pass Congress. When the president endorsed the Lecompton Constitution, Stephen Douglas denounced that decision and broke with the Buchanan administration.[39]

For Abraham Lincoln, this string of sensational events, dubbed "Bleeding Kansas," confirmed a suspicion he increasingly held. He believed that a coterie of proslavery forces, as well as too many sympathizers, were conspiring to undermine the aim of the Founding Fathers who had wanted to isolate the inconvenient institution of slavery where it existed. But the new proslavery forces wished to open the floodgates to allow slavery to flow unimpeded into new western territories. Lincoln was convinced that the attempt to encourage slavery in the areas gained at the end of the Mexican-American War was only the first step. Opposition to the Wilmot Proviso and a free California were the next. Much worse was Douglas's "popular sovereignty" doctrine to allow a vote on slavery in sections where previously it was excluded by the Ordinance of 1787 and the recently repealed Missouri Compromise. For Lincoln, attempting to oppose these rising forces was like arm wrestling an octopus; there were just too many strong opponents.[40]

During these depressingly uncertain times in August 1855, Lincoln wrote to his close friend Joshua Speed, now back in Kentucky and a slave owner. "I plainly see you and I would differ about the Nebraska-law," Lincoln told Speed. "I look upon that enactment not as a *law*, but as *violence* from the beginning. It was conceived in violence, passed in violence, is maintained in violence, and is being executed in violence." Then Lincoln revealed a parallel dilemma he was facing in defining his stance on slavery. "You enquire where I now stand. This is a disputed point. I think I am a whig; but others say there are no whigs, and that I am an abolitionist. When I was in Washington I voted for the Wilmot Proviso as good as forty times, and I never heard of any one attempting to unwhig me for that. I now do no more than oppose the *extension* of slavery. . . . I am not a Know-Nothing. That is certain."[41]

As he wrote to Speed, Lincoln was trying another tactic, running for the U.S. Senate in 1855 on an anti-Nebraska platform. Putting his political eggs in the no-expansion-of-slavery basket, Lincoln came within a half-dozen votes of winning the seat in the Senate. Unable to garner the last, needed votes, Lincoln urged his followers to swing their support to Lyman Trumbull, an antislavery, anti-Nebraska Democrat. Disappointed but not depressed about the outcome, Lincoln realized his Whig Party was moribund—if not already dead. As he wrote Owen Lovejoy on 11 August 1855, "I have no objection to 'fuse' with any body provided I can fuse on ground which I think is right; and I believe the opponents of slavery extension could now do this, if it were not for this K[now]. N[othing].ism."[42]

The debacle in Kansas following the introduction of the Kansas-Nebraska legislation shattered Lincoln's political home in late 1855 and early 1856. The controversies over slavery and its expansion destroyed the Whig Party, divided Democrats, and give rise to new coalitions. Characteristically, Lincoln did not move precipitously in finding a new political abode. He had been a loyal Whig for more than twenty years, so he was reluctant to abandon that party. Still, he certainly would not join the Democrats or the new Know-Nothing/American Party. And more radical—even fiery—abolitionists were too extreme for Lincoln's cautious and moderate temperament. When the Republicans, cohering around a no-expansion-of-slavery core, began to gather anti-Nebraska supporters from the Whigs and the Democrats, Lincoln thought about joining the new party but hesitated. Refusing to join in 1854 and 1855, he moved closer and by early 1856 supported organizational efforts for the Republicans. A few months later, he was a leading Republican in Illinois, immersed in the politics of the new party. That summer, when the national Republican Party nominated the famed western explorer John C. Frémont as its first presidential candidate, Lincoln even received 110 votes for the vice presidency.[43]

In June of 1858, the Illinois Republicans met to plan their campaign against Stephen A. Douglas, the two-time Democratic senator. The Republicans also crafted a platform (a "Declaration of Principles") that criticized the Democratic president, James Buchanan, flayed the recent *Dred Scott* Supreme Court decision, and called for no extension of slavery into the western territories. They also promised not to interfere with slavery in the South and elsewhere. Furthermore, the Illinois Republicans, showing their Whig backgrounds or making overtures to former Whigs, called for federal support for the improvement of harbors and rivers for trade, funding for the construction of a central highway connecting Illinois to the Pacific Coast, and censorship of ruthless land speculators and, conversely, support for land policies that encouraged individual western settlers. Lincoln embraced this platform and ran on it in his dramatic campaign, including the Lincoln-Douglas Debates.[44]

The evening of 16 June 1858, Republicans gathered to hear Lincoln deliver what became known as his "House-Divided" speech. Western issues were at the center of this memorable presentation. When Lincoln announced his political positions, some onlookers thought he veered toward a more radical position against slavery and its possible expansion. "In *my* opinion," Lincoln told his listeners, the country "*will* not cease, until a *crisis* shall have been reached, and passed." Then followed Lincoln's paraphrase of the New Testament words of Jesus in Mark 3:25: "if a house be divided against itself, that house cannot stand." Lincoln continued: "I believe this government cannot endure, permanently half *slave* and half *free*. I do not expect the Union to be *dissolved*—and I do not expect the house to *fall*—but I *do* expect it will cease to be divided. It will become *all* one thing, or *all the other*."[45] Here was Lincoln's prophetic warning about the West: if expansion continued as it had from the Kansas-Nebraska Act, through Bleeding Kansas, and on through the most recent *Dred Scott* decision (1857), the West—and perhaps most of the country—would become a proslavery nation.

The weeks and months immediately following Lincoln's House-Divided speech in mid-June were as full as any in his prepresidential politicking. Opening the campaign competition in July, Douglas and Lincoln energetically crisscrossed Illinois for the next four months. Although most students of history know about the seven famous debates stretching from 21 August to 15 October, they are unaware that, in all, Lincoln delivered more than sixty formal and informal speeches, and Douglas, by his own accounting, as many as one hundred thirty before the November election. The campaign quickly caught the attention of Illinois residents, and its drama soon spread to the East and elsewhere. Even in remote and faraway Texas, one journalist reported the debates were touted as "one of the most exciting political contests that has ever occurred."[46]

Each of the debaters followed several themes in making his points and in confronting his opponent. Douglas attacked Lincoln and "the Black Republicans" as radicals advocating dramatic change and racial equality. In making a case for his principle of popular sovereignty, Douglas tried ingeniously to link the idea with Henry Clay and Whig traditions. He likewise charged that Lincoln's tactics included supporting Buchanan, being dishonest, and trying to "abolitionize" everything. By contrast, Lincoln appealed to white residents of Illinois by calling for no extension of slavery into the new territories and saving those areas for free laborers. In turn he made Douglas into a radical, a proslavery radical. Increasingly, Lincoln also emphasized slavery was evil and immoral, although he shied away from the sociocultural implications of the "all men are created equal" phrase of the Declaration of Independence. Revealingly, the debates did not focus on the issue of internal improvements. Land policies, transportation expansion, and road and canal improvements are not mentioned, even though the platform of Lincoln's Republican Party in 1856 explicitly supported such measures.[47]

In the first debate, at Ottawa, Illinois, on 21 August, Douglas caught Lincoln off guard by accusing him of hobnobbing with abolitionists and by raising several probing questions. But six days later in Freeport, Lincoln launched his own attack, one as central to these debates as it was two years later in Lincoln's run for the presidency. The question put to Douglas was, "Can the people of a United States Territory, in any lawful way, against the wish of any citizen of the United States, exclude slavery from its limits prior to the formation of a State Constitution?" Attempting to explain away the tensions between his popular sovereignty doctrine and the Supreme Court's decision in the *Dred Scott* case, Douglas boldly asserted "the people have the lawful means to introduce it [slavery] or exclude it as they please, for the reason that slavery cannot exist a day or an hour anywhere, unless it is supported by local police regulations."[48] Known later as the Freeport Question and the Freeport Doctrine, Douglas's unsatisfactory answer, particularly alienating to southern slaveholders, helped solidify opposition against him in that region and, perhaps, kept Douglas from garnering eastern Republican support for the presidency in 1860.[49]

Later in September and through mid-October in debates at Jonesboro, Charleston, Galesburg, Quincy, and Alton, Lincoln and Douglas, by and large, elaborated on earlier questions and answers rather than raising new ones. Lincoln accused Douglas of having conspired with others to provide a means for expanding slavery into the territories and claimed that his Democratic opponent was blind to the evil of slavery, allowing it to be voted up or down without any moral qualms about the institution itself. Repeatedly Lincoln said Douglas's attempt to reconcile his popular sovereignty idea with the recent *Dred Scott* decision was, at bottom, a recipe for allowing slavery into the rest of the West. At Jonesboro, in southern Illinois, Lincoln pointed to Douglas's ideas about expanding slavery beyond the Mississippi as a violation of what the Founding Fathers had attempted to do, which was to limit slavery.[50]

Before the sixth debate in Quincy on 13 October, Lincoln took time to cross the Mississippi and deliver a speech at Burlington, Iowa. There he visited and conversed with Republican James W. Grimes, then governor and later senator. Grimes encouraged Lincoln to mount an offensive, go after Douglas, and not try to defend himself against Douglas's spurious attacks.[51] A few days later, Lincoln supporters from Iowa crossed over the Mississippi to hear his debate with Douglas in Quincy. In that exchange, Douglas complained that Lincoln refused to answer several of his pressing questions. For instance, would Lincoln, if elected to the senate, vote for admitting additional slave states (New Mexico, as an example) if the people there voted for slavery? Douglas, attempting to catch his opponent in trickery, said Lincoln changed his tone and content to suit the sentiments of abolitionist northern Illinois and more proslavery southern Illinois. In turn, Lincoln charged Douglas with so watering down his "squatter sovereignty" in his Freeport Doctrine that hadn't it now become "as thin as the homoeopathic soup that was made by boiling the shadow of a pigeon that had starved to death?"[52]

Lincoln's campaign goal was to capture Republican areas of northern Illinois, avoid losing huge numbers of voters in the Democratic south, and win over additional support in former Whig areas banded across central Illinois. He nearly accomplished his goal; in fact, Republicans won several statewide elections in late 1858. But faulty apportionment in the state that favored the Democrats won Douglas reelection to the U.S. Senate in the state legislature by a vote of 54 to 46.[53] Lincoln's dream of winning a coveted senate seat, so close in 1855 and now again so near in 1858, had eluded him once again. But it soon became clear that his debates with Douglas not only set the political prairies afire, but rumors and fallout from them had spread Lincoln's reputation far away through the North and into the East. Most importantly, stories of his reasoned, clear stance against the expansion of slavery into western territories and his increased emphasis on the moral repugnance of slavery soon stirred up calls for him to run for the presidency.

In the welter of increased political activity and the press of recouping his personal finances following the debates, Lincoln still found time in 1859 to make two, nine-day trips into the trans-Mississippi West. They were his only western jaunts beyond a one-day stay or other glancing touch-downs on the western shores of the Mississippi. The first trip, which extended from 9 to 18 August, was ostensibly to look over land in Council Bluffs, Iowa, that his Illinois Republican colleague Norman B. Judd had offered as collateral on a possible loan. While in Council Bluffs to examine Judd's land, Lincoln delivered a speech at the Concert Hall. The presentation, one sympathetic journalist reported, illustrated "the dexterity with which . . . [Lincoln] applied the political scalpel to the Democratic carcass . . . [and] beggars all description at our hands."[54] Of more future importance, Lincoln heard that Grenville M. Dodge, a young but experienced railroad engineer, was in town, and Lincoln engaged him in a two-hour conversation that markedly influenced his attitudes and plans about a transcontinental railroad nearly three years later in his presidency.[55]

A second western trip the following 30 November to 8 December took Lincoln through Missouri and into the eastern end of Kansas. He came to Kansas at the invitation of Kansas Republican Mark W. Delahay, a former Illinois resident and fellow lawyer and distant relative of Lincoln's. Delahay was convinced that Lincoln's presence and speeches would encourage the moderate Republicans of the territory and spark Free State sentiment there. After speeches at Troy, Doniphan, and Atchison, Lincoln rode south in freezing weather to Leavenworth. There he stayed four days, including through the Kansas territorial election on 6 December, and delivered three speeches to enthusiastic audiences.[56] Some have argued that Lincoln's major speech at Leavenworth, as much as his famed Cooper Union lecture the following February in New York City, launched his presidency, with Lincoln repeating in New York what he had already said in faraway Kansas. Probably even more significant than the content of the Leavenworth speech was Lincoln's presence there—where Bleeding Kansas had been nearly torn asunder by a violent civil war struggle over slavery and its extension into a newly formed western territory. Lincoln represented a more temperate approach to these disuniting debates. While in Kansas, he denounced the radical violence of Kansan John Brown, who had just been hanged on 2

December, for leading his attack on Harpers Ferry the previous October. The voice of moderation that Lincoln represented in frontier Kansas was the same moderate tone and spirit he would illustrate nearly three months later at Cooper Union. Revealingly, Lincoln also chose to deal solely with the slavery controversy while in Kansas and not to discuss local issues concerning internal improvements.[57]

The speech at Cooper Union in New York City on 27 February 1860, argues Lincoln scholar Harold Holzer, was "the speech that made Abraham Lincoln president."[58] Perhaps so, as others have similarly argued. In his diligently researched, powerfully presented speech, Lincoln hammered away at Douglas and the concept of popular sovereignty. The central question to consider, Lincoln argued, was, "Does the proper division of local from federal authority, or anything in the Constitution, forbid *our Federal Government* to control slavery in *our Federal Territories?*"[59] After carefully reviewing the available documentation, Lincoln concluded that a majority of the Founding Fathers did not *oppose* federal government control of slavery in the territories. In the Northwest Ordinance, the Constitution and first amendments, and in the Louisiana Purchase, most of the early leaders voted for the central government's right to limit slavery in the territories.[60]

The aim of keeping slavery out of the western territories, Lincoln reminded his large audience of fifteen hundred eastern Republicans, was the central tenet of their party. Republicans would not attack slavery where it already existed and was protected by the Constitution, Lincoln promised the South, and his party had not supported the fanatical John Brown, who was no Republican. Warning his fellow party members they must avoid bargaining away or watering down their major reason for being, Lincoln ended with a rousing ring of party loyalty: "LET US HAVE FAITH THAT RIGHT MAKES MIGHT, AND IN THAT FAITH, LET US, TO THE END, DARE TO DO OUR DUTY AS WE UNDERSTAND IT."[61] This powerful, one-sentence ending remains one of Lincoln's most memorable statements.

A few days before he accepted the invitation to speak at Cooper Union, Lincoln clarified why his position on the West focused so singularly on the no-expansion-of-slavery issue. When Ohio senator Thomas Corwin wrote to Lincoln to tell him that Republicans were too tied to the slavery controversy, Lincoln asked him what issues he thought were bringing Democrats into the Republican Party. Lincoln pointed out that it was not conflicts over internal improvements—"tariffs, extravagances, live oak contracts and the like . . . the very old issues upon which the Whig party was beat out of existence"—that attracted new party members. Slavery had to be the issue, but not an alienating abolitionism. Illinois Republicans, as well others in the party, needed a man "who does not hesitate to declare slavery a wrong, nor to deal with it as such; who believes in the power, and the duty of Congress to prevent the spread of it."[62] Surely Lincoln was thinking of himself in describing this needed Republican candidate.

The eight months following Lincoln's pathbreaking trip to New York City and New England and the run-up to his nomination and election as president were jammed with new demands. But his links with the West remained unbroken. The Republicans of Illinois met in Decatur in early May 1860 to nominate Lincoln as their favorite son and to adopt a political platform for the coming election. As the party's candidate, Lincoln almost certainly had a hand in a plank calling for homestead legislation in Congress and acceptance of Kansas into the Union as a free state. As already noted, it was also at this convention that Lincoln became known as the railsplitter candidate from the West.

A week later, the national Republican convention gathered in Chicago to nominate their presidential candidate. The convention also adopted several planks linked to the West. While crammed into the ramshackle, makeshift Wigwam, the Republicans hotly denounced Stephen Douglas's popular sovereignty that effectively allowed slavery into the territories. They also argued that neither the Constitution nor territorial legislatures could "give legal existence to slavery."[63] Five of the seventeen Republican planks dealt with slavery, but others provided support for the older Whig, or Henry Clay, measures. As they had earlier in their first nomination of a presidential candidate in 1856, the Republicans meeting in Chicago called for internal improvements and a railroad to the Pacific; they now added, as well, homesteads for incoming western settlers.[64]

Once nominated as the railsplitter candidate from the West, Lincoln remained at home in Springfield and yet participated, at a distance, in the maelstrom of the campaign. Most of Lincoln's time was taken up in deciding on a complicated cabinet—"a team of rivals," as Doris Kearns Goodwin calls them—to reflect the diverse interests of the Republican Party and those constituents who helped elect Lincoln in November of 1860.[65] A flood of office-seekers and patronage applicants engulfed Lincoln and his advisers, snatching away many of his daily appointments in his Springfield office.

Lincoln was also pressured to make statements to try to mollify southern states beginning their stuttering steps toward secession and the organization of the Confederacy in the weeks stretching from November 1860 to early March 1861. For the most part, Lincoln refused to make such compromising announcements. He explained his position in notes he wrote in mid-February 1861 for a "Speech Intended for Kentuckians." He had "steadily refused . . . to shift the ground upon which . . . [he] had been elected," Lincoln told them, because if a chief magistrate betrayed the platform on which he had been elected and allowed changes in policies to satisfy his carping critics, "this government and all popular government is at an end. Demands for such surrender, once recognized, are without limit, as to nature, extent and repetition. They break the only bond of faith between public and public servant."[66]

The central plank of the Republicans and of Lincoln's credo, the one which he refused to give way on, was his stance against the extension of slavery into western territories. Repeatedly in his first days as president-elect, Lincoln told advisers, friends, and fellow Republicans there would be "no compromise on the question of *extending* slavery." He restated that position in writing to Alexander H. Stephens, a former fellow Whig and later the Confederate vice president: Lincoln would allow slavery where it already existed and was protected by the Constitution, but he steadfastly opposed its extension into yet unformed western states.[67]

This meant Lincoln entered the White House abiding by the earlier Wilmot Proviso and later Republican doctrine of no extension of slavery into territories west of the Mississippi. Notably, historians and biographers of Lincoln rarely make clear that this position was as much a western stance as one on slavery. Just as an explanation of Lincoln's links with the American West must include his attitudes toward slavery, so comment on his antislavery emphases should contain reference to his connections with the trans-Mississippi West. This stage in Lincoln's relationship with the West had begun during his congressional years and lasted until his presidency. As president, Lincoln entered a third stage in his connections with the West in which his positions on slavery and the Civil War joined with his earlier Whig stance on federal support for internal improvements.

Lincoln's inaugural address on 4 March 1861 and his annual message to Congress eight months later on 3 December reveal Lincoln's western ties through his statements on slavery and war and on federal roles in lands beyond the Mississippi. In his inaugural address, Lincoln repeated the promises of his president-elect days: he would abide by the Constitution, so slavery was safe where it was but would not be extended into the new territories. He would also uphold the Union. When Congress gathered for its winter session of 1861–62, Lincoln provided his first annual message to Congress. Buried in the larger sections devoted to the problems of war and policies dealing with "disloyal citizens" were several references to the West. Lincoln observed that the recent insurrection had enlarged difficulties with Indians, but he furnished no blueprint for addressing these mounting questions. He did recommend, however, that the growing importance of agriculture in the country necessitated the establishment of a bureau or department of agriculture, which Lincoln thought "might profitably be organized." Noting too that the territories of "Colorado, Dakotah and Nevada" had been established, the president recommended the "interests and defence" of these territories "to the enlightened and generous care of Congress."[68]

Although these statements dealt with the major topics of slavery, the Civil War, and territorial organizations influencing the West, other western issues soon emerged and commanded Lincoln's attention. Congress would introduce and pass pathbreaking legislation dealing with a transcontinental railroad, a homestead bill, and agricultural education that the president would have to act upon. Even more time-consuming were the hundreds of patronage positions and the thousands of hungry politicians asking for Lincoln's political manna in the form of a position in the West. Vexing problems vis-à-vis western Indians and Mormons also forced themselves on the chief executive. And still other military and even later Reconstruction dilemmas kept Lincoln looking west. Together these several links identify the third stage of Lincoln's connections with the American West, stretching from his entrance into the White House in March 1861 to his death in April 1865.

In the midst of mounting pressures of a nearly all-encompassing war, the Thirty-seventh Congress passed a clutch of notable legislative bills of central importance to the American West. It would be a mistake to state that Abraham Lincoln kept his guiding hand on the legislative throttle that drove the enactment of bills dealing with a transcontinental railroad, a homestead bill, a college land-grant act, and a department of agriculture. He did not. It would be equally misleading to depict Lincoln as a disinterested bystander, uninvolved in their support or passage. With Lincoln's encouragement and sometimes explicit direction, the U.S. Senate and House passed a series of acts, as one Ohio congressman noted, "whose vision embraced the entire continent."[69]

Many scholars, following the lead of historian David Donald, refer to Lincoln as a "Whig in the White House."[70] In this reference, historians imply that Lincoln, like many early Whigs reacting to what they considered the excessive imperial leadership of President Andrew Jackson, preferred presidents who largely left legislative matters to Congress. Lincoln gave some substance to his Whiggish perspectives in a speech in February 1861 while on his way to Washington to take up the presidency. He told an audience in Pittsburgh that "By the Constitution, the executive may recommend measures which he may think proper, and he may veto those he thinks improper; and it is supposed he may add to these, certain indirect influences to affect the action of congress. My political education strongly inclines me against a very free use of any of these measures, by the Executive, to control the legislation of the country."[71] But it is an overstatement to argue that Lincoln "took little interest in a series of far-reaching laws that Congress passed in [1861–62] . . . to develop the West, fund the war, and organize the economy, and which he signed without a murmur."[72] Publicly, and even more privately, Lincoln supported and encouraged the congressional legislation dealing with the West.

A revealing incident of Lincoln's support for a transcontinental railroad occurred in late summer of 1859. It was while visiting in Council Bluffs, Iowa, that Lincoln met the young engineer Grenville M. Dodge, who was returning from a trip to examine possible rail lines to the west. In a two-hour conversation, Lincoln closely questioned Dodge about what the engineer thought concerning rail work in "the country west of the Missouri River." "He stated," Dodge wrote later about Lincoln, "that there was nothing more important before the nation at that time than the building of a railroad to the Pacific Coast." Before he left Council Bluffs, Lincoln walked up Cemetery Hill (later Lincoln Hill), from which he could view the lay of land to the north and south. Four years later, Lincoln declared the Union Pacific would begin there—near the mighty Missouri.[73] One of Lincoln's presidential secretaries, John Hay, also testified to Lincoln's enthusiastic support of railroads and reported that the chief executive may have even thought of supporting an "unrealistic proposal of simultaneously building three separate lines to the West Coast."[74] Among Lincoln's papers is a heavily annotated pamphlet, including an underlined phrase criticizing railroad opponents for "want of confidence in our ability as a government." So influential was Lincoln's support of the transcontinental railroad project and its funding that one wag concluded, "Abraham's faith moved mountains."[75]

After Congress passed the Pacific Railroad Act in June 1862, Lincoln quickly signed it on 2 July. This act stipulated that the federal government would grant rights of way and make generous land grants (10 alternating sections, or 6,400 acres, per mile of track laid) for a transcontinental railroad to be built to the West Coast. Other government financial aid would be forthcoming, too, for the railroad construction companies. When these unprecedented governmental financial incentives did not satisfy prospective investors and builders, Congress doubled the size of the land grants and added still further financial supports in a second act that Lincoln signed in July 1864. Although the president and many of his fellow Republicans shied away from government ownership of the railroads, these two enactments in 1862 and 1864 proved the Republican Party favored establishing a sound marriage between government and business to link the East and the West.

Lincoln supported and encouraged these decisions in 1862 and 1864. Indeed when the act of 1862 failed to attract needed investors, the president himself pushed for the much more favorable terms of 1864. The legislation of 1862 stipulated too that the chief magistrate would decide the eastern terminus of the transcontinental line and also determine its gauge (width) of rails. Lincoln did both. After speaking again with Grenville Dodge and others, Lincoln decided in November 1863, even though undoubtedly focused on the Gettysburg Address he was to give two days later, that the eastern starting point would be located within "so much of the western boundary of the State of Iowa as lies between the north and south boundaries of . . . the city of Omaha." Nine months earlier, in January, he had determined that the width of the rails should be 5 feet, but northern members of Congress, preferring their gauge of 4 feet 8½ inches, quickly overrode Lincoln's decision. The president acceded to their position, despite westerners' preference for the 5-foot width.[76]

Lincoln's support for the transcontinental railroad illuminates his western connections. He wanted California tied to the East and kept secure within the Union. He also wished the prairies and plains to be opened to settlers and western mineral wealth made available for financing the government. And his Whig and Republican principles, clearly linked to American System precedents, undoubtedly accounted for much of his attraction to a westward-moving rail line. As a man of his times, Lincoln might well have argued that the Pacific Railroad acts and the mighty railroads they launched would make the United States "the greatest nation of the earth," as another observer argued.[77] Critics, reading history backwards, have more often seen the acts as subsidization without regulation, as a "blueprint for the Gilded Age."[78]

Springing from far different origins was Lincoln's support for several agricultural measures. Although drawn to railroads early on, Lincoln showed little interest in—in fact, alienation from—agricultural life. That separation began as a youth with Lincoln's clear decision to abandon his father's agricultural occupation and, once made, never turning back. The nonfarming twig was bent by the time Lincoln arrived in New Salem in 1831. But apt and ambitious politician that he was, Lincoln also realized he could not alienate or cut off farmers. And so, early on Lincoln, who ambitiously aspired to achieve something in life, thought anyone should have open to them the possibility of landownership, if that was their dream of upward mobility.

During his prepresidential career, Lincoln did not say much about agriculture or farming, but he did support Whig and Republican platforms that called for homestead acts. In fact, during Lincoln's nearly twenty years of political participation in Illinois, he supported legislation beneficial to farmers. His internal improvement schemes for building networks of roads, canals, and railroads, he was convinced, would allow farmers to transport their goods to nearby markets, encouraging them to move beyond subsistence to commercial agriculture, if that was their goal.[79]

On the eve of his nomination and election to the presidency, Lincoln made his most important statement about American agriculture. He accepted an invitation to speak on 30 September 1859 before the Wisconsin State Agricultural Society, meeting at the Wisconsin State Fair in Milwaukee. The presentation was unusual in two ways: Lincoln rarely gave lectures—hundreds of political stump speeches, but almost never formal lectures. And the lecture in Wisconsin was his only extensive presentation on agriculture. Lincoln told his listeners he would not engage "in the mere flattery of the farmers, as a class," but rather provide "some general suggestions on practical matters." He encouraged the audience (1) to think about the latest agricultural technologies, especially steam plows; (2) to contemplate the need for free labor; and (3) to study and make better uses of varied soils. Improved education, diligent labor, and skillful uses of lands, Lincoln argued, would help agriculturists "secure an individual, social, and political prosperity and happiness, whose course shall be onward and upward, and which, while the earth endures, shall not pass away."[80]

Three important pieces of congressional legislation in 1862 conjoined agriculture, Lincoln, and the American West. These were the Homestead Act, the creation of the Department of Agriculture, and the Morrill Land-Grant College Act. The most significant of these—some think it the most important piece of legislation on land policies ever enacted in the U.S. Congress—was the Homestead Act. This pathbreaking legislation stipulated that a bona fide homesteader, after five years of residence ("proving up") and payment of a small registration fee, could gain 160 acres of land. Lincoln and most Republicans favored this legislation because they were convinced that the free land, like a powerful magnet, would draw ambitious farmers, help settle the West, and thus expand the nation's economy. In their view—Lincoln with them—the West belonged to upwardly mobile white farmers (and later, veterans) who deserved to benefit from nature's bounty and in turn add to it.[81]

Lincoln also called for the establishment of a department of agriculture in his annual message in December 1861. Congress quickly followed up on Lincoln's suggestion to organize a bureau to gather statistics and provide an annual report on U.S. agriculture. After a good deal of interparty and regional wrangling, the bill to establish a subcabinet Department of Agriculture passed Congress, and Lincoln signed the act on 15 May 1862. Soon thereafter Lincoln appointed Isaac Newton, a friend of the president's then serving in the agricultural division of the patent office, as head of the agricultural department. An ambitious and loyal bureaucrat, Newton moved with alacrity and thoroughness. Lincoln saluted his work and that of the new Department of Agriculture in his annual message in December 1862.[82]

The third of the agricultural measures to pass the Thirty-seventh Congress, the Morrill Land-Grant College Act, gained less explicit attention from Lincoln than the two other bills, but the enactment illustrated his ideas about the need for agricultural education. Passed in June 1862 by the Senate and House, the land-grant act provided as many 30,000-acre parcels of federal land in any state as the number of senators and representatives in each state for the establishment of colleges "to teach such branches of learning as are related to agriculture and the mechanic arts."[83] Ironically, Senator Justin Morrill of Vermont and other strong advocates of the bill had to overcome strong opposition from several western congressmen who feared that easterners would gobble up western lands to fulfill the grant's stipulations. When Lincoln signed the Morrill land-grant bill on 2 July 1862, he undoubtedly recognized echoes of his admonitions to the Wisconsin farmers in 1859. He believed that educational advantages for farmers, especially in the sciences and technology, would enhance agriculturists' advancement as well as that of the entire country.[84]

Reactions to Lincoln's attitudes toward railroads and agriculture and these legislative enactments during his presidency have shifted notably in the past century and a half. These changing viewpoints illuminate Lincoln's perspectives as well as the shifting sociocultural milieu of his supporters and critics. During the remainder of the nineteenth and the first years of the twentieth centuries, most observers praised Lincoln and his administration's transportation and agricultural achievements as beneficial acts opening up the West and making inexpensive and potentially fruitful lands available to farmers from within the United States and Europe. But beginning in the Progressive Era in the first two decades of the twentieth century and increasingly in the following decades, critics excoriated railroads and the railroad magnates as "Robber Barons" plundering the treasured public domain and lining their own pockets. In addition, some historians of agriculture criticized the Homestead Act as an "incongruous" land system that profited speculators and railroad corporations more than individual farmers.[85]

In the second half of the twentieth century, especially from the 1970s forward, revisionist historians increasingly pointed to the sociocultural costs of Lincoln's railroad and agricultural policies. Those policies, the critics argue, encouraged not only speculation but also misguided land policies and environmentally disastrous uses of western farming areas. Even worse, the faultfinders continue, were the effects of these policies on Native Americans: stealing their lands, forcing them onto reservations, and undermining their occupational and cultural patterns of existence.

So, by the early twentieth century, those who praised Lincoln's support for railroad and agriculture expansion in the West faced mounting criticism of the economic and social fallout of those policies.[86]

In Lincoln's presidency, even before his railroad and agricultural policies impacted Native Americans, he had to deal with several issues involving Indians. In late August of 1862, a few days before Lincoln announced his preliminary Emancipation Proclamation, telegrams arrived in Washington informing the president and cabinet that Minnesota was aflame in an Indian uprising. "Men, women, and children are indiscriminately murdered," read one telegram. Another from Gov. Alexander Ramsey told Secretary of State Edward Stanton and the president that "The panic among the people has depopulated whole counties."[87]

These dramatic events and the decisions that followed in the next few months revealed how little contact Abraham Lincoln had had with Indians and how minuscule was his knowledge about them. Before Lincoln entered the White House, his contacts with Indians were limited—some argued—to perhaps two events. Before Lincoln was born, an Indian had slain his grandfather Abraham Lincoln in Kentucky in 1786. The president's father, Thomas Lincoln, repeatedly told the story of that attack, so often that it became, his son said, "the legend more strongly than all others imprinted upon my mind and memory." The other incident occurred in 1832 when Lincoln volunteered to defend Illinois from returning Indians in the so-called Black Hawk War. Lincoln saw no combat against the Indians and later poked fun at his inconsequential role in this conflict. But from the war derives another story illustrating Lincoln's sympathetic reaction to Native Americans. When an old Indian wandered into the soldiers' camp, the story goes, some soldiers immediately came forward to kill him. Standing in front of the elderly man, Lincoln threatened to attack anyone who harmed the wanderer. None of the soldiers was willing to confront Lincoln, allowing the old Indian to escape.[88]

During his presidency, Lincoln was forced to deal with Indian affairs even while he was buried under a tsunami of civil war, political turmoil, and personal challenges. In his handling of the Sioux outbreak in Minnesota and his dealings with Cherokee leader John Ross, as well as in several other contacts with Indians, Lincoln provided glimpses of his attitude toward and policies concerning Native Americans. The road he traveled moved quickly from ignorance and lack of sympathy toward increasing understanding and expanding empathy.[89]

The Sioux outbreak in August 1862 reveals the contrasting pressures at work on Lincoln as well as his initial stance toward Indians. In Minnesota the flood of incoming settlers, unfulfilled treaty promises, and intratribal squabbles prefaced the violent Sioux rebellion against whites in southwestern and south central parts of the new state. After a few indecisive local and national actions, Lincoln named Gen. John Pope to lead the counterattack on the rebellious Sioux. When Pope asserted, "It is my purpose utterly to exterminate the Sioux if I have the power to do so," and added, "They are to be treated as maniacs or wild beasts," his viciously hard-nosed policy was clear from the beginning. Pope and other white military leaders, with superior numbers and weaponry at their command, quickly rounded up Sioux leaders, tried these captives before a five-man commission, and called for the summary execution of 303 prisoners. They telegraphed details to President Lincoln and urged him to support the mass hangings. Instead Lincoln requested more details on all those declared guilty and then proceeded to closely scrutinize all that evidence.[90]

Minnesota territorial officials, frontier military leaders, and numerous white traders and white settlers pushed for the immediate execution of all 303 Sioux captives. Lincoln put the brakes on the rush to hanging. In his telegraphs to General Pope, he asked for full reports on the bloodbath, particularly any information that might distinguish among Indians guilty of capital crimes such as murder and rape and those innocent of such violence.[91] Lincoln and his advisers found shocking evidence that some Indians were convicted on the flimsiest evidence, others on hearsay and rumors. Still, military and political leaders in Minnesota were calling for the precipitous hanging of all the captive Sioux, warning that if harsh treatment were not meted out settlers would rise up and slaughter other Indians wholesale. On the other hand, the humane and empathetic leadership of Episcopal bishop Henry Benjamin Whipple and Lincoln's able Indian commissioner, William P. Dole, opposed the mass executions and spoke forcefully for their position.[92]

Gradually, with much hesitation and reluctance, Lincoln made his tortured decision. On 6 December 1862, he forwarded to Gen. Henry Hastings Sibley the names of thirty-nine Sioux, those guilty of "massacres" (as opposed to those merely fighting in "battles") and those who "had been guilty of violating females."[93] Nearly three weeks later, on 26 December, the 38 Indian men (another gained a last-minute pardon) were hanged in Mankato, Minnesota, in the largest mass execution in U.S. history. Later Lincoln spoke of the Sioux outbreak and subsequent hangings as "a disagreeable subject" he wished to avoid. He had saved the lives of approximately 265 Indian captives, but he had also allowed the executions of 38 others to go forward. Some historians and biographers emphasize the Indian lives Lincoln saved; others point to those he sent to the gallows. Lincoln's interpreters seem as divided in their reactions as he was emotionally ambivalent in the momentous decision he had to make as the nation's chief magistrate.[94]

Lincoln's association with Cherokee chief John Ross provides a second example of his mixed feelings about Indian affairs. When Ross and the Cherokees, as well as members of the other Five Civilized Tribes, were left unprotected and unsupported during the opening months of the Civil War, they felt they must either join the Confederacy or flee north to Kansas as refugees. In the case of Ross and the Cherokees, they became, very hesitantly, Confederates. After being captured by Union forces, Ross came to Washington, D.C., where he met with Lincoln in September 1862. In subsequent meetings and through correspondence, Lincoln came to know Ross better than any other Native American, just as he was better acquainted with Frederick Douglass than with any other African American. But Lincoln was slow and indecisive on Ross's request for aid and support. He told the Cherokee leader that because of "the multitude of cares claiming [his] attention," he had been "unable to examine" the history of treaty relations between the Cherokee and the United States.[95] He promised to carry out the needed reading, but left most of those details to Commissioner Dole and Secretary of Interior Caleb Smith. Later, hoping to win back support of the Five Civilized Tribes and perhaps feeling guilty about his inattention to their real and pressing needs, Lincoln issued a "Pardon and Amnesty Proclamation." This message, part of a general act of pardon for all those involved in the rebellion against the Union, included the tribes of Indian Territory. Although the act indicated Lincoln's growing interest in the affairs of Native Americans in Indian Territory, the pardon accomplished very little because it came too late to avoid the strife that those tribes experienced throughout the Civil War.[96]

Most of these contacts do not redound well for Lincoln's dealings with Native Americans, even though his decisions concerning the Sioux uprising and the Five Civilized Tribes reveal a growing sympathy for Indian dilemmas in the West. Other actions add more positive details. When English reformer and writer John Beeson, who had spent several years on the Oregon frontier, finally met with the president, Lincoln told him he had heard his calls for needed changes in Indian policy. "I have said little but thought much," the president informed Beeson. "You may rest assured that as soon as the pressing matter of this war is settled the Indians shall have my first care and I will not rest untill Justice is done to their and your Sattisfaction."[97] Encouraged also by another reformer, Bishop Whipple, to make necessary changes, Lincoln stated in his annual address in 1862, "I submit for your especial consideration whether our Indian system shall not be remodelled. Many wise and good men have impressed me with the belief that this can be profitably done."[98] If these statements by Lincoln are taken at face value—and there is no compelling reason not to—the president obviously saw many flaws in the Indian system and hoped to reform it.

Lincoln and Commissioner Dole, close friends, often talked of the need to reform policies toward Indians and to make the reservation system more helpful for Native Americans. As one authority on the subject argues, "both men discussed affairs of state with such frequency and at such great length that Dole's Indian policy pronouncements can probably also be said to represent Lincoln's thinking."[99] Dole served as commissioner for Lincoln's entire presidency, and several of his ideas for the improvement of reservations for Indians were adopted, although the distracting Civil War and Reconstruction, the cupidity of Indian agents, and lack of military enforcement in the West delayed implementation of most of Dole's ideas. One dramatic incident revealed how much reform was needed—and soon. When a mean-spirited, bellicose contingent of soldiers, mainly Colorado Volunteers, invaded a sleeping camp of Cheyenne and proceeded to wantonly murder as many as 200 Indians (mostly children and women), the news of the Sand Creek Massacre in eastern Colorado sickened the American public, helped launch a congressional investigation, and undoubtedly upset Lincoln. An aspirant for Dole's job suggested that Lincoln was so disturbed about the murderous events at Sand Creek that he considering sacking Dole, but, if so, the assassination intervened before Lincoln could act.[100]

Lincoln was forced to act in another area linked to the American West, however. The Constitution mandated that Congress or the president must appoint several officials in each newly formed western territory. Over time, presidents had taken responsibility for most of this duty. For Lincoln these time-demanding and tension-ridden obligations turned out to be onerous, energy-consuming, and bittersweet experiences. He enjoyed providing positions for friends and worthy acquaintances, but the requests and importunities of thousands of office seekers were endless. They gathered around Lincoln like hordes of hungry ants in search of tasty morsels. The whirligig of politics and patronage undoubtedly occupied more of Lincoln's time than any other of his dealings with the West.[101]

The irresistible call of politics, as well as his duty to deal with western territories, led Lincoln to expand the reach of his Republican Party deep into the West. In several parts of the West, Lincoln became a virtual founding father of western politics. When he began his presidency on 4 March 1861, there were only nine states situated on the Mississippi and to the west. They were Louisiana (1812), Missouri (1821), Arkansas (1836), Texas (1845), Iowa (1846), California (1850), Minnesota (1858), Oregon (1859), and Kansas (1861). Louisiana and Texas had seceded by the beginning of Lincoln's presidency, and Arkansas would do so later that year. During Lincoln's four years in the White House, Nevada became a state, and Arizona, Idaho, and Montana were organized as new territories. In all or part of these years, New Mexico, Utah, Nevada, Washington, Dakota, Nebraska, Colorado, and Indian Territory retained their territorial status. This meant that during his administration Abraham Lincoln was charged, as president, with appointing political officials in eleven territories in the American West. Those opportunities allowed the ambitious politician in the White House to greatly enlarge the power of the Republican Party in the West even while he established the earliest political trends in these areas of the Far West.[102]

A few general patterns are discernable in the political links that Lincoln forged in western states and territories, even though most of those political connections reflected the varied histories of those heterogeneous peoples more than any other generalized patterns. Most of Lincoln's political appointees were former Whigs or new Republicans. Many came from his large pool of acquaintances, especially the lawyers he knew in Illinois or politicians from that state or eastern states whom he met during his nearly thirty years as a western and national politician. Others were acquaintances of cabinet members or leading Republicans. Some of the appointees served well as Lincoln's political missionaries in the West, others wobbled indecisively in their unfamiliar surroundings, and still others were first-rate rascals, sometimes failing to show up or even running off with government funds. Altogether in the years between 1861 and 1865, Lincoln may have appointed more than a hundred men to western posts, especially as governors, secretaries, judges, Indian agents, or surveyors-general.[103]

The two most recognizable of the several patterns that developed between Lincoln and the western states and territories were his political and personal contacts with the men he appointed or knew in the West. Consider, for example, the states of Missouri and Oregon. Political connections, troubled and vexing as they were, defined his links with Missouri. But in Oregon personal friendships most clearly shaped Lincoln's relationships with that new far-western state.

Lincoln's dealings with the disruptive state of Missouri were unlike those in any other western state. From the opening to the closing months of his presidency, he was beset with the inseparable political, military, and legal chaos in Missouri. In fact in Missouri there lurked a complex set of challenges that Lincoln did not have to face elsewhere in the West. Riven by conflicts between Unionist and Confederate diehard partisans and convulsed by more military battles than any other state save Virginia, Missouri boiled over with all the major problems that led to and continued during the Civil

War. Moreover, the moderate and Radical wings of the Republican Party were in nearly open warfare on how slavery, war, and reconstruction policies should be handled. Into this bubbling caldron of discontent fell President Abraham Lincoln.[104]

Lincoln's political connections with Missouri radically differed with those in Oregon, for example. In the latter state he had four close friends to rely on for news and suggestions about political decisions. With one or two exceptions he had no close personal friends in Missouri on which to rely thoroughly. The issues, the factional leaders, and the controversies were more complex, emotional, and constantly changing than elsewhere in the West. When a group of Missouri and Kansas Radical Republicans met with Lincoln in 1863, they demanded he harken to their wishes and make immediate changes. Lincoln's reply a few days later, in his seriocomic way, made clear the "perplexing compound" of issues and factions in Missouri. There are those in Missouri, he wrote, "who are for the Union *with*, but not *without* slavery—those for it *without*, but not *with*—those for it *with* or *without*, but prefer it *without*. Among these again, is a subdivision of those who are for *gradual* but not for *immediate*, and those who are for *immediate*, but not for *gradual* extinction of slavery."[105]

The internecine struggle in Missouri often revolved around the inflexibly divisive politicians of the state. The tinderbox situation exploded when the impetuous Gen. John C. Frémont, whom Lincoln had put in charge of the Department of the West, unilaterally declared martial law in Missouri on 30 August 1861. Without checking with the president, Frémont ordered the confiscation of the property of all enemies of the Union, the shooting of citizens who took up weapons, and, most controversial of all, the freeing of slaves. Lincoln first requested Frémont to countermand his order but then issued his own countermanding proclamation when Frémont refused initially to back down.[106] Lincoln also had to suffer through an embarrassing, late-night, combative set-to with Frémont's indomitable wife, Jesse Benton Frémont. Lincoln said of the testy interview that Mrs. Frémont "sought an audience with me at midnight and taxed me so violently with many things that I had to exercise all the awkward tact I have to avoid quarreling with her."[107] Reluctantly, General Frémont relented and obeyed the president, but after investigations revealed further evidence of Frémont's incompetence as a leader, Lincoln cashiered him two months later. To Lincoln's credit and indicative of his character, he found another military position for the troublesome Frémont in the eastern theater of the war.

Three factions weaved in and out of the Missouri political scene during the Civil War years. Each of the three, certain they knew how to run the state and their opponents did not, was clearly and loudly upset when Lincoln seemed inclined to follow one of the other factions. Understanding the major cause for the political upset in Missouri, Lincoln wrote to several of the state's Radical Republican leaders in May 1863: "It is very painful to me that you in Missouri can not, or will not, settle your factional quarrel among yourselves. I have been tormented with it beyond endurance for months."[108] The Democrats were often considered closet secessionists—unless proven innocent—but the two Republican factions needed and courted those same Democratic voters. The Conservative (or "softs") among the Republicans, influenced by their connections with Lincoln's attorney general, Edward Bates (who was from Missouri), and Postmaster General Montgomery Blair, usually supported Lincoln's policies. But the Radical Republicans (or "hards") were difficult partisans who increasingly opposed Lincoln.

When an outspoken Radical contingent, led by the pugnacious Charles D. Drake, visited Lincoln on 30 September 1863, he tried to reason with them. They arrived upset both with Lincoln's support for Gov. Hamilton Gamble, a moderate or soft, and the president's willingness to keep John Schofield in command. They also took umbrage with Lincoln's description of Missouri's political squabbles as a "pestilential factional quarrel."[109] The president spoke directly and clearly to the Missouri Radicals, pointing out that as long as a person supported the Union he was Lincoln's friend, even if he disagreed with Lincoln's policies. "I think it ungenerous[,] unjust and impolitic to make . . . [such a person's] views on abstract political questions a test of his loyalty. I will not be a party to this application of a pocket Inquisition." Following the definitions of the Radicals, who were calling themselves his friends, Lincoln continued, it must be "only so while I agree with you. According to that, if you differ with me you are not my friends."[110]

Gradually, the Radicals gained strength in Missouri and dominated the state by early 1865. But they were at best hesitant supporters of Lincoln. He had wanted gradual emancipation, while they had wanted immediate emancipation; he stood for compromise in allowing back into the state former Confederates now willing to take a loyalty oath to the Union, whereas they wanted to keep out such persons. But Lincoln promised not to force his opinions on the state, and he did not. Unfortunately, to the end of his administration, Lincoln was unable to win over the Missouri Radicals, or hards, to his viewpoint. One of Lincoln's longtime secretaries, John G. Nicolay, wrote

Lincoln in October 1864 that only "time will abate the disorder" in Missouri. Lincoln's time ran out before much of that disorder disappeared.[111]

Lincoln's links with Oregon were more personal and much less controversial. Although he had rejected an opportunity to become the territorial governor of Oregon in 1849, in the next decade four close friends moved to the territory or new state. The acquaintances of Lincoln who went to Oregon were David Logan, who arrived in 1849, Anson G. Henry in 1852, Simeon Francis in 1859, and Edward D. Baker in 1859–60. They became Lincoln's political eyes and ears on the West Coast. Most of all they reported on the political events of the Pacific Northwest and California, explaining the unique competitions in these areas and sometimes urging Lincoln to take new tacks.[112]

Lincoln's personal and political connections in Oregon often differed from those in other western areas. The controversies over slavery, the Civil War, and the earliest Reconstruction measures that embroiled the president and Missouri in a series of fractious disputes were muted or absent in Oregon. In addition, because Oregon had become a state in 1859 before Lincoln entered the White House, he did not appoint the dozens of officeholders he named in territories such as New Mexico, Colorado, and others across the northern West. But the quartet of longtime acquaintances that began moving to Oregon in 1849 linked Lincoln to the political party transformations in the 1850s and early 1860s in Oregon. All of these men—Logan, Dr. Henry, Francis, and Baker—were active Whigs and then Republicans. In the election of 1860, they played important roles in Lincoln's win in the state and in Baker's selection as one of the state's new senators.[113]

The career of David Logan was the longest and most controversial of Lincoln's friends in Oregon. Son of Lincoln's second law partner, Stephen Logan, David probably came west at the command of his imperious father. Logan quickly exhibited his first-class legal mind and was elected to the territorial legislature in 1854 and 1857. But his incipient alcoholism, questionable moral behavior, and political confrontations undermined his dream of winning a U.S. congressional seat. After Lincoln captured the presidency in 1860, Logan wrote to the president-elect suggesting he merited a political appointment. Lincoln never answered Logan's pushy letter but, through other friends in Oregon, encouraged Logan's political career. Later, Logan was elected mayor of Portland but died a young man of fifty, frustrated in fulfilling his dream of entering the U.S. House of Representatives.[114]

The most rabidly political of Lincoln's acquaintances in Oregon was Dr. Anson G. Henry. Although trained as a doctor, Henry spent most of his time as a controversial and combative Whig politico in Lincoln's Illinois. But he and his wife, Eliza, were close friends of Lincoln and his fiancée, Mary Todd, helping them through stuttering steps to marriage.[115] Hungry for new political and economic possibilities, Henry went to Oregon in 1852. There Dr. Henry's penchant for pugnacity soon resurfaced. He was quickly enmeshed in Oregon politics, telling his territorial neighbors how they should operate politically. Through dozens of letters and two arduous trips to Washington, Henry also lobbied Lincoln for new political posts.[116] He was at the capital when the president was assassinated in April 1865 and helped Mrs. Lincoln through her initial grieving.

As Paul Zall points out in a new essay, Henry sometimes acted as Lincoln's "junkyard dog."[117] He barked—even snarled—at the president's opponents. As one of the "Tribe of Abraham" and the self-appointed protector of Lincoln's interests, Henry kept critics at bay. Yet Lincoln understood the doctor and viewed him as a "great, big-hearted man . . . one of best . . . I have ever known. He sometimes commits an error of judgment," but, Lincoln added, "he is the soul of truth and honor."[118]

Simeon Francis was the third of Lincoln's close acquaintances to migrate to Oregon. A longtime Whig newspaper editor in Illinois, Francis sustained Lincoln's politics and opened his pages to Lincoln's journalistic writings. Francis and his wife, Eliza, also helped Abraham and Mary through their floundering months of courtship before Francis sold his Springfield newspaper and moved west.[119] Soon after his arrival in 1859, Francis wrote an important article in the *Oregon Argus* calling for Lincoln's election to the presidency. It may have been the first such call for Lincoln on the West Coast. Later, Francis briefly edited the *Portland Oregonian*, and Lincoln named him army paymaster at Fort Vancouver, a position Francis held until retiring in 1870. Like other friends in Oregon, Francis wrote Lincoln about the politics of the Oregon Country and suggested persons for political appointment.[120]

Edward D. Baker was the most influential nationally of Lincoln's personal connections in Oregon. His career there was also the briefest. An active Whig and U.S. congressman from Illinois, Baker moved to California in the 1850s but was unsuccessful in his run for public office in that new state. At the behest of David Logan, Dr. Henry, and other Republicans, Baker came to Oregon, made political compromises with popular sovereignty Democrats, and quickly won a seat as a Republican in the U.S. Senate in 1860. He was the first West Coast Republican elected to Congress.

Baker's closeness to Lincoln became apparent when the incoming president asked Baker to introduce him at the inauguration in March 1861. Soon thereafter Baker joined the Union army and helped raise a regiment. Sadly, in October 1861 he was killed at the Battle of Ball's Bluff near Washington. Serving but a few weeks in the Senate, Baker had nonetheless helped Lincoln forge an early link with the nascent Republican Party in the Far West.[121]

Even though Oregon was considered a Democratic stronghold, Lincoln narrowly and surprisingly won the state's vote in 1860 and again in 1864. His friends and political acquaintances were important links for Lincoln in Oregon as well as in the nearby territories of Washington, Idaho, and Montana. They enlarged his political prospects throughout the Pacific Northwest and helped establish the Republican Party in the area.[122]

Some of Lincoln's personal and political connections in Oregon stretched out, like his own long limbs, into other parts of the Pacific Northwest and the northern West. For example, Anson G. Henry, the indefatigable political doctor in Oregon, quickly jumped into the politics of the eight-year-old Washington Territory, after Lincoln named him surveyor general there in 1861. He and Senator Baker of Oregon evidently put together a list of possible appointees in Washington for Lincoln and urged the new president to name them to office. But a group of resident Republicans in Washington Territory also decided they should be chosen as officeholders. In 1861, they had nominated themselves for all the plumb positions in the territory—from governor to court justices to Indian agents and land office officials. They selected William Henson Wallace, Washington Territory's leading resident Republican, for their territorial governor and asked him to present their nominations to Lincoln for his selection. Wallace claimed to be a longtime friend of Lincoln's.[123]

Once the competing lists of Baker and Henry's choices and those of the Washington Republicans arrived in Washington, they were mixed and matched. Tradeoffs and compromises abounded. Wallace would be governor, Henry, surveyor general, but no office came to Simeon Francis, although later he received his paymaster position. In the end, many of the appointees in Washington Territory were friends of Lincoln, former Illinois residents, or acquaintances of cabinet members. Not surprisingly, Democrats and resident Republicans roundly criticized Lincoln's appointees, referring to them as "The Tribe of Abraham," as "importations," and, in the case of one official, "another Drunkard from Illinois." They aimed special animus at

Dr. Henry, whom they castigated as vain, tricky, and too inclined to view himself as Lincoln's special political envoy to the territory.[124]

In many regards, the political turmoil in Washington Territory clearly reflected what one historian has termed the "chaotic factionalism" of the western territorial system. No matter which nonresident ("carpetbagger") Lincoln selected for offices in Washington, those choices were unacceptable to residents who wanted the positions themselves. The "rival ambitions" between the outsiders and insiders in Washington, like similar conflicts throughout the western territories, complicated what Lincoln tried to do in his appointments.[125] On the other hand, were his choices good ones? In chapter 6, Robert W. Johannsen, a leading authority on Stephen Douglas, replies in the negative. He concludes that "as president, [Lincoln] simply implemented his assumption that territorial appointments were important only insofar as they served partisan ends." Another student of Washington territorial politics asserts, however, that the two governors Lincoln appointed, Wallace and William Pickering, were strong executives and that his judicial appointments were exceptional appointments.[126]

Other Lincoln friends and political contacts were involved in Idaho territorial politics. Soon after William Henson Wallace became territorial governor of Washington, he began lobbying, with his new political crony Anson Henry, for the organizing of a new territory to the east, in the booming mining areas beyond Walla Walla and stretching over the Rockies. Working elbow to elbow, Wallace and Henry, the latter probably Lincoln's most active lieutenant in the Pacific Northwest, pushed for the territory of Idaho, which Congress and the president established in March 1863. Lincoln named Wallace as Idaho's first governor, and then as happened in Washington, almost before the ink on Lincoln's nomination form was dry, Wallace was elected Idaho's territorial delegate to Washington.[127]

In two years—from March 1863 to April 1865—Lincoln selected about fifteen men to territorial offices in Idaho. Some like Wallace, Sam Parks (a lawyer from Illinois), Sidney Edgerton (an acquaintance of the president), and Alleck C. Smith (Dr. Henry's son-in-law) were longtime political or family friends. Others such as Caleb Lyon of New York were curious Lincoln selections. Flamboyant and incompetent, Lyon gave half-crazy speeches filled with ancient literary references to miners and refused to govern the territory. Nor could Lyon ever explain how $46,000 in funds for Indian aid went missing.[128]

With Idaho only months old, Pacific Northwest political leaders were agitating for a new territory to the east that would take in the new communities springing up in and around the northern Rockies. One of these ringleaders for what became Montana was Sidney Edgerton, the former chief justice of Idaho. Overall, Lincoln had little direct contact with Montana. After he signed the congressional bill making Montana a territory on 26 May 1864, he named Edgerton governor, but most of his other appointees declined their positions, did not serve, or held office briefly before Lincoln's death. Edgerton was unable to emulate the president's talents in dealing with divided constituents. A devout Unionist, Edgerton sometimes attacked opponents as Confederate sympathizers, of which there were many in Montana. Still, without needed funding for secretarial help, Edgerton soldiered on until the summer of 1865, when he left the territory. Obviously the chaos following Lincoln's assassination in April 1865 had spilled over into far-off Montana in the months immediately following the tragedy.[129]

Lincoln's connections with Dakota Territory followed similar patterns. Once Congress established the area as a territory in 1861, Lincoln appointed his neighbor, physician, and Illinois political adviser William Jayne as governor. But then a Deist-like strategy obtained, as it did frequently in western territories during Lincoln's administration. The president named the territorial governor, took his hands off, and largely allowed that official to succeed or flounder without much presidential direction or support. Jayne experienced difficulty in Dakota largely because as an outsider and loyal Republican he was unable to rally strong, ongoing political support in a territory becoming increasingly no-party in its politics. In addition, Jayne seemed unable to blunt the political strength of Captain John Blair Smith Todd, a relative of Mary Todd Lincoln and an earlier resident of Dakota. As one scholar has concisely explained, when Jayne and Todd later contested for the office of territorial delegate, "the main issue was over which of the candidates had the most influence with President Lincoln, his physician [Jayne] or his wife's cousin [Todd]."[130] Lincoln's attitude toward Jayne's successor as Dakota governor seemed particularly lukewarm—"I suppose [Newton] Edmunds better be appointed Governor of Dakota." But the selection of that resident Dakotan in 1863 seemed to set well with the territory, and political squabbles assumed a new calm in the next two years.[131]

Lincoln's dealings with Utah and Colorado illustrate other ways in which varied peoples and experiences influenced the president's policies in western territories. Lincoln had limited early acquaintances with the Latter-day Saints. Although he did not comment on the Mormons being driven out of the Illinois city of Nauvoo following Joseph Smith's assassination in 1844, he later pushed Stephen Douglas to show how the concept of popular sovereignty would impact polygamy in Utah. Once in the White House, Lincoln followed his normal procedures in Utah: he appointed territorial officials from outside the territory, usually naming political allies to those offices. He was urged on more than one occasion to name Brigham Young, the Mormon president, territorial governor, but he did not. At first Young was unhappy with Lincoln, misnaming him "Abel" and describing the president's power as "like a rope of sand, or like a rope made of water." Then, his dislike intensifying, Young labeled Lincoln "wicked."[132]

The Mormons were dissatisfied with Lincoln's handling of Utah up to early 1863. Adding to their initial uncertainly about Lincoln's leadership was his signing of antipolygamy legislation that Congress passed in 1862. But when Lincoln replaced the unpopular territorial governor Stephen S. Harding with the more acceptable James Duane Doty and when he asked Brigham Young to help protect overland mail routes, the negative attitudes of the Saints began to soften. Even more instrumental in encouraging a more sympathetic Mormon attitude toward Lincoln was the oft-quoted conversation he is said to have had with Mormon T. B. H. Stenhouse. When Stenhouse visited the White House, he queried the president about his plans for Utah. Lincoln paused and then told the Mormon visitor: "You go back and tell Brigham Young that if he will let me alone, I will let him alone."[133] Opinions toward Lincoln sharply shifted among the Saints once his "let alone" policy became known and implemented in Utah.

Lincoln's links with Colorado differed a good deal from those with the Mormons because the religious-political culture of Utah was never present in Colorado. Congress passed legislation to organize the territory of Colorado in the last week of the Buchanan administration, and Lincoln quickly appointed its first territorial governor, William Gilpin, by the end of March 1861. An experienced traveler in the Far West and a Colorado booster, Gilpin seemed a logical choice for its territorial leadership. But his experimentation with deficit spending, even before the federal government discovered it, got him into deep trouble. In the first year of his governorship, Gilpin signed hundreds of thousands of dollars of promissory drafts for needed supplies and thereby plunged Colorado into a deep well of debt. Gilpin evidently thought Lincoln and his fiscal agents would honor the notes, but those administrators refused to do so. After the governor's fiscal credibility plummeted, he committed another large faux pas when he opined that Colorado ladies "were so few they were not worth mentioning."[134] He also wrote an anonymous and self-serving story in the *New York Times* (27 January 1862) praising the work of Colorado's "excellent governor" and accused many of the territory's residents of being incipient secessionists. Whether it was the overspending, the insults of women, or the self-congratulations, Gilpin had stumbled and fallen on his own political sword. Increasingly pressed to recall the naive Gilpin, Lincoln did so and replaced him with Dr. John Evans of Illinois.

Lincoln's selection of Evans as the second governor of Colorado resulted in part from the president's connections with the Methodists. Leaders of that denomination, especially the influential Bishop Matthew Simpson, urged Lincoln to name Methodists to western territorial offices. Heeding that advice, Lincoln nominated Dr. Evans as Washington's territorial governor. When Evans rejected that position in the Pacific Northwest as too remote, Lincoln named him to Colorado's governorship.[135] A doctor from the family after which Evanston, Illinois, was named and instrumental in founding Northwestern University in Evanston, Evans was well connected and pleased Coloradoans in his initial actions, particularly his promotions of mines, railroads, and other economic endeavors. But once Indian-settler conflicts began to mount and Evans sided with the militant opponents of Indians, the less attractive side of the governor began to show itself.

Evans demonstrated his limited leadership capabilities by issuing unwise proclamations while an anti-Indian virus infected increasing numbers of Colorado's white population. These proclamations allowed—and perhaps encouraged—trigger-happy settlers and militiamen to pursue Indians defined as "hostile" (i.e., those Indians who did not follow one of Evans's pronouncements calling on all peaceful Indians to retreat to forts or "places of safety," where they would be protected and fed). In these acts, Evans added incendiary fuel to already-burning fires and clearly urged Colorado militia members to kill off Indians who refused to retire to the army posts and who were thus "hostile." Evans's faulty leadership and the militia's thirst to wipe out Indians helped lead to the murderous Sand Creek Massacre on 29 November 1864. Evans was hotly criticized for his muddled and sometimes vicious role in Colorado's Indian affairs, and calls for his quick removal circulated widely. But as late as a month before Lincoln's assassination, the president wrote to the beleaguered Evans without calling for his resignation and urged him to move on with political appointments in Colorado.[136]

As the only western area that transitioned from territorial status to statehood during Lincoln's administration, Nevada occupied a unique position in the president's web of political connections with the West. Lincoln was centrally involved in the unusual steps leading to Nevada's statehood. Like Colorado, Nevada became a territory in the closing hours of the Buchanan administration. In the first days of his presidency, Lincoln named James Warren Nye, a New Yorker and friend of Secretary of State William Seward, the first and only territorial governor of Nevada. For territorial secretary, following the advice of his attorney general, Missourian Edward Bates, Lincoln selected Orion Clemens, the older brother of Samuel L. Clemens (Mark Twain), who came west to Nevada as his brother's secretary.[137]

As national political and economic needs quickly came into focus, Lincoln pushed Nevada toward statehood, even though its number of residents was well below the 60,000 population threshold stipulated for statehood. Lincoln coveted the mineral wealth of Nevada to help fund the mounting costs of the North's war efforts, and he also wanted another antislavery state whose senators and representative would support the Republican Party and their legislation to end slavery. Residents of Nevada moved rapidly toward statehood, with more than three-fourths of the territory's 8,162 voters casting their ballots in favor of statehood in September 1863. In the same year, the U.S. Senate voted to enable Nevada, Colorado, Montana, and Nebraska to write constitutions for statehood, but the move for enablement languished in the House. Also in 1863, Nevadans rejected the first draft of their constitution, chiefly because it included taxation of the total assets of mines rather than merely their net worth.[138]

Although evidence is incomplete and historians differ in their conclusions, it is probable that Lincoln encouraged Nevadans to try again for statehood. One scholar seems closest to the truth in arguing that Washington, D.C.—and Lincoln—helped "instigate" the second attempt at Nevada statehood.[139] The president increasingly needed more votes in Congress to pass a constitutional amendment ending slavery; he worried about his own reelection in 1864; and he wanted another Republican state to support his war measures. In 1864 Lincoln promptly signed all bills Congress passed in moving Nevada toward statehood. Throughout the late summer and early fall of 1864, Nevadans, Congress, and the president were in a hurry-up mode to complete the necessary steps for Nevada statehood. A copy of the entire new Nevada state constitution was even wired to Washington, costing taxpayers $4,303.27, to satisfy the necessary deadlines. Following the stipulations of special congressional legislation, Lincoln proclaimed Nevada a new state in October 1864, and it was able, just a few days later, to participate in the election of 1864. Nevada's first senators hurried to Washington to support Lincoln, and its lone congressman voted on 31 January 1865 for the Thirteenth Amendment ending slavery. After the new state soon thereafter ratified the amendment, Nevada had, in the words of one historian, "paid the initial installment of its debt to Lincoln and Congress."[140]

Lincoln's connections to states and territories across the Southwest stretching from California to Louisiana, although varied, also illustrate his enormously important ties to these areas. Lincoln's military ties, especially with Texas, Arkansas, and Louisiana, were particularly strong. Links in other areas were nonmilitary.

Lincoln often expressed great interest in California. The California Gold Rush, the Mexican-American War and the Compromise of 1850, the move of his very close friend Edward Baker to the West Coast, even the thought of moving his wife and sons there—all these happenings and dreams enlarged Lincoln's interest in California. Once he was elected, those hopefuls lusting after California patronage positions invaded the White House to twist Lincoln's arm or sent their cheerleaders to persuade the president. His California links turned political, and they were very complicated.[141]

The double-barreled political challenges facing Lincoln in California were, for the most part, familiar competitions elsewhere in the West. But they seemed more intense—even cut-throat—in the Golden State. In the hectic and politics-filled weeks between the November 1860 election and Lincoln's first days as president, the new Oregon senator Edward Baker came to the White House with suggestions for patronage positions in California. Baker arrived as Lincoln's longtime intimate friend, as a recent California resident for nearly a decade, as the only Republican national officeholder on the West Coast, and as a believer in a spoils system that rewarded family and friends. It was a system of political appointments to which Lincoln also subscribed.

California Republicans then congregating in Washington to protect their own interests rushed to the White House when they heard of Baker's taking a list of possible appointees to the president. The Republicans had their list, including many of their own names, to bring to Lincoln's attention. Perhaps there was also a sense of urgency for all. In the first decade of its existence, California was primarily a Democratic state. Now the Republicans, for the first time, might have a new lease on officeholding with one of their own in the White House.[142] Rumors were still afloat, too, that California and perhaps Oregon might organize an independent "Pacific Republic." Governor

John B. Weller seemed to substantiate this threat when he declared in his annual address in 1860 that California "will not go with the South or the North, but here on the shores of the Pacific [will] found a mighty republic which may in the end prove the greatest of all."[143]

One day after Lincoln received endorsements for Baker's nominations from nearly a dozen of the Oregon senator's supporters, fifty-five Republicans invaded the White House to provide an alternative roster of candidates. Their list, they claimed, was "the expression of a majority of California Republicans now in Washington."[144] Knowing the intentions of this group, Lincoln invited Senator Baker to join him for breakfast in the White House and to stay over for the meeting with the disgruntled California Republicans. After presenting their protest, the Californians asked James W. Simonton, editor of the *San Francisco Bulletin*, to read a statement. It included a fiery attack on Baker and his son-in-law, Andrew J. Butler, a Democrat for whom Baker wished to win a political plum in California. Once Simonton finished his diatribe, so the story goes, Lincoln asked if he could have the comments, which he then threw into the fire as an unwonted attack on his friend Ned Baker. Later, Lincoln evidently apologized to Simonton for his emotional reaction.[145]

Even as these confrontations over California patronage were transpiring, Lincoln was attempting to deal with the fateful events surrounding Fort Sumter that eventually led to the first shots of the Civil War. Despite these mounting pressures, Lincoln found a way to balance the two groups making demands for California political appointments. Fortunately, Leland Stanford, occupying a middle-of-the road position between the two factions and then in Washington, provided Lincoln with good suggestions from both lists. Following some of these suggestions and his own balanced instincts, Lincoln named leaders from both groups to several positions in California. Neither the Baker supporters nor the California Republicans were entirely pleased, of course, but the California patronage squabbles settled down after Lincoln's adroit handling of a possible tempestuous situation. Nor were observers blind to what California's mineral wealth meant to the North. Month after month, one or two steamers left California ports with more than $1 million in gold on board. In 1864 alone, more than $46 million poured into the North's war chest from California. Gen. U. S. Grant, realizing how much California's loyalty and its mineral wealth meant, told others, "I do not know what we would do in this great national emergency were it not for the gold sent from California."[146]

Lincoln knew much less about New Mexico than California. Just as he was acquainted with few individual African Americans and Native Americans, so he may not have known any Hispanics before entering the White House. A handful of lawyer and political friends, as well as Radical Republicans in Congress, were Lincoln's informants as well as agents of pressure in his dealings with New Mexico. Lincoln's patronage appointments in New Mexico reveal he was more bipartisan there than in any other western territory, especially in the first year or two of his administration.[147]

New Mexico had been a territory for nearly a decade before Lincoln made his first appointments there. These initial nominations, signaling exceptions to Lincoln's usual patronage patterns in the western territories, indicate the unique pressures in the southwestern region. In 1861–62, growing pro-southern sentiments in Texas to the east and in the southern part of the New Mexico Territory stretching west into present-day Arizona shaped Lincoln's thinking about New Mexico. In light of these hovering Confederate influences, there were doubts that New Mexico could be kept in the Union. To offset the possibility of such a loss, Lincoln needed loyal Union leaders in New Mexico, no matter their party allegiance. Given this necessity, Lincoln appointed Dr. Henry Connelly as the new territorial governor. A Democrat who had lived in the Southwest since 1824, Connelly spoke for the Union and against the "Texan" threat.

Even more offensive to Republican loyalists than Connelly's Democratic politics was Lincoln's choice for territorial secretary, Miguel A. Otero.[148] An enthusiastic Democrat and a former New Mexico territorial delegate in the 1850s, Otero had supported proslavery legislation and roundly criticized the Republicans as "this horde of infidels" who held a "hostility to the death" toward native New Mexicans.[149] But Lincoln, thinking Otero could rally New Mexicans to the Union and help keep out the Confederates, sent Otero's nomination to the U.S. Senate for confirmation. (The Republican-dominated Senate rejected Otero's nomination in the summer 1861.) Lincoln retained a third Democrat, Kirby Benedict, as chief justice of the territory's supreme court. He had been acquainted with Benedict in Illinois, knew of his Union sentiments, and preferred to keep a stalwart supporter in the judicial position despite his political affiliation. These selections of Democrat Unionists were unusual for Lincoln and for the West and were powerfully upsetting to Republican Radicals.[150]

The patronage decisions in New Mexico owed much to the influence of John S. Watts. Appointed an associate justice in New Mexico in 1851, Watts had remained in the territory during the following decade. He wrote to Lincoln, urging him to avoid appointing nonresidents and to name the best leaders, irrespective of their political preferences. For Watts, Connelly was "the most able influential and popular man in New Mexico," and he was convinced that on "the appointment of Mr. Otero to this office [territorial secretary] depends the success or failure of the administration of New Mexico."[151]

But Lincoln's patronage decisions in New Mexico changed directions after Union forces held off a Confederate invasion from Texas in 1862. With the southern threat much diminished, the president, still feeling the persisting pressure from the Radicals, was less inclined to nominate other Democrats for available positions. Still, overall, Lincoln's decisions on patronage in New Mexico provide a revealing exception to most of his appointments in western territories. As he had in border states to the east, Lincoln tried, as Deren Earl Kellogg notes in chapter 5, "to build broad cross-party coalitions that would help ensure their citizens' loyalty. . . . New Mexico's experience proved that [Lincoln] could be flexible and inspired when the situation demanded."[152]

Lincoln's ties to Arizona were briefer and less controversial. Even before the Confederates were driven out of southern and western New Mexico, Ohio promoters supporting companies from their state with investments in the Southwest pushed for federal organization of an Arizona territory to protect those interests. Congress moved quickly on the Arizona Organic Act, and Lincoln signed it 24 February 1863. Most of Lincoln's first territorial nominees were former congressmen, including John A. Gurley, the governor appointee who died before coming to Arizona, and his replacement, John N. Goodwin.[153] Some wags might have pointed out, with only a bit of exaggeration, that the new territory had more politicians than other white settlers, since the latter numbered only 4,187 in the 1864 census. But Congress seemed convinced, and perhaps Lincoln too, that Arizona contained abundant mineral wealth, making it another California, Nevada, or Colorado to enrich the North's yawning war-effort coffers. Still, for the most part, Lincoln was less engaged with Arizona than with any other part of the West.[154]

Lincoln's isolation from political activities in Louisiana, Texas, and Arkansas stemmed from other sources. Louisiana (on 26 January 1861) and Texas (on 1 February 1861) had already seceded when Lincoln became president, and Arkansas followed soon thereafter (on 6 May 1861). Lincoln did remain connected militarily with all three during his administration and began to formulate some of his earliest plans for Reconstruction in these states.

In Texas an intriguing political link with Lincoln remained even after the state's secession. There his contact was with Sam Houston, the sitting governor when Texas withdrew from the Union. Houston was a Unionist, disinclined to join other southern secessionist states, and offered to resign rather than join the Confederacy. As rumors of Houston's and other Unionists' position trickled up to Washington from distant and isolated Texas, Lincoln decided to make surreptitious contact with Houston and to offer him aid and military support to keep Texas loyal. But the outgoing Texas governor, now on the verge of abdicating his position, rejected Lincoln's offer. It came too late, Houston told one messenger; he did not want to lead Texas Unionists into a fratricidal war with Texas supporters of the Confederacy. Houston's decision ended Lincoln's contact with Texas political leaders.[155]

These manifold political connections demonstrate that across the West, from California to Minnesota and from Washington Territory to Louisiana, Lincoln was deeply involved in western politics. He made dozens of political patronage appointments in the new territories, helped establish the Republican Party in territories and states alike, and influenced party politics directly in all western states. These political activities were Lincoln's most important links with the West during his presidency. He administered a larger combination of western states and new territories than any previous president. Like George Washington, Thomas Jefferson, and James K. Polk before him, Lincoln reshaped the political-geographical map of the United States.

Some historians think Lincoln's patronage appointments in the trans-Mississippi West undistinguished. Others are even more critical, accusing Lincoln of naming too many friends and hungry politicians to positions in the West. Appointees like Caleb Lyon of Idaho, William Gilpin of Colorado, and dozens of nominees to the Indian service were ineffectual leaders, political hacks, or downright crooks. But many others, among them governors James Nye of Nevada, Henry Connelly of New Mexico, and William Henson Wallace of Washington and Idaho, served well, leading western territories through challenging transitional times. When one considers that all these political contacts and appointments were made during the country's most traumatic years, the achievements of these appointees clearly outweigh their failures.

If Lincoln's political connections spread out like a new, self-expanding web during his presidency, his western links on the issue of slavery seemed to disappear—or move rapidly in other directions. During the second stage of

Lincoln's ties to the West, from the Mexican-American War until his entry into the White House in March 1861, his most important western involvement was his position allowing no extension of slavery into the territories. That stance changed early in his administration.

To reiterate, historians should emphasize more specifically that Lincoln's adamant position against the expansion of slavery into the territories when he arrived in Washington was a *western* as well as an *antislavery* position. In March 1861 all areas still not organized as territories lay west of the Mississippi. Thus, when Lincoln became president, he was speaking out against any further expansion of slavery *into the West*. His viewpoint about the nonextension of slavery into western territories, like that of many Whigs and later Republicans, was closely linked to their attitudes about the West. As historian Eric Foner has written, "In the eyes of many Republicans, the development of the West held the key to America's future."[156] If the West—those areas through which the Mississippi coursed and the huge, sprawling lands beyond the Mississippi—were to remain the promise of the future, it must be kept a free land, a free soil for free labor.

Lincoln's own decisions and congressional actions in the first two years of his administration radically changed his stance on the Wilmot Proviso that he had held to for nearly fifteen years. When he became president, Lincoln advocated colonization as the best solution for the future of free blacks as well as former slaves. He called for the voluntary immigration of blacks to Africa, to Panama, and to an island located just off Haiti. No group expressed large interest in these colonization schemes, and those that were tried ended disastrously, but Lincoln continued to encourage the idea—even after issuing the Emancipation Proclamation. He also urged border states and all slave states to consider compensated emancipation; if plantation owners would free their slaves, the U.S. government would compensate them at the current value of the slave. Neither did this idea catch fire despite Lincoln's strong support for it on several occasions.

Two congressional legislative enactments also helped change Lincoln's attitudes and actions concerning slavery in the West. On 19 June 1862, he signed a measure Congress passed that ended all slavery in U.S. territories, all of which, of course, were in the West. As Lincoln biographer Phillip Shaw Paludan points out, although there were less than a hundred "slaves in the territories, [and] the actual freedom proved minor, . . . the vindication of the long-treasured principle was sweet."[157] Shortly thereafter, on 17 July, Congress passed the Second Confiscation Act. This controversial legislation, about which Lincoln was decidedly lukewarm but nonetheless signed, defined Rebels as guilty of insurrection and allowed, among other provisions, the freeing of their slaves. The provision of emancipation not only contradicted the Republican platform of 1860 but, more importantly, implied that Congress had the power to end slavery in any state. Rather than veto the legislation and anger the largely Republican Congress, Lincoln decided to take his own route to the ending of slavery.

Lincoln's steps were gradual, sometimes reluctant, in the move toward emancipation. When Lincoln issued the preliminary form of his Emancipation Proclamation in September 1862 and the full and official proclamation on 1 January 1863, his actions impacted parts of the West. The final version stated that "all persons held as slaves within any State or designated part of a State, the people whereof shall then be in rebellion against the United States, shall be then, thenceforward, and forever free," and it specifically referred to Arkansas, Texas, and parts of Louisiana.[158] Shortly thereafter, the president began pushing for a constitutional amendment to end slavery in all parts of the nation. After being defeated in the House of Representatives in late summer 1864, the Thirteenth Amendment cleared Congress in January 1865, pushed adroitly along by Lincoln's extraordinary efforts to ensure its passage, including the vote from the new state of Nevada. The amendment's eventual ratification in December 1865 by three-fourths of the states meant that slavery was ended—in all western states, as elsewhere in the country.

When the Civil War erupted in April 1861, Lincoln did not include the trans-Mississippi West in much of his fumbling efforts at overall war strategy. Once events forced him to turn his attention to military events in the West, most of his decisions dealt with the actions of his generals, matters concerning Indian conflicts, or other strategic matters.

When the war came, Lincoln had no specific strategy in mind about how to assume or carry out his central role as commander in chief. Just as he lacked a design for national military affairs, so he had no strategy planned for the American West. But by the end of 1861 or early 1862, he had bit by bit begun to decide what roles the trans-Mississippi West would play in the Civil War. He wanted to make certain, first of all, that the Confederacy did not invade and capture the West, particularly New Mexico and Arizona, on their way to the California coast and the valuable mineral deposits and important seaports. Second, if possible, Lincoln hoped to divide southern dominion at the Mississippi, separating the western Confederate states of

Texas and Arkansas and parts of Louisiana from the Confederacy to the east. Third, he wanted to control the Mississippi River and keep it open for trade and troop movements up to Illinois. In addition, he wished to make sure the two new states of the Far West, California and Oregon, stayed with the Union. Of course, the unexpected consequences of the first months of the war, intraparty squabbles in Missouri and Kansas, Indian conflicts, and the idiosyncratic actions of Union military leaders served as central reminders that these goals might be difficult to achieve.[159]

As in the area of politics and patronage, no part of the West vexed Lincoln more militarily than Missouri. As a military consideration, the state was a lynchpin of Lincoln's preliminary strategy of foiling the Confederacy's attempts to move west, a key to keeping the Mississippi open for trade, and a gateway to the area where, the president hoped, he might begin to divide his opponents into isolated eastern and western wings. But the warring elements among pro-South and pro-Union forces and the internecine conflicts within his Republican Party gave Lincoln military and political headaches throughout his presidency. Politics and military decisions were so intertwined in Missouri that even a master leader such as Lincoln was unable to unravel them. And he got diverse and misguided suggestions from his friends and advisers.

The conflicting advice on Missouri began in his own backyard—in his cabinet. Atty. Gen. Edward Bates, a Missourian by heritage and a moderate Republican at most, urged cautious military control in Missouri, a control that would not disrupt the fragile economy of the state. In contrast, Postmaster Gen. Montgomery Blair, son of the eminent political patriarch Francis Preston Blair, understandably supported his brother Frank Blair, a Missouri political leader. At first a friend of Frémont and Radical Republicans in his policies, Monty Blair now backed his brother Frank and commander Nathaniel Lyon, who stormed through Missouri throwing out Confederate sympathizers and vigorously pursuing the reported ten thousand guerillas harassing Missourians and Union supporters in 1862. The "hards" like Blair and Lyon and the Radical Republicans told Lincoln he needed to act boldly in Missouri to root out "soft," more conservative leaders such as Governor H. R. Gamble, who often blamed Union invaders from Kansas and elsewhere, as well as the loathsome guerillas, for the state's major problems.[160]

Lincoln summed up his vexations with the Missouri scene when he wrote Gen. Samuel R. Curtis in early 1863: "I am having a good deal of trouble with Missouri matters."[161] Temperamentally more inclined toward the "softs" than the "hards," Lincoln told Curtis's replacement, Gen. J. M. Schofield, "Let your military measures be strong enough to repel the invader and keep the peace, and not so strong as to unnecessarily harrass and persecute people. . . . If both factions, or neither, shall abuse you, you will probably be about right."[162] Lincoln remained convinced that if the good men of Missouri would shake themselves and rise up in humanity and good will, peace would come to the state. He located few such good men. Those on site were more convinced that enforcing law and order with strong military measures and leadership was necessary to keep even an uneasy peace. The military-political squabbles continued unresolved throughout the Civil War and remained one of Lincoln's largest headaches in the West.

Lincoln's attempts to clear the Mississippi of Confederate control and to split the South into two, unconnected parts brought fewer nightmares. Still, in the spring of 1863, as Gen. U. S. Grant prepared to float down the Mississippi to engage the Confederates at Vicksburg, Lincoln "feared it was a mistake" when Grant laid plans to march overland on the western shores of the Mississippi until below Vicksburg, recross the river, march inland below the southern fortress, and attack. But news of Grant's startling victory at Vicksburg compelled the president to write to him on 13 July that though Lincoln had had his doubts about Grant's plans, he now wished to "make the personal acknowledgment that you were right, and I was wrong."[163] Two weeks later, the president was reporting emphatically, if a bit overconfidently, that "The Father of Waters again goes unvexed to the sea. . . . Peace does not appear so distant as it did."[164]

Solving the military dilemmas in Missouri and opening the Mississippi were high on Lincoln's agenda. Success came in the second goal but not in the first. The president also hoped to return Texas quickly to the Union and keep areas farther west from falling into Confederate hands. Again his successes were mixed. As Lincoln told General Grant soon after his victory at Vicksburg, "I am greatly impressed with the importance of re-establishing the national authority in Western Texas as soon as possible."[165] But despite Lincoln's encouragement and superior numbers of Union troops in some areas of Louisiana and Texas, the North was unable to drive the Confederates from these areas. Botched expeditions and flawed invasions of the Texas coast and up the Red River in Louisiana, rivalries between Union leaders, and mixed signals and conflicting goals of military leaders in Washington, D.C., and the East undermined attempts to reassume Union domination of Texas and all of Louisiana.[166]

For a few months early in the war, it looked as if Lincoln's desire to save New Mexico and Arizona would also go south. In the latter half of 1861 and early months of 1862, Confederate units under Lt. Col. John R. Baylor and Brig. Gen. Henry Hopkins Sibley launched campaigns from Texas into New Mexico that quickly gained control over the southern and central sections of the territory. After moving north to take Albuquerque and Santa Fe without major difficulty, the invading Confederates marched rapidly toward Fort Union in northern New Mexico. Then a southward-dashing group of Colorado Volunteers, in a surprising, end-run maneuver, caught the invading Texans unawares, routed them at the Battle of Glorieta Pass in late March 1862, and sent Sibley's forces in rapid retreat back to Texas. But in southern New Mexico, Texans under Colonel Baylor's command, after capturing Union troops stationed at Fort Fillmore, declared themselves the "Confederate Territory of Arizona," with headquarters at Mesilla, New Mexico. Confederate Arizona was short-lived in 1862 and soon fell before the California Column, moving eastward under the leadership of Col. James H. Carleton. Revealingly, Abraham Lincoln seemed unaware of most of these military activities, or at least did not mention them. He left most military decisions to others.[167]

But Lincoln was centrally involved in the events surrounding the Sioux uprising in Minnesota in 1862. His presidential moves there included several military decisions. Soon after Lincoln heard of the Sioux outbreak in August 1862, he sent Gen. John Pope to organize military operations against the Sioux. Pope found that the Indian annuity system was rancid with racism, bias, and outright thievery, typified by one agent who repeatedly said, "So far as I am concerned, if the [Indians] are hungry let them eat grass or their own dung."[168] Nevertheless, Pope assumed an aggressive military posture toward the Indians, culminating in the call for the summary execution of hundreds of them discussed above. Lincoln countered these militaristic decisions, following instead the more humane suggestions of religious leaders and his own, less harsh inclinations. The president's military and political actions in the fall of 1862 with regard to the Sioux uprising and its aftermath may have been the most significant he took concerning the West.[169]

On the evening of 11 April 1865, less than a week after the South surrendered at Appomattox, Lincoln appeared at a White House window to give a speech. Historians often point to this presentation as Lincoln's kickoff of his Reconstruction policies. But Lincoln had already floated parts of his plan for Reconstruction. Some of those details had been revealed in the West in sections of Louisiana and Arkansas.

Lincoln's plans for Reconstruction began to emerge, tentative and piece-meal, as soon as Union forces assumed control of formerly Confederate-held areas. Although other regions experienced some of these preliminary effects of Reconstruction, the state of Louisiana became the first full test of Lincoln's Reconstruction policies in the trans-Mississippi West. Lincoln's desire to return Confederate states to the Union as soon as possible, with a minimum of nods to "niceties of the law," emerged in his dealings with Reconstruction in Louisiana and elsewhere. They were testaments to Lincoln's pragmatic willingness to discover modes of action in the midst of a journey rather than superimposing a hard-and-fast series of demands from the beginning.[170]

Lincoln's Annual Message to Congress and his Proclamation of Amnesty and Reconstruction, both dated 8 December 1863, provided guidelines on how ex-Confederates and their states might become "reconstructed" and again part of the Union. The president's proposal, the so-called "10 percent plan," stipulated that a Confederate state could return to the Union when 10 percent of its qualified voters in 1860 took an oath of allegiance, received amnesty, rewrote their constitutions omitting slavery, and elected repre-sentatives to the U.S. Congress. Radical Republicans attacked Lincoln's plan of Reconstruction as far too lax, open to misuse by pragmatic and self-serving ex-Confederates, and blind to the needs of the newly freed slaves in the South. Recognizing the tensions within his own party and understanding the need to rally national support, Lincoln confessed that his plan was tentative and not the only blueprint the nation might follow. Still, moving ahead, he named military governors in the newly conquered areas of Arkansas, Louisiana, and Tennessee and urged leaders there to accept his 10 percent plan.[171]

Confederate control in Arkansas was short-lived. Within a year of Ar-kansas's secession in May 1861, Union forces began to push out the Con-federates. Northern victories at Pea Ridge (March 1862), the largest battle in the trans-Mississippi West, and at Prairie Grove (December 1862) and the fall of Little Rock in September 1863 essentially ended southern domi-nation of the state. Soon thereafter, Lincoln named Gen. Frederick Steele, a competent and generally kind administrator, to lead Arkansas through the Reconstruction process. When Lincoln's timelines proved out of sync with what Steele and provisional governor Isaac Murphy were planning for Arkansas, the president stepped back, saying he had "been constantly trying to yield my plan to them." Lincoln urged General Steele to do the same and work with Murphy and other Unionists in their convention to establish a new government in the state.[172] In March 1864, qualified voters supported Murphy as governor, ratified a new constitution, 12,177 to 226, and elected three congressmen. Later, the new Arkansas legislature named two U.S. senators, but Congress, greatly influenced by Radical Republican leadership, refused to seat any of these newly elected officials and called for their own system for reconstructing the South rather than following the president's too-lenient plan.[173]

Louisiana was an even more important symbol of Lincoln's attempts at restoring the Rebel states back into the Union. In April 1862, the troops of Gen. Benjamin Butler captured New Orleans, the largest and most cosmopolitan city of the Confederacy. General Butler moved to broaden support by backing Unionists and their Free State Association. So did Lincoln, in August 1863. He encouraged Gov. Nathaniel P. Banks, who had replaced Butler, to call a convention to rewrite the Louisiana constitution and end slavery. But political divisions within the Republican ranks and among other political factions doomed any quick movement toward Reconstruction. Radical Republicans particularly pushed for more involvement of blacks in the new government. Lincoln seemed to be moving in that direction too. "I barely suggest for your private consideration," Lincoln wrote to Michael Hahn, the newly elected governor from the Free State group, "whether some of the colored people may not be let in—as, for instance, the very intelligent, and especially those who have fought gallantly in our ranks. They would probably help . . . to keep the jewel of liberty within the family of freedom. But this is only a suggestion, not to the public, but to you alone."[174]

When the constitutional convention met, it displayed the complexities of the Reconstruction process in Louisiana as well as the ambiguities of the delegates' reactions to Lincoln's urgings. Slavery was ended, the old proslavery planters were absent and roundly criticized, and a few provisions concerning wages, labor, and educational benefits impacting emancipated blacks were adopted. But members of the convention did not take up Lincoln's "suggestion" that some blacks be allowed to vote. Some observers were especially surprised to learn that more than a few convention members who were abolitionists supported measures to transport all blacks out of Louisiana.[175]

Nationally and at the state level, clashes over a welter of issues divided the Republicans and other Union supporters, delayed Reconstruction, and disappointed Lincoln with respect to Louisiana. When Radical Republicans in Congress, dissatisfied with what they considered the extraordinary leniency of Lincoln's presidential Reconstruction, pushed through their own Wade-Davis bill demanding much more from the southern states, the president pocket vetoed it. When Lincoln made his last public address on 11 April 1865, he admitted that Reconstruction was "fraught with great difficulty." Reviewing what he had done especially in Louisiana and reiterating that his plan was "not the only plan which might possibly be accepted," he cut to what he consider two central questions: "Will it not be wiser to take it [the new Louisiana constitution] as it is, and help to improve it; or to reject, and disperse it?" and "Can Louisiana be brought into proper practical relation with the Union *sooner* by *sustaining* or by *discarding* her new State Government?"[176]

Lincoln spoke to listeners standing just outside the White House, but he was also speaking to Congress and the whole country. All must be flexible as they traveled uncharted territory to bring the newly refitted ship of liberty through the shoals of difference and competition. He counseled flexibility and promised "to make some new announcement to the people of the South. ... [He would not] fail to act, when satisfied that action will be proper."[177] What those words and actions would have been will never be known; the plans remained unfinished. Four days later, John Wilkes Booth assassinated Lincoln in Ford's Theater.

Abraham Lincoln was undoubtedly satisfied with some results of his connections with the trans-Mississippi West. To the end of his life, he defended his controversial opposition to the Mexican-American War and his notable role in opposing the expansion of slavery into the western territories. Although progress on launching the transcontinental railroad was slow and the taking up of homesteads barely begun, these were enactments about which he was pleased. Even though fractious political clashes still divided Missouri and several of his territorial appointees were rascals or flat failures, he had helped organize giant sections of the West and planted his Republican Party in the region. Governmental policies dealing with Indians remained a challenge, but the president hoped to reform that rancid system. He seemed to retain similar hopes about preliminary plans for Reconstruction across the country from Texas, Arkansas, and Louisiana in the west through the South to the East Coast. Quite possibly Lincoln would have pointed to more successes than failures in his record of unfinished business in the West.

If these thoughts entered Lincoln's mind in the last days of his life, they likely resonated with many mid-nineteenth-century Americans. His contemporaries would have remembered him as an "anti-Nebraska man," an opponent of slavery in new western territories, and a backer of the development of agricultural lands and transportation networks in the West. And, although he did not stand with the agents of Manifest Destiny in the 1840s and their vows to annex Texas, reannex Oregon, and take large sections of Mexico at the end of the Mexican-American War, he was an expansionist of another kind. He called for and helped put into place territorial governments in expansive parts of the West that eventually came into the Union as states, all of them by 1912. Few of his fellow Americans criticized his treatment of Native Americans as too harsh; in fact, many thought him too sympathetic to American Indians, particularly in Minnesota and Indian Territory.

But now, after a century and a half of hindsight, many historians and other students of our past view Lincoln's actions in the West through different eyes. We realize that his support of the Pacific Railroad and the Homestead Act and the implementation of those expansionist measures led to tragic consequences for Native Americans, especially in the loss of their lands and rights. Also, without proper fiscal safeguards, the huge federal financial outlays and land grants to the Union Pacific and Northern Pacific resulted in disastrous economic, political, and social consequences for the West. Nor was Lincoln able to deal satisfactorily with crises in governmental policies in regard to Native Americans during the Civil War. Like nearly all his contemporaries, he seemed blind to the full rights of Native Americans, Mexicans, and African Americans; his western policies sometimes reflected this blindness. From the perspective of many early twentieth-first-century Americans, sometimes with clouded and presentist views of their own, Lincoln's western connections seem more complex and less successful than the sixteenth president and his supporters thought.

Still, whatever observers conclude about Lincoln's links with the West— whether as successes, failures, or both—they are likely to agree that these connections reveal a good deal about our greatest president and our largest region. These ties with the West prove that among Lincoln's many designations, he deserves to be known as a Man of the West.

Notes

1. W. Emerson Reck, *A. Lincoln: His Last 24 Hours* (1987; Columbia: University of South Carolina Press, 1994), 20; Earl Schenck Miers, ed., *Lincoln Day by Day: A Chronology, 1809–1865*, 3 vols. (1960; Dayton, OH: Morningside, 1991), 3:329–30.
2. Douglas L. Wilson and Rodney O. Davis, eds., "Mary Todd Lincoln (WHH interview)," in *Herndon's Informants: Letters, Interviews, and Statements about Abraham Lincoln* (Urbana: University of Illinois Press, 1998), 357, 359; Justin Turner and Linda Turner, *Mary Lincoln: Her Life and Letters* (New York: Alfred A. Knopf, 1972), 276–78, 399–400.

3. Roy P. Basler et al., eds., *The Collected Works of Abraham Lincoln* (New Brunswick, NJ: Rutgers University Press, 1953–55), 8:410, 412 (hereafter CW); Reck, *A. Lincoln*, 15, 53–57.

4. The only discussion of books and essays dealing with Lincoln and the West appears in Samuel E. Bell and James M. Smallwood, "The Pragmatic Lincoln: A Historiographical Assessment of His Western Policy," *Lincoln Herald* 86 (fall 1984): 134–42. For a brief overview of Lincoln and the American West, see Richard W. Etulain, "Lincoln Looks West," *Wild West* 21 (April 2009): 26–35.

5. Unfortunately, the single book treating Lincoln and the territorial West is narrowly focused and inadequately researched: Ralph Y. McGinnis and Calvin N. Smith, eds., *Abraham Lincoln and the Western Territories* (Chicago: Nelson-Hall, 1994). The best recent biographies of Lincoln contain information on his connections with the West. See Ronald C. White Jr., *A. Lincoln: A Biography* (New York: Random House, 2009); and Michael Burlingame, *Abraham Lincoln: A Life*, 2 vols. (Baltimore: Johns Hopkins University Press, 2008).

6. Henry Nash Smith, *Virgin Land: The American West as Symbol and Myth* (Cambridge, MA: Harvard University Press, 1950); Richard W. Etulain, *Re-imagining the Modern American West: A Century of Fiction, History, and Art* (Tucson: University of Arizona Press, 1996).

7. Douglas L. Wilson, *Honor's Voice: The Transformation of Abraham Lincoln* (New York: Alfred A. Knopf, 1998), 53; Patricia Hochwalt Wynne, "Lincoln's Western Image in the 1860 Campaign," *Maryland Historical Magazine* 59 (June 1964): 165–81, quote on 178; Wayne C. Williams, *A Rail Splitter for President* (Denver: University of Denver Press, 1951), 141, 144.

8. Richard N. Current, *Speaking of Abraham Lincoln: The Man and His Meaning for Our Time* (Urbana: University of Illinois Press, 1983), 3–4.

9. CW, 4:48–49.

10. Williams, *Rail Splitter*.

11. CW, 1:89, 4:24; Harold Holzer, ed., *The Lincoln-Douglas Debates: The First Complete, Unexpurgated Text* (1993; New York: HarperPerennial, 1994), 86, 88; Isaac N. Arnold, *The Life of Abraham Lincoln* (1884; Lincoln: University of Nebraska Press, 1994), 82–83; Waldo W. Braden, "'A Western Man': Lincoln's Appearance and Delivery," in *Abraham Lincoln, Public Speaker* (Baton Rouge: Louisiana State University Press, 1988), 104–15.

12. The best recent discussion of Whig ideas and political philosophy appears in Daniel Walker Howe, *What Hath God Wrought: The Transformation of America, 1815–1848* (New York: Oxford University Press, 2007).

13. CW, 1:5

14. Gabor S. Boritt, *Lincoln and the Economics of the American Dream* (1978; Urbana: University of Illinois Press, 1994), viii.

15. Kenneth J. Winkle, *The Young Eagle: The Rise of Abraham Lincoln* (Dallas, TX: Taylor Trade, 2001), 202, 238.

16. CW, 1:382

17. Robert W. Johannsen, *Stephen A. Douglas* (New York: Oxford University Press, 1973), 139.

18. Ibid., 163.

19. CW, 1:337.

20. CW, 1:347, 348.

21. CW, 1:420, 421, 422.

22. CW, 1:432, 433, 439, 441–42.

23. Quoted in David Herbert Donald, *Lincoln* (New York: Simon and Schuster, 1995), 125.

24. William Herndon and Jesse W. Weik, *Herndon's Lincoln*, ed. Douglas L. Wilson and Jesse W. Weik (1889; Urbana: University of Illinois Press, 2006), 177. A letter from a longtime Illinois politico and close friend of Lincoln reveals how varied Whig politics were in Lincoln's home state; see Anson G. Henry to Abraham Lincoln, 29 December 1847, Abraham Lincoln Papers, Manuscript Division, Library of Congress (hereafter ALP), available online at <http://memory.loc.gov/ammem/alhtml/alhome.html>. All citations to the ALP are from this online site.

25. Gabor S. Boritt, "A Question of Political Suicide?: Lincoln's Opposition to the Mexican War," *Journal of the Illinois State Historical Society* 67 (February 1974): 79–100; Mark E. Neely Jr., "Lincoln and the Mexican War: An Argument by Analogy," *Civil War History* 24 (March 1978): 5–24 (reprinted in chapter 1 of the present volume).

26. For an early, extended discussion of Lincoln in Congress, see Albert J. Beveridge, *Abraham Lincoln, 1809–1858*, 4 vols. (Boston: Houghton Mifflin, 1928), 2:73–196. A more recent account is Paul Findley, *A. Lincoln: The Crucible of Congress* (New York: Crown, 1979).

27. Donald W. Riddle, *Congressman Abraham Lincoln* (Urbana: University of Illinois Press, 1957), 178.

28. For a discussion of Lincoln's run for commissioner of the land office, see Thomas F. Schwartz, "'An Egregious Political Blunder': Justin Butterfield, Lincoln, and Illinois Whiggery," *Journal of the Abraham Lincoln Association* 8 (1986): 9–19.

29. Documents dealing with Lincoln's rejection of the Oregon offers are printed in CW, 2:61–67, and in Roy P. Basler and Christian O. Basler, eds., *The Collected Works of Abraham Lincoln, 2nd Supplement, 1848–1865* (New Brunswick, NJ: Rutgers University Press, 1990), 2–6. See also Paul I. Miller, "Lincoln and the Governorship of Oregon," *Mississippi Valley Historical Review* 23 (December 1936): 391–94.

30. Walter B. Stevens, *A Reporter's Lincoln*, ed. Michael Burlingame (1916; Lincoln: University of Nebraska Press, 1998), 276–77; Michael Burlingame, ed., *An Oral History of Abraham Lincoln: John G. Nicolay's Interviews and Essays* (Carbondale: Southern Illinois University Press, 1996), 15, 136.

31. Robert W. Johannsen, *Frontier Politics and the Sectional Conflict: The Pacific Northwest on the Eve of the Civil War* (Seattle: University of Washington Press, 1955); Richard W. Etulain, "Lincoln's Links to a Distant Oregon," *Portland Oregonian*, 18 February 2008.

32. CW, 3:512.

33. Michael S. Green provides a very helpful survey of a large subject in his essay "Lincoln, the West, and the Antislavery Politics of the 1850s" (chapter 2 of the present volume). The development of the trans-Missouri West in the 1850s is treated in Richard W. Etulain, *Beyond the Missouri: The Story of the American West* (Albuquerque: University of New Mexico Press, 2006).

34. Don E. Fehrenbacher, *Prelude to Greatness: Lincoln in the 1850's* (1962; New York: McGraw-Hill, 1964), 3.

35. CW, 2:122, 125.

36. Beveridge, *Abraham Lincoln*, 3:218. (see chapter subtitle).

37. Stephen B. Oates, *With Malice toward None: The Life of Abraham Lincoln* (New York: Harper and Row, 1977), 114–18.

38. The full Peoria speech appears in CW, 2:247–83; the quotes are from 262, 264, 266, 275, 281.

39. The most useful account of the mini-civil war in Kansas in the 1850s is Nicole Etcheson, *Bleeding Kansas: Contested Liberty in the Civil War Era* (Lawrence: University Press of Kansas, 2004). See also the valuable chapters in Fehrenbacher, *Prelude to Greatness*, and William C. Harris, *Lincoln's Rise to the Presidency* (Lawrence: University Press of Kansas, 2007).

40. William Lee Miller, *Lincoln's Virtues: An Ethical Biography* (New York: Alfred A. Knopf, 2002), 360–61.

41. CW, 2:321, 322–23.

42. CW, 2:316.

43. For the most thorough study of the rise of the Republican Party, see William E. Gienapp, *The Origins of the Republican Party, 1852–1856* (New York: Oxford University Press, 1987).

44. Harris, *Lincoln's Rise to the Presidency*, 91–92.

45. CW, 2:461.

46. The most recent, and now best, general account of the Lincoln-Douglas debates is Allen C. Guelzo, *Lincoln and Douglas: The Debates That Defined America* (New York: Simon and Schuster, 2008). The comment from Texas appears in Guelzo, "Houses Divided: Lincoln, Douglas, and the Political Landscape of 1858," *Journal of American History* 94 (September 2007): 391.

47. Guelzo, "Houses Divided," 403; Harold Holzer, introduction to *The Lincoln-Douglas Debates* , 22.

48. Guelzo, "Houses Divided," 412; CW, 3:51.

49. Guelzo, *Lincoln and Douglas*, 160–64.

50. Harris, *Lincoln's Rise to the Presidency*, 129–33.

51. Wilson and Davis, *Herndon's Informants*, 377–78.

52. CW, 3:279; Harris, *Lincoln's Rise to the Presidency*, 139.

53. Holzer, introduction, 27.

54. Miers, *Lincoln Day by Day*, 2:258; Waldo W. Braden, "Lincoln's Western Travel, 1859," *Lincoln Herald* 90 (Summer 1988): 38–43.

55. Miers, *Lincoln Day by Day*, 2:258; CW, 3:396–97; E. R. Harlan, "Lincoln's Iowa Lands," *Annals of Iowa* 15 (April 1927): 621–23; William J. Peterson, "Lincoln and Iowa," *Palimpsest* 41 (February 1968): 81–103.

56. Carol Dark Ayres, *Lincoln and Kansas: Partnership for Freedom* (Manhattan, KS: Sunflower University Press, 2001); CW, 3:495–504; Charles Arthur Hawley, "Lincoln in Kansas," *Journal of the Illinois State Historical Society* 42 (June 1949): 179–92.

57. Unfortunately, Ayres, *Lincoln and Kansas*, exaggerates the importance of Lincoln's speeches in Kansas and underemphasizes how much the same ideas appeared in presentations before and after his trip to Kansas Territory. See M. H. Hoeflich and Virgil W. Dean, eds., "'Went to Hear Hon. Abe Lincoln Make a Speech': Daniel Mulford Valentine's 1850 Diary," *Kansas History* 29 (summer 2006): 100–115.

58. The quotation is the subtitle of Harold Holzer's *Lincoln at Cooper Union: The Speech That Made Abraham Lincoln President* (2004; New York: Simon and Schuster, 2005), the best study, by far, we have of this pathmaking Lincoln speech.

59. CW, 3:523.

60. Holzer, *Lincoln at Cooper Union*, especially chap. 6.

61. CW, 3:550.

62. Holzer, preface to the paperback edition, *Lincoln at Cooper Union* (2005), xviii, xix.

63. Harris, *Lincoln's Rise to the Presidency*, 205.

64. Ibid., 206; Don E. Fehrenbacher, *Lincoln in Text and Context: Collected Essays* (Stanford, CA: Stanford University Press, 1987), 56–57.

65. Doris Kearns Goodwin, *Team of Rivals: The Political Genius of Abraham Lincoln* (New York: Simon and Schuster, 2005).

66. CW, 4:200, 201

67. CW, 4:149, 160.

68. CW, 5:46, 47.

69. Allan Nevins, *The War for the Union*, vol. 2, *War Becomes Revolution, 1862–1863* (New York: Charles Scribner's Sons, 1960), 189.

70. In the 1950s, historian David H. Donald described Lincoln as "the Whig in the White House," an interpretation that still influences many American historians; for Professor Donald's earliest use of this phrase, see Donald, "Abraham Lincoln: Whig in the White House," in Norman A. Graebner, ed., *The Enduring Lincoln* (Urbana: University of Illinois Press, 1959), 47–66.

71. CW, 4:214.

72. William E. Gienapp, *Abraham Lincoln and the Civil War: A Biography* (New York: Oxford University Press, 2002), 106.

73. Grenville M. Dodge, *Personal Recollections of President Abraham Lincoln, General Ulysses S. Grant, and General William T. Sheridan* (1914; Denver: Sage Books, 1965), 11; John William Starr, *Lincoln and the Railroads: A Biographical Study* (New York: Dodd, Mead, 1927), 196.

74. Boritt, *Lincoln and the Economics of the American Dream*, 210–11.

75. Ibid., 211.

76. Stephen E. Ambrose, *Nothing Like It in the World: The Men Who Built the Transcontinental Railroad, 1863–1869* (New York: Simon and Schuster, 2000), 78; Louis Bernard Schmidt, "Abraham Lincoln's New Deal for the Argonauts," *Arizoniana* 3 (Winter 1962): 25–35.

77. Heather Cox Richardson, *The Greatest Nation on the Earth: Republican Economic Policies during the Civil War* (Cambridge, MA: Harvard University Press, 1997), 208.

78. Leonard P. Curry, *Blueprint for Modern America: Nonmilitary Legislation of the First Civil War Congress* (Nashville, TN: Vanderbilt University Press, 1968), 148.

79. I have benefited a good deal from the discussions of Lincoln and agriculture in Olivier Fraysse, *Lincoln, Land, and Labor, 1809–60*, trans. Sylvia Neely (1988; Urbana: University of Illinois Press, 1994); and Boritt, *Lincoln and the Economics of the American Dream*.

80. CW, 3:471–82, quote on 472, 473; Earle D. Ross, "Lincoln and Agriculture," *Agricultural History* 3 (April 1929): 51–66.

81. Lincoln's annual messages in 1862 and 1863 included his support for homestead legislation: CW, 5:25, 7:46–47. For capsule summaries of congressional actions on these agricultural measures, see Richardson, *Greatest Nation on Earth*, and Curry, *Blueprint for Modern America*.

82. Richardson, *Greatest Nation on Earth*, 150.

83. Phillip Shaw Paludan, *"A People's Contest": The Union and the Civil War, 1861–1865* (New York: Harper and Row, 1988), 132; Louis Bernard Schmidt, "Abraham Lincoln's New Deal for Industrial Education," *Arizoniana* 3 (Spring 1962): 10–15.

84. James G. Randall, a noted Lincoln authority from an earlier generation, provides a still useful summary of the Lincoln administration's contributions to agricultural legislation in *Midstream: Lincoln the President* (New York: Dodd, Mead, 1953), 143–48.

85. Two notable criticisms in the 1930s were Paul Gates, "The Homestead Law in an Incongruous Land System," *American Historical Review* 41 (1936); 652–81; and Fred A. Shannon, "The Homestead Act and the Labor Surplus," *American Historical Review* 41 (1936): 637–51.

86. Phillip Shaw Paludan, drawing on the interpretations of western environmental historian Donald Worster, points to the detrimental impact of Lincoln's western economic policies in *The Presidency of Abraham Lincoln* (Lawrence: University Press of Kansas, 1994), 116–18, 336.

87. David A. Nichols, *Lincoln and the Indians: Civil War Policy and Politics* (Columbia: University of Missouri Press, 1978), 78, 80. Of the several book-length studies of the Sioux uprising in Minnesota in 1862, two particularly include Native Americans in the story: Gary Clayton Anderson, *Little Crow: Spokesman for the Sioux* (St. Paul: Minnesota Historical Society Press, 1986); and Gary Clayton Anderson and Alan R. Woolworth, eds., *Through Dakota Eyes: Narrative Accounts of the Minnesota Indian War of 1862* (St. Paul: Minnesota Historical Society Press, 1988).

88. Donald, *Lincoln*, 90. William C. Harris provides a good section on Lincoln and Indians in *Lincoln's Last Months* (Cambridge, MA: Belknap Press of Harvard University Press, 2004), 168–95.

89. For a brief overview of Lincoln's handling of Indian relations, see David A. Nichols, "Lincoln and the Indians," in Gabor S. Boritt and Norman O. Forness, eds., *The Historian's Lincoln: Pseudohistory, Psychohistory, and History* (Urbana: University of Illinois Press, 1988), 149–69 (reprinted in chapter 9 of the present volume).

90. Francis Paul Prucha, *The Great Father: The United States Government and the American Indians*, 2 vols. (Lincoln: University of Nebraska Press, 1984), 1:443.

91. CW, 5:493.

92. Hank H. Cox, *Lincoln and the Sioux Uprising of 1862* (Nashville, TN: Cumberland House, 2005).

93. Nichols, *Lincoln and the Indians*, 112.

94. Among scholars studying Lincoln's Indian policies, Nichols is the most critical of the president. Much less negative are the conclusions in Harry Kelsey, "Abraham Lincoln and American Indian Policy," *Lincoln Herald* 77 (Fall 1975): 139–48.

95. CW, 5:439. The most extensive and best source on this subject is Gary E. Moulton, *John Ross: Cherokee Chief* (Athens: University of Georgia Press, 1978).

96. John Ross wrote several letters to Lincoln explaining the dilemmas he and the Cherokees faced. See, for example, Gary Moulton, ed., *The Papers of John Ross*, 2 vols. (Norman: University of Oklahoma Press, 1985), 2:516–18, 564, 614–15.

97. Prucha, *Great Father*, 468.

98. CW, 5:526.

99. Harry Kelsey, "William P. Dole and Mr. Lincoln's Indian Policy," *Journal of the West* 10 (July 1971): 484–85.

100. Elbert F. Floyd, "Insights into the Personal Friendship and Patronage of Abraham Lincoln and Anson Gordon Henry, M.D.: Letters for [*sic*] Dr. Henry to His Wife, Eliza," *Journal of the Illinois State Historical Society* 98 (Winter 2005–6): 236–38; Kelsey, "William P. Dole and Mr. Lincoln's Indian Policy," 491–92.

101. Harry J. Carman and Reinhard H. Luthin, *Lincoln and the Patronage* (New York: Columbia University Press, 1943). This thorough, fact-filled, and now somewhat dated source is still the beginning place for a study of Lincoln's political connections with the American West. Richard W. Etulain provides a brief summary of Lincoln's political roles in the trans-Mississippi West in his essay "Abraham Lincoln: Political Founding Father of the American West," *Montana: The Magazine of Western History* 59 (summer 2009): 3–22.

102. See the essays on eleven western territories in McGinnis and Smith, *Abraham Lincoln and the Western Territories.*

103. Earl Pomeroy, *The Territories and the United States, 1861–1890: Studies in Colonial Administration* (Philadelphia: University of Pennsylvania Press, 1947). This slim but extraordinary volume carries an invaluable "List of Territorial Officers, 1861 to 1890" (109–44), including the names of most of Lincoln's appointees.

104. Two helpful studies of Missouri during the Civil War are William E. Parrish, *Turbulent Partnership: Missouri and the Union, 1861–1865* (Columbia: University of Missouri Press, 1965); and Michael Fellman, *Inside War: The Guerilla Conflict in Missouri during the American Civil War* (New York: Oxford University Press, 1989).

105. Fehrenbacher, Don, and Virginia Fehrenbacher, eds., *Recollected Words of Abraham Lincoln* (Stanford, CA: Stanford University Press, 1996), 500.

106. CW, 4:506–7, 517–18.

107. Fehrenbacher and Fehrenbacher, *Recollected Words*, 220; Michael Burlingame and John R. Turner Ettlinger, eds., *Inside Lincoln's White House: The Complete Civil War Diary of John Hay* (Carbondale, IL: Southern Illinois University Press, 1997), 123.

108. CW, 6:218.

109. CW, 6:234.

110. Michael Burlingame, ed., *At Lincoln's Side: John Hay's Civil War Correspondence and Selected Writings* (Carbondale: Southern Illinois University Press, 2000), 57–64, quotes on 60, 64.

111. Michael Burlingame, ed., *With Lincoln in the White House: Letters, Memoranda, and Other Writings of John G. Nicolay, 1860–1865* (Carbondale: Southern Illinois University Press, 2000), 165.

112. Johannsen, *Frontier Politics and the Sectional Conflict*; Etulain, "Lincoln's Links to a Distant Oregon."

113. Robert W. Johannsen, "The Tribe of Abraham: Lincoln and Washington Territory," in David H. Stratton, ed., *Washington Comes of Age: The State in the National Experience* (Pullman: Washington State University Press, 1992), 73–93 (reprinted in chapter 6 of the present volume).

114. David Logan to Abraham Lincoln, 15 September 1861, Lincoln Collection, Huntington Library, San Marino, CA; Harry E. Pratt, ed., "22 Letters of David Logan, Pioneer Oregon Lawyer," *Oregon Historical Quarterly* 44 (September 1943): 254–85; David Alan Johnson, *Founding the Far West: California, Oregon, and Nevada, 1840–1890* (Berkeley: University of California Press, 1992).

115. Harry Edward Pratt, "Dr. Anson G. Henry, Lincoln's Physician and Friend," *Lincoln Herald* 45 (October 1943): 3–17, (December 1943): 31–40.

116. Of the numerous letters Henry wrote Lincoln about political, family, and friendship matters, see especially two for information about political complexities in the Pacific Northwest: A. G. Henry to Lincoln, 21 June 1861, and Henry to Lincoln, 11 November 1861, A. G. Henry Papers, SC 683, Abraham Lincoln Presidential Library, Springfield,

IL. CW, 6:111, refers to a ten-page letter that Henry wrote to Lincoln on 3 February 1863 about "affairs in Oregon and Washington Territory in general and Indian affairs in particular," but I have been unable to locate this letter.

117. See Paul M. Zall's previously unpublished essay, "Dr. Anson G. Henry (1804–65): Lincoln's Junkyard Dog" (chapter 7 in the present volume).

118. Quoted in Pratt, "Dr. Anson G. Henry," 34; Harry C. Blair, *Dr. Anson G. Henry: Physician, Politician, Friend of Abraham Lincoln* (Portland, OR: Binfords and Mort, 1950), 27.

119. Paul M. Zall, "Simeon Francis, 1796–1872," unpublished manuscript in the possession of Richard W. Etulain; Mark E. Neely Jr., *The Abraham Lincoln Encyclopedia* (New York: McGraw-Hill, 1982), 116–17.

120. *Oregon City (Ore.) Argus*, 31 March 1860; Simeon Francis to Abraham Lincoln, 26 December 1859, ALP.

121. Harry C. Blair and Rebecca Tarshis, *Colonel Edward D. Baker: Lincoln's Constant Ally* (Portland: Oregon Historical Society, 1960).

122. Johnson, *Founding the Far West*.

123. Johannsen, "Tribe of Abraham," 82–83; A. G. Henry to "My dear Genl," 30 October 1861, Bion F. Kendall Papers, University of Washington Library, Seattle.

124. Johannsen, "Tribe of Abraham," 83–86; Robert E. Ficken, *Washington Territory* (Pullman: Washington State University Press, 2002).

125. Kenneth N. Owens, "Pattern and Structure in Western Territorial Politics," *Western Historical Quarterly* 1 (October 1970): 373–92, and "Government and Politics in the Nineteenth-Century West," in Michael P. Malone, ed., *Historians and the American West* (Lincoln: University of Nebraska Press, 1983), 148–76.

126. Johannsen, "Tribe of Abraham," 89; Gerry L. Alexander, "Abe Lincoln and the Pacific Northwest," *Columbia: The Magazine of the Northwest History* 16 (Winter 2002–3): 3–6.

127. David H. Leroy, "Lincoln and Idaho: A Rocky Mountains Legacy," in Frank J. Williams et al., eds., *Abraham Lincoln: Sources and Style of Leadership* (Westport, CT: Greenwood Press, 1994), 143–62; A. G. Henry to Gov. W. H. Wallace, 6 December 1863, W. H. Wallace Papers, University of Washington Library, Seattle.

128. Ronald H. Limbaugh, *Rocky Mountain Carpetbaggers: Idaho's Territorial Governors* (Moscow: University of Idaho Press, 1982).

129. Clark Spence, *Territorial Politics and Government in Montana, 1864–89* (Urbana: University of Illinois Press, 1975), 17, 234–35; CW, 7:371–72, 403; Patricia Ann Owens, "Wyoming and Montana during the Lincoln Administration," *Lincoln Herald* 91 (Summer 1989): 49–57.

130. Howard R. Lamar, *Dakota Territory, 1861–1889: A Study of Frontier Politics* (New Haven, CT: Yale University Press, 1956), 91.

131. CW, 6:494–95.

132. E. B. Long, *The Saints and the Union: Utah Territory during the Civil War* (Urbana: University of Illinois Press, 1981), 29, 67.

133. Larry Schweikart, "The Mormon Connection: Lincoln, the Saints, and the Crisis of Equality," *Western Humanities Review* 34 (Winter 1980): 13 (reprinted in chapter 8 of the present volume). See also George U. Hubbard, "Abraham Lincoln as Seen by the Mormons," *Utah Historical Quarterly* 31 (Spring 1963): 91–108.

134. Thomas L. Karnes, *William Gilpin: Western Nationalist* (Austin: University of Texas Press, 1970); Duane A. Smith, *The Birth of Colorado: A Civil War Perspective* (Norman: University of Oklahoma Press, 1989), 24.

135. CW, 5:173–74; Harry E. Kelsey Jr., *Frontier Capitalist: The Life of John Evans* (Boulder, CO: Pruett, 1969).

136. CW, 8:356; Elliott West, *The Contested Plains: Indians, Goldseekers, and the Rush to Colorado* (Lawrence: University Press of Kansas, 1996), 290–307.

137. CW, 4:295.

138. Russell R. Elliott and William D. Rowley, *History of Nevada* (1973; 2nd ed., Lincoln: University of Nebraska Press, 1987), 69–89. For another view of Lincoln's desires for Nevada, see Earl S. Pomeroy, "Lincoln, the Thirteenth Amendment, and the Admission of Nevada," *Pacific Historical Review* 12 (December 1943): 31–40 (reprinted in chapter 3 of the present volume).

139. F. Lauriston Bullard, "Abraham Lincoln and the Statehood of Nevada," *American Bar Association Journal* 26 (March 1940): 210–13, 236; (April 1940): 313–17.

140. Elliott and Rowley, *History of Nevada*, 89; Merlin Stonehouse, *John Wesley North and the Reform Frontier* (Minneapolis: University of Minnesota Press, 1965), 172–77.

141. Milton H. Shutes, *Lincoln and California* (Stanford, CA: Stanford University Press, 1943). Also, see two well-researched essays by Robert J. Chandler, "Crushing Dissent: The Pacific Coast Tests Lincoln's Policy of Suppression, 1862," *Civil War History* 30 (September 1984): 235–54; and "The Release of the *Chapman* Pirates: A California Sidelight on Lincoln's Amnesty Policy," *Civil War History* 23 (June 1977): 129–43.

142. John Denton Carter, "Abraham Lincoln and the California Patronage," *American Historical Review* 48 (April 1943): 495–506.

143. Walton Bean, *California: An Interpretive History* (New York: McGraw-Hill, 1968), 177.

144. CW, 4:301, 302.

145. Carter, "Abraham Lincoln and the California Patronage."

146. CW, 4:304–6; Leonard L. Richards, *The California Gold Rush and the Coming of the Civil War* (New York: Alfred A. Knopf, 2007), 230.

147. Deren Earl Kellogg, "Lincoln's New Mexico Patronage: Saving the Far Southwest for the Union," *New Mexico Historical Review* 75 (October 2000): 511–33 (reprinted in chapter 5 of the present volume); Ralph Y. McGinnis, "New Mexico Territory," in McGinnis and Smith, *Abraham Lincoln and the Western Territories*, 71–83.

148. Vincent G. Tegeder, "Lincoln and the Territorial Patronage: The Ascendancy of the Radicals in the West," *Mississippi Valley Historical Review* 35 (June 1948): 77–90 (reprinted in chapter 4 of the present volume).

149. Kellogg, "Lincoln's New Mexico Patronage," 515, 514.

150. Howard R. Lamar, *The Far Southwest, 1846–1912: A Territorial History* (New York: W. W. Norton, 1970); Robert W. Larson, *New Mexico's Quest for Statehood, 1846–1912* (Albuquerque: University of New Mexico Press, 1968).

151. John S. Watts to Abraham Lincoln, 1 and 2 April 1861, quoted in Kellogg, "Lincoln's New Mexico Patronage," 523–24.

152. Ibid., 529.

153. Lamar, *Far Southwest*, 433, 435.

154. CW, 6:141; Deren Earl Kellogg, "'SLAVERY MUST DIE': Radical Republicans and the Creation of Arizona Territory," *Journal of Arizona History* 41 (Autumn 2000): 267–88; Walter N. Duffett, "Arizona Territory," in McGinnis and Smith, *Abraham Lincoln and the Western Territories*, 84–96.

155. Howard C. Westwood, "President Lincoln's Overture to Sam Houston," *Southwestern Historical Quarterly* 88 (October 1984): 125–44.

156. Eric Foner, *Free Soil, Free Labor, Free Men: The Ideology of the Republican Party before the Civil War* (1970; New York: Oxford University Press, 1971), 55.

157. Paludan, *Presidency of Abraham Lincoln*, 135.

158. CW, 6:29.

159. Alvin M. Josephy, *The Civil War in the American West* (New York: Alfred A. Knopf, 1991); Ray Colton, *The Civil War in the Western Territories: Arizona, Colorado, New Mexico, and Utah* (Norman: University of Oklahoma Press, 1959).

160. CW, 6:234

161. CW, 6:36

162. CW, 6:234.

163. CW, 6:326.

164. CW, 6:409, 410.

165. CW, 6:374.

166. Josephy, *Civil War in the American West*, 161, 186–94; William C. Harris, *With Charity for All: Lincoln and the Restoration of the Union* (Lexington: University Press of Kentucky, 1997), 91–95.

167. J. J. Wagoner, *Arizona Territory, 1863–1912: A Political History* (Tucson: University of Arizona Press, 1970); Andrew E. Masich, *The Civil War in Arizona: The Story of the California Volunteers* (Norman: University of Oklahoma Press, 2006).

168. Donald, *Lincoln*, 392.

169. In an attempt to head off a secessionist movement on the West Coast, Lincoln made sure that the Civil War draft was not implemented in California and Oregon. Lincoln's war policies for the West Coast are discussed in G. Thomas Edwards, "The Department of the Pacific in the Civil War Years" (Ph.D. dissertation, University of Oregon, 1963).

170. Eric Foner, *Reconstruction: America's Unfinished Revolution, 1863–1877* (New York: Harper and Row, 1988). For an innovative study of post-Lincoln Reconstruction policies and their impact on the American West, see Heather Cox Richardson, *West from Appomattox: The Reconstruction of American after the Civil War* (New Haven, CT: Yale University Press, 2008).

171. CW, 7:55.

172. CW, 7:189, 161.

173. Conrad Berry III., "Arkansas and Abraham Lincoln: Wartime Reconstruction and the President's Plan for the State" (Ph.D. dissertation, University of Mississippi, 1992); Don E. Fehrenbacher, "From War to Reconstruction in Arkansas," in *Lincoln in Text and Context*, 143–56; Harris, *With Charity for All*, 197–211.

174. CW, 7:243; Peyton McCray, *Abraham Lincoln and Reconstruction: The Louisiana Experiment* (Princeton, NJ: Princeton University Press, 1978).

175. Foner, *Reconstruction*, 46–50; William B. Hesseltine, *Lincoln's Plan of Reconstruction* (1960; Chicago: Quadrangle Books, 1967).

176. CW, 8:400, 403, 404.

177. CW, 8:405.

1 ➤ Lincoln and the Mexican War:
An Argument by Analogy

Mark E. Neely Jr.

Since Albert Beveridge's *Abraham Lincoln, 1809–1858* (1928), historians have regarded Lincoln's opposition to the Mexican War as a unique mistake, an ordinarily practical politician's case of political suicide. The unseasoned Sucker, they say, went to Washington for his first and only fling at national office (other than the presidency fourteen years later), was dazzled by the shining brilliance of his great Eastern Whig heroes, forgot the simple patriotic sentiments of his expansionist Midwestern constituents in Illinois's Seventh Congressional District, and opposed the war. The consequence was bipartisan outrage among his constituents and a tactical decision on Lincoln's part not to face the voters again for years. Indeed, his record *in* Congress was so odious to the voters that it doomed the next Whig to run for the district's congressional seat to defeat anyway—and that too in the only safe Whig district in this overwhelmingly Democratic state.

G. S. Boritt has entered an important challenge to the reigning interpretation. He notes that there is almost no evidence of popular disagreement with Lincoln's stand except in Democratic newspapers. Among Whigs who lived in the Seventh District, only two left evidence of dissent. One was Albert Taylor Bledsoe, who recalled decades later that Lincoln had made a political mistake by opposing the war. In the meantime, however, Bledsoe had been assistant secretary of war in the Confederacy and had become, for obvious reasons, a Lincoln-hater. The other was Lincoln's law partner, William H. Herndon, a witness who must be contended with. Boritt suggests that Herndon exag-

From *Civil War History* 24 (March 1978): 5–24.

gerated the importance of his influence on the great man by claiming greater political wisdom. Boritt hints at a complete reversal of the older view, seeing Lincoln's opposition not as opportunistic but as "the politics of morality" *and* seeing it as politically palatable to his constituents as well.[1]

The reappraisal of Lincoln's opposition to the Mexican War is only just beginning and needs a great deal of refinement. There is still a tendency to grant too much of the case to those who say he was politically maladroit and, therefore, to leap to the defensive position that he was being idealistic. The challenge to the older view is not based on any large body of evidence unavailable to Beveridge and his followers, and there may be some temptation to look upon the debate as a draw. This article will attempt to approach the problem by indirection, adding the weight of the actions of Lincoln's analogous peers in Congress to the balance and providing some refinements based on reading the documents in the light of post-Beveridge scholarship.

The first refinement that needs urgently to be made regards the interpretation of William Herndon's contemporary warnings to Congressman Lincoln that he had strayed onto dangerous ground in opposing the Mexican War. In his 1889 biography, Herndon recalled: "I warned him of public disappointment over his course, and I earnestly desired to prevent him from committing what I believed to be political suicide."[2] Even Lincoln's defenders have taken Herndon at his word on this point, and the term *political suicide* has influenced the literature ever since.[3]

Only Lincoln's letters to Herndon have survived, and one must infer what Herndon told Lincoln from the nature of Lincoln's responses. Though this leaves room for doubt on some points, happily it leaves no room for doubt in regard to the nature of Herndon's warning. Herndon wrote Lincoln on January 19, 1848, as soon as he heard that Lincoln had voted for George Ashmun's amendment (to a resolution of thanks to General Zachary Taylor for his victory at Buena Vista), which called the Mexican War "unconstitutional and unnecessary." Lincoln answered Herndon's letter the next day after he received it, saying, "The only thing in it that I wish to talk to you about at once, is that, because of my vote for Mr. Ashmun's amendment, you fear that you and I disagree about the war. I regret this, not because of any fear we shall remain disagreed, after you shall have read this letter, but because, if *you* misunderstand, I fear other good friends will also."[4] Thus it was Lincoln who suggested that the disease of political error might spread to Whig friends; Herndon had uttered only a personal disagreement with Lincoln's stand on the war.

Herndon complained again on January 29, and Lincoln again answered the next day after receiving the letter: "Your letter of the 29th. Jany. was received last night. Being exclusively a constitutional argument, I wish to submit some reflections upon it in the same spirit of kindness that I know actuates you."[5] Herndon seems to have quibbled with his partner on a constitutional point *exclusively*; he had apparently said nothing about the political effect of Lincoln's error on the district.

In his later biography, Herndon made his claim to superior "political" wisdom seem plausible by quoting Lincoln's letter in response to still another letter written on June 15, over four months after their disagreement over the Mexican War. In this letter, Lincoln did say, "how heart-sickening it was to come to my room and find and read your discouraging letter of the 15th." The discouraging news, if one judges from what followed in Lincoln's letter, however, had nothing to do with popular reactions to Lincoln's stand on the Mexican War. Answering Herndon's despair over the loss of certain men to the Whig cause in the district, Lincoln explained the cause of the problem: "Baker and I used to do something, but I think you attach more importance to our absence than is just. There is another cause. In 1840, for instance, we had two senators and five representatives in Sangamon; now we have part of one senator, and two representatives. With quite one third more people than we had then, we have only half the sort of offices which are sought by men of the speaking sort of talent. This, I think, is the chief cause." The letter went on to discuss the discontent of young men in the party (like Herndon) who felt they were being held back by the old fogeys. In fact, the problem, as Herndon obviously described it—far from being Lincoln's unpopularity—was the lack of his (and Edward Baker's) popular presence as a political speaker to rouse the Whigs to an election effort. Herndon also asked for information about the Mexican War, but the discussion remained unrelated to the political problems mentioned earlier in Lincoln's letter. Surely Herndon would not bemoan Lincoln's absence from the campaign and accuse him of driving voters away in the same letter.[6]

Remove William Herndon's claim to speak for disaffected Seventh District Whigs, and the evidence in regard to the political wisdom of Lincoln's opposition to the Mexican War is moot. Democratic newspapers attacked Lincoln for his stand, Whig newspapers defended him, and no editor broke partisan ranks. Lincoln did not stand the test of the voters in the next election (August 1848), and the man who did lose the seat, Stephen T. Logan, was a notoriously poor campaigner, fully capable of losing the district on his own.[7]

To evaluate the political wisdom of Congressman Lincoln's stand, one can only compare it to the course taken by similar men in similar circumstances. Unfortunately, Illinois affords no analogs, for Lincoln was the only Whig in the Illinois delegation to the Thirtieth Congress. Neighboring Indiana offers the nearest available basis for comparison. Politically and socially, the states were much alike, carved as they were out of the Old Northwest Territory by settlers from the same areas of the eastern, and southern United States. The Democracy dominated both states by the time of the Mexican War; in 1846, Illinois had one Whig congressman out of seven, and Indiana, two of ten. The Whig Party was stronger in Indiana, where it contested elections in every congressional district (though in two districts Whigs occasionally claimed a "no party" status in their campaign rhetoric); in Illinois, Whigs gave up the fight in some districts altogether. Nevertheless, the two delegations recognized their kinship and often cooperated (and competed) as the representatives of the interests of the Old Northwest.[8]

The comparison is complicated by the peculiarly unregularized status of American elections at that time. For the same Congress in which Lincoln served, elections were held in various states at various times over a period of a year and three months. Lincoln was elected in August 1846 and then waited more than a year to go to Washington to take his seat in the Thirtieth Congress, which convened in December 1847. Indiana's delegation to the same Congress was elected in August 1847, a full year later.[9]

Indiana's Whig congressmen thus stood election at the height of the Mexican War, during a period in which Congressman-elect Lincoln could, and did, remain silent on the issue. The Indiana Whigs could not remain silent, though they knew it was a thorny issue in the expansionist West. John D. Defrees, who edited the largest Whig newspaper in the state, thus advised a would-be Whig congressman from South Bend:

> This war question is rather a dangerous one to handle. It requires much prudence in its management. That the war is an outrage—and will forever be so regarded cannot be doubted. Corwin's speech on the subject, was pure, unadulterated Christianity, but, unfortunately, *that* has very little to do in determining elections.
>
> I think the true policy for you to take would be ... "that Congress should declare that, in the prosecution of the war, it was not our intention to ... dismember the Republic of Mexico, or to demand any portion of her territory, as the terms of a treaty of Peace—& that we were at all times ready to open negoti[ati]ons to conclude peace." So long as the War

lasts,—our *flag* and those who uphold it *must* be sustained—while, at the same time, those who placed that flag where it is, must be denounced &c. The doctrine of withholding supplies—proper enough in England where it always produces a change of Ministers, will not answer here, however it may be in theory.[10]

Of the two incumbent Whig congressmen in Indiana in 1847, only Caleb Blood Smith regained nomination. By far the most vociferous opponent of the war in the state, Smith came from a safe Whig district; Fayette, Henry, Union, and Wayne counties had consistently given majorities to Whig congressional candidates since 1837. When Smith ran for reelection against Democrat Charles Test in the summer of 1847, he described his campaign to Joshua Giddings this way: "[I am] in the field and canvassing the district in opposition to the war." The Democratic paper in Richmond, Indiana, called for Test's election "not because he is a democrat, not because he has claims on the democracy of the 4th district, but merely, because he is the advocate of his country's cause, the vindicator of her honor, the sworn foe of her enemy, and the supporter of her rights." In the issue immediately preceding the election, the rival Whig paper asked simply, "Are we for peace or war?" Smith won, 4,988 to 3,540, a better margin than in 1845. He even brought scorching Tom Corwin from Ohio to Richmond after the election. Three weeks after Lincoln gave his antiwar address in Congress, Smith gave his third antiwar speech in Congress.[11]

The other Whig incumbent chose not to run, and Terre Haute Whig Richard W. Thompson ran in his stead. Thompson's was a safe Whig district also, and this dictated an antiwar campaign. Thompson explained his strategy to a nervous supporter this way: "Of course, the *Whigs* have power to beat me—the *Locos* have not. Why should *Whigs* vote against me? There are a few *here* who do it from *personal* considerations—say 10 in this County. There are also 3 in Vermillion—but I know of no others of *this* sort in the district. Then, all other *Whigs* who vote against me must do it because of my *anti-war* notions—The question then resolves itself into this—is the District *for* the war or *against* it . . . I do not think the district in favor of the war—and shall think it *Whig* until *I am beaten*."[12] A constituent agreed, noting that "the war . . . was the only question of the canvass (of which any notice was taken)."[13] Thompson was running against a popular candidate who gave the Democracy confidence even in the Whiggish district. Whig J. S. Harvey, fretting about Thompson's campaign, advised Thompson that in Putnam County one "Captain Roberts was buried . . . lately, and they have been raising the very devil over there out of your opposition to the war. A whig from there the other day says he can count 20 Whigs in that vicinity who will not vote for you; I did not know the man, but there are those here (your friends) who say he is to be believed."[14]

Thompson's judgment was vindicated, for he defeated the popular Joseph A. Wright by some two hundred votes. This was a considerably smaller margin than that by which Whig Edward McGaughey had won the district two years previously, but factionalism in Whig ranks may have been a problem. H. G. Hilton wrote Thompson about two weeks before election day to warn him that he was in trouble because of his war stand and that, if Thompson would just give the word, McGaughey would save him. Thompson answered, "If I am to be beaten, because of my anti-war opinions, McGaughey would himself be equally objectionable—and I should scarcely think it probable that he could operate upon *war* men." Thompson added only a polite interest in having "the *active* support of McGaughey."[15] R. L. Hathaway was euphoric about Thompson's victory and argued that the Democrats' "defeat has shown them that the war is unpopular in this country and they now, for the *first time,* admit it. Not even the leaders deny it & some of the democrats this morning declare that they have always been anti-war men."[16] Thompson himself gave a more measured and temperate analysis of his victory to fellow Whig Elisha Embree just after the election: "I never doubted of my own success—although I ran against one of the most unscrupulous men in the State. My position in regard to the war was a very bold one, and kept some Whigs, who would not vote for Wright, away from the polls. But I was determined to carry it through. I knew my vote would be less than the usual Whig vote, but preferred to have it so, rather than to be elected by a different course. Hence my majority is only about 200—while I might have had, by a different course, a much larger one."[17]

Thompson's course of action in Congress was much like Lincoln's. Within days of arriving (on December 21, to be exact, the day before Lincoln introduced his famous "Spot Resolutions"), Thompson submitted a series of resolutions calling on the president to tell Mexico that peace could be settled on these terms: establishment of a boundary line in Texas that included the settlements south and west of the Nueces; purchase from Mexico of the territory west of the Rocky Mountains and north of the line 36°30′; settlement of United States claims against Mexico; and the surrender of all claims by the United States for indemnity for the expenses of war. On January 3, 1848, Thompson voted for resolutions to withdraw the army to the east bank of the Rio Grande and to make peace with no indemnity and with payment of all just claims due American citizens before the war. He voted for the Ashmun amendment. Then on January 27, just two weeks and a day after Lincoln's, Thompson gave a speech which argued that the United States had had no right to march troops as far as the Rio Grande, more or less the point of Lincoln's speech.[18]

Two other Indiana districts sent Whigs to Congress in 1847. In the First District, on the Ohio River, Elisha Embree upset Robert Dale Owen, a three-term Democratic incumbent of national reputation. George G. Dunn won a startling victory in the counties directly north of the First District. Winning by twelve votes out of almost fifteen thousand, he reversed a 64 percent Democratic landslide of 1845.

Dunn and Embree behaved differently than Thompson and Smith, probably because they did not come from safe Whig districts. Embree's campaign stressed the issue which had bred factionalism in the local Democratic Party and which brought defeat to Robert Dale Owen: one-man power and its ever-present accompaniment, nepotism. Owen was making his fourth consecutive run for Congress, and he had given too many patronage plums to too narrow a clique, including his brothers David and Richard (appointed director of the geological expedition to Wisconsin and captain of infantry, respectively) and his brother-in-law Robert Fauntleroy (as astronomer on the Coast Survey).[19]

Embree apparently dodged saying whether he admired Thomas Corwin's famous antiwar speech or not and answered most questions about his platform by saying that he would support Zachary Taylor's course—a dodge as well, because no one knew clearly where Taylor stood either. Democrats accused Embree of hypocrisy in crying over widows and orphans, some of whom were made by the very victories of Zachary Taylor he otherwise celebrated. He could not dodge the war issue altogether. Embree supported Taylor's defensive-line strategy, a plan to withdraw United States troops to a certain limited territory and leave it to Mexico to attack or sue for peace. He also gave a speech in the campaign in which he said it was not right to annex Texas because annexation brought on war. He did not stress the boundary issue, as Lincoln would later, but he did stress the war's origins. Avoiding an antiexpansionist position of any substance, Embree compared the situation of Texas to that of an underage youth wishing to marry. The United States, he said, should have got Mexico's consent. However, once the marriage was consummated, a parent need not annul it merely because the consent was not originally obtained, and Texas should be retained now.[20]

When he went to Congress, Embree avoided the war issue for a time and failed to be present at the vote on the Ashmun amendment. Finally, however, on May 3, 1848, amid rumors of peace, he gave a speech on a Bounty Land bill, in the course of which he called the Mexican War "a war of invasion and conquest, in opposition to the wishes and against the desires and interests of the great body of the people; a war, . . . of the President, and those of his party who expect to profit by it as individuals."[21]

George G. Dunn won in a traditionally Democratic district because the Democratic Party there split and had two candidates in the field against him until rather late in the contest. He apparently did not oppose the war in canvassing his two-thirds Democratic district. One constituent transmitted a Democratic dare to the new congressman: "If you have an opportunity to make a speech on the war question, you ought to do it, for the Locos say that you will not take the same ground on the war, in Congress, that you took last summer, when you canvassed the district."[22] Dunn did not take the dare; he made no speech on the war. When he did make his maiden speech (on the Oregon question) weeks after the war was over, Dunn carefully included a disapproval of dissent. "Some may have greatly *erred* in their views and expressions," the congressman said of Polk's opponents on the war issue, "—in my humble judgment, did; or when the war was recognized by Congress, it was then the lawful war of the country, whatever improprieties and irregularities may have previously existed, and as such demanded the united purposes and efforts of that country to ensure a speedy and honorable peace."[23]

Yet in the same speech Dunn treated the war with abusive language. He said the country was "improvidently and unnecessarily involved" in the war, a war rooted in "an insane and maddened avarice" and in "cupidity." He sneered at "high national considerations" as "the pretence for every international absurdity and insolent assumption of [the] right to interfere in the affairs of others, on our part." He added mocking phrases reminiscent of Tom Corwin: "We are resolved that henceforth there shall be no butchers upon this continent but ourselves."[24] Even in the midst of the war, Dunn had not deemed it inappropriate to vote for the Ashmun amendment, to send his constituents Albert Gallatin's *Peace with Mexico* (an antiwar pamphlet, which only grudgingly admitted that the United States might ask to adjust the Texas border and settle outstanding prewar claims against Mexico), or to frank John C. Calhoun's dissenting speeches, doubtless thought to be good antiwar medicine for a Democratic district.[25]

Abraham Lincoln did not share Smith's or the Whig Party's concerns about expansion. When the issue first surfaced in the form of the proposal to annex Texas in 1844, Lincoln called annexation on John Tyler's terms merely "inexpedient."[26] In a letter written to Williamson Durley in 1845, Lincoln left the only lengthy consideration of expansion which survives in his early correspondence: He denounced the "whig abolitionists of New York" for refusing to vote for Henry Clay in 1844 and thus making it possible for a Democratic president to annex Texas. But, Lincoln continued, "individually I never was much interested in the Texas question." On the one hand, he "never could see much good to come of annexation; inasmuch, as they were already a free republican people on our own model." On the other hand, "I never could very clearly see how the annexation would augment the evil of slavery. It always seemed to me that slaves would be taken there in about equal numbers, with or without annexation. And if more *were* taken because of annexation, still there would be just so many the fewer left, where they were taken from. It is possibly true, to some extent, that with annexation, some slaves may be sent to Texas and continued in slavery, that otherwise might have been liberated. To whatever extent this may be true, I think annexation an evil." Lincoln did "hold it to be . . . clear, that we should never knowingly lend ourselves directly or indirectly, to prevent . . . slavery from dying a natural death—to find new places for it to live in, when it can no longer exist in the old." This did not apply to Texas, which was already a slave republic. Therefore, Lincoln could conclude, "Liberty [Party] men . . . have viewed annexation as a much greater evil than I ever did."[27]

Acquisition of territory from Mexico was a different proposition. Slavery was forbidden by law there, and acquisition by the United States might give American slavery new areas to live in. On the other hand, the theory that expansion thinned the concentration of the slave population elsewhere and did not in and of itself increase total slave population was as applicable to New Mexico and California as it had been to Texas. Lincoln's ideas about the expansion of slave territory were not yet well thought out, and he would be challenged anew by the actions of the Polk administration in 1846.

Lincoln's ideas about expansion were not trammeled by any Federalist or Eastern residue of fear of expansion per se. Thus Texas annexation was largely a matter of indifference to him. He voiced no opposition to expansion of American territory into Texas as a policy which weakened the country's ability to improve and cultivate existing United States territory.[28]

Lincoln opposed expansion which would help slavery, but he never claimed that the Mexican War was a conspiracy to extend slave territory. In his famous congressional speech against the war, he refused to speculate about President Polk's motive for aggression against Mexico; he devoted the speech to proving simply that Polk was the aggressor. Campaigning for Taylor in the summer of 1848, Lincoln said he "did not believe with many of his fellow citizens that this war was originated for the purpose of extending slave territory." Rather, "it was his opinion, frequently expressed, that it was a war of conquest brought into existence to catch votes."[29]

Qualms about expansion itself would be a new development in Lincoln's thought. He had concentrated in the past on mastering the arguments for the Whig domestic program, which he felt underdeveloped Illinois needed badly; the party's foreign policy views were not stock parts of his political arsenal. It was the autumn of 1848 before Lincoln voiced a basically anti-expansionist position. In a campaign speech for Taylor, Lincoln claimed to be at one with "all those who wished to keep up the character of the Union; who did not believe in enlarging our field, but in keeping our fences where they are and cultivating our present possession, making it a garden, improving the morals and education of the people!"[30] Significantly, Lincoln was speaking to citizens of Worcester, Massachusetts, where the heritage of Federalist antiexpansionism among Whigs was as strong as any place in the Union. This partisan audience was the first to elicit antiexpansionist remarks from Lincoln.

Like most Western Whigs, Lincoln was better able to compromise with expansionism than the rest of the party. Since he did not oppose expansion, properly achieved, it was easier to compromise with expansion brought about by improper means. Lincoln protested those means—Polk's aggression—but expansion came to seem a sort of inevitability to him. In fact, that was the way he expressed his views in the spring of 1848: "As to the Mexican war, I still think the defensive line policy the best to terminate it. In a final treaty of peace, we shall probably be under a sort of necessity of taking some territory; but it is my desire that we shall not acquire any extending so far South, as to enlarge and agrivate the distracting question of slavery."[31]

One reason for this position was that Lincoln apparently shared the view of many that war between the United States and Mexico had been an inevitability even without the border incident involving Zachary Taylor on the

Rio Grande. Such would appear to be the meaning of this remonstrance to John Peck, an Illinois Baptist minister who had written what Lincoln deemed "a laboured justification of the administration on the origin of the Mexican War":

> [Y]ou say "Paredes came into power the last of December 1845, and from that moment, all hopes of avoiding war by negotiation vanished." A little further on, refering to this and other preceding statements, you say "All this transpired three months before Gen: Taylor marched across the desert of the Nueces." These two statements are substantially correct; and you evidently intend to have it infered that Gen: Taylor was sent across the desert, in *consequence* of the destruction of all hope of peace, in the overthrow of Herara of Paredes. Is not that the inference you intend? If so, the material fact you have excluded is, that Gen: Taylor was *ordered* to cross the desert on the 13th of January 1846, and *before* the news of Herara's fall reached Washington.[32]

On one occasion, Lincoln even uttered what was a typical apology for expansion—that the territory was better off in the hands of those who really knew how to put it to use for human advantage. In a lecture on discoveries and inventions in 1859, Lincoln sneered at Manifest Destiny, but he also praised the Yankee "*habit* of observation and reflection." "But for the difference in *habit* of observation," he said, "why did yankees, almost instantly, discover gold in California, which had been trodden upon, and over-looked by indians and Mexican greasers, for centuries?"[33] These remarks came more than ten years after the Mexican War, but they serve to remind us that Lincoln was not even at this late date an internationally minded man and that his dislike of that war stemmed mostly from a dislike of Democrats, from fears of the corruption of the Constitution's limits on executive war-making, and from fears that some territorial acquisitions would aggravate the slavery question. He worried not about Mexico and Mexicans but about the impact of the war on the domestic future of the United States.

Lincoln seems to have accepted the concept of territorial indemnity. Surely that concept underlay any belief that territorial acquisitions were "a sort of necessity." Moreover, in a speech in Wilmington, Delaware, on June 10, 1848, Lincoln chose to focus his criticism of the Democrats on the administration's desires for "a large sum of money to gain more territory than will secure 'indemnity for the past and security for the future.'"[34] This was a way to attack the administration for seeking something more than its announced war aim, indemnity, but it is worth noting that Lincoln nowhere questioned the concept of indemnity itself, which was surely an absurdity if the war were strictly a product of American aggression.

When Lincoln embraced the "defensive-line" strategy, he was embracing a plan that included, by 1848, considerable acquisitions of Mexican territory. Originally formulated by Taylor in 1846, it had been strictly a military strategy designed to achieve victory by putting the burden of attack on the Mexican army. Taylor had thought his small army incapable of invading central Mexico from the north because immense stretches of desert separated them from the prize, Mexico City. In a letter made public in January of 1847, Taylor had advocated the military virtues of assuming the defensive in the territory the United States already controlled.[35]

On February 9, 1847, John C. Calhoun gave a speech before the United States Senate which formulated the defensive-line strategy as a political rather than purely military plan. Calhoun transformed the idea into a stop-gap against any movement to acquire all of Mexico: "Mexico is to us the forbidden fruit; the penalty of eating it would be to subject our institutions to political death." He feared that an invasion of central Mexico would change the war from one for limited territorial indemnities to an unlimited war of conquest. He urged the United States to assume a stationary position running along the Rio Grande to the southern border of New Mexico and from there due west along the thirty-second parallel to near the head of the Gulf of California and then south through the gulf to the Pacific. Thus Calhoun's defensive-line strategy would acquire all the sparsely settled northern territories of Mexico which were said to be of great potential value to the United States and of little or no value to noncommercial Mexico. Taylor's plan was no longer a military strategy. Calhoun's version gained a maximum amount of territory into which Calhoun believed slavery would not enter because the land was too arid, and avoided the question of slavery expansion, which would rock the Union if territory further south were acquired.[36]

Lincoln embraced the strategy in all its guises. On the one hand, he said that territorial acquisitions were a necessity, and the strategy was a way of accepting them without agitating the slavery question. On the other hand, he once chided Whig Usher F. Linder, who had his doubts about opposing the war, this way: "By justifying Mr. Polk's mode of prossecuting the war, you put yourself in opposition to Genl. Taylor himself, for we all know he has declared for, and, in fact originated, the defensive line policy."[37] Thus it could be only a "mode of prosecuting the war."

That Lincoln regarded taking some territory as a "necessity" may have meant not that he endorsed the concept of indemnity but that he bowed to the political realities in the United States, where too many people wanted some sort of expansion for any realistic politician to resist. Such is the most charitable way to interpret Lincoln's vote *against* a resolution which called for ending the war by withdrawing the army to the east bank of the Rio Grande, relinquishing indemnity claims, settling the Texas boundary in the desert between the Nueces and the Rio Grande, and forcing Mexico to pay prewar claims adjudicated by a joint convention of the two nations. This was a no-territory resolution, in other words, and Lincoln voted against it even though it championed a boundary line for Texas which Lincoln felt very strongly to be correct. The resolution lost by a staggering 137–41 margin, and Lincoln, sensing the probable loss of the measure, may have seen nothing to be gained from hopelessly challenging the will of the congressional majority. The Hoosier congressmen from Democratic districts, Embree and Dunn, also voted against it. On the other hand, Caleb Smith and Richard W. Thompson voted for the resolution. If one assumes that these votes were meant to appeal to the constituents of their Whig districts, one can also assume that Lincoln's Whig district may have had more Democratic tendencies in rabidly expansionist and solidly Democratic Illinois. Whatever the reason, Lincoln was certainly among those Western Whigs who were most willing to compromise on expansion.[38]

In spite of the appearance of disunity in the vote on the no-territory resolution, Whigs in the Old Northwest reached near unanimity on the issue of expansion. Thompson had endorsed expansion (north of the 36°30′ line) previously in his own series of resolutions. Caleb Blood Smith came around reluctantly to supporting some expansion (just as he came around reluctantly to supporting Taylor for president). Although Smith supported the "no-territory" idea in the Twenty-ninth Congress and in the campaign for reelection that followed, he grudgingly changed his mind.[39] Recognizing the strength of the administration, he acknowledged, under the circumstances, the "wisdom and sound policy in the course marked out by the distinguished Senator from South Carolina [Mr. Calhoun]":

> If, however, the Administration intends to hold and retain permanently New Mexico and California—acknowledging, at the same time, that they constitute a larger measure of indemnity than we have any just right to demand—why not hold those provinces, and withdraw our forces from the other portions of Mexico? Why shall we keep an army of fifty thou-

sand men in the heart of Mexico, preying upon the vitals of the country, when with ten thousand men we can hold all that the Administration pretends it wishes to retain? Five thousand troops in New Mexico, and an equal number of Upper California, would hold those provinces against all the force which Mexico can bring into the field.[40]

Embree, Dunn, and Lincoln voted against the no-territory resolution. Embree had supported the moderately expansionist defensive-line strategy in the midst of his campaign for the House. Dunn distributed Calhoun's speeches to his constituents, and those documents were the *locus classicus* of the defensive-line strategy. Lincoln looked upon the defensive-line strategy as a near panacea.

Though all of the Western Whig congressmen made compromises in keeping with their expansionist constituencies, Western Whiggery also showed an impressive level of agreement in opposing the war. The Ashmun amendment took a position most could agree with: the war was unconstitutional and unnecessary. Only Embree failed to vote for this; he was absent. All agreed that the war was a war of conquest. All five men made their dissent from Polk's policies a matter of public record. The three from Whig districts made speeches directly on the subject of the war and proudly sent them home to their constituents. Dunn and Embree, in more delicate positions than Lincoln, Smith, and Thompson, commented on the war only in speeches on other subjects. Smith, Thompson, and Embree had criticized the war in their campaigns to get to the Thirtieth Congress. Only Dunn seems to have disapproved of far-reaching criticism of the war once it was declared, and he managed to join the rest in terming its declaration unconstitutional and unnecessary.

Lincoln, then, did not behave in an eccentric fashion for a Whig in a Western expansionist state. He bowed more to expansionist sentiment than any Whig from a Whig district, though his choice to make a speech directly on the war issue differed from the course followed by the two most conservative Whigs from basically Democratic districts. He was a mainstream Western Whig who exercised normal caution; why, then, did he not run again?

The principal reason, he said, was in order "to deal fairly with others, to keep peace among our friends, and to keep the district from going to the enemy." When Herndon wrote just after Lincoln's arrival in Washington that some hoped for his reelection, Lincoln replied that he would not object to reelection "although I thought at the time, and still think, it would quite as well for me to return to the law at the end of a single term." If, however, no one else wished to run, he "could not refuse the people the right of sending me again." Most often, historians have interpreted this only as the obligatory coyness of a man who always lusted after office, but there is reason to believe Lincoln's relative indifference to serving in the House and to believe that it increased through his term.[41]

Lincoln had left the state legislature in March of 1841. It was a long wait through the "turns" of John Todd Stuart, John J. Hardin, and Edward D. Baker to become the district's candidate in 1846. By 1843, he was openly voicing his desire to run.[42] Like many things long awaited, success seemed anticlimactic. Less than three months after his election, Lincoln wrote his close personal friend Joshua Speed, "Being elected to Congress, though I am very grateful to our friends, for having done it, has not pleased me as much as I expected."[43] No doubt the prospect of well over a year's wait to go to Washington served to make the impact on his life less dramatic.

Yet Lincoln could have gone to Congress sooner than he did, and he did not lift a finger to try to do so. Seventh District Congressman Edward D. Baker, who chose to go to Mexico to fight, was criticized for maintaining his military rank while a member of the House. In December of 1846, he resigned his seat, leaving two months of his term to be filled by another man. A special election to fill the seat was announced for January 20, 1847. Whig members of the state legislature from the Seventh District caucused to choose a nominee. Previous to the meeting, William Brown of Morgan County called on John Henry, the state senator from Morgan, expressing his interest in filling the vacancy and requesting his support. Henry rather disingenuously promised his support, thinking all along that Congressman-elect Lincoln would surely be a candidate for the nomination. At the meeting, Lincoln was present but declined consideration as a candidate. Shortly thereafter, Henry changed his mind, and Brown was forced by Whig leaders to withdraw his candidacy out of the consideration that Henry, if angered, could cause the Whigs to lose Morgan, Scott, and Cass counties (the two latter were formerly parts of Morgan County and all had only slim Whig majorities).[44]

What is of interest in all this, of course, is that Abraham Lincoln, in what would seem to be an uncharacteristic lack of zeal for elected office, declined to run. John Henry indicated that most people expected Lincoln would want to run as a matter of course. "It was then supposed that Mr. Lincoln would be a candidate for the nomination," Henry said in a letter to the *Sangamo Journal* defending his original willingness to support Brown. Lincoln certainly stood to lose nothing by going to Congress early. The mileage allowance given congressmen en route to and from Washington was so generous that Henry laid his whole claim to the Whig nomination on the fact that he was a poor man who needed the money from the mileage allowance (Brown was a well-to-do man). Nor was it inordinately troublesome to travel to the capital in such a short period of time. When Lincoln finally went to Congress, he came home in September after a recess and a campaign tour in Massachusetts, campaigned on a moderate schedule in October and returned to Congress by the first week in December for the short lame-duck session which ended the first week in March.[45]

Washington life did not appeal to Mary Todd Lincoln. After about four months, she packed up her children and went home to Kentucky. On April 16, 1848, Lincoln wrote her: "In this troublesome world, we are never quite satisfied. When you were here, I thought you hindered me some in attending to business; but now, having nothing but business—no variety—it has grown exceedingly tasteless to me. I hate to sit down and direct documents, and I hate to stay in this old room by myself. You know I told you in last sunday's letter, I was going to make a little speech during the week; but the week has passed away without my getting a chance to do so; and now my interest in the subject has passed away too."[46]

Most historians have disregarded this letter, dismissing it as a function of momentary loneliness, but there is good reason to believe that it betrays a more fundamental boredom with the tedium of being an obscure Western congressman. Although he nowhere else expressed dismay with the elaborate etiquette of sending documents (compiling a list of constituents in a book and not missing anyone of importance), Lincoln did in another letter say that giving speeches in Congress was no special thrill. Of his very first speech in the United States House of Representatives, Lincoln said to Herndon, "I find speaking here and elsewhere about the same thing. I was about as badly scared, and no worse, as I am when I speak in court."[47] Unless they had long tenure in the House and the power consequent to it, nineteenth-century congressmen did only three things. They sent documents and newspapers home to important constituents; they made speeches (intended, like Lincoln's, as much for home consumption as for influence on other congressmen); and they handled patronage (which was scarce when the president was of the other party). Of these three essential activities, Lincoln was bored by two.

One can add to the tedium of powerlessness the insecurity of identity for Western Whigs. Critics of Lincoln's stand on the Mexican War have recognized this insecurity as a force which could make even a customarily canny politician like Lincoln forget his constituents by cringing before the whims of the party's Eastern power brokers. There is some truth in this, perhaps, but it is no reason to condemn Lincoln. Nor did cringing before the East necessarily lead to opposition to the war.

Edward D. Baker took a very different course in regard to the Mexican War from that one taken by his friend and fellow Whig. Congressman Baker's response to the war was unreservedly patriotic and a function of his long-standing military interests and aptitudes.[48] He resigned his seat in the House to become the colonel of the Fourth Illinois Regiment of Volunteers for the Mexican War. Though his response thus contrasted with Lincoln's, Baker still carefully consulted the wishes of the powers in the Eastern wing of the party, even going so far as to ask Daniel Webster whether it was all right to go. Webster replied on May 18, 1846:

> In reference to our conversation this morning, I am quite free to say, that I approve your purpose of entering into the military service of the country, if your inclination & circumstances prompt such a design. We are in a state of war, that war must be fought thro'; the more vigorously it shall be prosecuted, the shorter it will probably prove. Whig young men, like other young men, may well bear a part in the service which the exigency of the country demands. A son of mine would take a commission tomorrow if he could obtain it. An existing public foreign war, is a subject equally interesting and important, to all parties; all should be equally desirous of carrying their country honorably through it, without sacrificing its honor or interests or tarnishing its military renown.[49]

So much for the vaunted independence of Westerners! Whoever they were, they were not powerful voices in the Whig Party, and they knew it. Nor should it be ignored that service in the Mexican War failed to make Baker any less a Whig than Lincoln in his views of the origins of that conflict. Lincoln told Herndon on February 1, 1848, that Baker was in Washington again and that the colonel agreed with the mass of Whigs that the president's conduct "in the beginning of the war" was "unjust."[50]

Nor must one infer Lincoln's lack of taste for his job only from casual references in his own correspondence. Outside corroboration comes from a fragment of a manuscript on Lincoln, written after his death, by his old House colleague Richard W. Thompson. Thompson recalled the similarities in the positions of Congressman Lincoln and himself: "We were within two months of the same age—our districts were not far apart—our constituents were the sharers of common interests—and we were members of the Whig party, alike impressed by the wonderfully magnetic influence of Henry Clay." About Lincoln's decision not to run again for Congress, Thompson said this: "At the close of his only term in Congress he hesitated somewhat as to his future course of life. He had made up his mind not to seek re-election. He did not doubt about his success, but found a Congressional life uncongenial to him. This I personally know, for being of the like opinion with regard to myself, we frequently conversed upon the subject. Having withdrawn from his profession he apprehended that possibly his practice might not be recovered as speedily as his circumstances demanded." And, therefore, Thompson said, Lincoln sought a lucrative appointment in the land office.[51]

There are reasons to mistrust the document. Thompson was reminiscing about events of as much as two decades earlier, and he was probably wrong about Lincoln's decision not to run at the end of his term. Lincoln had decided long before, and there was no congressional election in Illinois in 1849 to provoke a new decision. Still, it confirms reliable strands from Lincoln's own letters and does constitute a memoir of an eyewitness whom Lincoln, remembered as an "old friend" in 1860, though he had not seen him since their days in the Thirtieth Congress. Thompson had been a genuine friend, too, the only man outside Illinois to put substantial effort towards getting Lincoln an appointive office from the Taylor administration in 1849.[52]

Finally, a brief footnote to the question whether Lincoln caused Stephen Logan's defeat in the congressional election in 1848 seems in order. Defenders of Lincoln's political prowess say Logan was a poor campaigner and by implication concede the facts in the other side's case, namely, that the Democrats tarred Logan with Lincoln's record on the Mexican War.

In truth, this is more a matter of assumption on the historians' part than of evidence of the campaign as seen in local newspapers. In May 1848, over two months before the election, the *Illinois State Register* accused the Whigs not of being traitors but of taking a vacillating and opportunistic approach toward the war. At first they condemned it; when Taylor's popularity rose, they supported it; when Taylor faded a bit and Clay made his antiwar speech, they criticized the war once more. The *Register* termed Logan's position on the war "equivocal" and predicted that he would eventually oppose it because Lincoln and John Henry had not made up their minds before they left, and they eventually opposed it.[53]

By mid-July, Suckers knew the war was over; Mexico City had fallen on September 14, 1847. Gradually, other issues replaced the Mexican War in the columns of Seventh District newspapers. By the third week in June, still over a month before the election, the *Register* began to attack Logan as a pro-British Whig. Logan had criticized Democrat Lewis Cass for opposing a quintuple treaty against the slave trade. The *Register* defended Cass on the grounds that the treaty was really aimed at making Great Britain the "mistress of the seas" because it allowed British ships to stop and search American ships suspected of engaging illegally in the slave trade. These charges mounted in a steady crescendo up to election time. Just two weeks before the election, a long article on Logan in the *Register* mentioned Lincoln and John Henry in passing but focused most of its attention on Logan and England. This issue, rather than Lincoln's record, received the lion's share of Democratic attention in the newspaper and ignoring it grants too much to the case against Lincoln and slights the degree to which Logan made his own issues.[54]

The comparative method makes Lincoln's opposition to the Mexican War more understandable and makes our descriptions of its nature and tone more precise. He did not err politically, for virtually every Whig congressman (and candidate, for that matter) in Indiana and Illinois acted as he did. Opposition to the war was a party issue; therefore, Whigs went to Congress and opposed the war, no matter where they came from. There were concessions, of course, to local feelings. Whigs in the Old Northwest compromised easily with expansion; there was no residue of Federalist nonexpansionism in this wing of the party. Lincoln was more willing to compromise on expansion than Hoosier Whigs from similarly safe districts. In other words, his dissent was not the least bit shrill under the circumstances, and he picked his way through the political solutions to the Mexican War with a politician's care. On the other hand, then, his stand on the war was not idealistically principled or internationally minded. It was a party stand, not an antiexpansionist stand, and his major concern about the war's result was what it would do to the domestic peace of the United States.

The episode gives a surprising insight on Lincoln's biography. In one case for certain, he failed to pursue an office, and there is some evidence that he did not care for the duties of an obscure Western Whig congressman. Lincoln did not fear his constituents, but he did tire of serving them in return for little thanks. It exasperated him to find, after his diligent and tedious efforts at franking, that only two of the five Whig newspapers in the district published his speech. It made him "a little impatient" that no paper carried "a single speech, or even an extract from one" of the others he had sent.[55] When David Davis wrote him near the end of his term, a weary and frustrated Lincoln answered his letter by saying, "I have more cause to thank you for it, than you would suppose. Out of more than three hundred letters received this session, yours is the second one manifesting the least interest for me personally."[56]

Lincoln contentedly returned to Springfield and his law practice. The lesson of his congressional career was doubtless plain to him but misunderstood by most historians since. He had tried to distinguish himself by speaking up in Congress. His constituents had not rejected his message: they simply had not heard it at all.

Notes

1. G. S. Boritt, "A Question of Political Suicide? Lincoln's Opposition to the Mexican War," *Journal of the Illinois State Historical Society* 67 (Feb. 1974): 79–100, also includes an exhaustive historiographical discussion, which makes the customary review of the literature superfluous here.
2. Paul M. Angle (ed.), *Herndon's Life of Lincoln* (Cleveland, 1965), 226.
3. Boritt, for example, claims that "The extant half of the Lincoln-Herndon correspondence on the subject suggests that Lincoln discounted his law partner's evaluation of Illinois sentiment on the war." "Question of Political Suicide?" 92.
4. Lincoln to Herndon, Feb. 1, 1848, in Roy P. Basler (ed.), *The Collected Works of Abraham Lincoln* (New Brunswick, N.J., 1953–55), 1:446. Hereafter cited as Lincoln, *Coll. Works.*
5. Lincoln to Herndon, Feb. 15, 1848, ibid., 451.
6. Lincoln to Herndon, June 22, 1848, ibid., 490–491.
7. Boritt, "Question of Political Suicide?," 93
8. Such regional cooperation is evident, for example, in Lincoln's quest for appointive office from the Taylor administration. See Donald W. Riddle, *Congressman Abraham Lincoln* (Urbana, 1957), 214–15.
9. Brian G. Walton, "The Elections for the Thirtieth Congress and the Presidential Candidacy of Zachary Taylor," *Journal of Southern History* 35 (May 1969), 186–87.
10. John D. Defrees to Daniel D. Pratt, Apr. 17, 1847, Daniel D. Pratt Papers, Indiana Division, Indiana State Library, Indianapolis.
11. Hal W. Bochin, "Caleb B. Smith's Opposition to the Mexican War," *Indiana Magazine of History* 69 (June 1973): 98–99, 107, 109, 110.
12. Richard W. Thompson to H. G. Hilton, July 16, 1847, Richard W. Thompson MSS, Lilly Library, Indiana University, Bloomington.
13. R. L. Hathaway to Abiathar Crane, Aug. 3, 1847, Crane Papers, William Henry Smith Memorial Library, Indiana Historical Society, Indianapolis.
14. J. S. Harvey to Richard W. Thompson, July 15, 1847, Illinois State Historical Society, Springfield.
15. Richard W. Thompson to H. G. Hilton, July 16, 1847, Thompson MSS.

16. R. L. Hathaway to Abiathar Crane, Aug. 3, 1847, Crane Papers.

17. Richard W. Thompson to Elisha Embree, Aug. 14, 1847, Lucius C. Embree Papers, Indiana State Library.

18. *Congressional Globe*, 30th Cong., 1st sess., 1847–48, 61, 94, 95; Appendix, 263–67.

19. Factionalism is apparent in articles quoted in the *Princeton Democratic Clarion*, Mar. 13 and 27, 1847. See also Richard William Leopold, *Robert Dale Owen: A Biography* (Cambridge, Mass., 1940), 234–35. The need for rotation in office as a cause of Democratic loss of the district is discussed in the *Madison Courier*, Aug. 7, 14, and 21, 1847. See also Lawrence N. Powell, "Rejected Republican Incumbents in the 1866 Congressional Nominating Conventions," *Civil War History* 19 (Sept. 1973): 219–37.

20. Embree's speeches are known principally from hostile reports in the *Princeton Democratic Clarion*, June 12, June 26, and July 10, 1847.

21. *Speech of Hon. Elisha Embree of Indiana, on Bounty Land Bill, Delivered in the House of Representatives, Wednesday, May 3, 1848* (Washington, 1848), pamphlet in Lucius Embree Papers, Indiana State Library.

22. Isaac E. Johnson to George G. Dunn, Apr. 17, 1848, George G. Dunn MSS, Lilly Library, Indiana University, Bloomington.

23. *Congressional Globe*, 30th Cong., 1st sess., 1847–48, Appendix, 973.

24. Ibid., 969, 971.

25. See Williamson Dunn to George G. Dunn, Feb. 4, 1848; Austin Ward to George G. Dunn, Feb. 8, 1848; and J. G. McPheiters to George G. Dunn, Apr. 20, 1848, George G. Dunn MSS. The popularity of Gallatin's pamphlet is discussed in John G. Schroeder, *Mr. Polk's War: American Opposition and Dissent, 1846–1848* (Madison, 1973), 144–45.

26. "Speech on Annexation of Texas," May 22, 1844, in Lincoln, *Coll. Works*, 1:337.

27. Lincoln to Williamson Durley, Oct. 3, 1845, ibid., 347–48.

28. Frederick Merk says that "Whigs, as a party, were fearful of spreading out too widely." *Manifest Destiny and Mission in American History: A Reinterpretation* (New York, 1966), 40. See also Major L. Wilson, *Space, Time, and Freedom: The Quest for Nationality and the Irrepressible Conflict, 1815–1861* (Westport, Conn., 1974), 108, 115–16, 118.

29. "Speech at Wilmington, Delaware," June 10, 1848, in Lincoln, *Coll. Works*, 1:476.

30. "Speech at Worcester, Massachusetts," Sept. 12, 1848, ibid., 2:4.

31. "Fragment: What General Taylor Ought to Say," [March?] 1848, ibid.

32. Lincoln to John M. Peck, May 21, 1848, ibid., 1:472.

33. "Second Lecture on Discoveries and Inventions" [Feb. 11, 1859], ibid., 3:358.

34. "Speech at Wilmington, Delaware," June 10, 1848, ibid., 1:476.

35. See Otis Singletary, *The Mexican War* (Chicago, 1964), 45.

36. See Schroeder, *Mr. Polk's War*, 69–71.

37. Lincoln to Usher F. Linder, Feb. 20, 1848, Lincoln, *Coll. Works*, 1:453.

38. *Congressional Globe*, 30th Cong., 1st sess., 94.

39. Bochin, "Caleb B. Smith's Opposition to the Mexican War," 99, 105, 108.

40. *Congressional Globe*, 30th Cong., 1st sess., 325.

41. Lincoln to Herndon, Jan. 8, 1848, Lincoln, *Coll. Works*, 1:431.

42. Donald W. Riddle, *Lincoln Runs for Congress* (New Brunswick, N.J., 1948), 9–10.

43. Lincoln to Joshua Speed, Oct. 22, 1846, Lincoln, *Coll. Works*, 1:391.

44. *Sangamo Journal*, Jan. 14, 1847.

45. Ibid.; Riddle, *Congressman Lincoln*, 137–40.

46. Lincoln to Mary Todd Lincoln, Apr. 16, 1848, Lincoln, *Coll. Works*, 1:465.

47. Lincoln to Herndon, Jan. 8, 1848, ibid., 1:430.

48. Harry C. Blair and Rebecca Tarshis, *Colonel Edward D. Baker: Lincoln's Constant Ally* (Portland: Oregon Historical Society, 1960), 21.

49. Daniel Webster to Edward D. Baker, May 18, 1846, Anson Miller Papers, Illinois State Historical Society.

50. Lincoln to Herndon, Feb. 1, 1848, Lincoln, *Coll. Works,* 1:447.

51. Richard W. Thompson, MS on Abraham Lincoln, Thompson MSS, Illinois State Historical Society, Springfield.

52. Lincoln to Schuyler Colfax, May 26, 1860, Lincoln, *Coll. Works,* 4:54; Riddle, *Congressman Lincoln,* 214.

53. *Illinois State Register,* Mar. 3 and May 14, 1848.

54. Ibid., June 26 and July 21, 1848.

55. Lincoln to Herndon, June 22, 1848, Lincoln, *Coll. Works,* 1:491–92.

56. Lincoln to David Davis, Feb. 12, 1849, in Roy P. Basler (ed.), *The Collected Works of Abraham Lincoln: Supplement, 1832–1865* (Westport, Conn., 1974), 14.

2 ▷ Lincoln, the West, and the Antislavery Politics of the 1850s

Michael S. Green

On February 27, 1860, a large crowd sat at New York City's Cooper Union as William Cullen Bryant, the poet and Republican editor of the *New York Evening Post*, introduced that evening's speaker. Bryant said, "The great West, my friends, is a potent auxiliary in the battle we are fighting, for Freedom against Slavery." He added, "These children of the West, my friends, form a living bulwark against the advance of Slavery, and from them is recruited the vanguard of the armies of liberty. One of them will appear before you this evening in person," and with that, he presented a politician and lawyer from Illinois, Abraham Lincoln.[1]

That night, the audience heard what Harold Holzer has called "the speech that made Abraham Lincoln president." Lincoln had spent weeks scouring historical and contemporary accounts of the Founding Fathers to prove their opposition to slavery—"As if," Holzer wrote, "not only 'the Cause,' but his own political life, depended on it." That may have been the case. Bryant and another Republican sitting on the platform, *New York Tribune* editor Horace Greeley, shared a distaste for Senator William Henry Seward, the front-runner for the party nomination, and they hoped to find another candidate. Compared with Seward, Lincoln had the advantages of political moderation, a reputation for probity, and, since he came from a swing state, geography. The question was whether he had the ability and the gravitas. That night, he abandoned the style of stump speech he had mastered back home to deliver a long, scholarly treatise in which he satisfied himself and his listeners that the Founding Fathers intended to avoid the spread of slavery into new territories—the issue on which Republicans had united. Lincoln's success at Cooper Union laid important groundwork for his nomination that spring and his election that November.[2]

While Lincoln struck his fellow Republicans favorably, he also struck them in another way. "The first impression of the man from the West did nothing to contradict the expectation of something weird, rough, and un- cultivated," one observer remembered. Others commented on his personal appearance. Holzer explained, "Cooper Union gave Lincoln the opportunity to prove his universal appeal beyond the confines of the western frontier that produced him. It demonstrated to the entire eastern region, through newspaper reprints and subsequent personal appearances, that he was a serious, learned, dignified public figure, far more civilized than the prai- rie-bred storyteller who had mesmerized rowdy crowds on the debate trail in 1858."[3]

At Cooper Union, New Yorkers encountered a different Lincoln from the one familiar in Illinois, but what Lincoln said that night represented not a break with the past, but a continuation of it. Lincoln was a child of the fron- tier, born in Kentucky, raised in Indiana, and matured in Illinois. There he married Mary Todd, a Kentucky native of higher social origins, who spent two decades trying to domesticate his relaxed, rustic manners, with mixed results. In his appearance, dress, speech patterns, and folksiness, Lincoln cut a far different figure from the politicians familiar to easterners. But in Illinois, with its more racist and frontier culture, Lincoln faced a different situation than his eastern counterparts—or, to put it more accurately, he had to face the same issues and opinions in different ways. As he once told a Massachusetts audience, Illinoisans opposed slavery just as much as they did, but people of his state "did not keep so constantly thinking about it." Lincoln thought about it more and more as the issue became increasingly important nationally—and as settlement increased in the West. Living and working there, he understood the West's importance to the nation's future. In the years before he became president, he often expressed and demon- strated that importance and, in the process of trying to shape the West, revealed its importance in shaping him.[4]

The Western Whig

From his political beginnings, as Lincoln sought to shape the West, the West was shaping him. His view of the West was partly what would become Frederick Jackson Turner's West of equality and opportunity, which Lin- coln exemplified in his rise from storekeeper to political leader, advocacy of democratic ideals, and declaration in 1836 that "I go for admitting all whites to the right of suffrage, who pay taxes or bear arms, (by no means excluding females)." It resembled Patricia Limerick's West of conquest, inherent in Lincoln's support for Whig doctrines about internal improvements to make the resources of the Old Northwest accessible and profitable, and in his joining the militia in 1832 to defeat Chief Black Hawk. Having grown up along the portion of the Cumberland Road that included the Louisville to Nashville turnpike in Kentucky, and in promoting first the development of New Salem and then of Springfield in Illinois, he also would have understood Richard Wade's declaration in *The Urban Frontier* that "towns were the spearheads of the frontier." The son of a yeoman farmer of the sort that Jefferson celebrated, but with no desire to follow in his father's footsteps, Lincoln advocated the kinds of transportation and development that would do for Illinois what the Erie Canal had done for cities like Rochester, New York.[5]

Similarly, the most studied of Lincoln's early works revealed the role of the West in his thinking. He delivered "The Perpetuation of Our Political Institutions" before Springfield's Young Men's Lyceum on January 27, 1838. Some scholars have dissected this as his political lodestar in its celebration of reason, or as a psychological study in the need to outdo the Founding Fathers, but it also discussed issues that alternately vexed and explained westerners. His lengthy assault on "mobocratic spirit" spoke for and to large numbers of frontier settlers who had to build their institutions before federal, state, and territorial governments took hold. While his subject matter ranged from recently martyred abolitionist Elijah Lovejoy to a variety of urban uprisings, he also recited what would become a history of vigilantism that often characterized western settlements.[6]

Nor did Lincoln object to perpetuating western stereotypes. In the first presidential campaign in which he participated extensively, in 1840, Whigs capitalized on the Democratic depiction of Whig William Henry Harrison, an old Virginia slave owner, as living in a log cabin and drinking hard cider. Lincoln joined in making the most of the myth. While Democrats claimed to be for the common man and accused Whigs of being the party of big business, Lincoln contended that Whig policy made it possible for people to own their own homes and land—a Jeffersonian and free labor view, and a precursor to the whole idea behind the Homestead Act. Lincoln and other Whigs also signed an anti-Van Buren letter in which they promised to "meet, conquer and disperse Gen. Harrison's and the country's enemies, and place him in the chair, now disgraced by their effeminate and luxury-loving chief." If ever a statement was meant to influence western frontiersmen, that was it.[7]

Lincoln's desire for western settlers to be free laborers required that slavery not move west with them, and his first recorded statement on the subject foreshadowed his opposition to the growth of slavery as the Civil War approached. Responding to an antiabolition resolution in the Illinois legislature, he and fellow Sangamon County legislator Dan Stone declared "that the institution of slavery is founded on both injustice and bad policy; but that the promulgation of abolitionist doctrines tends rather to increase than to abate its evils," a frequently quoted passage that underscores Lincoln's tendency toward moderation. But a less quoted passage also spoke to Lincoln's future political ideology. While agreeing that slavery could be banned in Washington, D.C., if its residents wanted, Lincoln and Stone questioned the legislative branch's right to limit slavery "in the different States"—a significant phrase. At no time did Lincoln say that Congress could not interfere anywhere else, a harbinger of his opposition to slavery expanding into the territories.[8]

This issue came to the fore with Manifest Destiny. The question of whether the United States should annex Texas became crucial to the 1844 election, and Henry Clay's waffling on the subject cost the Whig nominee the support of enough antislavery northern Whigs and members of the antislavery Liberty Party to throw the election to Democrat James Polk. While Lincoln questioned adding so much potential slave territory, Clay's defeat troubled him more, at least in part because it made that addition more likely. Nearly a year later, he remained agitated enough to write, "If the whig abolitionists of New York had voted with us last fall, Mr. Clay would now be president, whig principles in the ascendent, and Texas not annexed; whereas by the division, all that either had at stake in the contest, was lost." What had been lost, he feared, was the ability of the free states to block the growth of slavery: "we should never knowingly lend ourselves directly or indirectly, to prevent that slavery from dying a natural death—to find new places for it to live in. . . ." Before the next presidential election, he continued to criticize abolitionists who "professed great horror at the proposed extension of slavery territory" but "aided in the election of Mr. Polk; for which, and its disastrous consequences, they were responsible, as they held the balance of power." As it turned out, this idea about the growth of slavery into the West, and how to fight it, would form the basis of the political ideology of Lincoln and the party he eventually would lead.[9]

The Making of "a Western Free State Man"

When Lincoln arrived in Washington, D.C., late in 1847 for his first session in the House of Representatives, slavery had supplanted internal improvements and Clay's American System as foremost in Whigs' minds. Polk supported annexing Texas and began a war with Mexico in his quest to acquire California. Both parties and sections, and factions within them, sought to resolve whether slavery could or would spread into whatever lands the United States acquired in the war, which it clearly was about to win. While David Wilmot of Pennsylvania won support from many antislavery northern Democrats and Whigs with his Proviso, which would have banned slavery from newly acquired territory, southern and centrist northern Whigs adopted the policy of "No Territory," reasoning that without new territory added, the slavery controversy would die down.[10]

For his part, Lincoln deplored Polk's actions. Before the House, Lincoln accused Polk in all but word of lying and wanting to acquire not just what became the state of California but "the whole province of lower California to boot, and to still carry on the war—to take *all* we are fighting for, and *still* fight on"—voicing the kinds of doubts about the president's intent that he and other Republicans later would express about the Slave Power and the South. Lincoln's comments and his "Spot Resolutions," demanding to know exactly where "American blood had been shed on American soil," as Polk claimed, were not antiterritorial or antiwar so much as anti-Polk and antislavery, although the Whig in Lincoln evinced more interest in developing existing American lands than acquiring new ones. They also demonstrated his concerns about the West's development: if slave labor spread into new lands, free labor might not.[11]

Lincoln's party loyalty trumped his antislavery views in 1848, when he showed no inclination to join the Free-Soil Party and stuck with the Whigs. But, perhaps influenced by the preponderance of Democrats in the new party, he also argued that the Whigs had the best chance of stopping slavery in its tracks. He told the House, "I am a Northern man, or rather, a Western free state man, with a constituency I believe to be, and with personal feelings I know to be, against the extension of slavery." To concerns that Zachary Taylor, a slave owner, disagreed with those views, he expressed doubts that the Whig nominee would encourage the growth of slavery, in part because Whig ideology dictated that a president defer to Congress, and if Congress approved antislavery legislation—as the House had done with the Wilmot Proviso and the Senate had refused to do—he could expect Taylor to sign it.

He also assailed the Democratic nominee, Senator Lewis Cass of Michigan. That Cass would let settlers in territories vote on whether to allow slavery, Lincoln warned, increased the chances of "new wars, new acquisitions of territory and still further extensions of slavery." Nor did Lincoln hold out hope for the third party, telling a New England audience during a campaign tour that opposition to slavery in the territories seemed to be all that Free-Soilers believed in. In the unlikely event that they won, their lack of positions on other issues could paint them into corners "calculated to break down their single important declared object." Just as bad, from Lincoln's perspective, "The 'Free Soil' men in claiming that name indirectly attempted a deception, by implying the Whigs were *not* Free Soil men." He was living proof of the commitment among at least northern antislavery Whigs to stopping the spread of slavery into new western lands.[12]

Lincoln proved both optimistic and prescient. Before the next congressional session, Taylor acted unwhiggishly in trying to bring California into the Union without slavery and present Congress with a fait accompli, and later threatened to veto the compromise measures that Lincoln's idol, Henry Clay, introduced as the Compromise of 1850. By then, Lincoln had returned to Illinois, where he kept his hand in Whig and western politics, but with only marginal success. As Taylor prepared to take office, Lincoln told a Boston Whig, "In these days of Cabinet making, we out West are awake as well as others." Suggesting his friend Edward Baker for the cabinet, he added that "the West is not only entitled to, but is in need of, one member of the cabinet." That effort failed, as did his attempt to influence the Taylor administration's patronage decisions affecting Illinois. Lincoln even declined the chance to move west as governor of Oregon Territory, reasoning that its Democratic majority would do nothing for his political aspirations. Nor did much happen in Illinois to further them: after leaving Congress, he remained a loyal Whig but devoted most of his attention to his law practice.[13]

Between his departure from Congress and his battle against the effects of the Kansas-Nebraska Act, if Lincoln seemed shunted aside and easily ignored, his views of the issues of slavery and westward expansion in this period could be discerned through a pair of eulogies. When Taylor died, Lincoln spoke in Chicago. "I fear the one *great* question of the day, is not now so likely to be partially acquiesced in by the different sections of the Union, as it would have been, could Gen. Taylor have been spared to us," he said. If that suggested he shared Taylor's unwillingness to accept the Compromise of 1850, he also praised Clay, his "beau ideal of a statesman," when the Kentuckian died in 1852. "In all the great questions which have agitated the country, and particularly in those great and fearful crises, the Missouri question—the Nullification question, and the late slavery question, as connected with the newly acquired territory, involving and endangering the stability of the Union, his has been the leading and most conspicuous part," Lincoln said. While Clay's positions on some issues remained open to debate, "there are many others, about his course upon which, there is little or no disagreement amongst intelligent and patriotic Americans. Of these last are the War of 1812, the Missouri question, Nullification, and the now recent compromise measures," all of which were more controversial than Lincoln's eulogy would have its listeners and readers believe.[14]

What Lincoln thought about the compromise and its meaning bubbled to the surface of one of his speeches for Whig presidential candidate Winfield Scott in 1852. When Stephen A. Douglas claimed that the Whigs endorsed the compromise after Democrats did, and therefore had taken the idea from them, Lincoln was aghast. Not only had his idol Clay been denied his due, but the denier had been a Democrat. "I had thought that the pen of history had written, acknowledged, and recorded it as facts, that Henry Clay, more than any other man, or perhaps more than any other ten men, was the originator of that system of measures . . . ," he told the Springfield Scott Club. "I knew, or supposed I knew, that democrats, numerous and distinguished, gave it able and efficient support; and I have not sought, or known of any whig seeking to deprive them of the credit of it," and he still was complaining six years later that Douglas had arrogated credit for Clay's actions to himself. If Lincoln was out of the political mainstream, he remained well aware of its currents—and he was about to be swept up in them.[15]

The Making of a Republican, 1854–60

If Lincoln's comments in the early 1850s were limited by time and his seeming unimportance, what he had to say upon his return to active politics in 1854 was clear—William Gienapp aptly described his speeches as "more crisp and lean, like the man himself"—and revealed that he had been reading and thinking a great deal. That January, Douglas introduced the Kansas-Nebraska Act. By letting residents of the two territories vote on whether to add slavery, the bill repealed the Missouri Compromise of 1820, which had banned slavery north of latitude 36°30′, except in Missouri. It served other, unintended purposes. It dissolved the Democrats and Whigs as they then existed, leading to a kaleidoscopic era of party movement that culminated in a more prosouthern Democratic Party and an almost entirely northern Republican Party opposed to the extension of slavery. It also reenergized Lincoln politically and ideologically. Retaining his whiggish economic views, he still supported industrial development to breed a more urban, educated West. But now, in connection with that goal, he could more fully voice and hone his antislavery principles, continuing his opposition to the spread of the institution into western territories.[16]

Central to his opposition to slavery in western territories was his disgust with Douglas's idea of popular sovereignty. But neither the idea of voting on whether to own a human being or the politician it was associated with fully explained Lincoln's opposition. As important as they were, his views were rooted in his sense of the West and his sense of history. Lincoln's opposition to the spread of slavery was obvious, and his speech at Cooper Union explained the historical forces behind that opposition. But Lincoln spent the six years leading up to that speech, and his election as president later in 1860, constructing a historical argument that the Cooper Union speech fortified. His argument can be traced to the westward growth that had been crucial to his success and his commitment to Whig policies promoting economic growth, which slavery threatened. That Lincoln found slavery abhorrent was evident, but he also found disturbing that its expansion contradicted what he considered the ideals the Founding Fathers had for the country—ideals that he saw slavery and its supporters driving to ruin.[17]

Lincoln had a more detailed explanation for why slavery became important to him. "Although I have ever been opposed to slavery, so far I rested in the hope and belief that it was in course of ultimate extinction. For that reason, it had been a minor question with me. I might have been mistaken; but I had believed, and now believe, that the whole public mind, that is the mind of the great majority, had rested in that belief up to the repeal of the Missouri Compromise," he said during his Senate campaign in 1858. From his study of history and law, he concluded that federal policy had been to keep slavery out of new territories. "All I have asked or desired anywhere is that it should be placed back again upon the basis that the fathers of our government originally placed it upon. I have no doubt that it *would* become extinct, for all time to come, if we but re-adopted the policy of the fathers by restricting it to the limits it has already covered—restricting it from the new Territories," he said in the third debate with Douglas. But when the Kansas-Nebraska Act passed, and the Supreme Court issued the *Dred Scott* decision in 1857, "I became convinced that either I had been resting in a delusion, or the institution was being placed on a new basis—a basis for making it perpetual, national and universal. . . . I believe that bill to be the beginning of a conspiracy for that purpose. So believing, I have since then considered that question a paramount one. So believing, I have thought the public mind will never rest till the power of Congress to restrict the spread of it, shall again be acknowledged and exercised on the one hand, or on the other, all resistance be entirely crushed out."[18]

Lincoln's study of the history of slavery began long before he prepared to speak at Cooper Union. He saw the effort to spread slavery as threatening to deprive the western territories of their best chance for prosperity. Thus, even before he joined the Republican Party, he shared its ideology, equating free labor with advancement and slave labor with decrepitude. Mixing earnestness and sarcasm in analyzing the Founding Fathers just before the 1854 election, Lincoln saw the ban on slavery in the Old Northwest territories as "the *best* exposition of their views of slavery as an institution. It was also a most striking commentary of their political faith, and showed how the views of those political sages, to whom we owe liberty, government, and all, comported with the new-fangled doctrines of popular rights, invented in these degenerate latter days to cloak the spread of slavery." According to Lincoln, as "tyrannical and oppressive as its principle, in these evil days, has come to be considered," its results were clear: "No States in the world have ever advanced as rapidly in population, wealth, the arts and appliances of life, and now have such promise of prospective greatness, as the very States that were born under the ordinance of '87, and were deprived of the blessings of 'popular sovereignty,' as contained in the Nebraska bill, and without which the people of Kansas and Nebraska cannot get along at all!" He concluded that "we of the north western States, never knew the depth of our political misfortunes imposed by the ordinance of '87—we never knew how miserable we were!"[19]

Unsurprisingly, in Lincoln's opinion, the blame for upsetting the historical applecart rested with Democrats truckling to the South. Another argument that Douglas and his defenders used on behalf of popular sovereignty was that Congress implicitly repealed the Missouri line by giving the Utah and New Mexico territories the right to decide slavery for themselves in 1850. Lincoln responded with a history lesson linking slavery and westward growth. "There was no more agitation of the subject till near the close of our war with Mexico, when three millions were appropriated with the design that the President might purchase territory of Mexico, which resulted in our obtaining possession of California, New Mexico, and Utah. This was new territory, with which Jefferson's provision and the Missouri Compromise had nothing to do," Lincoln declared. "It had no more direct reference to Nebraska than it had to the territories of the moon." But with the United States about to win Mexican territory, Douglas moved to extend the compromise line to the Pacific. "The Proviso men in the House, including myself, voted it down, because by implication, it gave up the Southern part to slavery, while we were bent on having it *all* free," Lincoln said. But Douglas tried to give slavery room to grow in what had been free territory and did it to appease the South: "The South had got all they claimed, and all the territory south of the compromise line had been appropriated to slavery; they had gotten and eaten their half of the loaf of bread; but all the other half had not been eaten yet; there was the extensive territory of Nebraska secured to freedom, that had not been settled yet. And the slaveholding power attempted to snatch that away."[20]

Lincoln offered another interpretation of the Compromise of 1850 that suggested a different approach for opponents of slavery to take to its defenders. The trigger for the compromise was California's need for a government for the thousands who migrated there in search of gold. Throughout 1849, though, neither Taylor nor Congress could work out a plan that satisfied both northerners and southerners. "The Proviso men, of course were for letting her in, but the Senate, always true to the other side would not consent to her admission. And there California stood, kept *out* of the Union, because she would not let slavery *into* her borders," Lincoln said. But other questions remained, and the Compromise of 1850 helped solve them by ceding ground to the North (a new free state, the end of the District of Columbia slave trade) and the South (a tougher fugitive slave law). "For all these desirable objects the North could afford to yield something; and they did yield to the South the Utah and New Mexico provision. I do not mean that the whole North, or even a majority, yielded, when the law passed; but enough yielded, when added to the vote of the South, to carry the measure," Lincoln said. "Now can it be pretended that the *principle* of this arrangement requires us to permit the same provision to be applied to Nebraska, *without any equivalent at all*?" To Douglas's claim that the Compromise was not "a system of equivalents," as Lincoln put it, "This is mere desperation. If they have no connection, why are they always spoken of in connection. . . . Why has he constantly called them a SERIES of measures? Why does everybody call them a compromise?"[21]

Lincoln's argument had the virtue of being both simple and complex. First, in taking Clay's position that both sections needed to compromise, he voiced his continued hopes for preserving the Whig Party at a time when its salvation still might have been possible. Second, long before any Freeport Doctrine, he sought to hoist Douglas on his own petard: he knew that the Little Giant played a key role in passing the compromise that Clay articulated, and pointed to the contradiction and immorality in his effort to repeal the Missouri Compromise of 1820 through the Kansas-Nebraska Act. Third, whether or not Lincoln even knew it, he made a pair of subtle points: California extended south of the old Missouri line, meaning the North had not only received a free state, but also avoided the present or future creation of a southern slave state out of southern California; and Utah statehood was unlikely as long as Mormons believed in polygamy, so that northerners could reasonably expect not to gain another free state in that bargain.

Finally, Lincoln reminded an audience that hardly needed the reminder that American history was a series of compromises, and this time the South was demanding its own way while giving nothing in exchange. That was unacceptable. Whatever gains the North had enjoyed in population and industry had been of its own volition, and the South had failed to take advantage of the opportunity. The simplistic part of his argument was that he had to try to find a way to explain why allowing popular sovereignty or its equivalent in Utah was not an implicit repeal of the Missouri line, because it clearly was. By repealing the Missouri Compromise, Douglas led an effort that "opens the door for slavery to enter where before it could not go. This is practically legislating for slavery, recognizing it, endorsing it, propagating it, extending it," which Lincoln deemed "a woeful coming down from the early faith of the republic"—and, by implication, making it impossible for the region it entered to enjoy the fruits of freedom that Lincoln saw in free territory.[22]

Lincoln pondered the issue in one of the drafts he wrote over the years for use in a future speech. Kansans had approved the proslavery Lecompton Constitution, but only after violence and intimidation. President James Buchanan wanted to accept the constitution, which Douglas saw as a corruption of popular sovereignty. Trying to counter any Republican inclination to support Douglas—after all, since he had broken with Buchanan, they had a common enemy—Lincoln asked whether Douglas wanted an antislavery constitution in Kansas or opposed slavery. "Nothing like it. He tells us, in this very speech, expected to be so palatable to Republicans, that he cares not whether slavery is voted down or voted up," Lincoln answered. "His whole effort is devoted to clearing the ring, and giving slavery and freedom a fair fight. With one who considers slavery just as good as freedom, this is perfectly natural and consistent." He also detected another motivation: a desire to avoid the issue by forcing it into the territories and beyond the consideration of Congress. That may have been acceptable when neither of the two parties actively sought to spread slavery, but times had changed. Lincoln wrote, "I, too, believe in self-government as I understand it; but I do not understand that the privilege one man takes of making a slave of another, or holding him as such, is any part of 'self-government.' To call it so is, to my mind, simply absurd and ridiculous."[23]

Nor did Lincoln doubt that slavery interests would assure that their institution spread into western territories. Douglas supporters had claimed that a vote of the people would keep Kansas and Nebraska free of slavery. While sympathetic toward the slaveholder's predicament, reminding audiences that they might act similarly if they lived in the South, Lincoln understood the slaveholder mind better than he let on. After all, if Douglas would sacrifice the Missouri line, why would slaveholders be unwilling to cross it, too? To his oldest friend, Joshua Speed, who supported slavery, Lincoln said, "You say if Kansas fairly votes herself a free state, as a Christian you will rather rejoice at it. All decent slave-holders *talk* that way; and I do not doubt their candor. But they never *vote* that way." Lincoln all but predicted the result in Kansas when he disdained predictions that slavery would not spread into the West. He asked, "Will it not go, then, into Kansas and Nebraska, if permitted? Why not? What will hinder? Do cattle nibble a pasture right up to a division fence, crop all close under the fence, and even put their necks through and gather what they can reach, over the line, and still refuse to pass over into that next green pasture, even if the fence shall be thrown down?" He also proved prescient when he said, "Each party WITHIN, having numerous and determined backers WITHOUT, is it not probable that the contest will come to blows, and bloodshed? Could there be a more apt invention to bring about collision and violence, on the slavery question, than this Nebraska project is?" He captured what he considered Douglas's illogic when he mused, "When we voted for the Wilmot Proviso, we were voting to keep slavery *out* of the whole . . . acquisition; and little did we think we were thereby voting, to let it *into* Nebraska, laying several hundred miles distant. When we voted against extending the Missouri line, little did we think we were voting to destroy the old line, then of near thirty years standing."[24]

While Lincoln questioned the fairness of voting on slavery, he also questioned the fairness of letting slavery alter the political system. The structure that Douglas and his allies had set up struck him as untidy, to say the least. He noted an often ignored danger of the Kansas-Nebraska Act: "The people are to decide the question of slavery for themselves; but WHEN they are to decide, or HOW they are to decide; or whether, when the question is once decided, it is to remain so, or is it to be subject to an indefinite succession of new trials, the law does not say." He also saw that behind the push to expand slavery lay a political motivation that offended his sense of democracy and fair play: more slave states meant more southerners in Congress and the Electoral College, thus assuring that the Slave Power would elect its own to the presidency or force northerners to accede to its wishes. The *Illinois Journal* reported his saying that "he was unwilling that his neighbor, living on an equality by his side in Illinois, should by moving over into Kansas be elevated into a state of superiority over himself" by having slaves count for an additional three-fifths of a voter under the Constitution. While Lincoln's references to democracy often were implicit, his observation leaned as strongly in that direction as any of Douglas's utterances.[25]

If the Nebraska issue and his sense of unfairness and immorality revitalized Lincoln rhetorically and intellectually, the measure had the same effect politically, revealing the importance of the issue of slavery in the West to him. Late in 1854, with the Democrats divided in the wake of Douglas's bill and old Democrats and Whigs starting to reconstitute themselves into new parties, Lincoln returned to electoral politics. He sought a legislative seat to help the anti-Douglas, anti-Nebraska ticket, then withdrew to seek a U.S. Senate seat. The old Whig lost to an old Democrat, Lyman Trumbull, despite originally having far more support in the Illinois legislature. Lincoln was a victim of old party faithful shrinking from throwing their support to someone who used to be in the opposition. But as he told Elihu Washburne, the long-term cause mattered more than the short-term result of electing Trumbull, especially since those supporting Douglas on the Nebraska issue "confess that they hate it worse than any thing that could have happened. It is a great consolation to see them worse whipped than I am."[26]

But in victory or defeat, Lincoln faced a problem: what to do about the collapse of the Whigs? Between their poor showing in the 1852 elections, their inability to maintain sectional unity on slavery, and the rise of the anti-immigrant American or Know-Nothing Party, the Whig Party dissolved. Lincoln understood party loyalty and the need to belong to a party to influence affairs, but he was no Democrat or Know-Nothing, and Republicans had yet to coalesce. As Lincoln told the more radically antislavery Owen Lovejoy, "Not even *you* are more anxious to prevent the extension of slavery than I; and yet the political atmosphere is such, just now, that I fear to do any thing, lest I do wrong," especially with the Know-Nothings still strong. "Of their principles I think little better than I do of those of the slavery extensionists. Indeed I do not perceive how any one professing to be sensitive to the wrongs of the negroes, can join in a league to degrade a class of white men. I have no objection to 'fuse' with any body provided I can fuse on ground which I think is right," and he saw fusing with Know-Nothings as wrong. He mused to Speed, "I think I am a whig; but others say there are no whigs, and that I am an abolitionist. When I was at Washington I voted for the Wilmot Proviso as good as forty times, and I never heard of any one attempting to unwhig me for that. I now do no more than oppose the *extension* of slavery."[27]

In May 1856, Sangamon County Republicans called a party convention, and William Herndon, his more radical law partner, signed Lincoln's name atop the list—and Lincoln approved, making it official that he had joined a party that stood for what he had believed all along. He drew support at that year's convention for vice-president and backed presidential nominee John C. Frémont, whose western explorations had done so much to build interest in acquiring the territory that so deeply concerned Lincoln. Speaking in Michigan for the party ticket, Lincoln declared, "The question is simply this:—Shall slavery be spread into the new Territories, or not?" He also made an appeal with racist undertones, an approach that he took out of concern he often voiced during the campaign that Republicans needed to attract as broad a group of supporters as possible, and his awareness of western racism: "Have we no interest in the free Territories of the United States—that they should be kept open for the homes of free white people?"[28]

Early in 1857, with Buchanan newly ensconced in the White House, Chief Justice Roger Taney's opinion in the *Dred Scott* case claimed that slavery could enter any territory. While Lincoln was caught up in the fever over *Dred Scott* and responded accordingly with criticism of Taney and the Court, events in Utah also captured his attention. Historians have paid far less attention to his speech on this subject than to his carping about *Dred Scott*, but it revealed a great deal about what he thought about slavery and the West, Douglas, and popular sovereignty. When Buchanan replaced Brigham Young as Utah territorial governor, Young's Mormon followers ignored the new appointee, Alfred Cumming, who accused them of rebelling against the government. Buchanan sent troops toward Utah, and Young issued a call to Mormons to return to defend their Zion. Douglas suggested repealing the law creating Utah Territory, eliminating its government structure, and adding Utah to an adjoining state. While "not now prepared to admit or deny that the Judge's mode of coercing them is not as good as any"—damning Douglas with the faintest praise he could muster—Lincoln agreed that "if they are in rebellion, they ought to be somehow coerced to obedience." But he pointed out that "it would be a considerable backing down by Judge Douglas from his much vaunted doctrine of self-government for the territories." He asked, "If the people of Utah shall peacefully form a State Constitution tolerating polygamy, will the Democracy admit them into the Union?" After all, he noted, no federal law existed against plural marriage, so "why is it not a part of the Judge's 'sacred right of self-government' for that people to have it, or rather to *keep* it, if they choose?"[29]

More important to Lincoln was what the battle over Utah symbolized: the hypocrisy in Douglas's idea of popular sovereignty. Douglas claimed democracy for territories, but his democracy, Lincoln noted, had its limits. He declared that Douglas opposed Mormons' freedom to have multiple wives, offering "only additional proof of what was very plain from the beginning, that that doctrine [of popular sovereignty] was a mere deceitful pretense for the benefit of slavery. Those who could not see that much in the Nebraska act itself, which forced Governors, and Secretaries, and Judges on the people of the territories, without their choice or consent, could not be made to see, though one should rise from the dead to testify." What Lincoln left unmentioned was his party's position in their 1856 platform, which lumped together slavery and polygamy as "twin relics of barbarism." But he could remain consistent by opposing the spread of both.[30]

Lincoln's criticism of Douglas over Utah concerned a bigger issue—not just Mormons or even the spread of slavery, but the Republican Party's soul. In the same speech, Lincoln distinguished between the ways the two parties addressed the black man's humanity. "The Republicans inculcate, with whatever of ability they can, that the negro is a man; that his bondage is cruelly wrong, and that the field of his oppression ought not to be enlarged," he said. "The Democrats deny his manhood; deny, or dwarf to insignificance, the wrong of his bondage; so far as possible, crush all sympathy for him, and cultivate and excite hatred and disgust against him; compliment themselves as Union-savers for doing so; and call the indefinite outspreading of his bondage 'a sacred right of self-government.'" But just as an ex-Whig like Lincoln could unite with ex-Democrats like Trumbull in a new party, so could others unite with Douglas if they agreed. By June 1857, when Lincoln delivered these sallies, relations between Buchanan and Douglas showed signs of strain. By the end of the year, with Buchanan accepting the Lecompton Constitution and Douglas denouncing it, that strained relationship had snapped.[31]

While Lincoln wanted his nascent party to spread its tent as broadly as possible, he had several problems with allowing Douglas to enter. Complaining that Horace Greeley of the *New York Tribune* engaged in "constant eulogizing, and admiring, and magnifying Douglas," he asked, "Have they concluded that the republican cause, generally, can be best promoted by sacrificing us here in Illinois? If so we would like to know it soon; it will save us a great deal of labor to surrender at once." After the election, he told Trumbull that "the Republican principle can, in no wise live with Douglas; and it is arrant folly now, as it was last Spring, to waste time, and scatter labor already performed, in dallying with him." His moral objection to working with Douglas was that he and Republicans differed on the party's fundamental principle: popular sovereignty in the western territories rather than legislating to stop slavery from going there at all. Lincoln's political objection was that he had spent the better part of two decades in political battle with Douglas and had no faith in him as an ally. His personal objection was that he wanted to be a U.S. senator, Douglas was up for reelection, and for Republicans to reach an accommodation with the Little Giant would be suicidal for their party and homicidal for Lincoln's aspirations.[32]

Battling slavery and party divisions, Lincoln entered the 1858 Senate campaign, including his "House Divided" speech and the debates with Douglas, all of which made him a national figure. As Don Fehrenbacher and Ward McAfee wrote, "Given that Douglas had effectively stolen the political center with his anti-Lecompton heroics, Lincoln knew that uncharacteristically he himself would have to take advanced antislavery positions to create any significant difference for the voters." But while making a moral appeal, Lincoln engaged Douglas in a battle over whether the western territories would be slave or free—whether the nation would be, as he suggested in his "House Divided" speech, all slave or all free. In his first debate with Douglas, he asked, "What is Popular Sovereignty?" and answered, "I will state—and I have an able man to watch me—my understanding is that Popular Sovereignty, as now applied to the question of Slavery, does allow the people of a Territory to have Slavery if they want to, but does not allow them *not* to have it if they *do not* want it." He worried that the argument for extending slavery into western territories would be used to restore the constitutionally banned African slave trade. Worse, the Kansas-Nebraska Act and the Supreme Court's *Dred Scott* ruling meant Douglas and his sympathizers would have no problem with expanding it into states—thus his observation in the "House Divided" speech, "We shall lie *down* pleasantly dreaming that the people of *Missouri* are on the verge of making their State *free*; and we shall *awake* to the *reality*, instead, that the *Supreme* Court has made *Illinois* a *slave* State." Thus, to allow slavery to spread would "blow out the moral lights around us . . . penetrating the human soul and eradicating the light of reason and the love of liberty in this American people."[33]

Lincoln also revealed his ability to appeal to western racial prejudice—and try to overcome any that Douglas sought to build against him. One of his most famous speeches showed the subtlety with which he approached the touchy issue of race in Illinois and how it related to the spread of slavery into the western territories, showed the contradictions in Douglas's argument, assured his audiences that he was less radical on race than Douglas and other Democrats would argue, and demonstrated that the Republican position on the spread of slavery differed considerably from that of the abolitionists. In one of his early drafts to a speech in Chicago, he declared that "I protest, now and forever, against that counterfeit logic which presumes that because I do not want a negro woman for a slave, I do necessarily want her for a wife"—a sentiment to which he returned during the debates. But he used racial fears to advantage and turned Douglas's racism against him when he said, "The Judge regales us with the terrible enormities that take place by the mixture of races; that the inferior race bears the superior down. Why, Judge, if we do not let them get together in the Territories they won't mix there."[34]

Indeed, Lincoln argued not that Douglas would allow voters to decide whether they wanted slavery, but that he wanted to force slavery upon them—an appeal to free labor and to racial prejudice. According to Lincoln, "he and every one knows that the decision of the Supreme Court, which he approves and makes especial ground of attack upon me for disapproving, forbids the people of a territory to exclude slavery," although Lincoln's arguments against slavery in the territories and Douglas's belief that popular sovereignty would keep it out meant that their positions may have been more similar than Lincoln preferred to admit. But since Douglas had waffled as much as possible on *Dred Scott*, and publicly declared his ambivalence on the spread of slavery, he left room for Lincoln to attack him. And Lincoln took advantage of the opportunity, pointing out that "the Judge is not sustaining popular sovereignty, but absolutely opposing it. He sustains the decision which declares that the popular will of the territories has no constitutional power to exclude slavery during their territorial existence."[35]

It has become common to say that Lincoln lost the battle but won the war. Douglas won in 1858 but Lincoln's performance against him made him a national force in time for Republicans to nominate him for president in 1860. Meanwhile, Lincoln spent part of 1859 and early 1860 delivering speeches that introduced him to more Republicans, whether for "the cause" or because he had "the taste" of the presidency "in my mouth." In Illinois, Ohio, Indiana, New York City, and New England, he continued making the points he had made since the introduction of the Kansas-Nebraska Act: the Founding Fathers proved in the Northwest Ordinance that they wanted to limit slavery, the Compromises of 1820 and 1850 continued their tradition, Douglas broke with that tradition, and popular sovereignty was an evil. He kept warning against surrendering "the *object* of the Republican organization—the preventing the *spread* and *nationalization* of Slavery. This object surrendered, the organization would go to pieces." He lamented the "gradual and steady debauching of public opinion, this course of preparation for the revival of the slave trade, for the territorial slave code, and the new Dred Scott decision that is to carry slavery into the free States" in popular sovereignty. "Did you ever five years ago, hear of anybody in the world saying that the negro had no share in the Declaration of National Independence; that it did not mean negroes at all; and when 'all men' were spoken of negroes were not included?"[36]

In September 1859, he went to Cincinnati to speak. Politically, his trip could do him no harm. In 1860, Ohio would support its radical and well-known Republican, Salmon Chase, for president. If Lincoln proved to be a favorite son candidate from Illinois, though, he might gain Ohio's delegates on a later ballot, and anything he said would help the Republican cause. Lincoln's speech encapsulated a great deal of Republican dogma, and what he had been arguing:

> It is as easy to prove that the framers of the Constitution of the United States, expected that Slavery should be prohibited from extending into the new Territories. . . . There was nothing said in the Constitution in regard to the spread of Slavery into the Territory, I grant that, but there was

something very important said about it by the same generation of men in the adoption of the old Ordinance of '87, through the influence of which you here in Ohio, our neighbors in Indiana, we in Illinois, our neighbors in Michigan and Wisconsin are happy, prosperous, teeming millions of free men. (Continued applause.) That generation of men, though not to the full extent members of the Convention that framed the Constitution, were to some extent members of that Convention, holding seats, at the same time in one body and the other, so that if there was any compromise . . . , the strong evidence is that that compromise was in favor of the restriction of Slavery from the new territories.[37]

Five months later, Lincoln boarded the train to New York to make a similar point at Cooper Union. There, he spoke in a more scholarly way, based on months of research that began not long after the publication of his Cincinnati remarks. But what he said in New York and afterward evolved over three decades in politics, especially during the 1850s. When slavery played a smaller role in public discourse, Lincoln had less to say about it but made clear his opposition to it as economically unsound, politically dangerous, and morally wrong. Then slavery superseded all other issues in his and the nation's mind, and the Mexican-American War, the Wilmot Proviso, the Compromise of 1850, and the Kansas-Nebraska Act redefined the party system and political ideology. These changes forced him to find a new political home and enabled him to find a new political voice. The issue, for him and for most other Republicans, was not whether slavery could be eliminated where it existed, but whether it could be kept from existing elsewhere—in the new territories of the West, where they feared that the presence of slavery would make a prosperous future impossible. Those new territories were not the scene of major military battles during the Civil War. But it was over those territories as an Illinois politician in the 1850s and as president during the Civil War that Lincoln fought the political and ideological battle for the future.

Notes

1. *New-York Times*, February 28, 1860, 1.
2. Harold Holzer, *Lincoln at Cooper Union: The Speech That Made Abraham Lincoln President* (New York: Simon & Schuster, 2004), superbly analyzes the speech, what led up to it, and what followed. See quotation at 27. On the history of federal relations to the Founding Fathers and slavery, see Don E. Fehrenbacher, *The Slaveholding Republic: An Account of the United States Government's Relations to Slavery,* edited by Ward M. McAfee (New York: Oxford University Press, 2001).

3. Holzer, *Lincoln at Cooper Union*, 108–9, 234–35.

4. "Speech at Worcester, Massachusetts," September 12, 1848, in *Boston Daily Advertiser*, September 14, 1848, in Roy P. Basler, ed., *The Collected Works of Abraham Lincoln*, 9 vols. (New Brunswick: Rutgers University Press, 1953–55), 2:1–5, at 3 (hereafter cited as *CW*). On Lincoln's evolution, see esp. David Herbert Donald, *Lincoln* (New York: Simon and Schuster, 1995); and Douglas L. Wilson, *Honor's Voice: The Transformation of Abraham Lincoln* (New York: Alfred A. Knopf, 1998).

5. "To the People of Sangamo County," March 9, 1832, in *Sangamo Journal*, March 15, 1832, in *CW*, 1:5; "To the Editor of the *Sangamo Journal*," New Salem, June 13, 1836, in *Sangamo Journal*, June 18, 1836, in *CW*, 1:48. See also Patricia Nelson Limerick, *The Legacy of Conquest: The Unbroken Past of the American West* (New York: W. W. Norton, 1987); Richard C. Wade, *The Urban Frontier: Pioneer Life in Early Pittsburgh, Cincinnati, Lexington, Louisville, and St. Louis* (Chicago: University of Chicago Press, 1968); Paul E. Johnson, *A Shopkeeper's Millennium: Society and Revivals in Rochester, New York, 1815–1837* (New York: Hill and Wang, 1978).

6. "The Perpetuation of Our Political Institutions," Address before the Young Men's Lyceum of Springfield, Illinois, January 27, 1838, *Sangamo Journal*, February 3, 1838, in *CW*, 1:108–15, at 111–12.

7. Pamphlet, Illinois Historical Society, Springfield; and *Sangamo Journal*, March 6, 1840, "Speech on the Sub-Treasury," December 26, 1839, in *CW*, 1:159–79, at 163; "Communication to the Readers of *The Old Soldier*," in *Sangamo Journal*, February 28, 1840, in *CW*, 1:203–5, at 205; Campaign Circular from Whig Committee, "Address to the People of Illinois," March 4, 1843, in *North Western Gazette and Galena Advertiser*, March 17, 1843, in *CW*, 1:309–18.

8. "Protest in Illinois Legislature on Slavery," *House Journal*, 10th General Assembly, 1st sess., March 3, 1837, 817–18, in *CW*, 1:74–75.

9. "Speech on Annexation of Texas," May 22, 1844, in *Sangamo Journal*, June 6, 1844, in *CW*, 1:337; Lincoln to Williamson Durley, Springfield, October 3, 1845, in *CW*, 1:347–48; "Speech at Lacon, Illinois," November 1, 1848, in *Illinois Gazette*, November 4, 1848, in *CW*, 2:14. See Michael F. Holt, *The Rise and Fall of the American Whig Party* (New York: Oxford University Press, 1999); and Daniel Walker Howe, *The Political Culture of the American Whigs* (Chicago: University of Chicago Press, 1979).

10. Sean Wilentz, *The Rise of American Democracy: Jefferson to Lincoln* (New York: W. W. Norton, 2005), 547–632.

11. *Congressional Globe*, 30th Cong., 1st sess., 1848, n.s., 10:154–56, 64; *Congressional Globe Appendix*, 30th Cong., 1st sess., 159–63; Lincoln to William H. Herndon, Washington, February 2, 1848, in *CW*, 1:448, also in *CW*, 1:431–48; Gabor S. Boritt, *Lincoln and the Economics of the American Dream* (Memphis: Memphis State University Press, 1978), 258–59.

12. Lincoln speaking to the House of Representatives, July 27, 1848, *Congressional Globe Appendix*, 30th Cong., 1st sess., 1041–43, also in *CW*, 1:501–16, at 505; "Speech at Worcester, Massachusetts," September 12, 1848, in *Boston Daily Advertiser*, September 14, 1848, in *CW*, 2:1–5, at 3; "Speech at Boston, Massachusetts," September 15, 1848, in *Boston Atlas*, September 16, 1848, in *CW*, 2:5; "Speech at Lowell, Massachusetts," September 16, 1848, in *Lowell Daily Journal*, September 18, 1848, in *CW*, 2:6; "Speech at Taunton, Massachusetts," September [21?], 1848, in *Bristol County Democrat*, September 29, 1848, in *CW*, 2:6–9, at 7.

13. *Congressional Globe*, 30th Cong., 2nd sess., 1849, 533, in *CW*, 2:26–27; Lincoln to William Schouler, Washington, February 2, 1849, in *CW*, 2:25; Donald, *Lincoln*, 137–43.

14. "Eulogy on Zachary Taylor: Eulogy Pronounced by Hon. A. Lincoln, on the Life and Services of the Late President of the United States, at Chicago, July 25th, 1850," in *Chicago Weekly Journal*, August 5, 1850, and *Chicago Daily Journal*, July 27, 1850, in *CW*, 2:83–90, at 89; "Eulogy on Henry Clay," July 6, 1852, in *Illinois Weekly Journal*, July 21, 1852, in *CW*, 2:121–32, at 125–27; "First Debate with Stephen A. Douglas at Ottawa, Illinois," August 21, 1858, in *CW*, 3:1–37, at 29; Donald, *Lincoln*, 142–61.

15. "Speech to the Springfield Scott Club," August 14 and 26, 1852, in *Illinois Weekly Journal*, September 22, 1852, in *CW*, 2:135–57, at 137–38. See also "Speech at Peoria, Illinois," September 17, 1852, on Pierce, in *CW*, 2:158,. "Speech at Springfield, Illinois," July 17, 1858, in pamphlet reprint and *Illinois State Journal*, July 20 and 21, 1858, in *CW*, 2:504–21; "Speech at Bath, Illinois," August 16, 1858, in *Chicago Daily Press and Tribune*, August 21, 1858, in *CW*, 2:543–44; "Speech at Lewistown, Illinois," August 17, 1858, in *CW*, 2.544–47, on Clay and Douglas.

16. William E. Gienapp, *Abraham Lincoln and Civil War America* (New York: Oxford University Press, 2002), 50, and *The Origins of the Republican Party, 1852-1856* (New York: Oxford University Press, 1987); Eric Foner, *Free Soil, Free Labor, Free Men: The Ideological Origins of the Republican Party* (New York: Oxford University Press, 1970, 1995).

17. See Boritt, *Lincoln and the Economics of the American Dream*, and John S. Wright, *Lincoln and the Politics of Slavery* (Reno: University of Nevada Press, 1970).

18. "Speech at Springfield, Illinois," July 17, 1858, in pamphlet reprint and *Illinois State Journal*, July 20 and 21, 1858, in *CW*, 2:504–21, at 514; "Fragment: Notes for Speeches," ca. August 21, 1858, in *CW*, 2: 547–53, at 551; "Third Debate with Stephen A. Douglas at Jonesboro, Illinois," September 15, 1858, in *CW*, 3:102–44, at 117.

19. "Speech at Springfield, Illinois," October 4, 1854, in *Illinois Journal*, October 5, 1854, in *CW*, 2:240–47, at 240–43. See also "Speech at Kalamazoo, Michigan," August 27, 1856, in *Detroit Daily Advertiser*, August 29, 1856, in *CW*, 2:361–66, at 361, 363–64; Foner, *Free Soil, Free Labor, Free Men*, 40–72.

20. "Speech at Bloomington, Illinois," September 12, 1854, in *Bloomington Weekly Pantagraph*, September 20, 1854, in *CW*, 2:230–33, at 232–33, after the Missouri Compromise; see also "Speech at Bloomington, Illinois," September 26, 1854, in *Peoria Weekly Republican*, September 26, 1854, in *CW*, 2:234–40; "Speech at Peoria, Illinois," October 16, 1854, in *Illinois Journal*, October 21 and 23–28, 1854, in *CW*, 2:247–83, at 252–53, 259.

21. "Speech at Peoria, Illinois," October 16, 1854, in *Illinois Journal*, October 21 and 23–28, 1854, in *CW*, 2:247–83, at 259 and 279.

22. "Speech at Springfield, Illinois," October 4, 1854, in *Illinois Journal*, October 5, 1854, in *CW*, 2:240–47.

23. "Fragment of a Speech," ca.. May 18, 1858, in *CW*, 2:448–54. See also Lincoln to Elihu B. Washburne, Springfield, May 27, 1858, in *CW*, 2:455; to Stephen A. Hurlbut, Springfield, June 1, 1858, in *CW*, 2:456; and to Charles L. Wilson, *CW*, 2:456–57. See James A. Rawley, *Race and Politics: "Bleeding Kansas" and the Coming of the Civil War* (Philadelphia: J. B. Lippincott, 1969), and Nicole Etcheson, *Bleeding Kansas: Contested Liberty in the Civil War Era* (Lawrence: University Press of Kansas, 2006).

24. Lincoln to Joshua F. Speed, Springfield, August 24, 1855, in *CW*, 2:320–23, at 322; "Speech at Springfield, Illinois," October 4, 1854, in *Illinois Journal*, October 5, 1854, in *CW*, 2:240–47, at 244, 246–47; "Speech at Peoria, Illinois," October 16, 1854, in *Illinois Journal*, October 21 and 23–28, 1854, in *CW*, 2:247–83, at 258, 262, 271–72, 279.

25. "Speech at Springfield, Illinois," October 4, 1854, in *Illinois Journal*, October 5, 1854, in *CW*, 2:240–47, at 244, 246–47; "Speech at Peoria, Illinois," October 16, 1854, in *Illinois Journal*, October 21 and 23–28, 1854, in *CW*, 2:247–83, at 258.

26. Lincoln to Elihu B. Washburne, Springfield, February 9, 1855, in *CW*, 2:304–6, at 306; Donald, *Lincoln*, 162–85.

27. Lincoln to Owen Lovejoy, Springfield, August 11, 1855, in *CW*, 2:316–17; Lincoln to Speed, Springfield, August 24, 1855, in *CW*, 2:320–23, at 322. See also Lincoln to Edward Lusk, Springfield, October 30, 1858, in *CW*, 3:333.

28. *Illinois State Journal*, May 10, 1856; and William H. Herndon and Jesse W. Weik, *Herndon's Lincoln: The True Story of a Great Life*, 3 vols. (Chicago: Belford, Clarke & Co., 1889), 2:382, cited in *CW*, 2:340; "Speech at Bloomington, Illinois," May 29, 1856, in *Alton Weekly Courier*, June 5, 1856, in ibid.; Lincoln to Lyman Trumbull, Springfield, June 7, 1856, in *CW*, 2:342–43; Lincoln to James Berdan, Springfield, July 10, 1856, in *CW*, 2:347–48; see also Lincoln to John Bennett, Springfield, August 4, 1856, in *CW*, 2:358; Lincoln to Hezekiah G. Wells, ibid.; Lincoln to Trumbull, Springfield, August 11, 1856, in *CW*, 2:359–60; "Speech at Kalamazoo, Michigan," August 27, 1856, in *Detroit Daily Advertiser*, August 29, 1856, in *CW*, 2:361–66; Eugene H. Berwanger, *The Frontier against Slavery: Western Anti-Negro Prejudice and the Slavery Extension Controversy* (Urbana: University of Illinois Press, 1967); and Michael A. Morrison, *Slavery and the American West: The Eclipse of Manifest Destiny and the Coming of the Civil War* (Chapel Hill: University of North Carolina Press, 1997).

29. "Speech at Springfield, Illinois," June 26, 1857, in *Illinois State Journal*, June 29, 1857, in *CW*, 2:398–410, at 398–99. See Norman F. Furniss, *The Mormon Conflict, 1850–1859* (New Haven: Yale University Press, 1960); and Sally Denton, *American Massacre: The Tragedy at Mountain Meadows, September 11, 1857* (New York: Alfred A. Knopf, 2003).

30. "Speech at Springfield, Illinois," June 26, 1857, in *Illinois State Journal*, June 29, 1857, in *CW*, 2:398–410, at 398–99.

31. Ibid., 409. See Robert W. Johannsen, *Stephen A. Douglas* (New York: Oxford University Press, 1973), 551–52.

32. Lincoln to Trumbull, Chicago, November 30, 1857, and Bloomington, December 28, 1857, in *CW*, 2:427, 430. See also Lincoln to Elihu B. Washburne, Urbana, April 26, 1858, and Springfield, May 10, 1858, in *CW*, 2:443–44, 445–46; Lincoln to Jediah F. Alexander, Springfield, May 15, 1858, in *CW*, 2:446–47; Lincoln to Trumbull, Springfield, December 11, 1858, in *CW*, 3:344–45; Lincoln to W. H. Wells, Springfield, January 8, 1859, in *CW*, 3:349; Lincoln to Salmon P. Chase, Springfield, April 30, 1859, in *CW*, 3:378.

33. "'A House Divided': Speech at Springfield, Illinois," June 16, 1858, in *Illinois State Journal*, June 18, 1858, in *CW*, 2:461–69; "First Debate with Stephen A. Douglas at Ottawa, Illinois," August 21, 1858, in *CW*, 3:1–37, at 18–19, 23–24, and 29; "Speech at Bloomington, Illinois," September 4, 1858, in *Bloomington Pantagraph*, September 6, 1858, in *CW*, 3:85–90, at 88. See Lincoln to Samuel Galloway, Springfield, July 28, 1859, in *CW*, 3:394–95. See Fehrenbacher, *Slaveholding Republic*, 285; although McAfee completed and edited the book, and is not credited as a coauthor, he cowrote the chapter in which the quotation appears. On the debates, the most recent fine contribution to an extensive literature is Allen C. Guelzo, "Houses Divided: Lincoln, Douglas, and the Political Landscape of 1858," *Journal of American History* 94:2 (September 2007): 391–417.

34. "Speech at Chicago, Illinois," July 10, 1858, in *Chicago Daily Democrat*, July 13, 1858, and *Chicago Daily Press and Tribune*, July 12, 1858, in *CW*, 2:484–502, at 498.

35. "Speech at Springfield, Illinois," July 17, 1858, in pamphlet reprint and *Illinois State Journal*, July 20 and 21, 1858, in *CW*, 2:504–21, at 508.

36. Lincoln to Mark W. Delahay, Springfield, May 14, 1859, in *CW*, 3:378–79; "Speech at Columbus, Ohio," September 16, 1859, in *Illinois State Journal*, September 24, 1859, in *CW*, 3:400–425, at 423; "Speech at Dayton, Ohio," September 17, 1859, in *Dayton Journal*, September 19, 1859, in *CW*, 3:436–37; "Speech at Indianapolis, Indiana," September 19, 1859, in *Indianapolis Atlas*, September 19, 1859, in *CW*, 3:463–70.

37. "Speech at Cincinnati, Ohio," September 17, 1859, in *Illinois State Journal*, October 7, 1859, in *CW*, 3:438–62, at 448–49 and 454–57.

3 ➤ Lincoln, the Thirteenth Amendment, and the Admission of Nevada

Earl S. Pomeroy

The scholars and the debunkers have pared away much of the "Lincoln legend"—the hagiography which not only canonized the man but presented him posthumously with a united and sympathetic party. Today the schoolboy knows that Lincoln was both political manager and statesman, and he knows that Lincoln had bitter enemies and outspoken critics among those who elected him. But the legend dies hard: it is a blend of truth, error, and fabrication in which the revisionists themselves have not disdained to quarry. Most of them accept a story of the admission of Nevada whose best claim to acceptance is that it seems to confirm aptly both legend and revision.

The proposal of the Thirteenth Amendment was to President Lincoln one of the great political objects of 1864–65. "The passage of this amendment," he told Representative James Rollins of Missouri in January 1865, "will clinch the whole subject. It will bring the war, I have no doubt, rapidly to a close."[1] The crucial vote was in the House, where the amendment failed on June 15, 1864,[2] and passed on January 31, 1865, by the narrow margin of 119 to 56—2 over the required two-thirds.[3] Ratification was easy and uneventful.[4]

Charles Anderson Dana, assistant secretary of war under Stanton and later editor of the *New York Sun,* published *in McClure's Magazine* for April 1898 a temptingly graphic and circumstantial story, which has led many to identify Lincoln's strategy toward the Thirteenth Amendment with the passage of the Nevada Enabling Act:

From *Pacific Historical Review* 12 (December 1943): 362–68.

Lincoln was a supreme politician. He understood politics because he understood human nature. I had an illustration of this in the spring of 1864. The administration had decided that the constitution of the United States should be amended so that slavery should be prohibited. . . . In order thus to amend the constitution, it was necessary first to have the proposed amendment approved by three-fourths of the States. When that question came to be considered, the issue was seen to be so close that one State more was necessary. The State of Nevada was organized and admitted to answer that purpose. . . .

In March, 1864, the question of allowing Nevada to form a State government finally came up in the House of Representatives. . . . For a long time beforehand the question had been canvassed anxiously. . . .

"Dana," he [Lincoln] said, "I am very anxious about this vote. It has got to be taken next week. The time is very short. It is going to be a great deal closer than I wish it was."

"There are plenty of Democrats who will vote for it," I replied. "There is James E. English of Connecticut; I think he is sure, isn't he?"

"Oh, yes; he is sure on the merits of the question."

"Then," said I, "there's 'Sunset' Cox of Ohio. How is he?"

"He is sure and fearless. But there are some others that I am not clear about. There are three that you can deal with better than anybody else, perhaps, as you know them all. . . ."

. . . One man was from New Jersey and two from New York. . . .

"Here [said Lincoln] is the alternative: that we carry this vote, or be compelled to raise another million, and I don't know how many more, men, and fight no one knows how long. It is a question of three votes or new armies."[5]

Dana recalled that he secured those three votes for Nevada by judicious promises of presidential patronage, which Andrew Johnson, as president, refused to honor.

Though Nevada happened to be the only new western state of the Civil War years, the admission of new states had attracted interest and suspicion among Republicans. Thaddeus Stevens, while favoring the West Virginia bill on its passage, suggested that originally it had been a phase of a presidential conspiracy to control Congress;[6] he and Roscoe Conkling had been instrumental in delaying consideration in the House from July to December of 1862.[7] Attorney General Bates, however, later said that the admission of West Virginia was "conceived, as a fraudulent party trick, by a few unprincipled

Radicals, and the prurient ambition of a few meritless aspirants urged it, with indecent haste, into premature birth."[8]

By 1864 there was little question of the Radical attitude toward new Republican states. When Nevada appeared as a candidate for statehood, it appeared not alone, as one might suppose from Dana's account and from the accounts following on Dana,[9] but in company with Colorado and Nebraska. Chairman James M. Ashley of the House Committee on Territories had introduced enabling bills for all three on December 22, 1862,[10] while the West Virginia bill still lay before Lincoln. The Senate failed to act on the bills at that session[11] but displayed more interest in 1864: bills for Nevada and Colorado introduced in the Senate on February 8[12] became laws on March 21.[13] Lincoln signed a bill for Nebraska on April 19.[14]

Colorado and Nebraska failed to become states in 1864 because of divisions in intraterritorial rather than congressional politics.[15] When citizens of the two territories changed their minds in 1865 and 1866, Congress overrode a presidential veto to admit Nebraska,[16] but not Colorado.[17] A political accident, rather than the policy of the Thirty-eighth Congress, thus withheld statehood from these two states till 1867 and 1876, respectively, and gave it to the least populous member of the Union.

Did Congress admit Nevada in order to insure passage of the Thirteenth Amendment? It is improbable that Congress admitted Nevada to fill the quota of three-fourths of the states for ratification, as Dana says. Ratification proceeded rapidly enough, with states to spare. Lincoln's impromptu speech celebrating the amendment's proposal on January 31, 1865, reflects general satisfaction and confidence after a difficult step.[18] Senator Cornelius Cole later recalled that no difficulty was apprehended in ratification and that the trouble lay in the House.[19]

Dana probably confused events of March 1864 with those of January 1865. Both Dana and Cox in their reminiscences discuss the question of Cox's voting with the administration. Cox, however, instead of being "sure and fearless" from the administration's point of view with respect to Nevada, objected strongly to the Nevada, Colorado, and Nebraska bills in March 1864.[20] He campaigned vigorously against the administration that fall.[21] In the winter; however, "during the holidays," he promised Lincoln his help with the Thirteenth Amendment, provided that the administration make a sincere effort for peace.[22] As a Democrat, feeling as he did toward both Lincoln and the Radicals, Cox could more reasonably promise to support a single measure such as the amendment than an admission bill or group of admission bills that would create Republican votes in the electoral college and Republican votes in Congress applicable to any measures. Again, Cox wrote that "in that winter of 1864–'65"—the winter of the final vote in the House—"Mr. Seward and the President considered this amendment worth an army."[23] These words are strikingly similar to Dana's when he spoke of the president's feeling in March of 1864.

Still other details of Dana's story are obviously more applicable to January 1865 than to March 1864. Dana's story that Johnson refused to concede patronage, which Dana had promised on Lincoln's authority,[24] makes it seem unlikely that the vote in question occurred as many as thirteen months before Lincoln's death. James E. English, whom Lincoln, according to Dana, described as "sound on the merits of the question," was outstanding as one of the few Democrats who supported the amendment.[25] Representative John B. Alley's account of Lincoln's concern over the vote of January 31, 1865,[26] resembles Dana's in a general way. Sandburg mentions the possibility of a bargain for New Jersey Democratic votes in preparation for the vote of January 31;[27] Dana recalled securing a New Jersey Democratic vote by promises of patronage.[28]

The real objects of the admission of Nevada and Nebraska and of the attempt to admit Colorado were undoubtedly not confined to the single amendment. Nor is it clear that the chief object was electoral votes. The presidential election was in prospect; on the importance of Republican victory, the president and the Radicals could agree, if not on the candidate, in March of 1864. "We supposed," said Senator (former Governor) Nye of Nevada in 1866, "that we must be admitted before the election in the fall, or our work would be void."[29] Yet the original enabling acts of March 1864 provided that the state constitution should be submitted to popular vote on October 11; Governor Nye, a close friend of Seward, suggested an earlier date so that the state might take part in the presidential election;[30] and Congress only then passed an amendment specifying September 7.[31] The original enabling act would have permitted Nevada to add to the Republican strength in Congress; there might not have been time enough for Nevada to add to the Republican strength in the presidential election. Lincoln was curiously slow to take advantage of the change, refusing to proclaim Nevada a state until he had received copies of the constitution and ordinances sent after ratification, even though he already had copies sent before ratification.[32] Governor Nye telegraphed the constitution, at a cost of $4,303.27, on October 26 (received October 28).[33] Lincoln did not issue the proclamation until October 31[34]—eight days before the election!

Statements of congressional leaders in the years just following suggest a broad concern in 1864 over Republican strength in general, not confined to the issue of the presidency or of any amendment. By 1865 and 1867, when Colorado and Nebraska were candidates for statehood, many Republicans felt the need less pressing. This was not simply because these were not presidential election years. Senator Howe of Wisconsin attributed his earlier favor for Colorado (in 1864) to "temporary" reductions of the majority in the Senate: "I began to look about for reinforcements. I did not see exactly where they were to come from unless we drew on the West. . . . It was that necessity resting on me that finally induced me to vote for the admission of Colorado. But that emergency has passed by. We have two-thirds of both Houses assured men."[35]

By this time, the Radicals themselves were divided in victory. Pomeroy defended Colorado's leaders as "the most radical, loyal, devoted, and earnest men,"[36] but Sumner objected to irregularities in procedure, to the small population, and to the constitutional provisions on suffrage.[37] Wade also stood at this time (March 1866) against admission,[38] but two months later was for it again, in opposition to President Johnson.[39] Johnson himself publicly conceded the propriety of admitting Nevada under "some high public necessity," while denying such necessity in the case of Colorado.[40]

As Johnson concurred in the admission of Nevada, so could Lincoln. Apart from Dana's story, there is no reason to suppose that Nevada was a favorite project of Lincoln or that he viewed it with great warmth. Senator Buckalew said in 1866 that, according to plans of Chairman Wade of the Senate Committee on Territories, the enabling acts of 1864 "were passed for the purpose of heading off Mr. Lincoln . . . in his policy of establishing State governments in the South and obtaining their recognition and representation in this government."[41]

Ashley, chairman of the House Committee, later claimed that his own objects had been "to establish a new principle of the admission of States . . . negativing, so far as I could in the enabling acts, the old idea of State rights," and also to secure extra votes in case the presidential election should be thrown to the House.[42] Ashley and his colleagues, in demanding that the new states satisfy certain conditions before admission, prepared the devices of reconstruction; some suggested returning the Southern states to territorial status; and the committees on territories reported reconstruction bills. If such were the motives in Congress, it is indeed ironical that Charles Anderson Dana, journalistic champion of Radicalism, should have succeeded in planting the story that the admission of Nevada was a cherished project of Abraham Lincoln. It is not impossible that Lincoln may have realized and merely tolerated such Radical motives in the belief that the general need of the moment overshadowed the party's internal divisions.

Notes

1. Carl Sandburg, *Abraham Lincoln; The War Years* (New York, 1939), 4:7. Richard Nelson Current refers to the amendment as Stevens's measure, "anti-Lincoln or at least un-Lincolnian." *Old Thad Stevens: A Story of Ambition* (Madison, 1942), 204, 206. I shall not discuss here the question of Lincoln's decision for unqualified abolition.

2. The vote was 93 ayes to 65 nays, 23 not voting. The Senate passed it, 38 to 6, on April 8, 1864. Sandburg, *Abraham Lincoln,* 4:6.

3. Eight not voting. According to Cornelius Cole, several members violently opposed to it failed to vote after seeing that passage was assured. *Memoirs of Cornelius Cole, Ex-Senator of the United States from California* (New York, 1908), 221.

4. It was completed by Georgia on December 9, 1865. Five states followed Georgia in the next seven weeks, Texas in 1870. Mississippi, Kentucky, Delaware, and Maryland rejected. Nevada ratified on February 16, 1865, the fifteenth state to do so.

5. "Reminiscences of Men and Events of the Civil War," *McClure's Magazine,* April 1898, 564. The articles in *McClure's* appeared later with some additions in Dana's *Recollections of the Civil War: With the Leaders at Washington and in the Field in the Sixties* (New York, 1902).

6. *Congressional Globe,* 37th Cong., 3rd sess., December 9, 1862, 50–51.

7. Ibid., 37th Cong., 2nd sess., July 16, 1862, 3397. Conway of Kansas charged that admission would "consolidate all the powers of government in the hands of the executive," there being no logical limit to the setting up of Union governments. Ibid., 37th Cong., 3rd sess., December 9, 1862, 37–38.

8. Howard K. Beale, ed., *The Diary of Edward Bates, 1859–1866,* Annual Report of the American Historical Association, 1930 (Washington, 1933), 4:508. Bates's suspicions doubtless were quickened by his feeling that loyal Virginia should remain a "constitutional nucleus" for reconstruction. Bates to A. F. Ritchie, August 12, 1861, in Virgil A. Lewis, *How West Virginia Was Made: Proceedings of the First Convention of the People of Northwestern Virginia at Wheeling, May 13, 14 and 15, 1861 . . .* (Charleston [1909]), 219–20.

9. Carl Russell Fish, "Lincoln and the Patronage," *American Historical Review* 8 (October 1902): 66–67; Effie Mona Mack, *Nevada: A History of the State from the Earliest Times through the Civil War* (Glendale, 1936), 255–56, 266; Sandburg, *Abraham Lincoln,* 4:7.

10. *Congressional Globe,* 37th Cong., 3rd sess., 1862–63, 166. Ashley had similar bills introduced in the Senate on February 12, 1863; they passed on March 3 but were not considered in the House. Ibid., 37th Cong., 3rd sess., 1863, Part 2, 905, 1512; *House Journal,* 37th Cong., 3rd sess., March 3, 1863, 611; *Congressional Globe,* 39th Cong., 1st sess., May 3, 1866, 2372.

11. Albert Watkins, ed., *Official Report of the Debates and Proceedings in the Nebraska Constitutional Convention Assembled in Lincoln, June Thirteenth, 1871, Concluded . . . ,* Nebraska State Historical Society Publications, ser. 2, no. 8 (1908): 476.

12. *Congressional Globe,* 38th Cong., 1st sess., 1863–64, 521. In the meantime, Nevada had approved statehood at an election held September 2, 1863, but rejected the proposed state constitution on January 19, 1864. Mack, *Nevada,* 249; Hubert Howe Bancroft, *History of Nevada, Colorado, and Wyoming, 1540–1888,* in *Works* (San Francisco, 1890), 25:178–79.

13. *Congressional Globe,* 38th Cong., 1st sess., 1864, Part 2, 1228.

14. Ibid., 1607.

15. Delegates to the Nebraska convention having been pledged not to form a constitution, the convention adjourned immediately after organizing. Watkins, *Official Report,* 486. The Colorado constitution was defeated on September 13, 1864. Elmer Ellis, "Colorado's First Fight for Statehood, 1865–1868," *Colorado Magazine,* January 1931, 24.

16. February 9, 1867, 14 *Stats at Large* 391–92.

17. The attempt to override Johnson's veto stopped after March 1, 1867, when it mustered 29–19 votes in the Senate. *Congressional Globe,* 39th Cong., 2nd sess., 1867, 1927. The light and close vote on statehood in Colorado, the small population, and the overwhelming opposition to Negro suffrage probably all operated against a larger vote for admission.

18. John G. Nicolay and John Hay, *Abraham Lincoln: A History* (New York, 1890), 10:87–88.

19. *Memoirs of Cornelius Cole,* 219–20.

20. *Congressional Globe,* 38th Cong., 1st sess., March 11, 1864, 1044; March 17, 1864, 1166–67.

21. *New York Herald,* November 1, 1864.

22. *Three Decades of Federal Legislation, 1855 to 1885* . . . (San Francisco, 1885), 310. For an explanation of Cox's last-moment decision to vote against the amendment, see his *Eight Years in Congress, from 1857–1865: Memoirs and Speeches* (New York, 1865), 397–98.

23. *Three Decades,* 320.

24. *McClure's,* April 1888, 565–66.

25. Jarvis M. Morse in *Dictionary of American Biography* (New York, 1931), 6:166.

26. Sandburg, *Abraham Lincoln,* 4:7.

27. Ibid., 9. Only one New Jersey representative, a Republican, voted for the amendment. *Congressional Globe,* 38th Cong., 2nd sess., 1865, 531.

28. *McClure's,* April 1898, 565–66.

29. *Congressional Globe,* 39th Cong., 1st sess., April 24, 1866, 2145.

30. Mack, *Nevada,* 257.

31. The act of May 21, 1864, reported on May 5 by B. F. Wade in the Senate. *Congressional Globe,* 38th Cong., 1st sess., 2118, 2358, 2372, 2385, 2405.

32. Seward to Nye, October 14 and October 18, 1864, Domestic Letters, 66:479, 428. Copies of the constitution addressed to the president on August 15 were received on October 5. J. Wesley Johnson to President, August 15, 1864, Territorial Papers, Nevada, vol. 1, no. 75. There is some interest, if not significance, in the fact that in estimating the electoral vote on October 13, Lincoln forgot to count the Nevada votes. Sandburg, *Abraham Lincoln,* 3:275.

33. Territorial Papers, Nevada, vol. 2.

34. Seward to Nye, October 31, 1864, Domestic Letters, 66:543.

35. *Congressional Globe,* 39th Cong., 2nd sess., January 7, 1867, 317.

36. Ibid., 39th Cong., 1st sess., March 13, 1866, 1352.

37. Ibid., March 12, 1866, 1327. Cf. Edmund's position. Ibid., April 25, 1866, 2176.

38. Ibid., March 13, 1866, 1359.

39. Ibid., May 21, 1866, 2712.

40. James D. Richardson, ed., A *Compilation of the Messages and Papers of the Presidents, 1789–1897* (1900), 6:415–16, entry for May 15, 1866.

41. *Congressional Globe,* 39th Cong., 2nd sess., December 20, 1866, 221.

42. Ibid., 1st sess., May 3, 1866, 2372. John Conness's language in January 1864 also coupled the ideas of attacking states' rights and of increasing party strength. In telegrams urging ratification of the proposed Nevada constitution, he emphasized that "Her votes are wanted here, and every loyal man impatiently awaits her application for admission. She has the great honor of being the first to rebuke the pretense that the States are mere partners, as well as of having set National over State sovereignty." Conness to J. T. Goodman, January 16, 1864. Another message suggests that at that time Lincoln was not known as actively working for Nevada: "We have inquired, and there is no doubt the Administration would be glad to have Nevada a State. They have no doubt it would be a loyal State, and they understand its Constitution has provisions of superior national importance." William Rigby and John Conness to J. T. Goodman, January 16, 1864. Clippings in Bancroft Scraps, Nevada Miscellany, 1; set W, 95: 1:47, Bancroft Library, University of California, Berkeley. Ashley's reference to the possibility of a presidential contest in the House suggests that between March and May 5 of 1864, when Wade introduced the bill to admit Nevada in time for the November election, Radical campaign strategy may have shifted. The outcome of the Cleveland convention (May 31, 1864) may have been apparent earlier in the month.

4 ▷ Lincoln and the Territorial Patronage: The Ascendancy of the Radicals in the West

Vincent G. Tegeder

"How pleasant to think of, and how delightful to enjoy are those nice fat offices that our generous Uncle has provided." In these words, Jared Benson, an influential Minnesota Republican, alluded in 1859 to the interest of his party in the federal patronage.[1] The Republican victory of 1860 placed the selection of a host of officials in the hands of triumphant party leaders; they were now afforded an opportunity to appoint the various territorial governors, secretaries, judges, land agents, revenue officials, and officers of the Indian service. Since the days of Jackson, except when the Whigs were victorious, Democrats had controlled the distribution of territorial appointments. Success in 1860 gave the new Republicans opportunity to distribute these lush positions as they might desire.

President Lincoln, however, was faced with a complex problem when he began to distribute the spoils of victory. The Republican Party of 1860 contained former Whigs, old Free-Soilers, antislavery Democrats, eastern protariff manufacturers, western free-trade farmers, hardened machine politicians, and visionary reformers in its ill-assorted ranks. Already, too, a division of the party into moderates and Radicals had appeared. The president-elect, Orville H. Browning, James R. Doolittle, and Jacob Collamer represented the moderate wing; Benjamin F. Wade, George W. Julian, Charles Sumner, Zachariah Chandler, Thaddeus Stevens, and Owen Lovejoy led the Radicals. Although these two segments of the Republican Party diverged in opinion about the treatment of the southern "slaveocracy," a common attitude toward the West provided a bond of unity during the

From *Mississippi Valley Historical Review* 35 (June 1948): 77–90.

election of 1860. Moderates and Radicals alike favored northern control of the territories and endorsed subsidies for railroads, free access to the rich resources of the public domain, free homesteads, and federal aid for internal improvements.[2] No matter whom Lincoln appointed to offices in the West, the Radicals could expect genuine support for their program.

In attempting to carry out his maxim, "Justice to all,"[3] Lincoln gave reasonable attention to the demands of the Radicals for a share in the territorial patronage. His appointments in the Interior Department favored their western interests. The officials of this department, including the General Land Office, the Bureau of Indian Affairs, and the Bureau of Mines, controlled the operation of the territorial system.

The position of secretary of the interior was awarded to Caleb B. Smith, one of the key advocates of Lincoln's nomination at Chicago in 1860. As the leader of the Indiana delegation, Smith promised Judge David Davis that he would support Lincoln's candidacy in return for a cabinet position.[4] Even though Smith was not closely affiliated with the Radicals, he shared the common Republican interest in keeping slavery out of the territories and in fostering internal improvements. While in Congress during the 1840s, he had served as a member of the House Committee on Territories, succeeded Stephen A. Douglas as its chairman in 1847, and stamped himself as an advocate of federal aid for the construction of railroads and canals. During the 1850s, he attained the presidency of the Cincinnati and Chicago Railroad Company.[5]

Smith retained his cabinet post until December 1862, when he persuaded Lincoln to grant him a lifetime judgeship in Indiana and to appoint the assistant secretary, John P. Usher, a fellow Indiana politician, as his successor.[6] Usher was entirely satisfactory to Lincoln, for they had ridden the Illinois circuit together and Usher had campaigned vigorously for Lincoln during the 1860 contest in the critical middle western states.[7] Although Usher, too, was not a Radical, he was interested in opportunities for Northerners in the West. As a member of the Indiana legislature in the early 1850s, he had supported railroad interests, and as secretary of the interior he became closely identified with the movement to amend the Pacific Railroad Act of July 1, 1862, and promoted the passage of the revised bill of July 2, 1864.[8] In 1865 he resigned his cabinet position to become general solicitor of the Eastern Division, Union Pacific Railroad Company. In this capacity, Usher worked to complete the branch line of the Union Pacific from Kansas City via Denver to Cheyenne, Wyoming, and defended the company in its various land controversies during the Reconstruction era.[9]

The Radicals had even greater reason to rejoice when Lincoln appointed one of their number, James M. Edmunds of Detroit, as commissioner of the General Land Office, a key position in the Interior Department.[10] Besides being an "astute politician," Edmunds was known as Chandler's "right-hand man."[11] The Michigan Radicals, with the aid of the Lincoln-appointed surveyor general, George D. Hill of Ann Arbor,[12] also a political ally of Commissioner Edmunds, reaped many advantages in the exploitation of Dakota Territory by nonresident northern groups. Hill imported Michigan residents and granted them choice surveying contracts.[13]

The Radicals gained another territorial position in the appointment of William Jayne of Springfield, Illinois, as governor of Dakota Territory. Brother-in-law of Senator Lyman Trumbull and one of Lincoln's key supporters in 1860,[14] Jayne had been mayor of Springfield and a state senator. He readily pleased the Radicals by calling for the passage of an antislavery law and a memorial for a Pacific railroad in his first message to the Dakota territorial legislature.[15] The Radicals also attempted to profit from his ambition to become the Republican congressional delegate from Dakota. Already in 1862 the Michigan appointees, such as Hill and his associates, supported Jayne in preference to the successful candidate, General John B. S. Todd, a cousin of Mary Todd Lincoln.[16] Between 1856 and 1861, Todd had been one of the leading promoters in the creation of Dakota Territory. While serving as captain of a United States infantry force located at Fort Pierre, he became interested in the possibilities of the upper Missouri region. In 1856 he resigned his commission to enter business with Daniel M. Frost, a merchant and trader in St. Louis. They carried on trade with the Yankton Indians, won their confidence, organized the Upper Missouri Townsite Company in 1858, and during the next year lobbied for ratification of the Yankton Treaty in Washington. Their next step was to promote the creation of Dakota Territory, and, notwithstanding the fact that the new territory contained only 2,600 settlers, they achieved their objective by 1861.[17] In 1862 Todd and his supporters were unwilling to relinquish political and economic control of Dakota Territory to the Michigan Radicals. They organized the People's Union Party and campaigned on a platform that condemned the evils of nonresident territorial rule, which the Jayne and Hill forces fostered.[18]

Governor Jayne and the Radicals encountered much difficulty in their attempt to curb Todd's influence in Dakota's affairs. Even though the governor obtained a certificate of election from the territorial board of canvassers, he failed to persuade Congress to seat him as delegate from Dakota.[19] Not until the fall of 1864 did the Radicals succeed in ousting Todd and in electing their own candidate, Walter A. Burleigh.[20] Meanwhile, however, the Jayne-Todd controversy produced one important result for the Radicals. In order to defend his case better in Washington, Governor Jayne resigned his position. The Michigan Radicals Zachariah Chandler and Commissioner James Edmunds immediately petitioned Lincoln to appoint Edmunds's brother, Newton Edmunds, as the new governor of Dakota.[21] Samuel C. Pomeroy, Henry S. Lane, James Harlan, Lyman Trumbull, and James Doolittle increased the Republican pressure on the president.[22] Lincoln heeded the appeal and sent Newton Edmunds as the new governor of the territory.[23] By the close of 1863, the Radicals enjoyed a favored position in the territory with a brother of the commissioner of the General Land Office as governor and the control of surveying activities by Michigan residents under the direction of Surveyor General Hill.

In Nebraska Territory, the Radicals also obtained friendly appointees. Lincoln's choice for governor, Alvin Saunders of Mt. Pleasant, Iowa, became a staunch antislavery politician and promoted the growth of the Republican Party.[24] As a candidate for the Nebraska appointment, he enjoyed the unqualified support of John P. Hale, James Harlan, and Charles Sumner.[25] Saunders had hardly entered upon his new duties when he identified himself with the development of the Union Pacific Railroad project by encouraging the construction of the line across Nebraska.[26] The Radicals likewise approved of Lincoln's appointment of an old political friend, Mark Delahay, as surveyor general of the Kansas-Nebraska land district. During the Kansas struggles of the 1850s, his antislavery vigor as editor of a Republican newspaper in Leavenworth had provoked the proslavery forces to raid his office and hurl his press into the Missouri River.[27]

In nearby Colorado Territory, Lincoln's first appointee for the governor's post was William Gilpin, who had cooperated with Francis P. Blair Jr. and B. Gratz Brown in organizing the Republican Party in Missouri and in opposing the proslavery maneuvers of Senator David R. Atchison and his associates.[28] Between 1840 and 1860, Gilpin had also done much exploring in the West and had written a book on the central gold regions of the Rocky Mountains. He especially favored the construction of a central transcontinental railroad.[29] Two of the leading Radicals, Benjamin Wade and George Julian, supported him for the Colorado governorship.[30] Gilpin's political career as governor, however, was cut short in the early days of the Civil War when the people of Colorado discovered that the secretary of the treasury would not honor his drafts on the United States government to defray the expenses for outfitting the First Colorado Regiment. Although the issue involved was only technical, the Lincoln administration abandoned Gilpin in 1862 and sent a new governor, John Evans, a Chicago friend of the president.[31]

The new appointee was approved by such Radicals as Samuel Pomeroy, James H. Lane, and Schuyler Colfax.[32] Evans's desire to promote the rapid development of the West and to make Colorado a strong Republican outpost fitted in well with the Radical program. Although a prominent medical man in Chicago, he had exhibited greater interest in railroad, townsite, and real estate ventures than in practicing his profession. During the antebellum era, he had promoted the growth of the Fort Wayne and Chicago Railroad project and had served for many years as the director of the Chicago terminal.[33] Dr. Evans collaborated with Lincoln and the Radicals in their attempt to make Colorado a state when they needed more votes in Congress to assure the passage of the Thirteenth Amendment.[34] He enthusiastically supported western railroad undertakings and in 1868 became president of the Denver Pacific Railroad and Telegraph Company. During the next year, his aid helped the passage of the Denver Pacific land grant bill.[35]

The Radicals closely watched Lincoln's appointments in New Mexico Territory. Their supporters in Kansas, such as Charles Robinson, Thomas Ewing Jr., and William F. M. Arny, wanted to reap the benefits of the rich Santa Fe trade and to gain possession of railroad land grants.[36] The Radicals vigorously opposed Lincoln's nomination of Miguel A. Otero, member of a prominent Spanish family in New Mexico and a stalwart Democrat, as territorial secretary. They looked upon him as a proslavery man and a representative of those who labored to preserve local control of territorial affairs. While in Congress as territorial delegate during the 1850s, Otero had championed statehood for New Mexico. The radicals feared that if such action were permitted at this time, New Mexico would come into the Union as a slave state and they would lose the opportunity for the political and economic exploitation of the Southwest. Nor were they ready to forgive the New Mexican territorial legislators for having passed, in 1859, an act to protect slavery, and they denounced Otero as the chief supporter of the bill.[37]

Further, the New Mexican delegate incurred the displeasure of the Republican Party in January of 1861 when he answered Horace Greeley's charges of December 31, 1860, in the *New York Tribune*. "Uncle Horace" attempted to prove that New Mexico was not a fit territory for statehood, for the slave power was in complete control. In his reply, Otero denied Greeley's assertion and condemned the program of the Republican Party in no uncertain terms. This party, he charged, "represented a minority of the American people, and had succeeded in gaining control of the federal government—'if any Government exists at all'—by concentrating its whole strength in one section of the country. By nurturing the prejudices, inflaming the passions, exciting the animosities, and bribing the interests of the free states, the Republican party has so strengthened itself that it could now attack the rights, the character, and the interests of the South."[38]

In July 1861, the Senate rejected Otero's nomination by a decisive vote. Greeley, on receipt of this announcement, headed his report, "Rejection of a Traitor's Nomination."[39] Faced with the necessity of proposing another nominee, Lincoln this time favored the interests of the Kansas politicians and the Radicals and appointed James H. Holmes, a rabid New York Republican whom Lane and Sumner recommended.[40] The local politicians denounced the appointment and soon petitioned the president for his removal on grounds that Holmes delayed his arrival in the territory, slandered local officials, used federal funds for his own advantage, and promoted abolitionist fury in New Mexico.[41] Lincoln thereupon named Arny to succeed Holmes. The new secretary was a thoroughgoing Radical who had led the Kansas antislavery movement of the 1850s and favored the interests of northern railroad groups and other nonresident outsiders in the Southwest. As secretary, he promoted the aims of the Leavenworth merchants, the Topeka railroad group, and New York mining companies.[42]

The Radicals were less pleased with the president's retention of Chief Justice Kirby Benedict in New Mexico. Lincoln had become acquainted with him as a member of the Illinois bar during the 1840s. Benedict, however, had supported Stephen A. Douglas in 1860. Nevertheless, Lincoln, who was willing to use Unionist Democratic leaders in New Mexico in an effort to hold the territory against the secessionists,[43] reappointed him over Radicals' protests. The president explained that he knew Benedict "too well, and had spent many pleasant hours with him."[44] Later Judge Benedict clashed with General James H. Carleton, the Union commander who inaugurated military rule in New Mexico during the summer of 1862 after the departure of the Confederate general, Henry H. Sibley. Arny and his associates, who were using military force to gain control of New Mexico's political and economic development, made a determined effort to have Benedict ousted. They sent a protest to Lincoln, charging the judge presided in court while under the influence of liquor. New Mexico's territorial delegate and some army officers in Washington transmitted the message to the president. He replied: "Well, gentlemen, I know Benedict. We have been friends for thirty years. He may imbibe to excess, but Benedict drunk knows more law than all the others on the bench in New Mexico sober. I shall not disturb him." Judge Benedict's position remained secure during Lincoln's administration.[45]

The president's appointee as governor of New Mexico, Henry Connelly, another Democrat, proved less obnoxious to the Radicals. In his first message to the territorial legislature, Governor Connelly recommended that capitalists be encouraged to invest in the mines of New Mexico.[46] He approved of a severe policy toward the Navajo Indians and later collaborated with Secretary Arny and General Carleton in the Bosque Redondo reservation venture in an attempt to benefit the miners by ridding the mountains of Indians.[47]

For Nevada Territory, much to the disgust of the western settlers, Lincoln chose James W. Nye, a friend of William H. Seward, as the first territorial governor.[48] "The president," one western editor complained, "has also followed the beaten track in appointing a Governor for Nevada Territory. He floats a man from the State of New York into the Territory for Governor, instead of appointing a citizen of the Territory, as he should have done."[49] When Lincoln and the Radicals later showed great concern about having Nevada admitted as a state to assure passage of the Thirteenth Amendment, they found Governor Nye a very effective agent. He foresaw the possibility of obtaining a Senate seat and was elected to that position in the fall of 1864.[50] The Radicals obtained favored men in other territorial offices. For the position of secretary, Lincoln selected Orion M. Clemens of Missouri, whom Attorney General Edward Bates recommended for an office. Clemens, who had studied law in Bates's office in St. Louis, was an active antislavery politician in Missouri.[51]

The Radicals could also expect cooperation from Lincoln's judicial appointees. In Nevada Territory, these positions were especially important, for territorial courts had the final decision in cases involving miners' claims. With the approval of Wade and the Ohio Radicals, the president appointed George Turner chief justice.[52] As associate justices, Lincoln selected Horatio Jones of Missouri and Gordon N. Mott of California. Such Radical Republicans of California as Leland Stanford, Charles C. Washburn, and Ira P. Rankin petitioned the president to make Mott a judicial official in Nevada in the hope that California mining interests would be more secure.[53] The judges evidently served the outside patrons well, for by 1864 thousands of Nevada residents were ready to petition Lincoln for a change in the territorial judiciary. They complained "that the prevailing want of confidence in our highest judicial officers is operating most injuriously upon all interests and classes in our Territory, and is a prominent cause of the present distressing depression in all kinds of business, and particularly of the ruinous stagnation in mining enterprises and the consequent loss of employment by our laboring population."[54]

John W. North, the surveyor general of Nevada Territory, was unanimously endorsed by the Minnesota congressional delegation. Cyrus Aldrich, Morton S. Wilkinson, and William Windom told Lincoln that North was "a Republican of long standing, who had done good service in the Republican cause" in Minnesota.[55]

The Radicals likewise sought to install sympathetic officials in Utah Territory. Lincoln declared that he intended to leave the Mormons alone, and he compared the problem "to a knotty, green hemlock log on a newly cleared frontier farm. The log being too heavy to remove, too knotty to split, too wet to burn, he proposed like a wise farmer to plow around it."[56]

Lincoln's intentions may have been good, but his first appointees, especially the governor, John W. Dawson, and two of the judges, Robert P. Flenniken and Henry R. Crosby, left their posts before a year elapsed.[57] Governor Dawson, who came from Indiana, arrived in Utah in December 1861. He had hardly taken up his new duties when he fell into public disrepute and on the last day of the month made a hurried exit from the territory.[58] Lincoln was relieved when the Senate refused to confirm Dawson's nomination.[59] Even before the Dawson episode, the Indiana Radicals Colfax and Julian urged the appointment of their friend Stephen S. Harding as governor of the territory.[60] Julian described Harding to Lincoln as an "old free soiler,"[61] and other Indiana Republicans pictured him as a vigorous antislavery politician who had labored long and hard to break the Democratic power in one of Lincoln's supporting states.[62] Writing to Lincoln early in 1862, Harding reminded him of his visit to see the president the preceding December, along with Lane and Julian, and that Lincoln had promised, after hearing that Dawson's nomination "had been brought about by some unfair means," to give Harding the post if the Senate rejected Dawson.[63]

After the Dawson fiasco, Lane and Julian again joined Harding in urging Lincoln to honor his promise, and in March 1862, Harding received the governorship of Utah. Lincoln also named Thomas J. Drake of Michigan and Charles B. Waite of Illinois as the new associate justices to fill the positions that Flenniken and Crosby had vacated.[64] Both these appointees proved staunch supporters of Harding and the Radicals in their attempt to gain control of the affairs in Utah.

The newly appointed governor went to the territory posing as a friend of the Mormons. He claimed to have known Joseph Smith and to have preserved the title page of the Book of Mormon from destruction. In 1847, by his own assertion, he presented the sheet to Robert Campbell, who deposited it in the Mormon church historian's office. He also boasted that he had entertained Mormon elders in his Indiana home.[65] Harding, therefore, expected a kind reception in Utah. A Mormon elder related an interview with the new governor and recorded his impression of the man: "The governor tells me he hopes we would take as good care of him as he did that paper [the title page of the Book of Mormon]. I told him we should certainly do it for he had placed it in a box where the rats could get access to it, and we would not do worse than that. He appears to be a pleasant fellow, a thorough-going black Republican; a dyed-in-the-wool abolitionist; but has some faint glimmerings that 'Mormonism' is to rule the destinies of nations, and that there was a great miracle in the preservation of the title page."[66]

The Mormon leaders, however, were soon irked by Harding's conduct. In December 1862, they became especially incensed when his first message to the territorial legislature indicated that he intended to work with the Radicals to destroy Mormon supremacy in Utah. On this occasion, he defended the antipolygamy act, which Congress had just passed, accused the Mormons of a lack of loyalty to the federal government in wartime, criticized the territorial laws, and suggested wholesale changes in the management of Utah. The legislators were so vexed that they refused to have the governor's message printed.[67] Harding provoked additional popular opposition by launching a movement in Congress to amend Utah's Organic Act of 1850 by limiting the jurisdiction of the probate courts, which the Mormons controlled. In this endeavor, he was supported by Associate Justices Drake and Waite. He also recommended the complete control of the militia by the governor.[68] These changes were necessary if the Radicals were to break the strength of the Mormon power. By March 1863, Brigham Young and his followers became so dissatisfied that at a mass meeting in Salt Lake City they dispatched a petition to Lincoln demanding the instant removal of the governor and his judicial supporters.[69] The president, attempting to appease both the Mormons and the Radicals, transferred Harding to Colorado Territory as chief justice and removed Secretary Frank Fuller and Chief Justice John F. Kinney, both of whom had been accused of pro-Mormon sympathies.[70] The Mormons expressed their esteem for Judge Kinney in the fall of 1863 by electing him Utah's congressional delegate.[71]

For governor of the territory, Lincoln selected James D. Doty, a Michigan and Wisconsin politician and land speculator, who had been superintendent of Indian affairs in Utah since 1861. Even though Doty improved federal relations with the Mormons, the Radicals also benefited by his rule. Secretly he wrote to Secretary Seward about the unwholesome state of affairs in Utah and sent the new territorial secretary, Amos Reed, to Washington to report actual conditions in the territory. Doty ordered this action without applying for an explicit leave of absence from the State Department for Reed in order to prevent the mission from becoming known to the "so-called authorities" in Utah.[72] The governor also wrote at length to Seward concerning the immense power the Mormons possessed in the territory. He made it clear that Young and his associates were not content to confine their activities to religious matters, that they exercised complete direction of territorial politics, and that there was little hope for improvement until the power of the Mormon Church was curbed.[73] Doty thus furnished propaganda for the Radicals in their nationwide campaign against the residents of Utah.

In Washington Territory, the gubernatorial appointees of Lincoln readily supported the efforts of the Radicals to organize the new territories of Idaho and Montana and to develop the Northern Pacific Railroad[74] in which Thaddeus Stevens was especially interested.[75] William H. Wallace, Lincoln's first selection for governor of Washington Territory, early resigned to campaign as the Republican candidate for territorial delegate. After his election, he spent much time working with the Radicals in Washington to organize the Territory of Idaho.[76] For Wallace's successor, Lincoln chose William Pickering, another Illinois friend of long standing.[77] In his first message to the territorial legislature, Pickering advocated federal aid for the construction of a transcontinental railroad from Lake Superior to Puget Sound.[78]

The position of collector of customs at Port Townsend in Washington Territory was awarded the ardent abolitionist Victor Smith, a close political associate and Ohio friend of Secretary of the Treasury Salmon P. Chase.[79] Smith worked with Chase to have the port of entry changed to Port Angeles, where they had mutual interests in a townsite development. The completion of this transfer and other forceful measures on Smith's part evoked much opposition in the Puget Sound district. When Lincoln attempted to remove Smith, Chase threatened to resign but finally approved of a change on the condition that Smith remain as a special agent of the Treasury Department.[80]

The disposition of the territorial patronage by the Lincoln administration resulted in placing numerous staunch supporters of the Radicals' program in important positions. With favorable governors in every one of the territories, well-disposed secretaries, amenable judges, a speculator as customs collector in Washington Territory, and sharp surveyor generals, the Radicals were prepared to reconstruct the West for their own benefit and the northern interests that they represented. The Radicals could use their territorial allies to promote the supremacy of the Republican Party in the West, to create new territories and states for their political and economic advantage, to control the disposition of the public domain, and to foster the domination of the trans-Mississippi region by northern political, mining, railroad, and other economic interests. In many of their activities, the Radicals used the territories as "pilot plants" for the later reconstruction of the South.

Notes

1. Jared Benson to Alexander Ramsey, April 6, 1859, Alexander Ramsey Papers, Minnesota Historical Library, St. Paul.
2. T. Harry Williams, *Lincoln and the Radicals* (Madison, 1941), 9–15.
3. John G. Nicolay and John Hay (eds.), *Abraham Lincoln: Complete Works*, 2 vols. (New York, 1894), 1:657.
4. Newton D. Mereness, "Caleb Blood Smith," in *Dictionary of American Biography*, edited by Allen Johnson, Dumas Malone, and Harris E. Starr, 21 vols. and index (New York, 1928–44), 17:244–45.
5. Ibid., 245.
6. Thomas L. Harris, "John Palmer Usher," in Johnson et al., *Dictionary of American Biography*, 19:134–35.
7. *President Lincoln's Cabinet, by Honorable John P. Usher, Secretary of the Interior, January 7, 1863–May 15, 1865*, foreword and sketch of the life of the author by Nelson H. Loomis (Omaha, 1925), 6–7.
8. Ibid., 9.
9. Ibid., 10.
10. "James M. Edmunds," *Michigan Biographies*, 2 vols. (Lansing, 1924), 1:266.
11. Wilmer C. Harris, *Public Life of Zachariah Chandler, 1851–1875* (Lansing, 1917), 112.
12. James M. Edmunds to George D. Hill, March 27, 1861, Letters to and from the Surveyor Generals, Division of the Interior Department, National Archives.
13. *Yankton Weekly Dakotian*, August 11, 1863.
14. Ibid., July 22, 1862.
15. Annual Message of Governor William Jayne, March 17, 1862, Territorial Papers of Dakota, 1:62, Division of the State Department, National Archives.
16. *Yankton Weekly Dakotian*, July 22, 1862.
17. Clement A. Lounsberry, *Early History of North Dakota* (Washington, 1919), 218, 225, 263–64.
18. *Yankton Weekly Dakotian*, July 29, 1862.

19. Ibid., March 1, 1864.

20. Ibid., October 16, 1864.

21. James M. Edmunds to Abraham Lincoln, February 9, 1863; Zachariah Chandler to Lincoln, February 24, 1863, Application and Recommendation Papers of the State Department, National Archives (hereafter ARPSD-NA).

22. Republican congressmen to Lincoln, June 21, 1863, ARPSD-NA.

23. Territorial Papers of Dakota, 1:93.

24. Benjamin F. Gue, *History of Iowa from the Earliest Times to the Beginning of the Twentieth Century*, 4 vols. (New York, 1903), 4:233.

25. John P. Hale, Charles Sumner, and James Harlan, Petition to Lincoln in favor of Alvin Saunders, 1861, ARPSD-NA.

26. Gue, *History of Iowa*, 4:233.

27. James H. Lane and others to the Senate Judiciary Committee, December 23, 1863, Records of Executive Proceedings: Nomination Papers, National Archives.

28. *Omaha Daily Nebraska Republican*, April 16, 1861.

29. *Denver Rocky Mountain News*, August 21, 1862.

30. Petition in favor of William Gilpin to Lincoln, 1861, ARPSD-NA.

31. Hubert H. Bancroft, *History of Nevada, Colorado, and Wyoming* (San Francisco, 1890), 426–29; W. B. Vickers, *History of the City of Denver, Arapahoe County, and Colorado* (Chicago, 1880), 413.

32. John Evans, Senate group to Lincoln, February 19, 1862, ARPSD-NA.

33. Vickers, *History of the City of Denver*, 413.

34. *Denver Rocky Mountain News*, August 30, 1864.

35. Vickers, *History of the City of Denver*, 414.

36. Daniel W. Wilder, *Annals of Kansas* (Topeka, 1886), 305.

37. Ralph E. Twitchell, *The Leading Facts of New Mexican History*, 5 vols. (Cedar Rapids, 1911–17), 2:309–10.

38. Loomis M. Ganaway, *New Mexico and the Sectional Controversy, 1846–1861,* Historical Society of New Mexico, Publications in History 12 (Albuquerque, 1944), 83.

39. *Santa Fe Gazette*, August 17, 1861.

40. James H. Holmes, Congressional Petition to Lincoln, July 15, 1861, ARPSD-NA.

41. John S. Watts to Lincoln, February 17, 1862, ibid.

42. *Santa Fe Gazette*, February 6, 1864.

43. Ganaway, *New Mexico and the Sectional Controversy*, 86–87.

44. Ralph E. Twitchell, "Chief Justice Kirby Benedict," in *Old Santa Fe: The Story of New Mexico's Ancient Capital* (Santa Fe, 1925), 83.

45. Ibid., 85.

46. Territorial Papers of New Mexico, 2:93, Division of the State Department, National Archives.

47. Henry Connelly to William H. Seward, September 13, 1863, ibid.

48. Bancroft, *History of Nevada, Colorado, and Wyoming,* 157.

49. *Sacramento Daily Union*, April 5, 1861.

50. Effie M. Mack, *Nevada: A History of the State from the Earliest Times through the Civil War* (Glendale, 1936), 248.

51. Edward Bates to Seward, March 12, 1861, ARPSD-NA.

52. Benjamin F. Wade recommendation in favor of George Turner, n.d., Application Papers of the Justice Department, No. 16, National Archives.

53. Petition in favor of Gordon Mott, n.d., ibid.

54. Petition of the Citizens of Storey County, August 19, 1864, Nevada Territory, ibid.

55. Minnesota delegation, Petition in favor of John W. North, n.d., ARPSD-NA.

56. Orson F. Whitney, *History of Utah*, 4 vols. (Salt Lake City, 1892–1904), 2:25.

57. Brigham H. Roberts, *A Comprehensive History of the Church of Jesus Christ of Latter-day Saints: Century One*, 6 vols. (Salt Lake City, 1930), 5:14. Roberts is a Mormon apologist.

58. Whitney, *History of Utah*, 2:25.

59. Roberts, *Comprehensive History of the Church*, 5:14.

60. Indiana Delegation to Lincoln, July 16, 1861, ARPSD-NA.

61. Julian to Lincoln, n.d., ibid.

62. Morton C. Hunter to Lincoln, March 4, 1861; Miles J. Fletcher to Lincoln, March 5, 1861, ibid.

63. Stephen Harding to Lincoln, February 16, 1862, ibid.

64. Roberts, *Comprehensive History of the Church*, 5:14.

65. Ibid., 15.

66. George A. Smith to Hosea Stout, July 30, 1862, quoted in ibid.

67. Ibid., 19.

68. Ibid., 21.

69. Petitions of Utah Citizens to Lincoln, March 10, 1863, ARPSD-NA.

70. Roberts, *Comprehensive History of the Church*, 5:24–25.

71. Ibid., 25.

72. James D. Doty to Seward, January 30, 1865, Territorial Papers of Utah, 2:618 National Archives.

73. Doty to Seward, January 28, 1865, ibid.

74. *Congressional Globe*, 38th Cong., 1st sess., 1864, 2349.

75. Hill to J. H. Hawes, January 26, 1864, Letters to and from the Surveyor Generals, Division of the Interior Department, National Archives.

76. Thomas C. Donaldson, *Idaho of Yesterday* (Caldwell, 1941), 230.

77. Clinton A. Snowden, *History of Washington: The Rise and Progress of an American State*, 4 vols. (New York, 1909), 4:144.

78. Charles M. Gates (ed.), *Messages of the Governors of the Territory of Washington to the Legislative Assembly, 1854–1889* (Seattle, 1940), 106.

79. Snowden, *History of Washington*, 4:168–69.

80. Ibid., 170–76.

5 ▷ Lincoln's New Mexico Patronage: Saving the Far Southwest for the Union

Deren Earl Kellogg

N ew Mexico Territory receives scant mention in connection with the administration of President Abraham Lincoln. Historians have generally concluded that Lincoln and other federal officials attached no great value to the territory and mostly neglected it. It is true that Lincoln could devote little attention to the administration of the western territories during the Civil War, which threatened the very future of the country. However, evidence suggests that Lincoln did care about saving New Mexico for the Union and should be given some credit for achieving this goal. Although Lincoln's western patronage record was generally undistinguished, his appointments to the New Mexico Territory were popular men who had experience in the Southwest and who often did not identify themselves with the Republican Party. In fact, the patronage record of New Mexico was, in some ways, more similar to those of the crucial border states of Kentucky, Missouri, and Maryland than that of the remaining western territories.

Even among historians of the Southwest, there has been a conception that the region was mostly ignored by the federal government during the Civil War. Those who mention the attitudes of Washington officials at all usually stress their apathy in this matter. For instance, Ray C. Colton, writing on the war in the southwestern territories, argues that the federal government assigned no "strategic importance" to New Mexico until 1862. Alvin Josephy, historian of the Civil War in the West, states that "the western territories, and particularly New Mexico, were treated at times as if they

From *New Mexico Historical Review* 75 (October 2000): 511–33.

were a nuisance." Likewise, James A. Howard II, discussing the war in New Mexico and Arizona, concludes that the government viewed New Mexico "as a burden rather than as an attribute."[1]

Neither Lincoln scholars nor southwestern historians have examined Lincoln's New Mexico patronage to any great degree. J. G. Randall's classic multivolume biography of Lincoln and important biographies by David Herbert Donald and Philip Shaw Paludan note New Mexico in connection with attempts to compromise the secession crisis in 1861, but these scholars say nothing about Lincoln's appointments to federal offices there. In their study of Lincoln's patronage, Harry J. Carman and Reinhard H. Luthin assert that Lincoln's appointment of Henry Connelly as governor of New Mexico Territory in 1861 was the only gubernatorial appointment "not tinged with party politics," but their work barely touches on territorial patronage. Histories of the West and Southwest by Ralph Y. McGinnis and Howard Roberts Lamar do give some information on the men Lincoln appointed to New Mexico offices but fail to fit these appointments into the broader context of territorial patronage. Loomis Morton Ganaway's work on New Mexico's place in the prewar slavery controversy and Vincent G. Tegeder's article on territorial patronage give Lincoln credit for appointing loyal Democrats to office in New Mexico, but Ganaway does not discuss territorial patronage in general, while Tegeder fails to mention Connelly.[2]

Territorial patronage made up a large percentage of federal patronage in the mid-nineteenth century. In each territory, a governor was chief executive, and a territorial secretary carried out many of the same functions as state lieutenant governors. In addition, each territory was divided into three federal judicial districts, each of which was presided over by a federal district judge. When sitting together, these three judges formed the territorial supreme court. Other positions included the territorial marshalcy and land office commissioner. All positions were filled by presidential appointment subject to confirmation by the Senate. Each territory also had the right to send a nonvoting delegate to the U.S. House of Representatives; these were elected by the territorial voters.[3]

Lincoln's policy regarding civil appointments to the territories was not notably different from that of his predecessors and successors. Partisan political considerations played the major part in deciding who would be appointed. Patronage was a successful presidential candidate's main method of rewarding his supporters. In Lincoln's case, his appointments had to be acceptable to powerful eastern Republicans. At the beginning of Lincoln's first term, there were eight western territories: New Mexico, Dakota, Colorado, Nebraska, Utah, Nevada, Washington, and Indian Territory. The last of these did not have a traditional civil government since it was administered by the Bureau of Indian Affairs, the branch of the Interior Department that oversaw administration of Indian tribes. After his inauguration, then, Lincoln had the opportunity to fill thirty-five major territorial posts, five in each territory. He appointed residents to posts in their own territories in only nine instances, four being in New Mexico. In the other western territories, Lincoln appointed only five residents out of thirty total appointees and never more than two residents in any one territory. New Mexico was the only territory in which residents were appointed as both governor and territorial secretary. The only other territory to receive a resident as governor was Washington, but he was replaced by an Illinoisan before the year was out.[4]

In the Lincoln administration, major territorial posts also tended to go to Republicans. Many of Lincoln's appointments to territories were associated with Radical Republicans, men with very strong antislavery and politically partisan feelings. For instance, William Jayne, appointed to the Dakota governorship, was favored by Radicals because of his strong antislavery views and his advocacy of a federally subsidized transcontinental railroad. Governor William Gilpin of Colorado, who also supported the idea of a government-financed transcontinental railroad, was supported by powerful Radical Republican senator Benjamin F. Wade of Ohio. William H. Wallace, Lincoln's first appointment as governor of Washington, supported the Radicals' goal of territorial organizations for Idaho and Montana. However, some unfortunate territories were dumping grounds for men who were clearly incompetent. For instance, Lincoln's first appointee as governor of Utah, John W. Dawson, was a political hack from Fort Wayne, Indiana, of such dubious character that Republican leaders of that community had submitted his name for a territorial office mainly to get rid of him. Outside New Mexico in 1861, the only Democratic governor Lincoln appointed was James W. Nye, a New Yorker who became Nevada's first and only territorial governor. Despite his party affiliation, Nye was a close friend of Secretary of State William H. Seward and a strong antislavery and pro-Union advocate. Even chauvinistic Republican Horace Greeley, influential editor of the *New York Tribune*, could approve of Nye. Lincoln's need to reward his supporters, Republican and Democratic, was often the main impetus behind his choice of territorial officers.[5]

Lincoln's New Mexico patronage, however, dramatically diverged from this pattern. A prime example was Lincoln's bestowing the governorship upon Dr. Henry Connelly, a Democrat. Born in Virginia in 1800 but raised in Kentucky, Connelly had been a resident of New Mexico and Chihuahua since 1824. A prosperous and influential merchant in the territory when it still belonged to Mexico, Connelly had helped arrange the surrender of New Mexico by Mexican governor Manuel Armijo to American general Stephen W. Kearny during the war with Mexico. In 1850 Connelly was elected governor of New Mexico during an abortive attempt to win statehood. From 1853 to 1859, he served in the upper house of the territorial legislature and had close ties with some of the most prominent Hispanic families of the territory. He married twice; both of his wives were Hispanas. When he was sworn in on 4 September 1861, he became the first resident to serve as territorial governor of New Mexico under the United States.[6]

Lincoln's choice for territorial secretary, the second highest territorial office, was Miguel Antonio Otero Sr., another New Mexico resident identified with the Democrats. Born into a powerful New Mexican family, Otero had been educated in St. Louis and New York after the territory's transfer to the United States. In 1852–53, Otero served in the territorial legislature and defeated incumbent Manuel Gallegos in the 1855 election for territorial delegate. In Washington, D.C., Otero considered himself a Democrat and supported the Kansas-Nebraska Act and Senator Stephen A. Douglas. He married a woman from South Carolina and became known as a proslavery man. Otero won reelection to his post in 1857. Two years later, he was instrumental in convincing the territorial legislature to pass a law protecting slave property in New Mexico. He served as a delegate to the Democratic convention in Charleston in 1860, supporting Douglas for the presidential nomination. Lincoln's victory with less than 40 percent of the popular vote drove Otero to criticize the election for thwarting the will of the majority of the American people and bringing a party of dangerous fanatics to power. In a manifesto "to the people of New Mexico" dated 15 February 1861, Otero strongly censured the Republican Party for its opposition to New Mexico's slave code, warning New Mexicans of the "hostility to the death" that Republicans held toward New Mexico and its people. He urged the election of anti-Republican legislators and delegates and predicted, "After a short duration of their power, this horde of infidels will be driven from the Capital, and you, as well as your fellow citizens of the States whose rights are menaced will be left in peace and prosperity." However, Otero did not openly advocate the secession of the territory, instructing New Mexicans that "the faculties with which the law has clothed the Legislative Assembly are sufficiently ample for your protection." Likewise, he believed that Lincoln's antislavery tendencies would be moderated through Congress and that the election results were not sufficient cause to destroy the Union. However, western newspapers reported that Otero allegedly favored joining California and Oregon should they secede to form a "Pacific Republic."[7]

Lincoln retained Kirby Benedict, another Democrat, as chief justice of the territorial supreme court. Benedict was one of the few New Mexico officers whom the president knew personally. Although born in Connecticut, Benedict had been an attorney in Illinois two decades earlier and knew Douglas as well as Lincoln. Since becoming a judge in New Mexico in 1853, Benedict had gained a reputation as a political supporter of Douglas and had been appointed chief justice of New Mexico by President James Buchanan in 1858. Despite Benedict's Democratic affiliation, Lincoln had faith in his Unionism and knowledge of the law and refused to remove him, even when Radical Republicans protested.[8]

For the other two supreme court justices in New Mexico, Lincoln chose Sydney A. Hubbell and Joseph G. Knapp. Hubbell, a resident of Bernalillo County, New Mexico, had served on the Territorial Council, in the upper house of the legislature, during the 1860–61 session. Although not a public figure as well-known as Connelly or Otero, he was respected in the territory's legal community. A correspondent of the *New York Times* reported that the new justice enjoyed "the full confidence of the bar and the public in devotion to his country's service." The correspondent also praised Hubbell's "just discrimination and good sense." Knapp, a resident of Wisconsin, was recommended to Lincoln by Senator James R. Doolittle, a Republican of that state, and other members of Wisconsin's congressional delegation. Knapp's appointment received little notice at the time, but he would later become the center of one of New Mexico's most acrimonious public debates when he criticized the policies of Brig. Gen. James H. Carleton, the commander of the Department of New Mexico.[9]

In appointing Connelly and Otero to office in New Mexico, Lincoln faced substantial opposition within his own party. Several Republicans in both New Mexico and the states were wary of Connelly. William Need, a soldier in the territory, wrote Secretary of State Seward to protest Connelly's nomination. According to Need, the nominee had been a friend of slavery—technically legal in New Mexico—and had himself been a slaveholder. Only changing his allegiance in response to circumstances, Connelly was "now a professed *neutral* Union man, provided the Union cause is strongest." A correspondent for the *New York Tribune* made similar charges in October 1861. He alleged that Connelly was "at heart a secessionist," had been a prime advocate of New Mexico's slave code, and had aided secessionists in the territory. Instead of offering evidence, the correspondent claimed that these charges could "be proved if necessary." In point of fact, the allegations of both Need and the *Tribune's* correspondent contained some truth. Connelly was indeed a former slaveholder and, as a member of the 1859 territorial legislature, had voted in favor of the territorial slave code.[10]

Like many Democratic Unionists, Connelly did not actively oppose the institution of slavery at the war's beginning, but neither did he ever make any public statements or take any action in support of secession. Most Republicans came to accept Connelly as his commitment to the Union became apparent. On Christmas Day, the *Tribune* published, without editorial comment, a portion of Connelly's 1861 annual message, in which the governor lauded New Mexicans' efforts on behalf of the Union and promised to continue the fight against the Confederacy. The same column and one published three days later also mentioned that Connelly favored the repeal of the territorial slave code. The *New York Times*, more moderate than the *Tribune* yet still a pro-Lincoln paper, printed an excerpt from Connelly's inaugural address, calling it "an able and patriotic document." A correspondent of the *Ohio State Journal* complimented Connelly on the antisecessionist tone, labeling his annual message "most excellent." These impressions of Connelly were strengthened when the New Mexico slave code was repealed in December and he continued to speak out on the need for New Mexicans to support the Union's war effort.[11]

Otero's nomination was not at all popular among Republicans, due to his strong identification with the proslavery South and his open excoriation of the Republican Party. The same William Need who had warned Seward against Connelly also charged Otero with being lukewarm in his support of the Union. Need wrote, "I think he is a *neutral* Union man, and can 'jump on either side of the fence.'" Greeley went a step farther, bluntly calling Otero a "traitor." When Otero's nomination was just a rumor, Greeley reminded *New York Tribune* readers of his role in formulating a slave code for the territory and implied that Otero's appointment to a territorial office would jeopardize New Mexico for the Union. Greeley concluded, "There has been no more pliant tool of the Slavery Extensionists than this same

Otero." The *Tribune* printed Otero's February manifesto without comment in November 1861 under the headline, "Secession in New Mexico." Although Otero did not explicitly call for New Mexico to join the Confederacy, this document was generally considered secessionist in tone by Republican sympathizers. "Luz," a *New York Tribune* correspondent in New Mexico, claimed that Otero had sent the manifesto to wealthy Hispanos, "urging on them strongly the claims of the Southern Confederacy to their support." So pervasive was this interpretation of the manifesto that it was passed on to historians. Benson J. Lossing's *Pictorial History of the Civil War,* a popular history that went through several editions in the late nineteenth century, stated that the purpose of the manifesto was "to incite the inhabitants of New Mexico to rebellion." In 1889 the well-known historian of the West, Hubert Howe Bancroft cited Lossing's statement, although Bancroft did not study the address himself. As late as the 1920s, New Mexico historian Ralph Emerson Twitchell accused Otero of being "disloyal to the core," mainly on the basis of the manifesto. Twitchell's assessment apparently agreed with that of Otero's Republican contemporaries, for in July Otero's nomination was decisively defeated in the United States Senate. The three-term delegate very quickly faded from the New Mexico political scene; he had already decided to pursue mercantile interests in Missouri. He had delayed his departure only to serve as territorial secretary. With nothing further to hold him in New Mexico, Otero moved to Missouri in 1862.[12]

Why did Lincoln break with his usual territorial policy so dramatically in making appointments to New Mexico? New Mexico was a unique territory at the outset of the Civil War. It was still relatively new, most of its geographical area only becoming part of the United States in 1848 as a result of American victory in the war with Mexico. The area bounded by the Rio Grande on the east, the Colorado River on the west, the Gila River on the north, and the Mexican border on the south was an even more recent acquisition officially purchased from Mexico in 1854. Commonly called the Gadsden Purchase, this parcel of land was known popularly as "Arizona," although it was part of New Mexico Territory and not a separate political entity. Alone among western territories, New Mexico had a non-Indian population made up mostly of Hispanos, former citizens of Mexico who retained their own culture and Spanish language under American jurisdiction. The census of 1850 counted fewer than six hundred English-speaking whites, or Anglos, out of a total non-Indian population of nearly fifty-seven thousand people in New Mexico.[13]

Lincoln had to make patronage decisions against a backdrop of public pessimism in the North over New Mexico's loyalty. It was widely believed in the loyal states that New Mexico was in great danger of becoming a part of the Confederacy. Greeley asserted that New Mexico's leading men and officeholders were all southern sympathizers and that "the masses are their blind, facile tools." In February 1861, Greeley declared that "the secession rebellion is in full blast" in southern New Mexico. The *New York Tribune* reported that pro-Confederate leaders were mounting an effort to take New Mexico into the Confederacy. "With the help of Texas and of Gen. Twiggs [they] may perhaps hope to succeed," Greeley concluded.[14]

Their apprehension had some foundation; a number of factors tied New Mexico to the South. The 1859 slave code had been passed to create an alliance with southern legislators to help New Mexico win a transcontinental railroad route. In addition, many men who held important federal positions in the territory had been appointed by Democratic administrations and were of southern origins or had expressed sympathy for the slave states. Col. William W. Loring, who became the commander of the Military Department of New Mexico in March 1861, was a North Carolinian, as was Governor Abraham Rencher, Connelly's predecessor. Rencher, called by Greeley's *New York Tribune* "a useful tool of the Slave Power," was the latest in a line of southern men to hold the top executive office in the territory; all three of his predecessors as civil governor had been residents of slave states at the time they were appointed to office. Territorial secretary Alexander M. Jackson, whom Otero was to replace, had been born in Ireland, but was raised in Mississippi and openly supported the Confederacy. Many of the men who owned mines in the southern and southwestern parts of the territory, such as Granville Oury and Sylvester Mowry, were sympathetic to the South. Otero himself, who was finishing his third term as territorial delegate in 1861, openly declared his alliance with southern legislators in Washington. Greeley concluded that "zealous Slavery Propagandists fill all the important Federal offices" in New Mexico. On 2 April, echoing Greeley, the *St. Louis Republican* published an anonymous letter charging Governor Rencher with leading a prosouthern "revolution" in Santa Fe and capturing nearby Fort Marcy.[15]

The rumor lacked even a shred of truth, but the *Tribune* and *Republican* articles typified Union public attitudes toward New Mexico. In addition, the president of the Confederate States of America, Jefferson Davis, was known to have a marked interest in the Far Southwest. As President Franklin

Pierce's secretary of war, Davis had ordered the exploration and survey of the region and urged the Gadsden Purchase to pave the way for a transcontinental railroad through the region, a route that would have benefited the slave states. There was some suspicion that he had deliberately stocked the territory with military officers whom he knew to be secessionists. From New Mexico, Need wrote to Secretary of War Simon Cameron that Davis's "military prototypes and protégés . . . were placed here purposely to second and forward his ulterior designs." The *New York Tribune* charged, "Pro-Slavery Army officers have been sent there, taking slaves with them."[16]

It was not unusual for easterners to question the devotion of western residents to the Union in 1861, but in New Mexico hard evidence demonstrated that disloyalty was a serious problem. Although rumors of pro-Confederate activity in the Santa Fe area were false, resentment against the North was strong in the Gadsden Purchase area known as Arizona—although this resentment was directed as much against the territorial government as against Washington. Because this area was so far distant from the territorial capital and could only be reached through land occupied by hostile tribes, the territorial government never established regular courts or law enforcement there. Disgusted with this state of affairs, Arizonans had been agitating since 1856 to have the region declared a separate federal territory. In 1860 a public convention met at Mesilla, a town on the Rio Grande in southern New Mexico, and founded the Territory of Arizona. On 16 March 1861, its leaders declared Arizona's attachment to the Confederacy. Later that spring, another convention in Arizona's other population center, Tucson, seconded this initiative. Aiding this process were Arizona's commercial ties to Texas and the Texans themselves, who sent representatives to encourage the Arizona secessionist movement.[17]

Another danger was that New Mexico was the only western territory, excepting Indian Territory, to border on a rebellious state. Texans had long dreamed of acquiring an outlet to the Pacific, and the Confederacy was aiming at an alliance with, or a military takeover of, the northern Mexican states, which would endanger New Mexico. New Mexico stood on the route of any invasion that the South might launch against mineral-rich California as well.[18]

Lincoln, then, was aware that the Far Southwest was highly vulnerable to Confederate and pro-Confederate influence. Appointing officials sent from eastern states, he surmised, would only cause local resentment that might very well tip the balance of popular feeling against Washington and toward the secessionists. Yet, if Lincoln desired to appoint residents to federal New Mexico posts, he would have to do so at the expense of strengthening the Republican Party in the territory. Because New Mexico had been Mexican territory until 1848, traditional American party organizations were of little importance in the territory. Throughout the 1850s, the vast majority of legislators in New Mexico were of Mexican origin, and few had ever been exposed to or had a chance to take part in the American party system. Parties in New Mexico tended to be semiformal groupings based on specific regional issues. The first political factions under U.S. governance had formed around 1851 over the issue of whether Hispanos or Anglos should hold key territorial offices. Later, attempts to reform the Roman Catholic Church in the territory provided another issue that fractured the existing factions. Although prominent New Mexicans occasionally identified themselves with national parties, loyalties to family and to local and regional factions were of much more importance and overshadowed national political allegiances. Given that Democratic administrations had been in power for all but the first two years of New Mexico's tenure as a territory, most of the experienced New Mexico politicians from the states were Democratic officeholders. Although a few individuals in New Mexico claimed allegiance to the Republican Party, there was no effective party organization from which Lincoln could draw appointments.[19]

Under these conditions, Lincoln proved willing to give serious weight to patronage recommendations from residents of the area. His main correspondent from New Mexico was John S. Watts, a former federal justice in the territory. Watts came from the same Whig-Republican background as the president. A lawyer in Indiana in the 1840s, he had served as a Whig in Indiana's House of Representatives from 1846 to 1847 and had been appointed an associate justice in New Mexico by Whig president Millard Fillmore in 1851. After resigning in 1854, Watts stayed on to practice law. By 1861, he was known as one of the territory's leading Unionists. In several letters to both Lincoln and Seward, Watts emphasized that placing nonresidents in New Mexico's territorial offices would have serious consequences. "If you or your cabinet are of the opinion that you have not friends enough in New Mexico to fill the little worthless places to be filled in it," Watts informed the president, "so long as that opinion is entertained and acted upon you will never have votes enough to win an election in it."[20]

Watts recommended both Connelly and Otero for their territorial posts. He called the former "the most able influential and popular man in New

Mexico." Watts's recommendation for Otero was even more emphatically stated: "Upon the appointment of Mr. Otero to this office depends the success or failure of the administration in New Mexico." Dr. Michael Steck, a longtime resident of the territory who would become its superintendent of Indian affairs the following year, concurred with Watts. Both men claimed that Otero would, in Steck's words, "favour the views of the present administration," a surprising statement in view of Otero's clearly stated antipathy to Republicanism. However, the two men believed that Otero could help solidify the ostensibly doubtful Unionism of New Mexico's Hispanos, who were, after all, the dominant population of citizens in the territory, at least in a numerical sense. "Had the question of disunion not presented itself I should not have recommended the appointment of Mr. Otero," Watts informed Lincoln, "but the issue now is with New Mexico, Texas and slavery or the United States and freedom and in that battle I shall find Mr. Otero and the large mass of his people on the side of the Union and freedom." Watts believed that having Otero as secretary would "preserve the Territory from internal discontent." He explained to Lincoln, "If [Otero] is appointed the large majority of the contending parties are united and success is easy. If he is not appointed he will be run for Delegate and party issues will be deepened and intensified." Steck succinctly summed up the point: "[Otero] is a native of this territory and connected with the most wealthy and influential families in the Country and enjoys the entire confidence of his people."[21]

President Lincoln put a great deal of stock in Watts's judgment. His western origins, his Whig political background, his well-known Unionism, and his appointment to federal office by the Fillmore administration for which Lincoln vigorously campaigned may well have made the president favorably inclined toward the frontier lawyer. In addition, by providing a detailed list of recommendations, Watts relieved Lincoln of the tedious task of finding for himself men fit to govern a distant territory about which Lincoln had little firsthand knowledge. Still, Lincoln's decision to be guided by Watts shows a good deal of consideration toward New Mexico. Acting on Watts's recommendation, Lincoln both defied elements of his own party and broke with his usual policy for appointing territorial officials.[22]

Congress's refusal to confirm Otero's appointment left Lincoln with the problem of finding a replacement. His choice, James H. Holmes, was a more typical Lincoln territorial appointee than Otero. A Republican and native of New York, Holmes had been nominated for office by two powerful Republican senators, James H. Lane of Kansas and Charles Sumner of Massachusetts.

On the other hand, Holmes had lived in New Mexico for three years before his appointment; so he presumably had some familiarity with the territory before taking the job. Holmes proved to be an unfortunate choice for Lincoln. The new secretary was widely unpopular in the territory and provoked a battle between a coalition of moderate Republicans and Democrats, led by Watts (now territorial delegate), and Radical Republicans. In February 1862, Watts charged Holmes with leaving New Mexico without State Department permission at a time when the territory was under threat of conquest by Texas. According to Watts, Holmes had gone to Washington "to slander the Governor, the Superintendent of Indian Affairs, myself, and other friends of your administration because we are not rabid abolitionists." Watts also preferred against Holmes a long list of formal charges encompassing both personal misconduct and official corruption. The former included allegations that Holmes had owned a brothel and a "Whiskey Shop" near Fort Union, New Mexico. The latter encompassed accusations that the secretary had given to relatives and acquaintances drafts from public funds and secured an appointment as New Mexico's U.S. marshal for his brother-in-law, who was neither qualified for the post nor a resident of the territory. Watts even went so far as to state that Holmes was "utterly condemned & despised as unworthy of the association of gentlemen by all the Federal Officers in N. Mexico." In addition, Holmes attempted to found a newspaper in Santa Fe, which appeared to be a conflict of interest to many New Mexicans, given that the territorial secretary awarded government printing contracts.[23]

Holmes's supporters charged that the campaign against him was part of an overall effort to discredit Republicans in the territory and open it to domination by men whose loyalty to the Union was dangerously unreliable. Watts's remark about abolitionism was almost certainly a response to attempts by Holmes to bring the issue of the repealed 1859 slave code into the battle. Writing in defense of Holmes was Eliakim Persons Walton, a Republican congressman from Vermont. Walton was also a personal friend of S. B. Watrous, a leading Republican in New Mexico. The Vermont politician stated of Governor Connelly, Superintendent James L. Collins, Chief Justice Benedict, and their supporters, "I know some of them as the tools of Reuben Davis of Mississippi in foisting the notorious and abominable pro-slavery act upon an unwilling people, and some of them as sympathizers with rebels." Augustus Wattles, an Indian agent in the territory, charged that the opposition to Holmes was a politically motivated response to his efforts to build "a Republican press and Republican Party in New Mexico," and thus to resist the passage of New Mexico into Democratic and, implicitly, disloyal ranks. Senator Sumner reminded Lincoln that Holmes had founded "a Republican paper" in Santa Fe, and Senator Samuel C. Pomeroy of Kansas warned Lincoln that removing Holmes "would be disastrous to the best interests" of New Mexico.[24]

Lincoln's previous appointments, especially those of Connelly and Otero, had been opposed by the Radical Republicans both in Congress and New Mexico, but Holmes's appointment prefigured the greater success Radicals would have in influencing New Mexican affairs after the Union repulse of the Confederate invasion in 1862. It soon became clear, however, that Watts's influence with the administration had not ended, for by January 1862 Lincoln and Seward had already decided to remove Holmes. An anonymous note on the State Department's copy of the charges against Holmes hints at the trust Watts still inspired in Washington: "Mr. Watts bases his application for the removal of Mr. Holmes upon facts communicated to him from sources known to be true." A striking sign of Lincoln's concern for public opinion within the territory was that he held it above the wishes of such influential Republicans as Sumner and Pomeroy.[25]

To evaluate the role that New Mexico's distinctive situation may have played in Lincoln's appointments, it is useful to examine briefly his patronage record in New Mexico's neighbor to the north. Colorado Territory shared some characteristics with New Mexico. Although not contiguous to any seceded state, fewer than fifty miles lay between Colorado's southeastern corner and the nearest point in Texas, across the panhandle of Indian Territory. Also, rumors of pro-Confederate initiatives in Colorado were rife in the early days of the conflict. A few secessionists in the territory made no secret of their sympathies, causing Unionists to fear widespread anti-Unionist conspiracies. Shortly after taking office in May 1861, Governor William Gilpin warned Col. Edward R. S. Canby, the commander of the Department of New Mexico in Santa Fe, of "the strong and malignant element within this Territory," whose object was a takeover of Colorado as a prelude to a Confederate invasion of New Mexico. Rumors of secessionist sentiment in Colorado had already reached Lincoln's ears in Washington by the spring of 1861. He had given face-to-face instructions to Gilpin that the latter's mission as governor would be to keep Colorado from falling into the hands of the secessionists.[26]

Lincoln appointed territorial officials to Colorado with much the same discernment that was evident in the New Mexican appointments. For example Gilpin, although a resident of Missouri, was an acknowledged expert on Colorado. While serving in Col. Alexander Doniphan's command during the Mexican War, Gilpin had traveled extensively in the area. In 1860, he authored a book praising Colorado's mineral potential, even going so far as to predict that the territory would one day become the center of world civilization. So closely was Gilpin identified with Colorado that a Lincoln-authored memorandum on territorial appointments identified him as being "of Colorado" although he lived in Missouri. Gilpin's appointment was a popular one in the territory. The territorial secretary, Lewis L. Weld, was also very familiar with Colorado, working as an attorney in Colorado for several years, and practicing law for a time in Denver and then in the gold-mining region of Gregory. Thus, the two most important federal officials in Colorado were men who were knowledgeable about the region and familiar to residents of the territory. Only one other Coloradan was appointed to a federal post—Denver businessman Copeland Townsend—as U.S. marshal. The remainder of territorial offices went to outsiders, but Lincoln's slate of appointments generally met with widespread approval in the territory. His patronage in Colorado reflected his policy in New Mexico: appointing well-known figures with creditable qualifications to the most important offices. Also as in New Mexico, Lincoln's appointment took strongly into account the perception that Colorado was vulnerable to Confederate attack.[27]

The experience of New Mexico in federal patronage resembled that of the border slave states more than that of other western territories. In the crucial states of Missouri, Kentucky, Maryland, and Delaware—slave states that did not secede—Lincoln also concentrated on appointing strong Unionists regardless of party. Although the president could not appoint high executive officials to the states, he did control important federal offices such as United States postmasters, district attorneys, and marshals and, of course, appointments to the highest level of the military. For instance, Kentucky's United States district attorney, James Harlan, was a Unionist Whig, as were many of the appointments to federal offices in that state. Lincoln split his Maryland patronage almost equally between the followers of his Republican postmaster general, Montgomery Blair, and the faction loyal to powerful congressman Henry Winter Davis, a political gadfly who had supported the Constitutional Union Party in the 1860 presidential election. In Missouri, Lincoln allowed himself to be guided in patronage matters by Francis P. Blair Jr., brother of the postmaster general. The Blairs were Republicans, but moderate ones; family patriarch Francis P. Blair Sr. was a slaveholder, and the family enjoyed credibility among Democrats. Their dedication to the Union cause was not in question in the Lincoln administration, but his commitment to the Blairs angered many Radical Republicans. Lincoln also removed Gen. John C. Frémont, a hero to many Radicals, from command in Missouri after the general issued an unpopular proclamation freeing the slaves of Confederate sympathizers.[28]

New Mexico fits into this pattern quite neatly, although in some ways Lincoln went farther in the territory to appease non-Republicans than he did in the border states. Many non-Republicans he appointed to office in the states were Constitutional Unionists or Whigs, but most New Mexico appointments went to Democrats, and few appointees in border states had the kind of prosouthern history that Otero could claim. Of course, far less was at stake in New Mexico than in Missouri, Kentucky, or Maryland. The secession of Maryland would have left the national capital entirely surrounded by Confederate territory, and Lincoln was convinced that the loss of Kentucky would make the entire Union military position untenable. It is likely that Lincoln carefully struck a balance between Unionism and local acceptance even more in the border states than in New Mexico. Still, the similarity of Lincoln's patronage policy in New Mexico to that in the border states suggests the territory's strategic importance in Lincoln's thinking.[29]

Although New Mexico was not an economically critical territory in 1861, Lincoln considered it important enough to abandon partisan considerations in his initial appointments in order to ensure that the territory stayed loyal to Washington. Confederate troops from Texas invaded New Mexico and captured Mesilla late in the summer of 1861. After a winter break, Confederate general Henry Hopkins Sibley, who had served in the U.S. Army in New Mexico, resumed the offensive in February 1862. Although Sibley hoped to win converts from New Mexico to his cause, he received almost no support north of secessionist Arizona. Two complete New Mexico volunteer regiments were raised from the Hispanic population to fight the invaders. Many Hispanos were motivated by a profound hatred of Texans harking back to Texan filibustering expeditions against New Mexico in the 1840s and the Texas–New Mexico boundary dispute at the end of the Mexican-American War. However, Lincoln's appointees certainly helped the cause of Unionism in the territory. Governor Connelly in particular was instrumental in rallying New Mexicans to resist the Confederate invasion, mostly by appealing to their enmity toward Texans. The Texans were initially successful, even managing to capture Santa Fe. However, by July 1862 they were pushed out of the territory by the New Mexicans, augmented by troops from Colorado and California.[30]

Once the Confederate threat was removed, Lincoln's appointment policy in New Mexico became more typical of his territorial patronage as a whole. After this point, Lincoln's appointments seemed motivated by partisan politics to a greater degree. The discredited Secretary Holmes was replaced by William F. M. Arny, who had formerly resided in Illinois, where he was an acquaintance of Lincoln, and in Kansas. He had lived in New Mexico for only a year after being appointed the Indian agent for the Ute and Jicarilla Apache agency in the northern part of the territory. A well-known Radical Republican, Arny heightened political tension in the territory by attempting to counteract the influence of the earlier Democratic appointees such as Connelly. The governor and Justice Benedict were allowed to maintain their posts for the rest of Lincoln's life, but many lesser offices went to men of powerful Republican connections. For instance, Nathaniel Usher, brother of Secretary of the Interior John Palmer Usher, was appointed a Federal district justice in New Mexico in 1864. This later switch in policy helped demonstrate that during the early crisis months Lincoln was less concerned with creating political allies among the Republicans—Radicals particularly—than with trying to ensure the loyalty of New Mexico's residents. The appointments of Connelly and Otero to federal office alienated some Republicans but won the Lincoln administration friends in New Mexico. Once that crisis was over, patronage in New Mexico became motivated more by political partisanship, especially as Lincoln looked toward reelection in fall 1864.[31]

It would certainly be difficult to argue against the prevailing notion that the federal government assigned relatively little importance to New Mexico in 1861. And yet, perhaps Lincoln should be given more credit for foresight on the issue than he has been. Throughout most of the nineteenth century, territorial patronage was granted for partisan considerations, and Lincoln's appointments were, on the whole, no exception to this rule. His early appointments to New Mexico Territory's offices, however, did constitute an exception. New Mexico's unique position as a territory with a non-Anglo majority among U.S. citizens, proximity to a seceded state, and a strong secessionist movement made enough of an impression to justify Lincoln's abandoning his usual territorial policy and defying his own party to ensure that the territory stayed loyal to the Union. His New Mexico patronage policy did bear some similarities to his policies in the border states, where he sought to build broad cross-party coalitions that would help ensure their citizens' loyalty. Although Lincoln's record as a territorial administrator was generally unexceptional, New Mexico's experience proved that he could be flexible and inspired when the situation demanded.

Notes

1. Ray C. Colton, *The Civil War in the Western Territories* (Norman: University of Oklahoma Press, 1959), 12; Alvin M. Josephy, *The Civil War in the American West* (New York: Alfred A. Knopf, 1991), 390; James A. Howard II, "New Mexico and Arizona Territories," *Journal of the West* 16 (April 1977): 88.

2. J. G. Randall, *Lincoln the President: Springfield to Gettysburg* (New York: Dodd, Mead & Co., 1945), 1:235, 240; David Herbert Donald, *Lincoln* (New York: Simon & Schuster, 1995), 268–69; Philip Shaw Paludan, *The Presidency of Abraham Lincoln* (Lawrence: University Press of Kansas, 1994), 32; Harry J. Carman and Reinhard H. Luthin, *Lincoln and the Patronage* (New York: Columbia University Press, 1943), 107; Ralph Y. McGinnis, "New Mexico Territory," in *Abraham Lincoln and the Western Territories,* ed. Ralph Y. McGinnis and Calvin N. Smith (Chicago: Nelson-Hall, 1994), 74–77; Howard Roberts Lamar, *The Far Southwest, 1846–1912* (New York: W. W. Norton, 1970), 104–5; Loomis Morton Ganaway, *New Mexico and the Sectional Controversy, 1846–1861* (Albuquerque: University of New Mexico Press, 1944), 94–95; Vincent G. Tegeder, "Lincoln and the Territorial Patronage: The Ascendancy of the Radicals in the West," *Mississippi Valley Historical Review* 35 (June 1948): 83–84.

3. Calvin N. Smith, "Overview," in McGinnis and Smith, *Abraham Lincoln and the Western Territories*, 2, 4–5.

4. Fred Burnell and Ralph Y. McGinnis, "Western America during Lincoln's Tenure," in McGinnis and Smith, *Abraham Lincoln and the Western Territories*, 62–64, 119–29.

5. Tegeder, "Lincoln and the Territorial Patronage," 79, 82, 90; Eric Foner, *Free Soil, Free Labor, Free Men: The Ideology of the Republican Party before the Civil War* (New York: Oxford University Press, 1970), 103–6; Calvin N. Smith, "Utah Territory," in McGinnis and Smith, *Abraham Lincoln and the Western Territories,* 116; "From Nevada Territory," *New York Tribune,* 24 July 1861; William Need to Simon Cameron, 27 September 1861, in *The War of the Rebellion: A Compilation of the Official Records of the Union and Confederate Armies* (Washington, D.C.: Government Printing Office, 1880–1901), ser. 1, 50 (1):638 (hereafter *Official Records); Carman and Luthin, Lincoln and the Patronage,* 107; Smith, "Overview," 1.

6. John S. Watts to Abraham Lincoln, 2 April 1861, Robert Todd Lincoln Collection of the Papers of Abraham Lincoln (1809–1865), Library of Congress, Washington, D.C. (hereafter Lincoln Papers); Calvin Horn, *New Mexico's Troubled Years* (Albuquerque: Horn & Wallace, 1963), 93–98; Josephy, *Civil War,* 42; Tegeder, "Lincoln and the Territorial Patronage," 85.

7. Ganaway, *New Mexico,* 60–61, 67–71, 88–89; Miguel Antonio Otero Jr., *My Life on the Frontier, 1854–1882* (New York: Press of the Pioneers, 1935), 283; Donald, *Lincoln,* 256; "Secession in New-Mexico," *New York Tribune,* 12 November 1861; "Pacific Confederacy," *San Francisco Alta California,* quoted in *National Intelligencer,* 12 January 1861.

8. Ralph Emerson Twitchell, *Old Santa Fe* (Santa Fe: Santa Fe New Mexican Publishing, 1925), 348–51; Tegeder, "Lincoln and the Territorial Patronage," 84–85.

9. Hubert Howe Bancroft, *History of Arizona and New Mexico, 1530–1888* (San Francisco: History Co., 1889), 636; "Affairs in New Mexico," *New York Times,* 8 November 1862; Memorandum, Appointment of Joseph G. Knapp, ca. 15 July 1861, Abraham Lincoln to Edward Bates, 5 August 1861, *The Collected Works of Abraham Lincoln,* ed. Roy P. Basler et al., 9 vols. (New Brunswick, N.J.: Rutgers University Press, 1953–55), 4:449, 471 (hereafter *Collected Works); Biographical Directory of the American Congress* (Washington, D.C.: Government Printing Office, 1961), 822.

10. Ganaway, *New Mexico,* 95–96; "From New Mexico," *New York Tribune,* 30 November 1861.

11. "From Santa Fe," *New York Tribune,* 25 December 1861; "From New Mexico," *New York Tribune,* 28 December 1861; "Inaugural Address of Gov. Connelly of New-Mexico," *New York Times,* 22 October 1861; "New Mexico," *Ohio State Journal,* quoted in *New York Times,* 26 December 1861; Ganaway, *New Mexico,* 95–99; Governor's Message, 4 December 1861, roll 2, State Department Territorial Papers: New Mexico, 1851–1872, microcopy no. 17, General Records of the State Department, Record Group 59, National Archives, Washington, D.C. (hereafter New Mexico Territorial Papers).

12. Tegeder, "Lincoln and the Territorial Patronage," 83–84; "New-Mexico Arizona," *New York Tribune,* 28 March 1861; "Secession in New-Mexico," *New York Tribune,* 12 November 1861; "From New-Mexico," *New York Tribune,* 30 November 1861; Benson J. Lossing, *Pictorial History of the Civil War in the United States of America* (Philadelphia: G. W. Childs, 1880), 2:186; Bancroft, *History of Arizona and New Mexico,* 684n; Twitchell, *Old Santa Fe,* 368–69; Otero, *My Life,* 1–2.

13. Alvin R. Sunseri, *Seeds of Discord* (Chicago: Nelson-Hall, 1979), 38; Bancroft, *History of Arizona and New Mexico,* 491–92, 503–5; Edward H. Peplow Jr., *History of Arizona* (New York: Lewis Historical Publishing, 1958), 1:348–49.

14. "New-Mexico," *New York Tribune,* 31 December 1860, 28 February 1861. Gen. David E. Twiggs, commander of the Department of Texas, had surrendered his command to the Confederates early in 1861. He subsequently joined the Confederate army. Ezra J. Warner, "David Emmanuel Twiggs," *Generals in Gray* (Baton Rouge: Louisiana State University Press, 1959), 312.

15. Lamar, *Far Southwest,* 105, 109–12; Ganaway, *New Mexico,* 61, 86; Josephy, *Civil War,* 36; William I. Waldrip, "New Mexico during the Civil War," pts. 1 and 2, *New Mexico Historical Review 28* (July/October 1953): 274–75; "New-Mexico–Arizona," *New York Tribune,* 28 March 1861, "New-Mexico," *New York Tribune,* 31 December 1860; Abraham Rencher to the Editor, *St. Louis Republican,* 20 April 1861, roll 2, New Mexico Territorial Papers.

16. Lamar, *Far Southwest,* 110–11; Need to Cameron, 27 September 1861, *Official Records,* ser. 1, 50 (1): 637; "New Mexico," *New York Tribune,* 31 December 1861.

17. Lamar, *Far Southwest,* 421–23; "Save Us From Our Friends, We Can Watch Our Enemies," *Mesilla Times,* 16 March 1861; "Political Position of Arizona," *Mesilla Times,* 30 March 1861; Bancroft, *History of Arizona and New Mexico,* 511.

18. Charles S. Walker, "Causes of the Confederate Invasion of New Mexico," *New Mexico Historical Review* 8 (April 1933): 76–80.

19. Lamar, *Far Southwest,* 100–104.

20. *Biographical Directory of the American Congress,* 1784; Rebecca Shepherd et al., eds., *A Biographical Directory of the Indiana General Assembly,* 2 vols. (Indianapolis: Select

Committee on the Centennial History of the Indiana General Assembly, 1980–84), 1:410; Watts to Lincoln, 1 April 1861, Lincoln Papers.

21. Watts to Lincoln, 1 April, 2 April 1861, Lincoln Papers; Steck to William H. Seward, 14 March 1861; Watts to William H. Seward, 13 March, 20 March 1861, in Letters of Application and Recommendation during the Administrations of Abraham Lincoln and Andrew Johnson, 1861–1869, National Archives, Washington, D.C. (hereafter Application and Recommendation).

22. Watts to Lincoln, 2 April 1861, Lincoln Papers.

23. Tegeder, "Lincoln and the Territorial Patronage," 84; Abraham Lincoln to William H. Seward, 22 January 1862, Collected Works, 5:107; Statement of the Secretary of the Territory of New Mexico (undated), Watts to Lincoln, 14 February 1862, Application and Recommendation. For Watts's changes against Holmes, see Secretary of the Territory of New Mexico, James H. Holmes, Abstract of charges preferred against him by Hon. John S. Watts, Delegate from New Mexico (undated), Application and Recommendation; Lawrence R. Murphy, Frontier Crusader: William F. M. Arny (Tucson: University of Arizona Press, 1972), 117.

24. Walton to William H. Seward, 3 March 1862, Wattles to William H. Seward, 24 February 1862, Sumner to Lincoln, 30 July 1862, Pomeroy to Lincoln, 1 March 1862, roll 23, Application and Recommendation.

25. Lincoln to Seward, 22 January 1862, Seward to Lincoln, 22 January 1862, Collected Works, 5:107; Secretary of the Territory of New Mexico, James H. Holmes, Abstract of charges preferred against him by Hon. John S. Watts, Delegate from New Mexico (undated), roll 23, Application and Recommendation.

26. Josephy, Civil War, 292–93; Lamar, Far Southwest, maps (following p. 20), 211, 223, 226; Gilpin to Canby, 26 October 1861, Official Records, ser. 1, 4:73.

27. Lamar, Far Southwest, 223–24; Memorandum on Appointments to Territories, 20 March 1861, Collected Works, 4:294; Frank Hall, History of the State of Colorado (Chicago: Blakely Printing, 1889), 1:264–66.

28. Carman and Luthin, Lincoln and the Patronage, 186–89, 194, 197–98, 205–7; Paludan, Presidency of Lincoln, 41–42, 86–87.

29. Carman and Luthin, Lincoln and the Patronage, 191, 207; Paludan, Presidency of Lincoln, 83.

30. Bancroft, History of Arizona and New Mexico, 688, 691–99; Lamar, Far Southwest, 114–15; Connelly to William H. Seward, 17 November 1861, Governor's Message, 4 December 1861, roll 2, New Mexico Territorial Papers; Otero, My Life, 63; Darlis A. Miller, "Hispanos and the Civil War in New Mexico: A Reconsideration," New Mexico Historical Review 54 (April 1979): 108–9; T. T. Teel, "Sibley's New Mexico Campaign: Its Objects and the Causes of Its Failure," in Battles and Leaders of the Civil War, ed. Robert Underwood Johnson and Clarence Clough Buel (New York: Thomas Yoseloff, 1956), 2:700.

31. Murphy, Frontier Crusader, 37–38, 68–69, 102; Horn, New Mexico's Troubled Years, 110; Elmo R. Richardson and Alan W. Farley, John Palmer Usher: Lincoln's Secretary of the Interior (Lawrence: University Press of Kansas, 1960), 38; Earl S. Pomeroy, The Territories and the United States, 1861–1890, 2d ed. (Seattle: University of Washington Press, 1969), 112; Bancroft, History of Arizona and New Mexico, 704n.

6 ➤ The Tribe of Abraham:
Lincoln and the Washington Territory

Robert W. Johannsen

On November 6, 1860, the day American voters cast their ballots for a new president, a politically active farmer living on Puget Sound asked, "Who is Elected? or is any one Chosen? If the People have made a choice, which is probable, that Choice has undoubtedly fallen on Lincoln." The prospect did not seem reassuring. "I have faint hope that Lincoln may be defeated," the farmer wrote. "Yet I scarcely allow myself to believe Such can be the fact."[1]

Although Washington Territory had no voice in national elections, its people felt a keen interest in the outcome in 1860. Party feelings ran deep, in spite of the territory's geographic isolation and the slow, haphazard means of communication that tied it to the rest of the nation. Party divisions, conforming roughly to the national pattern, appeared early on this frontier, and the fact that two of the region's political leaders had achieved national prominence gave partisan organization in the territory a relevance it might not otherwise have had. Joseph Lane and Isaac I. Stevens (or "Ancient Joseph" and "Two-Eyed" Stevens, as they were often called) had both been territorial officeholders, Lane in Oregon and Stevens in Washington, and both represented their respective territories in Congress. Both were also principal figures in the 1860 election, unusual for men from a far-distant and sparsely settled frontier. Lane was the vice presidential candidate on the southern-backed Breckinridge Democratic ticket, and Stevens headed that party's national campaign committee. Because of their aggressive leadership

From David H. Stratton, ed., *Washington Comes of Age: The State in the National Experience* (Pullman: Washington State University, 1992), 73–93.

and close ties with national party leaders, and because the party of Andrew Jackson seemed more responsive to frontier interests and concerns, Democrats had dominated Pacific Northwest politics.[2]

Twelve days after the Puget Sound farmer had expressed his anxiety lest Lincoln be elected, the picture cleared. Fragmentary news reports filtering into the territory pointed to a Lincoln victory. "This is bad news for Democrats," the farmer shrugged, "but I suppose will have to be borne."[3]

The territory's leading Democratic newspaper searched desperately, if unsuccessfully, for some good that might come from the election of a Republican president. Republicans, on the other hand, made up for their lack of numbers with loud rejoicing. A one-hundred-gun salute was fired in the village of Tumwater to celebrate Lincoln's triumph, following which the townspeople marched to the nearby territorial capital of Olympia, ringing bells, blowing horns, and cheering all the way. Olympia's new Republican newspaper, the *Washington Standard*, boasted unconvincingly that Washington Territory had always been "Republican at heart." And from the territory's remote eastern mining region came an enthusiastic word: "Old Abe must certainly be elected President, for . . . we have not had a cloudy day for the past week."[4]

The Republican Party had won its first national victory, and there was no doubt among its partisans in Washington Territory that the country now stood on the threshold of a new and wonderful age. "A day of brightness is about to dawn on our Territory," crowed the *Standard*. "The dark shadows of locofocoism," which had long "blighted and withered" the Northwest, were about to be dispelled. The *Port Townsend North-West* proved unable to control its excitement: the Republican triumph marked "the inauguration of a new era, in which a prosperity unparalleled shall commence with our people." But, asked many puzzled Pacific Northwesterners, who is Abraham Lincoln?[5]

Lincoln was virtually unknown in the Pacific Northwest. Indeed, it had only been since his race for Stephen A. Douglas's Senate seat two years before that his name was recognized at all beyond the borders of his home state of Illinois. On the northwest frontier, Lincoln evoked only a dim response. Even then, most people knew him simply as the man whom Douglas defeated. His name had rarely been included among those who sought the Republican nomination for the presidency. When Oregon's Republicans met in April 1859 to select delegates to the national convention, they turned first to the well-known senator from New York, William H. Seward—a choice both premature and ill-advised. Seward not only was *not* identified with the

West and western interests but he also bore the burden of what appeared to be a radical antislavery stance, a definite liability on the frontier.

The real choice of the state's Republicans was Missouri's Edward Bates. Hailing from a border slave state, free from the taint of slavery agitation, Bates appealed to the conservative sensibilities of the far western frontier. Furthermore, he supported issues close to the hearts of westerners, like the Pacific railroad and free homesteads. "The great West, which has never had a President," predicted one Oregonian, "would hail his nomination with unparalleled enthusiasm." Early in 1860, Oregon Republicans, many of whom had emigrated from Missouri, instructed their delegation to support Bates as their first choice for the nomination.[6]

As a result, Lincoln's nomination took Pacific Northwest Republicans by surprise. They reacted at first with disbelief. "This may or may not be correct," warned the *Weekly Oregonian*. Democrats were gleeful. Lincoln, gloated one paper, "is but little known. . . . As a statesman, Mr. Lincoln takes rank nowhere." Douglas's coattails, it appeared, had served Lincoln well, stretching all the way to the Republican convention. "Had it not been his good fortune to be vanquished by the Little Giant," commented one editor with remarkable sagacity, "it is highly probable that his name would never have been thought of . . . in connection with the Presidency." Those who remembered Lincoln at all recalled him as a loser whose abstract arguments on the slavery question had cost him election to the Senate.[7]

Republicans tried to put the best face possible on the situation. As they raised Lincoln's name to their mastheads, Pacific Northwest Republican editors printed biographical sketches of the candidate, invariably getting the facts of his early life all wrong. Men who claimed to have known Lincoln in Illinois came forth with information, frequently misleading. One boasted that he knew "all the history of Abraham Lincoln" and found the candidate to be "one of God's noblemen." Another praised Lincoln's "proverbial honesty" and his "integrity of character." It was not possible, they agreed, that Lincoln could do anything as president that would harm the nation.

But what of Lincoln's attitude toward the West? Republicans groped for information. Lincoln, some said, was a "frontier man" who knew the needs of the Pacific Coast. He was "identified to his very heart's core with every interest of the great west," wrote another. Anything more specific was apparently not available. Editors took pains to portray Lincoln as a man of Jacksonian character and temperament—and even appearance! His humble beginnings, early poverty, and hard work marked him as the one person above all others who "could set the Western prairies on fire." That Lincoln was a frontiersman seemed beyond dispute when the editor of the *Oregonian* announced that he had received a black walnut rail that Lincoln had split, complete with a certificate of authenticity, and that he would place the rail on display for all doubters to see. While Lincoln's western orientation was on all Republican lips, however, no one could be really certain about it.[8]

In fact, Lincoln's name, unlike that of his rival Douglas, had never been linked in the public mind with the promotion of western development and interests. Douglas, from the moment he first entered Congress in 1843, had labored long and hard for western measures. As chairman of the committee on territories in both House and Senate, he had written, modified, and sponsored the bills that organized seven western territories, including Oregon and Washington. All the territories of the Union, he was once told, "bear the impress of your Statesmanship." Most appealing to westerners was his doctrine of popular sovereignty, his insistence that the people of the territories be allowed to decide all matters of local or domestic policy, including slavery, for themselves. The Northwest hailed this doctrine as an important step toward the "emancipation of the Territories" from the restrictive control of the national government. So popular was Douglas's position among Pacific Northwesterners that their political leaders, even Republicans, felt obliged to endorse it.[9]

Lincoln did not share Douglas's devotion to western development, which is surprising, for Lincoln more than Douglas was a child of the frontier. To be sure, Lincoln had not enjoyed a national forum in which he could address western issues, but this can hardly account for his singular lack of concern for measures that convulsed his own state. Illinois was in the forefront of agitation for western expansion and settlement, but Lincoln seemed to be immune to the fever that burned in so many of his fellow citizens. Throughout his life, he felt uncomfortable with, even embarrassed by, his backwoods upbringing. Consumed by ambition to overcome what he believed to be a deprived childhood, he sought an urban environment, pursued a professional career, and married into an aristocratic family. More telling was his early affiliation with the party of wealth and aristocracy, the party whose members, it was said, knew one another by the instincts of gentlemen. He deliberately separated himself from the rough-and-tumble of frontier life and never quite overcame his distrust of Andrew Jackson's "common man democracy." Whatever the reason, it was clear that Lincoln's look, unlike that of so many of his generation, was not westward.

The 1840s were marked by a quickening of the American pulse as the nation contemplated its role and mission in the world. Looking beyond their boundaries, many Americans became convinced that the fulfillment of their national promise lay in territorial expansion, in "extending," as they said, "the area of freedom." Thousands followed the lure of abundant land to newly independent Texas, and thousands more made the long trek to the promised land in the Pacific Northwest. "Oregon Fever" assumed epidemic proportions in Illinois. Town after town held "Oregon meetings," and farmers from all over the state made plans to begin life anew in a land where the living was easy and hard times unknown. New meaning was given to an old idea, and a phrase was invented to describe it—*manifest destiny*. America's claim to Oregon, wrote New York editor John L. O'Sullivan in 1845, was "by the right of our manifest destiny to overspread and possess the whole of the continent which Providence has given us for the development of the great experiment of liberty."

Lincoln remained remarkably detached from all this excitement, neither joining it nor opposing it. On Texas, he professed indifference: "I never was much interested in the Texas question." On Oregon, one searches in vain for a comment or a reaction. Like many Whigs, he could not quite make up his mind on the Mexican War. He followed the Whig party line and opposed its origins (waiting, however, until the war was virtually over), but expressed pride in the victories won by America's volunteers. He conceded rather vaguely that "we shall probably be under a sort of necessity of taking some territory" from Mexico. Years later, as he looked back on these stirring times, he offered only scorn and ridicule for the spirit of Young America that had actuated so many of his fellow citizens.[10]

Lincoln's silence on Oregon was the more surprising because many of his acquaintances, including some very close friends, left Illinois for Oregon's greener pastures, and Lincoln himself was offered the opportunity to make the trip. Following Zachary Taylor's election as president in 1848, only the second Whig to occupy the White House, Lincoln not only felt he was entitled to a government office but also believed that he should be consulted on all patronage matters relating to Illinois. An early supporter of Taylor, Lincoln had campaigned for the old general in New England and the Midwest; more importantly, he was Illinois's only Whig member of Congress—the "Lone Star of Illinois," as one Whig paper put it. Soon after Taylor's inauguration, Lincoln urged the removal of the state's Democratic officeholders, arguing that partisan reasons were sufficient to justify the changes. Furthermore, he insisted that his activities on behalf of Taylor entitled him to a political reward. His reelection to Congress appeared remote, and a government office, he believed, would further his career and enhance his stature among his constituents. He was not interested, however, in just any office. Only a first-class position would do, Lincoln confided to a friend, for a second-class appointment would not be worth "being snarled at by others who want it themselves." He had his eye on the post of commissioner of the General Land Office, a position of considerable responsibility and political clout, and he was confident that the appointment would be his for the asking.[11]

It was Lincoln's first brush with executive patronage, and everything went awry. Competition for the General Land Office was keen, partly due to his own earlier indiscretion in encouraging others to apply for the position. "I fear the Land Office is not going as it should," he wrote, "but I know nothing I can do." Not only were his own chances for the appointment slipping away but also those of the friends he had encouraged. Lincoln's distress turned to outrage when the office went to Justin Butterfield, a Chicago Whig who, Lincoln protested bitterly, had never "lifted a finger" to promote Taylor's election. On the contrary, Butterfield had remained loyal to Henry Clay throughout the campaign, and it was Clay's recommendation that won him the post. For Lincoln, it was an ironic twist. He had abandoned his own preference for Clay because Taylor, the hero of the Mexican War, appeared to be the sure winner. Had he stuck with Clay, he might have received the appointment.

Lincoln not only lost the appointment, but the president and his advisers also treated his recommendations for other posts in the administration with a marked indifference. He protested repeatedly that the president was wrongfully ignoring Illinois, even taking his case directly to Taylor, but his appeals were to no avail. It was a bitter lesson for Lincoln, and one he did not soon forget.[12]

Perhaps to soothe Lincoln's feelings and allow him to save face with his constituents, the administration offered a consolation prize—the office of secretary of Oregon Territory. It was a menial position, and Lincoln knew it. He quickly declined, whereupon the administration offered him the territorial governorship. This too he unhesitatingly declined. The offers, coming so soon after his rejection for the one office he really wanted, seemed insulting. The posts carried little political weight and would be of doubtful value to the advancement of his career. They were, moreover, precisely the second-class appointments Lincoln vowed he would not accept. To assume an office in

Oregon, moreover, was tantamount to voluntary exile, a conviction that was strengthened by his wife's refusal to exchange the social amenities of the Illinois capital for a life in the wilderness.[13]

Among those who Lincoln recommended for government appointments during the early days of Zachary Taylor's administration were three close friends, each of whom would later move to the Pacific Northwest—the vanguard of what would later be derisively termed the "tribe of Abraham." Simeon Francis, longtime resident of Springfield and the somewhat erratic editor of Illinois's principal Whig newspaper, was recommended for the office that Lincoln had just declined, secretary of Oregon Territory. Francis did not get the position; he did not leave for Oregon until 1859, amid rumors of scandal.

Anson G. Henry was Lincoln's doctor, a Springfield physician upon whom Lincoln had come to rely so heavily that he once wrote that "Dr. Henry is necessary to my existence." But with Henry's medical practice in decline, the doctor thought politics would be more congenial to his talents. Lincoln recommended him for secretary of Minnesota Territory in language that revealed a desperate urgency: "I am *exceedingly* anxious," he wrote. "On other matters I am anxious [only] to a common degree; but on *this*, my solicitude is extreme." In spite of Lincoln's entreaties, Taylor did not appoint Henry. He later crossed the plains to Oregon in 1852, after failing to qualify for an appointment as Indian agent two years before (although he drew the salary from the government).[14]

Edward Dickinson Baker was the most prominent of the three and the closest to Lincoln, so close indeed that Lincoln named his second son after him. Their friendship, in Lincoln's words, had been of a "long personal & intimate" character. A man of consuming ambition (he reputedly wept when told that his English birth barred him from election as president), Baker moved to Springfield in 1835 and shortly thereafter entered the Illinois state legislature. A Whig, Baker was never one to hew too closely to the party line if by so doing he put his career at risk. Elected to Congress from the Springfield district two years before Lincoln, and a strong expansionist, Baker left his seat in midterm to command a regiment of Illinois volunteers in the Mexican War. Following the war, he moved to the northern Illinois town of Galena, where the chances for election seemed better, and returned to Congress for a second term. Like Lincoln, Baker believed he was entitled to an office in the Taylor administration, although his claims were less modest. He set his sights on a seat in Taylor's cabinet and even traveled to

Washington to present his credentials to the president in person. Lincoln strongly supported Baker's pretensions, but Taylor was not impressed.

Always on the lookout for the main chance, Baker, like many others of his generation, turned his attention to California. With the population of that new El Dorado increasing dramatically, political opportunities seemed manifold. Baker proposed that the Taylor administration send him to the Pacific to organize the Whig Party and insure California's admission as a Whig state. Taylor did not respond, but Baker went anyway. To his disappointment, he could not crack the Democratic Party's hold on California politics, so when his friends Simeon Francis and Anson Henry invited him to move to Oregon and run as a Republican for United States senator, he jumped at the opportunity. Lincoln, delighted with Baker's decision, tried to persuade Oregon's Republicans to back his friend. Baker won election in September 1860, but only after he endorsed Douglas's doctrine of popular sovereignty, drawing the state's Douglas Democrats to his side.

Not all of Oregon's Republicans, however, were pleased. Some disliked Baker's overtures to the Democrats. Baker was a stranger to the state and its interests; he was, moreover, a Californian, and even in those days Oregonians resented the intrusion of Californians. There were disquieting reports that he had brought with him a "corruption fund" of $30,000 to be used to carry Oregon for the Republicans in the presidential election. Furthermore, it appears that he used his friendship with Lincoln to gain support, promising offices if Lincoln should be successful. History has been kind to this political adventurer, for Baker's career was abruptly and tragically ended by the Civil War when, in October 1861, he was killed while leading his troops at the Battle of Ball's Bluff. Ironically, he is now remembered as the Pacific Northwest's link with America's greatest president and as a martyr to the Union cause.[15]

Francis, Henry, and Baker kept Lincoln informed of political developments in the Pacific Northwest. They also represented Lincoln's interests and took a lead in solidifying support for his presidential candidacy. Their work bore fruit when Oregon's voters gave Lincoln a plurality in the three-cornered race for the presidency. Oregon was one of only two states (the other being California) in which the two opposing Democratic candidates, Breckinridge and Douglas, together received a majority of the votes. If this gave Republican leaders pause, it was not evident. For more than a decade they had lived in the shadow of the Democratic Party. Lincoln's election meant that they could at last come out into the sunlight and share in the spoils of victory. One despairing Democrat noted that "swarms of hungry, starving republicans" now stood ready to "devour all the places the administration of Abraham" had at its disposal. Another predicted that "every Republican in Oregon" would be an applicant for office. With Oregon's recent transition to statehood, the number of patronage positions had been severely reduced. North of the Columbia River, however, there still lay a rich field for would-be officeholders.[16]

By 1860, territorial offices were among the tastiest plums a chief executive could bestow, invariably granted to party workers as rewards for party loyalty or to repay old political debts, or as was too often the case, to old hacks who were best put out of the way. With each new presidential administration, a new set of officers usually descended on the territories, "a speckled array of political adventurers," according to one Oregonian, "from all the defeated camps in the country." By midcentury this frequent imposition of officeholders and the inability of the territories to select their own executive and judicial officers were the most irritating features of the territorial system. Oregonians had protested vehemently against the practice of using their territory as a dumping ground for "all the worthless needy and recreant" of the president's party, but their complaints were ignored. Statehood offered the only solution.[17]

Washington Territory had no statehood option in 1860. Lincoln's election, however, seemed to promise a new direction for the territory, Republicans being confident the offices would now be filled from among their own number. "We believe there are enough independent men in Washington Territory," urged one Republican paper, "to select persons to fill the few offices of honor or emolument . . . without the intervention of Federal authorities at Washington [D.C.]." With Lincoln in the White House, some Republicans even expected that the people of the territory would soon be allowed to elect their own officers.[18]

Lincoln, of course, was well aware of the riches that lay in the executive patronage. Although his taste had been too fastidious to accept one of the plums twelve years before, he had recommended many of his friends to territorial positions. There was no reason to believe Lincoln would regard the territories any differently than had his Democratic predecessors. There is, on the other hand, ample evidence that he viewed the disposal of government offices as one of his principal tasks as president.

Ever since Andrew Jackson had incorporated what he called "rotation in office" into his democratic thinking, presidents saw their control over the offices as an important source of political power, and Lincoln was no exception. Indeed, he replaced a larger percentage of officeholders than any president before him, the "cleanest sweep," according to one authority, in all of American history. It was one of the anomalies of his administration that with the Union crumbling about him and with civil war looming, he should give such high priority to the matter of appointments. "There is a throng here of countless spoilsmen who desire [a] place," declared Oregon's Senator James W. Nesmith, "forty thousand office seekers fiddling around the Administration for loaves and fishes, while the Government is being destroyed." Republicans had won their first national election, and they were determined that the spoils not be denied them. Carefully cultivating the notion that all members of the opposition party must be suspected of disloyalty, they called for wholesale removals. "The odor of disunion," wrote one applicant for position, "is rank among the old office holders!"[19]

Lincoln firmly believed, as he had advised President Taylor in 1849, that the president should maintain control over all the offices rather than farming out the responsibility to his cabinet members. Even so, there were plenty of good Republicans who stood ready to help him make his choices. As soon as Lincoln's election became certain, Oregon's Republicans proposed a meeting to draw up a slate of candidates for federal offices in their state. Petitions on behalf of individual office-seekers began to circulate. Some expressed the uneasy feeling that Senator Baker had already divided the offices among his supporters.[20]

Whether true or not, it was clear that the senator had not been idle. As the only Republican member of Congress from the Pacific Coast, he insisted that his recommendations concerning California, Oregon, and Washington Territory be heeded. Baker took his Senate seat early in December 1860, and later that month Lincoln invited him to spend Christmas in Springfield. There is no doubt that they discussed Lincoln's appointments. Republicans on the Pacific Coast believed, Baker later wrote the president, "that my advice would have great weight with the Executive. I have shared in that belief." Relations between the two men were indeed close, and Lincoln's request that Baker introduce him at his inauguration surprised few. Baker exploited his close friendship with the president to urge that his relatives and friends be given preferred consideration for government positions. In California, Baker urged an appointment for his son-in-law, a Democrat, outraging California Republicans. Fully expecting to control the appointments in their state, some sixty or more Californians gathered in the national capital to argue their cases. They lodged a vigorous protest with Lincoln against Baker's interference in the politics of their state, but Baker was not to be deterred. "I do not desire to control power or patronage in California," the senator explained, "except where past relations kindle gratitude or the requirements of the party in my judgment demand it." He drew up his list for Oregon and California and submitted it to the president.[21]

Baker also had candidates for Washington Territory's two top offices. Who else—but his friends and Lincoln's, Simeon Francis and Anson G. Henry. Both resided in Oregon, but, as the editor of Olympia's *Overland Press* remarked sourly, Baker did not dare give them places there because of their bad reputations. Francis, who had already moved to Olympia to await word from the president, was to be territorial governor; Henry, ready to move on a moment's notice, was to have the post of surveyor general, itself an office rich in patronage.

A group of Olympians, including several members of the territorial legislature, the self-styled leadership of Washington's Republican Party, challenged Baker's choices. Meeting "in a small room adjacent to a stable," the men proceeded to vote "each other into an office under the administration of Mr. Lincoln." It was a closed meeting, presumably secret, for as one of the men remarked, if any more were admitted there would not be enough offices to go around. At stake were several positions, including governor, surveyor general, superintendent of Indian affairs, collectors of customs and internal revenue, territorial secretary, three members of the supreme court, United States marshal, United States attorney, several Indian agents, and officials of the federal land offices. After assigning the offices, the Republicans chose William H. Wallace, whom they had selected as governor, to carry the list to the president. Wallace had moved to Washington from Iowa in 1853, had helped organize the Republican Party in the territory, and had twice been defeated for territorial delegate. Aside from being Washington's most prominent Republican, he also claimed friendship with Abraham Lincoln, and this bond doubtless dictated his selection. An old Illinois friend of Lincoln's accompanied Wallace to the East: John Denny of Seattle, whose son Arthur had been assigned the post of register of the Olympia land office. Counting on their ties with Lincoln, Wallace and Denny felt they need only present their list to the president and the whole matter would be settled.[22]

The plan began to unravel as soon as the two men arrived in the capital. First, they encountered Senator Baker and his list. They then struck a compromise whereby Wallace would retain the governorship and Henry the surveyor generalship, while Francis would be moved to superintendent of Indian affairs. Secondly, Wallace and Denny found the national capital in such a turmoil that gaining an audience with Lincoln proved no easy matter. A meeting was finally arranged with the help of another of Lincoln's friends, an Illinoisan named Leander Turney, who was in Washington seeking an office for himself. Turney's price came high; Wallace and Denny agreed to support him for secretary of Washington Territory in return for his aid. And lastly, Wallace himself apparently struck some of the names from his list and "traded off" others, an action those back home viewed with some consternation.

Lincoln followed many of Baker's and Wallace's recommendations, but not all. He appointed Wallace governor, and Henry, Lincoln's former doctor, won the office of surveyor general. But he left out Francis, a development Baker could not explain. "Mr. Lincoln," wrote the senator, "has acted peculiarly." Rumors floated about that Francis had defaulted on his debts when he moved to the Northwest. As one politician explained, there were too many Illinois Republicans in the capital who knew Francis to allow Lincoln to appoint him. Lincoln later appointed Francis to the much less prestigious post of army paymaster, with headquarters at Fort Vancouver, an odd position for a man suspected of fiscal irresponsibility.[23]

In making his appointments, Lincoln responded to other pressures, demonstrating further that he accepted the traditional view of the territorial patronage as a convenient means for rewarding friends and satisfying party demands. The lucrative post of superintendent of Indian affairs, originally earmarked for Francis, went instead to a former Democrat, a native of Maine who had lived in Washington Territory for eight years—a gesture toward Lincoln's vice president, Hannibal Hamlin, who also happened to be a former Democrat and a Maine native. The offices of secretary of the territory, the three justices of the territorial supreme court, and United States attorney all went to present or former residents of Illinois; four of the five appointees were personally acquainted with Lincoln. Of the seven Indian agents Lincoln appointed during his administration, two were friends who had lived in Illinois, two were Portland merchants interested in mining and land speculation, and one was a recent arrival from California. Of the four officials in the territory's two land offices, two had known Lincoln in Illinois and one was appointed from Maryland to satisfy Postmaster General Montgomery Blair.

Thus did the patronage wheels turn, not untypically for the mid-nineteenth century, and Washington Territory received its first set of federal officeholders under the Lincoln administration. It is clear that personal friendship with Lincoln became the primary qualification for office in Washington Territory. Washingtonians did not receive the "tribe of Abraham," as the appointees were now called, with much enthusiasm. Territorial Republicans complained that Lincoln's attitude toward the patronage was no different from that of his Democratic predecessors. They were deeply disappointed that the president had ignored their wish that only long-term residents of the territory be appointed, while the large number of Lincoln's friends in the group cast doubt on his motives. The territory, protested one editor, had been visited once again by the "quadrennial shower of Egyptian frogs." Lashing out at the "superannuated hangers-on" with which presidents peopled the territories, he charged that Lincoln had converted Washington Territory into a political poorhouse for broken-down Illinois politicians.[24]

There were other, more serious repercussions. Dissension between the "imported officials" and local politicians threatened Republican unity. Clearly a minority party, Republicans could not afford to lose their grip on territorial politics, yet Lincoln's policy seemed to be taking them in that direction. Wallace was strongly criticized for his failure to secure offices for all the aspirants. "There is a terrible ado because of the threatened importation of officials," commented the *Puget Sound Herald*. "Patriotism is fast getting at a discount among the Republicans in this Territory." Expressing their sense of betrayal by the president, some who had worked hard to build the party now threatened to make no further efforts "to sustain the Republican cause." Democrats seized on Lincoln's appointments with glee and pointed out the disparity between Republican promises and Republican practice. The dismay of local Republicans evoked no sympathy from the other side. "They are ravenous for the loaves and fishes," wrote one Democrat, "and if their demands are not satisfied, we expect some of them will go over to Jeff Davis's side of the house."

To make matters worse, many of Lincoln's appointees felt little identification with the interests of the territory, viewing both the region and its people with haughty distaste. They acted, complained a Republican editor, "as if their very feet were contaminated by contact with our soil, and their souls vulgarized by mingling with the plebian throng who in their opinion have peopled these benighted regions." Some of the appointees were found to be sadly lacking in competence, character, and morality, more attentive to the bottle than to the territory's problems.[25]

Anson Henry, as the closest friend of Lincoln in the "tribe," tried to reassure the critics that Lincoln's intentions were good, that he was "too good a politician not to appreciate the great importance of having the Patronage in the hands of men who will cordially and zealously sustain his administration." But Henry himself was a large part of the problem. Arrogant and vain, constantly boasting of his intimate friendship with Lincoln and of his strong influence on Lincoln's decisions, Henry fancied himself the territory's political mastermind. He had taken to heart Senator Baker's instruction to use the power of his position as surveyor general to serve Baker's friends; following Baker's death, Henry believed that the senator's mantle of leadership had fallen on his shoulders and that he now had become the president's representative in all matters relating to the Pacific Coast. Some Pacific Northwesterners saw through Henry's pretensions and viewed his strutting with mild amusement. "He thinks he is boring with a big augur," wrote an Oregonian, "but it would be just like his luck to make himself odious."

For most, however, there was nothing funny about Henry's claims. He would indeed have cut a pathetic figure had it not been for the fact that he enjoyed Lincoln's confidence to an incredible degree. Henry kept a steady stream of correspondence flowing to the White House, as he informed the president of personal and political developments and tendered advice on administration policy. In the spring of 1863, he traveled to Washington to confer with Lincoln and to enjoy, as he boasted, the "familiar hospitalities of the White House." He returned, "breathing threatenings and slaughter against all" who would not acknowledge his role as the president's spokesman.

Lincoln's uncritical support of Henry's posturing raised serious questions regarding the quality of his judgment and seems baffling when placed alongside his reputation as a shrewd judge of men. To many supporters it was disillusioning in the extreme. "It is hard to lose confidence in the integrity of one, who has been fully trusted," moaned one Republican. His faith that Lincoln would return the nation "to the purity and virtue of the fathers," he conceded, had been misplaced and he now realized that he had been mistaken about the "Honest Abe" he had so enthusiastically supported in 1860. He was astonished that an "honest and discreet President" could so easily be hoodwinked.[26]

If the people of Washington Territory expected matters to improve, their expectations were destined for disappointment. Even the one bright spot in the otherwise gloomy picture—Wallace's appointment as governor—soon faded. Nominated for territorial delegate while absent in the national capital, Wallace declined to assume the duties of the governorship, thus leaving that position vacant pending the election. A short time later, he was elected as delegate to represent Washington Territory in Congress, a much more advantageous post for a politically ambitious man than the governor's office in Olympia. The unexpected vacancy unleashed a wild scramble among local Republicans for the office, but they might just as well have saved their energy.

Lincoln appointed another friend from Illinois, and the editor of the *Puget Sound Herald* exploded: "We know nothing of this gentleman, but he is supposed to be another relative of Abraham's, or at least to have slept in the same bed with him at some period in the course of his life. Can Illinois furnish any more Federal officials? There is room for a few more of the same sort." The reaction to the appointment even bothered Anson Henry. "I don't blame you for taking care of your old Friends," he confided to Lincoln, but "the common talk about Town now is, 'that you have imported upon the Territory another Drunkard from Illinois.'" The new governor was William Pickering, a sixty-three-year-old southern Illinois farmer who had served with Lincoln in the state legislature. Pickering had applied for a minor diplomatic post, bearer of dispatches to England, but changed his mind when he learned of the vacancy in Washington Territory. Lincoln did not hesitate to oblige him. With Pickering's appointment, the territory's executive and judicial departments—governor, secretary, and the supreme court—were firmly in the hands of the president's personal friends.[27]

Other changes were to come. "The tribe of Abraham," noted the *Overland Press*, "unlike the laws of the Medes and Persians, appears to be moveable and susceptible of change." Even Illinois friends could no longer endure Leander Turney, secretary of the territory and acting governor until Pickering arrived. Lincoln replaced him in 1862 with a local resident who, to the surprise of everyone, did not belong to that "much hated class of officials known as 'importations.'" But dissension and accusations had become the rule, and even the new secretary soon found himself the target of those who felt themselves better qualified for the post. The important office of superintendent of Indian affairs turned over three times before Lincoln finally allotted it to the State of Wisconsin and allowed his friend Senator James R. Doolittle to name the appointee.[28]

People in the territory closely watched the behavior of Lincoln's office-holders, and every step or stumble they took usually generated a crisis. One of the most notorious episodes involved the controversial Victor Smith, former editor of the *Cincinnati Commercial* and an acquaintance of Salmon P. Chase, Lincoln's secretary of the treasury. Smith went to Washington Territory not only as collector of customs for the Puget Sound district but also as a special treasury agent—a treasury spy, in other words, charged with overseeing the spending of government money in the territory. Smith, moreover, was an outspoken radical abolitionist who did not try to hide his views. From the moment of his arrival, he was a *"blazing firebrand."*

Controversy erupted when Smith announced the removal of the customshouse from Port Townsend to Port Angeles, where he had a speculative interest in the townsite. Charges that he had embezzled a large sum of money from the government quickly followed, leading in turn to a bizarre incident in which Smith, from the deck of a revenue cutter, threatened to bombard Port Townsend. Demands for his removal increased in number and intensity, but did not move Lincoln, although Henry became worried. Each day that Smith remained in office, he warned, was one more reproach to those who supported the president. Lincoln did not act until mid-1863, and even then only tentatively, probably because he wanted to avoid offending Secretary Chase. He was needlessly concerned: Chase, outraged anyway, submitted the first of his several resignations as treasury secretary. He was mollified only when Lincoln allowed him to name Smith's replacement. The new collector of customs proved no more satisfactory; some said he was nothing more than the "pliant tool" of both Smith and Chase. No one became more disturbed by Lincoln's efforts to appease Chase than Anson Henry. Fearing Lincoln's action would have a damaging effect on the territory's elections, he confided to Wallace that "it can't be possible that the President knowingly allows himself to be used to compass the ruin of his best friends, and yet such is the fact."[29]

Territorial politics in its early stages, one scholar has suggested, was often marked by a "type of disruptive, confused, intensely combative, and highly personal form of politics," which he labeled "chaotic factionalism."[30] Washington Territory provided a good example. Although the early settlers adopted the nomenclature of the national parties, party organization by 1860 remained indistinct, fluid, and highly informal. The clash of rival ambitions, the strong desire for office, and the power it brought dominated the political scene; the leavening influence normally identified with a more mature party system had not developed. The chaos was exacerbated by the imposition of federal officeholders on the territory from the outside, a policy that stirred cries of resentment and outrage by settlers determined that their officials should be selected from among their number. If the nation's leaders appreciated this determination at all, they casually dismissed it in favor of the more traditional view of territorial patronage as a convenient instrument for satisfying the claims on the chief executive.

How can one assess the impact of Lincoln's use of the patronage to oil the territory's political development? Local Republicans remained convinced that the president's policies undermined their organization and eroded support for his administration. "The *foreign importations . . .* now being crowded upon us, when we have *patriots here willing and fully as competent to serve*," shouted one Republican, "are now hurled in our teeth." Their fears were first realized early in 1862 when Washington's territorial legislature rejected by a two-to-one margin a series of resolutions endorsing the Lincoln administration. Wallace, representing the territory's interests in Congress, reported his embarrassment and predicted that the rejection would hamper his efforts to obtain "any thing for the Territory." The *Washington Standard*, in its outrage, charged members of the legislature with "lurking, covert treason," and their action as having practically effected the secession of the territory from the Union.[31]

Republican anxiety escalated the following year when a Democrat who pledged to have all the officeholders removed won election as territorial delegate. It did not matter that George E. Cole was a former Douglas supporter and a Union Democrat. A newcomer to eastern Washington, but recently arrived from Oregon, Cole was denounced as an "imported web-foot," the Vallandigham of Walla Walla County. Nor was the impact of Lincoln's appointment policy limited to Washington Territory. Oregon's supporters of Lincoln's prosecution of the war, Republicans and Democrats alike, believed the president's patronage in Washington Territory would be used against them by the state's Peace Democrats. One anxious Oregonian, visiting in Olympia, reported that "the whole batch of Federal officials located at this place are 'by the ears.' Never have I witnessed such singular and disgraceful conduct. . . . The President should be informed that some of his officers are either insane, or drunken vagabonds, or else designedly act to give aid and comfort to the traitorous *peace* democracy."[32]

None protested Lincoln's appointments more vehemently than the *Olympia Overland Press*. The paper charged Lincoln with sending out a "class of men for public servants who ignorantly assume . . . to dictate to the people," men who had been kept out in the cold so long that "political starvation had shrivelled" their judgment. Each one vied to become the "mouth-Piece for the people." Close behind the Olympia paper, however, was Walla Walla's *Washington Statesman*. Eastern Washington Territory, the paper complained, was becoming infested with "errant politicians" who had fallen out with the Puget Sound crowd, or "Clam Eaters," as they were called. The editor, although generally outspoken in his denunciation of the "political bummers from Olympia," or the "tribe of Olympia swindlers," reserved his choicest invective for Anson Henry—the "Old Gorilla," "that slippery old hypocrite."

There was good reason for indignation east of the mountains. A band of conspirators among the officeholders, reported the *Statesman's* editor, had for months sought a division of the territory. It was a political move, promoted by politicians for political ends—and its ringleader was Henry. When Henry traveled east in the spring of 1863 to enjoy the hospitality of the White House, he also lobbied for the creation of a new territory out of the mining districts in eastern Washington Territory. "Old Henry quarters at the White House with our Uncle Abe," it was noted. "It must be worse than taking calomel to have the old scamp about." But the editor feared the worst. An Illinois congressman introduced the bill creating the Territory of Idaho, Congress passed it, and the president signed it.

With Lincoln's blessing, Anson Henry and Oregon congressman John R. McBride controlled patronage in the new territory. William Wallace moved from Washington Territory to assume the governorship of Idaho Territory, although once again he quickly left that post for the more desirable position as Idaho's territorial delegate in Congress. Henry was delighted. With Washington Territory represented by a Democrat, Wallace's election "from our Territory of Idaho" became all the more important. McBride's brother-in-law filled the office of secretary of Idaho Territory, and Henry's son-in-law won appointment to the territorial supreme court. It was clear that Lincoln's attitude toward the territorial patronage had not changed.[33]

Lincoln's disposal of the patronage in Washington Territory was not one of his finer hours. Handicapped in dealing with the Far West by his own lack of interest in western settlement and development, he was unfamiliar with the needs and desires of the far western frontier. His attitude toward territorial patronage, moreover, had been formed in 1849 when he rejected appointments for himself while seeking appointments in the territories for his friends. His thinking, it appears, had not changed in the interim; as president, he simply implemented his assumption that territorial appointments were important only insofar as they served partisan ends.

Washington Territory's citizens claimed that Lincoln hardly differed from Franklin Pierce, under whom the territory had been organized. That Lincoln should follow the example of his Democratic predecessors would not have surprised them, had not they expected better of Lincoln. "The people of no part of the United States," they had been assured in 1860, "have more reason to rejoice at his election than those of Washington Territory." Expectations had been raised by the tone of Lincoln's campaign. He would root out corruption from the government and eliminate the "hangers-on" who had been feeding at the public trough. Lincoln, they were told, would "do justice to and build up the Pacific States and Territories," ending the Democratic practice of maintaining a "set of government officers" in the West who "render the administration 'a hissing and a by-word.'"

One downhearted settler remarked during the last year of the Civil War, "I don't believe Congress will pay much attention to a few thousand people so far away, and out of the great trouble that now afflicts the land." What he said of Congress applied also to the president. In 1860, Washington Territory's population numbered only 11,594. Remotely situated in the far northwest corner of the nation, distant both geographically and temperamentally from the bloody conflict tearing the country apart, the people were easily ignored by a president desperately trying to save the Union. Even Lincoln's old friend Anson Henry confessed in one of his many appeals to the president that Washington Territory was probably not very important "in a political point of view."[34]

Lincoln, it appears, agreed.

Notes

1. Winfield Scott Ebey Diary, No. 6, 373 (November 6, 1860), University of Washington Library, Seattle.

2. For a summary of political developments in the Pacific Northwest during the decade before the 1860 election, see Robert W. Johannsen, *Frontier Politics and the Sectional Conflict: The Pacific Northwest on the Eve of the Civil War* (Seattle: University of Washington Press, 1955).

3. Winfield Scott Ebey Diary, No. 6, 378 (November 18, 1860).

4. *Olympia Pioneer and Democrat*, November 30, 1860; *Olympia Washington Standard*, November 23, 17, 1860, January 5, 1861.

5. *Olympia Washington Standard*, November 17, 1860; *Port Townsend North-West*, November 1, 1860.

6. *Portland Weekly Oregonian*, April 30, 1859; *Oregon City Oregon Argus*, October 1, 29, 1859; Howard K. Beale, ed., *The Diary of Edward Bates, 1859–1866*, Annual Report of the American Historical Association, 1930 (Washington: Government Printing Office, 1933), 4:124.

7. *Salem Oregon Statesman*, June 26, 1860; *Portland Weekly Oregonian*, June 16, March 17, 1860.

8. *Portland Weekly Oregonian*, June 16, July 14, 21, August 25, 1860; *Oregon City Oregon Argus*, June 23, February 11, July 14, August 11, 1860.

9. For Douglas's commitment to western development see these two works by Robert W. Johannsen: *Stephen A. Douglas* (New York: Oxford University Press, 1973), and *The Frontier, the Union, and Stephen A. Douglas* (Urbana: University of Illinois Press, 1989), 103–19.

10. *New York Morning News,* December 17, 1845, quoted in John William Ward, *Andrew Jackson: Symbol for an Age* (New York: Oxford University Press, 1955), 136; Roy P. Basler et al., eds., *Collected Works of Abraham Lincoln,* 9 vols. (New Brunswick, N.J.: Rutgers University Press, 1953–55), 1:347, 454 (hereafter *Collected Works*). In early 1859, Lincoln remarked in a public address, "We have all heard of Young America. He is the most *current* youth of the age. . . . He is a great friend of humanity; and his desire for land is not selfish, but merely an impulse to extend the area of freedom. . . . He knows all that can possibly be known; inclines to believe in spiritual rappings, and is the unquestioned inventor of *Manifest Destiny*. His horror is for all that is old, particularly 'Old Fogy'; and if there be any thing old which he can endure, it is only old whiskey and old tobacco." Ibid., 4:356–57.

11. Ibid., 1:475, 2:28–29.

12. Ibid., 4:65, 2:29, 41, 43, 49, 54.

13. Ibid., 2:61, 65, 66; Justin G. Turner and Linda Levitt Turner, *Mary Todd Lincoln: Her Life and Letters* (New York: Knopf, 1972), 39–40.

14. *Collected Works,* 2:61, 62, 64 (Francis), 1:228, 2:31 (Henry); Harriet Rumsey Taylor, "Simeon Francis," *Transactions of the Illinois State Historical Society, 1907,* 329–31; Harry E. Pratt, "Dr. Anson G. Henry: Lincoln's Physician and Friend," *Lincoln Herald* 45 (October 1943): 3–17, (December 1943): 31–40. See also Harry C. Blair, *Dr. Anson G. Henry: Physician, Politician, Friend of Abraham Lincoln* (Portland: Binfords & Mort, 1950).

15. *Collected Works,* 2:25, 38, 4:90; *Oregon City Oregon Argus,* December 8, 1860; *Portland Weekly Oregonian,* April 14, October 13, 1860; *Salem Oregon Statesman,* November 30, 1858, October 22, 1860; *Collected Works,* 4:89–90, 101. Baker has been the subject of much adulatory and uncritical writing; for example, see Harry C. Blair and Rebecca Tarshis, *Colonel Edward D. Baker, Lincoln's Constant Ally* (Portland: Oregon Historical Society, 1960).

16. Joseph W. Drew to Matthew P. Deady, January 18, 1861, Matthew P. Deady Papers, Oregon Historical Society, Portland; *The Dalles Mountaineer,* quoted in *Oregon City Oregon Argus,* September 1, 1860.

17. Deady to Asahel Bush, December 14, 1856, Deady Papers. See also Johannsen, *The Frontier, the Union, and Douglas,* 3–18.

18. *Port Townsend North-West,* July 5, 1860.

19. Carl Russell Fish, "Lincoln and the Patronage," *American Historical Review* 8 (October 1902): 56; *Congressional Globe,* 37th Cong., special sess., March 23, 1861, 1496; H. A. Goldsborough to Montgomery Blair, May 20, 1861, Abraham Lincoln Papers, Library of Congress (microfilm, University of Illinois Library).

20. *Collected Works,* 2:60; J. W. P. Huntington to Medorem Crawford, January 11, 1860 [1861], Medorem Crawford Papers, University of Oregon Library, Eugene; Jesse Applegate to Nesmith, December 25, 1860, Jesse Applegate Papers, Oregon Historical Society, Portland; *Oregon City Oregon Argus,* November 24, 1860.

21. Baker to Lincoln, April 3, 1861, California Republicans to Lincoln, March 28, 1861, Lincoln Papers; John Denton Carter, "Abraham Lincoln and the California Patronage," *American Historical Review* 48 (April 1943): 495–506.

22. *Olympia Overland Press,* December 15, 1862.

23. Ibid.; Baker to Henry, July 9, 1861, Anson G. Henry Correspondence (transcripts), Oregon Historical Society, Portland; *Oregon City Oregon Argus,* October 13, 1860; Amory Holbrook to David Craig, March 6, 30, 1861, Amory Holbrook Papers, Oregon Historical Society, Portland.

24. *Olympia Overland Press,* November 17, June 16, 1862.

25. *Steilacoom Puget Sound Herald,* November 28, 1861; Henry to William P. Dole, October 28, 1861, Lincoln Papers; Alexander Abernethy to Elwood Evans, March 9, 1862, Elwood Evans Papers (microfilm), University of Washington Library, Seattle; *Port Townsend North-West,* March 1, 1862.

26. Henry to Wallace, October 24, 1861, Lincoln Papers; Baker to Henry, July 9, 1861, Henry Correspondence (transcripts); Deady to Nesmith, May 16, 1861, Deady Papers; Holbrook to Lincoln, July 11, June 13, 1863, Lincoln Papers.

27. *Steilacoom Puget Sound Herald,* January 23, 1862; Henry to Lincoln, February 3, 1862, Lincoln Papers; William Pickering to Richard Yates, July 14, 1861, Richard Yates Papers, Illinois State Historical Library, Springfield.

28. *Olympia Overland Press,* May 26, 1862; *Olympia Washington Standard,* November 22; 1862.

29. John J. McGilvra to Lincoln, February 14, 1863, Henry to Chase, April 13, 1863, Lincoln Papers; Lincoln to Chase, May 8, 1863, *Collected Works,* 6:202; Chase to Lincoln, May 11, 1863, Lincoln Papers; Lincoln to Henry, May 13, 1863, *Collected Works,* 6:215; Henry to John R. McBride, August 7, 1863, Lincoln Papers; Henry to Wallace, December 6, 1863, William H. Wallace Papers, University of Washington Library, Seattle. For the incident at Port Townsend, see Hubert Howe Bancroft, *History of Washington, Idaho and Montana, 1845–1889* (San Francisco: History Company, 1890), 219–22.

30. Kenneth N. Owens, "Pattern and Structure in Western Territorial Politics." *Western Historical Quarterly* 1 (October 1970): 377.

31. Evans to Father, February 2, 1862, Evans Papers; Wallace to George A. Barnes, April 13, 1862, Wallace Papers; *Olympia Washington Standard,* February 1, 8, March 15, 1862.

32. John G. Sparks to Wallace, December 16, 1863, Wallace Papers; *Olympia Washington Standard,* June 13, 27, 1863; *Steilacoom Puget Sound Herald,* June 11, 1863; W. H. Farrar to James W. Nesmith, March 4, 1862, James W. Nesmith Papers, Oregon Historical Society, Portland.

33. *Olympia Overland Press,* September 29, 1862; *Walla Walla Washington Statesman,* April 4, May 2, 9, March 21, January 10, 17, 1863; Henry to Wallace, December 6, 1863, Wallace Papers; Ronald H. Limbaugh, *Rocky Mountain Carpetbaggers: Idaho's Territorial Governors, 1863–1890* (Moscow: University of Idaho Press, 1982), 25–29.

34. *Portland Weekly Oregonian,* December 8, August 18, 1860; J. H. Munson to Wallace, January 28, 1864, Wallace Papers; Henry to Lincoln, February 3, 1862, Lincoln Papers.

7 ▷ Dr. Anson G. Henry (1804–65): Lincoln's Junkyard Dog

Paul M. Zall

In July 1865, still mourning the murder of Lincoln, the Pacific Coast suffered more sorrow when the wooden-hulled, double side-wheel steamer *Brother Jonathan* went down in the roiling surf off Crescent City in northern California. For a dozen years and more, she had set speed records on both coasts and was still recognized as the swiftest between San Francisco and Washington Territory. Only nineteen passengers and crew made it to shore. The two-hundred-and-twenty-five lost were never found.

Among the lost was Lincoln's longtime friend, sixty-one-year-old Dr. Anson G. Henry, incorrectly named on the passenger list as governor of Washington Territory. President Andrew Johnson had only just nominated him for that post. The Senate had yet to confirm him. He surely deserved the reward after three decades of unrequited loyalty as a sort of Whig and Republican junkyard dog, snarling or snapping at Democrats in their faces or in print, "making two bitter enemies for each warm friend."[1] He was the first to acknowledge his duty as dismal, but somebody had to do it: "You need not expect [John T.] Stuart, [E. D.] Baker or Lincoln to do this kind of work. . . . I am the only working man of *this sort* in Springfield."[2]

Henry sacrificed medical practice for political action at the risk of the safety, health, and welfare of his family and himself. Had he survived to govern Washington Territory, justice would have been served. When he went down with the *Brother Jonathan*, Dr. Henry was still laboring for his party as ever, "without hope of fee or reward."[3]

Henry was born of otherwise undistinguished parents, 3 October 1804, in bucolic Richfield, a postcard-pretty village in upstate New York that boasted two thousand hardy souls. They became healthier still when physician Dr. Horace Manley, discovering that Richfield Springs had medicinal properties, developed a flourishing spa. Prosperity enabled Dr. Manley to build a new home south of Main Street and to mentor apprentices like twenty-two-year-old schoolteacher Anson Henry. This was at a time when critics complained, "Almost any man with an elementary education could take a course of lectures for one or two winters, pass an examination," and be licensed as a physician.[4] Henry's old-fashioned apprenticeship at Richfield took two years; his lectures at respected Dr. David Drake's medical school in Cincinnati only one.

Given the loose licensing laws, the field was bound to be overcrowded. Dr. Henry prospected for a practice through the border states and even Springfield, Illinois, with no success. He also failed at mining lead in Michigan. He even ran for the legislature, with no better luck. After two years, he went back to Richfield, taught school again, and waited for something to turn up. Patience paid with a post in Louisville, where he settled for two years. Five years later, he would look back on those years for the *Sangamo Journal* (6 June 1835). "Went into business on a salary," he wrote, "under the direction of the principal house Surgeon of the Hospital—set up shop for myself . . . in October, 1831—'fell dead in love' about the same time."[5] She was seventeen-year-old Eliza Dudley Bradstreet, descended from first families of Massachusetts Bay, though now impoverished. With an eye to their future, twenty-eight-year-old Dr. Henry invested $27.50 to open a drugstore that he stocked thanks to bank loans totaling $5,000. Winter rains came, he wrote later, flooding the shop: "Was drowned out in February; and while the water was falling got married—the notes became due, the Bank got suddenly out of funds, and I was left to paddle my own canoe."[6]

In late 1831, the Henrys relocated to Springfield with two trunks and $5.30. There they were embraced by local surgeon Dr. Elias H. Merryman, who seldom allowed medical practice to interfere with partying or drilling the local artillery company and parading with Captain Edward D. Baker's sharpshooters. Henry slid into Springfield's lively political life via columns of invective in the local press. It would surprise no one if the Democratic establishment spirited him out of town by making him postmaster of neighboring Sangamo Town. But when after a mere year the office vanished, Dr. and Mrs. Henry went back to Springfield, where he would promote Whig politics for the next twenty years, and she would raise five children—Margaret, Gordon, Eliza, Dudley, and Zachary—while the practice of medicine was supposed to sustain them.

With the irony that shadowed Dr. Henry's life, Asiatic cholera brought death to thousands but gave Henry new life. In summer 1832, the disease, new to Americans, swirled up the Hudson to Albany, to Buffalo through the Erie Canal, and thence across the nation east of the Mississippi. The mortality rate reached 75 percent among the aged and children. The next year it reached New Orleans, and a half-dozen years after that, San Francisco, where it took a thousand victims a month.[7] Dr. Henry, however, not believing Asiatic cholera contagious, went to St. Louis as early as the winter of 1832–33 to study the disease at close range there and at Jacksonville, Illinois.

Dr. Henry's reports back to the *Sangamo Journal* soon endowed him with an aura of expertise. He prescribed bloodletting of course, but his strength was in relieving pain with compounds of laudanum and easing discomfort with ointments compounded of camphor, cayenne pepper, and calomel. His pills became a staple in Springfield's medicine chest. On an informal board of health along with five other physicians, he prescribed keeping on hand compounds of opium, capsicum, and camphor. He was not without detractors but mocked them as tyros with the invective common in journalism of the day—"Does he feel himself competent to pronounce upon the efficiency of my remedies in cholera? Has he ever treated a case of 'real cholera'?"[8]

Dr. Henry could not live on medicine alone. He subordinated his passion for pills to his passion for politics in the *Sangamo Journal*. Trailing his usual irony, his major entry to state politics was a gubernatorial campaign for General James D. Henry (no kin). Initiated by Dr. Henry's widely reprinted "Address to the Freeman of Illinois," the general's campaign terminated with his untimely death. In subsequent campaigns, Dr. Henry teamed with the Springfield Junto, or what today would be called the Springfield Mafia—the fearsome foursome of Edward Baker, Abraham Lincoln, Stephen Logan, and John Todd Stuart. When they muscled the state capital from Vandalia to Springfield, Dr. Henry, as a loyal Whig activist, was named to the four-man commission responsible for building the new statehouse.

The office put him in the crossfire for political dominance in the new capital. He was also a candidate for probate judge to replace longtime incumbent Democratic candidate General James Adams. His progress reports in the *Sangamo Journal* drew fire from *Illinois Republican* editorials apparently written by Democratic leader Stephen A. Douglas. They claimed that Henry was as ignorant of managing construction projects as he was of pushing pills.[9] The *Sangamo Journal* counterblasted with columns by Lincoln and friends writing letters as "Sampson's Ghost." They charged General Adams with real estate fraud and supplied the evidence in an article that the *Sangamo Journal* printed only as a handbill signed by Lincoln. After six weeks of sniping back and forth, Adams won the election, leaving Henry still standing fire.

Democrats accused Henry of "squandering" public funds "disadvantageously and uselessly" on the statehouse project. He called a public meeting to answer the charges,[10] and Lincoln sponsored the investigating committee that cleared him of malfeasance. Lincoln's committee could hardly answer complaints that the state was paying Henry $3.00 a day for playing politics. Since being named to the commission, Henry had anchored the Whigs' statewide organizing campaign, corresponding with units throughout the state while Lincoln, Baker, and Stuart took the show on the road. They peaked in the presidential campaign for William Henry Harrison with Dr. Henry publishing a party newspaper (February–November 1840) to supplement the friendly *Sangamo Journal*. Called *The Old Soldier* in tribute to the candidate and "superintended" by Henry, Baker, Lincoln, and Joshua Speed, it had an unaudited circulation of eight thousand copies.[11]

Joy over Harrison's election was soon cooled by Henry's failure to be named Springfield postmaster. He had, though a father of five growing children, sacrificed medical income to promote "Old Tippecanoe's" victory. Lincoln appealed to Congressman John Todd Stuart, his old law partner, saying he wished Henry could have the office out of sheer self-interest. Dr. Henry had been treating Lincoln for severe depression brought on apparently by breaking an engagement to wed socialite Mary Todd because he lusted instead for her visiting cousin, Matilda Edwards,[12] of whom Mary Todd said, "A lovelier girl I never saw."[13] A "fanciful"[14] tradition features Henry in a starring role as intermediary, carrying Lincoln's note that broke the engagement, but there is no doubt that he acted as emergency-room physician when Lincoln suffered, "two Cat fits, and a Duck fit."[15] That hyperbole by friends sounds as though Henry had fed Lincoln some narcotic with effects as described by a contemporary writer: "A shock, as of some unimagined vital force, shoots without warning through my entire frame, leaping to my fingers' ends, piercing my brain, startling me till I almost spring from my chair."[16] Most likely the effects also consisted of the retching and vomiting of someone not used to mercury or opium.

From his days as cholera expert, Dr. Henry prescribed both substances in various compounds such as calomel, laudanum, and even paregoric. "Blue pills" compounded of mercury were household remedies for pain. His medicines for cholera were listed as "small doses of camphor and laudanum, and mercurial ointment." Witnesses concur that he cured Lincoln's "morbid stupor" with large doses of brandy.[17] When he prescribed the narcotics for "hypochondriasis,"[18] the blanket term for melancholy or depression, Henry put Lincoln at risk for addiction. Addiction could account for the eccentric behavior ingrained in Lincoln legend—mood swings from geniality to self-absorption, joviality to gloom, joy to dejection. A description by his former apprentice Jonathan Birch has Lincoln's eyes "sparkling with fun" as he told a knee-slapping joke to a circle of friends and then hours later "sad and downcast" as he sat with knees-clasped, alone "the very picture of dejection and gloom . . . a barrier so dense and impenetrable that no one dared to break through."[19] The consensus today is that Lincoln ceased taking narcotics on becoming president,[20] but effects such as vivid dreams and hallucinations lingered on to the end.

At a time when drugs were considered more cure than curse, Americans were consuming legally an estimated 65,000 pounds a year.[21] Dr. Henry found opium and mercury merely drugs on the market. Without income from the post office in 1840 he would have had to leave town. Lincoln tried to save him. "I have," he confessed, "within the past few days, been making a most discreditable exhibition of myself in the way of hypochondriaism and thereby got an impression that Dr. Henry is necessary to my existence."[22]

Lincoln's influence did not secure an office. Nevertheless, politics trumped poverty. Henry stayed in Springfield to help organize Whigs for Henry Clay in the next presidential race. He wrote letters and another campaign newspaper, the *Olive Branch*, chaired the party's county convention and its central committee. Resigned to his supporting role, he said that someone had to do it, and he was "the only working man of *this sort* in Springfield." He added: "I have all my life beat the bush for others to catch the bird, and as I am a Whig from principle, I shall continue . . . to labour faithfully for the triumph of those principles. . . ."[23]

Henry's labors yielded victory for Clay in the town and county, but the Democrats took the state and the presidency. Four years after Lincoln worried that his doctor would leave town, Henry was still chanting a lugubrious litany—"I owe it to my family to abandon politics and return to my profession and this I can't do and remain in Springfield."[24]

With James K. Polk's victory blocking federal largesse like the post office, Henry uprooted the family once more, this time for three years to the lively town of Pekin on the Illinois River in Tazewell County, with potential as a hub for river and rail commerce. The family or a flourishing practice may have prevented his soldiering as surgeon with Colonel E. D. Baker's regiment of volunteers in the Mexican War, but in the summer 1846 he did manage to bring thirty wounded volunteers home from the Rio Grande. In what was becoming a familiar pattern, Henry would turn to Lincoln, elected to Congress, for help in recouping out-of-pocket costs of $430, but Lincoln once more could do him no good.[25]

In 1847 Henry edited another newspaper, the *Tazewell Whig*. His columns were among the first to promote Lincoln for Congress. At the beginning of 1848, the same columns also proclaimed that, preferring pills to politics, Henry was moving back to Springfield in the spring. The move coincided with another outbreak of cholera. Besides dispensing the opium-based pill that had established his reputation as a cholera expert in the 1830s, he now sat on the newly created Board of Health. As part of its public health program, the board also prescribed the pill: equal parts of tinctures of opium, capsicum, and camphor.[26] Other than that, the epidemic did Dr. Henry no good since, along with other physicians, he waived fees for treating cholera.

Given his political past, Henry also sat on the Whig Central Committee. He was named presidential elector, a post that required riding across central Illinois with Lincoln every day and speaking for Zachary Taylor. Taylor lost in Illinois but won the country, a victory that ought to have justified Henry's great expectation of a federal office—and Lincoln's too. Carried away by his ardent spirit, Henry asked Cyrus Edwards to support Lincoln for the lucrative office of commissioner of the General Land Office. But Lincoln had earlier promised his support to Edwards for that office. When Henry's letter revealed the double cross, Edwards threw his support to Justin Butterfield, who accordingly won. Lincoln had been no less a loser a few months earlier in trying to secure a Minnesota land office post for Henry.[27]

Finally in March 1849, "with particular anxiety about it," Lincoln urged "appointing Dr. A. G. Henry to some Indian Agency." His meritorious service entitled Dr. Henry to a prime appointment: "Dr. Henry was at first, has always been, and still is, No. One with me. I believe, nay, I *know*, he has done more disinterested labor in the Whig cause, than any other one, two, or three men in the state."[28] Henry finally won his first federal appointment—since his brief term as postmaster of Sangamon Town—as Indian agent in Oregon; but interrupted by a Panama adventure, he did not reach the West Coast.

That winter, as he had in the Mexican War, Dr. Henry served as a travel escort. His friend Congressman E. D. Baker contracted to supply laborers for a railway across Panama. Henry and Baker's brother Alfred, another physician, were hired to shepherd a projected four hundred men from New York to the Chagres River.[29] When Colonel Baker caught the local fever, Dr. Henry was by his side with his pills but then had to return to Springfield and recruit more men to fill the ranks that would empty as soon as they experienced the Panamanian swamps.

Rumblings from the West about Indian agents who never visited their agencies must have reached Dr. Henry. Returning to Springfield, he recruited a wagon train to join pioneers from Springfield settled in Lafayette, Oregon. The year 1852 was to see the most devastating cholera outbreak on the Oregon Trail. Henry with his wife and five children and a train of ten ox-drawn wagons left Springfield in April. Three months later, after two hundred miles on the trail, conceivably dispensing his pills along the way, he filed a report to the *Illinois Journal* from Fort Kearney, Nebraska. Despite "considerable cholera . . . on the plains, judging from the numerous small graves we are passing daily," the folks from Springfield had not suffered "the slightest accident." They were enjoying very pleasant company, although Mrs. Henry had not gotten "used to camp life yet."[30]

Besides sending dispatches to the *Journal*, Dr. Henry kept a journal on the trail as a guide for those who would follow. It took six months to reach The Dalles on the Columbia River. During two weeks of rest and recreation at that Oregon site, the overlanders cut logs readily available in the enveloping woods for a raft to carry the women and children down to the falls, where they could catch a steamer. The men plodded on with the wagons except for Dr. Henry and three others. The men were supposed to manage the raft in the rough water, but the heavy winds that funneled through the narrow Columbia Gorge held them back. The winds pinned them down for another week until the morning they met Indians who dwelt in the gorge. The Natives shepherded them to the falls before night fell. Shortly after the next day began to brighten, the detached party of men appeared and all jogged aboard the small steamer *Multnomah* that carried them to Portland.[31] Walking another 25 miles southwest to Lafayette took 3 days, hardly worth counting after 152 days on the Oregon Trail.

For Dr. Henry, Oregon proved a Paradise Found. Planting the family at a 320-acre farm just outside Lafayette, he could hardly wait to resume politics—helping to organize Yamhill County's agricultural society, being appointed deputy surveyor of the county, running for the seat in the territory legislature, which he won in 1853, and rising to become leader of seven other

Whigs in a predominantly Democratic house. The next year he was on the territorial payroll at $300 a month "to take charge in part of the volunteer force" of Oregon militia recruited to put down opposing Indians. He managed the services, materiel, and supplies for the troops as commissary and quartermaster general.

Besides indulging his passion for politics and public office, Henry did not forget his old profession. He signed on as surgeon of volunteers. And once the Indians were suppressed in 1856, he was named physician to the neighboring Grande Ronde Reservation at $2,000 a year.[32] At the same time, he was able to sustain the flow of letters-to-editors that had been, so to speak, his stock in tirade against Democrats since Springfield days. Now, during 1855, they appeared in the *Oregon Statesman,* including his snappish exchange of insults with Democratic power broker Delazon ("Delusion") Smith of Eugene. Oddly enough, Henry himself had been a member of the Democratic Party[33]—at least until 1858, when his condolences to Lincoln on losing the Senate race to Douglas elicited Lincoln's celebrated reply: "I am glad I made the late race. It gave me a hearing on the great and durable question of the age."[34] Thereafter, Henry became a kind of western correspondent during Lincoln's march to the presidency, exchanging bicoastal news and notes on the campaign and, ultimately, its success.

Henry played a vital role on the western front, especially in persuading Colonel Edward D. Baker, now in California, that Oregon was ripe for Republican leadership against a Democratic Party split over slavery.[35] It took Henry three years to persuade his old comrade to pack his carpetbag, propelling him to the United States Senate and positioning Lincoln to win the West. With two old pals secure at the center of power, Henry was poised to be rewarded for thirty years as a third force—promoter, publicist, and protector "without hope of fee or reward."[36]

Battered by battalions of office seekers nationwide, Lincoln relied on Baker's counsel in parceling out political plums in the West. Henry also applied for a position, offering his experienced skills as surgeon, but, as Baker acknowledged, in following an evenhanded policy Lincoln "acted peculiarly," disappointing both of them—"although my very good friend and yours still, he has not done what you or I would have expected."[37] The best Baker could win for Henry was appointment as surveyor general of Washington Territory at $3,000 a year as of July 1861. "I have done what I thought right and best," wrote Baker and asked Henry in return to use the office "to serve my friends."[38] In a volatile time of contested land claims,

Henry controlled the surveying of enormous public lands, the drawing of township lines and subdivisions, the determining of meridians and parallels, and the registering of claims in territory that included huge parts of present-day Idaho and Montana. Henry was positioned to serve friends aplenty in a population of 11,500. He moved his family to the capital, Olympia, whence via rivers, the sea, and new wagon roads from Walla Walla and Coeur d'Alene, he or more usually two assistants—his sons—visited all he surveyed in season.

In season or off, he picked up his old passion for polemics, now in the columns of the *Oregon Statesman,* which he assured Lincoln was "the most zealous & efficient supporter you have in Oregon if not on the Pacific Coast."[39] Olympia offered outlets in the *Overland Press* and, most handily, the *Washington Standard,* of which Henry was also a proprietor. With the death of Colonel Baker in the early days of the Civil War, Henry assumed the mantle of guardian over Lincoln's interests in the West. Keeping a keen watch on Federal officeholders, he monitored loose loyalties among Republicans and censored or criticized with an even hand Republicans or Democrats on their performance in office.[40]

Both the *Puget Sound Herald* and the local *Overland Press* counterblasted with suggestions that Henry himself had swindled the government seven years earlier when, after taking $750 on being appointed surgeon for Indians of Oregon, he had not come farther west than Panama. Dr. Henry's bile overflowed. Abandoning print, he attacked the editor of the *Puget Sound Herald,* A. M. Poe, for being the original source of the canard. Catching Poe at coffee, Henry caned him on the head and shoulders. Poe fought him back, blow for blow. Infuriated, Henry unsheathed his Bowie knife, waving it wildly as he pulled back to pick up a pen. Although the grand jury indicted him for caning Poe and brandishing a knife, Henry escaped going to trial.[41]

Henry wrote to newly elected President Lincoln introducing newly elected local congressman John McBride. Later, McBride told the *Portland Oregonian* about Lincoln's reaction to Henry's letter: "What a great, big-hearted man he is. Henry is one of the best men I have ever known." But McBride's recollection makes it seem that Lincoln did not know about the knife-wielding incident. "He sometimes commits an error of judgment, but I never knew him to be guilty of a falsehood or of an act beneath a gentleman. He is the soul of truth and honor."[42]

Henry's friendship with the president established him as Oregon's designated gatekeeper for access to the White House. The gate swung both ways. Besides writing letters of introduction and easing appointments for congressional delegates from the West Coast, Henry also acted as conduit for complaints about public officials. The most notorious instance was winning dismissal of Victor Smith as Puget Sound customs collector. Henry was caught in the middle of a power play between the president and Secretary of the Treasury Salmon P. Chase, who insisted on controlling his own appointments.

As Chase's personal friend from Cincinnati, Smith was an eccentric autocrat who told newsman Noah Brooks that he had "so intertwined himself in the fibers of the government that his removal from office was an impossibility."[43] His bizarre conduct proved otherwise. Over loud objections from the local population numbering ten, he moved the customshouse from Port Townsend to Port Angeles, brazenly sailing into the harbor in August 1862 brandishing cannon and demanding the official files. Dr. Henry called him "a swaggering, conceited egotist, making himself offensive and odious to all who come in contact with him,"[44] and in February 1863 wrote Lincoln a ten-page report. Henry himself carried to the nation's capital a bundle of complaints, memorials, and petitions demanding Smith's removal.

Despite the presidential friendship he advertised, Henry's initial attempt at a hearing looked futile. He sat in the waiting room with two senators and a representative—"After waiting 1½ hours . . . we backed out." Next he tried a back door assault. "Then I sent my cards into *Bob* and Mrs. Lincoln. Ten minutes after [that] I was shown into Robert's room."[45] Robert and Mary Lincoln even invited him to stay at the White House while in town, the best access to the president. The Lincoln family had been his intimates since Springfield days when, tradition alleged, it was Dr. Henry who had mediated the Lincolns' star-crossed wedding. In any case, Henry's personal diplomacy mediated Smith's defeat. Lincoln sent Chase a personal note telling him he had placated Oregon's demands by replacing Smith—"the degree of dissatisfaction with him there is too great to be retained."[46] Chase, disgusted, threatened to resign. Lincoln held firmly to presidential control of patronage for the public good and old friends.

As Lincoln's self-professed "old confidential friend" who would share confidences "never yet named to anybody else,"[47] Henry duly impressed congressional delegations from the Far West. He made a spectacular public appearance as a member of the presidential party visiting Gen. Joe Hooker before the Battle of Chancellorsville. Alas, in private he was with the president when news came of Hooker's miserable defeat. As Lincoln reacted—

"ashen, trembling, dispirited, ghostlike"—Dr. Henry in solidarity "burst into a passion of tears."[48]

Besides engineering the removal of Victor Smith as collector of customs, Henry had officially come to the capital to lobby for splitting Idaho from Washington Territory. That question would not be resolved in 1863, but he and Smith would meet again the next year.

After brief visits to his brother in New York and old friends in Springfield, Anson Henry headed home overland in the spring of 1864. He retraced the route of twelve years earlier when a new land lay all before him awaiting his survey. If fortune had eluded him, he had found considerable fame as the man to see—Lincoln's man in the Pacific Northwest. His recent stay at the White House gave substance to that fame as he traveled the Northwest promoting the president's reelection. While California's popular vote for Lincoln receded slightly from that in 1860, Oregon's remained steady in his favor. The best was yet to come. As final election results were reported to the White House, Lincoln as promised gave "his friend on the far-off Pacific coast a clear and exact idea of what had happened,"[49] thus validating Henry's claim to honor if not profit in his own state.

With Lincoln secure at the pinnacle of power, Henry at sixty was no longer satisfied to persevere without hope of fee or reward. He speculated on another visit to the White House, risking about three hundred dollars and his life in sailing to the East Coast on winter seas. On the first leg of the venture, he reported to his wife, "For 48 hours the wind was so strong that a man could not stand upon the deck without holding on to something."[50] Two weeks later, he reported a near-catastrophe as their steamer, the *Constitution,* saved another that had lost a rudder in the "heavy rollers, the largest of which broke with terrible power" that would have sent her to the bottom in ten minutes. Henry imagined the scene if the rescue had failed: "They gave up all as lost, & such a wail as they sent for help was enough to rent the heart."[51]

Like the experience of confronting the Columbia River on entering Oregon a dozen years earlier, this scene foreshadowed his fate six months later.

Henry spent those six months solidifying his intimacy with the Lincoln family by squiring Mary Lincoln to the Congress or riding with the president and first lady in their carriage. Back home, a correspondent (probably Henry himself) assured readers of the 21 August *Oregon Statesman* that he was embedded with the Lincolns: "Last winter we scarcely saw the President that he was not in company with Dr. Henry," even arm-in-arm, leading the cabinet to the Senate, where "his position was next to the President."[52] He told his wife how Mary Lincoln had assured him that their future was secure: "Mr. Lincoln won't refuse anything you ask for."[53]

And yet he had to depend on West Coast congressmen to press his case for a place in the new cabinet. Lincoln told them he needed no testimony to his competency. He had known Dr. Henry long and well, but because the cabinet was already filled, the only suitable openings were in the Land Office or Indian bureaus. Henry expected to be named commissioner of Indian Affairs. In the hectic months of March and April, as war's end neared, Lincoln had other matters on his mind, leaving Henry in enforced idleness visiting friends and touring. He was visiting City Point near Richmond when news of Lincoln's assassination told him he had lost both a beloved friend and a promising future.

He replayed his sorrow for his wife: "I was so stunned by the blow that I could not realize that he was dead until I saw him lying in the Guests Chamber cold & still in the embrace of Death. Then the terrible truth flashed upon me, & the fountain of tears was broken up and I wept like a child refusing to be comforted, remaining riveted to the spot until led away. . . . I had never before realized the luxury of tears, & I never before wept in the bitterness of heart & soul, & God grant that I may never have cause to so weep again."[54]

Reassuring Henry of his future, the new president, Andrew Johnson, promised that he would honor Lincoln's intentions. In reinforcing their friendship, Henry told Mary Lincoln that he would remain by her side to ease the pain of her loss. In the cortege, he rode with the family in the third carriage and joined their mourning in the East Room. Most remarkable to Henry were the wild swings in Mary's grief that he described to his wife: "I found her in bed more composed than I had anticipated but the moment I came within her reach she threw her arms around my neck and wept most hysterically for several minutes. . . . My sympathy was to her most consoling and for a half hour she talked most composedly."[55]

Mrs. Lincoln's intimacy with Henry could have been based on a mutual interest in spiritualism she had acquired since the death of young Willie three years earlier. Henry said that because he was "a half way spiritualist," he could be "the best comforter she finds, and I spend several hours a day with her."[56] Just as likely, her dependence on Dr. Henry could have been connected to his dispensing pills laced with mercury or opium for her husband's depression or for the migraines she had suffered since childhood. Whatever the circumstances, she demanded his presence, sent him on errands, such as going to New York to settle her accounts, engaged him as her escort to Chicago and as her agent in reserving Lincoln's tomb for Oak Ridge Cemetery in Springfield. "I believe in my heart," she told him, "you are really the only disinterested, sincere friend, left us. . . . Alas, alas, our families are both situated alike, nothing but disappointments before us."[57]

On the first of July, he returned to the capital and an uncertain future. Disgusted with the delay in an appointment promised by both Lincoln and Johnson, and "more and more homesick,"[58] he sailed for home the next day via Panama. But disappointment would not be denied. At Panama Bay, where his ship took on survivors from the wreck of the *Golden Rule*, Henry found himself assigned to the same cabin as Victor Smith—the victim of his only successful mission to the White House the previous year: "I wouldn't dare to sleep in the same room with that viper. . . . He might get up and kill me in the night."[59]

Both found separate cabins as far as San Francisco, where they landed on 25 July. The next day the *San Francisco Alta California* reported that Dr. Anson G. Baker had been named governor of Washington Territory—though not yet confirmed. Then, on the last of their three-day layover, Dr. A. G. Henry and Victor Smith sailed for home on the *Brother Jonathan*. Besides passengers on this day she carried gold, hardware, railroad ties and rails, a huge ore crusher, 346 barrels of whiskey, and two camels—so overladen that only high tide could hoist her hull out of San Francisco Bay mud. After offloading heavy machinery at Crescent City, she faced ferocious winds and seas so fierce that Captain DeWolf sought safety in the breakwater, where an uncharted rock split her hull and sent that great ship down to the bottom of the Pacific sea.

The surf did not yield Dr. Henry's remains, yet his militant advocacy of Lincoln's political faith affected the future of the Pacific Northwest. As long-standing friend and functionary, Henry stood in relation to Lincoln as a director of communications supplying intelligence while protecting and promoting Lincoln's views. Lincoln's ultimate success rewarded Henry with patronage for himself and, more importantly, patronage for faithful cohorts. In Oregon the doctor fused like-minded splinter groups to break the grip of secession-minded Democrats. In Washington Territory as surveyor general and in Washington, D.C., as the region's lobbyist in the White House, Henry helped to anchor the Union in safe harbor at the Pacific Northwest.

Notes

1. Paul M. Angle, *"Here I Have Lived": A History of Lincoln's Springfield* (New Brunswick, NJ: Rutgers University Press, 1950), 65.
2. A. G. Henry to John J. Hardin, 11 November 1843, quoted in Harry E. Pratt, "Dr. Anson G. Henry: Lincoln's Physician and Friend," *Lincoln Herald* 45 (October 1943): 3–17, quote on 11; Part 2 (October 1943): 31–40.
3. Pratt, "Dr. Anson G. Henry," 11.
4. Richard Harrison Shryock, *Medicine in America: Historical Essays* (Baltimore: Johns Hopkins Press, 1966), 152.
5. Pratt, "Dr. Anson G. Henry," 4.
6. Ibid., 4–5.
7. Olaf Larsell, *The Doctor in Oregon* (Portland: Oregon Historical Society, 1947), 102–3; James O. Breeder, ed., *Medicine in the West* (Manhattan, KS: Sunflower University Press, 1982).
8. Pratt, "Dr. Anson G. Henry," 6.
9. John Richard Weber, "An Episode in Journalism in 1840," *Journal of Illinois Historical Society* 23 (1930–31): 506.
10. Pratt, "Dr. Anson G. Henry," 10.
11. Roy P. Basler, Marion D. Pratt, and Lloyd A Dunlap, eds. *The Collected Works of Abraham Lincoln*, 9 vols. (New Brunswick, NJ: Rutgers University Press, 1953–1955), 1:204; Pratt, "Dr. Anson G. Henry," 10.
12. Basler, *Collected Works*, 1:282.
13. Angle, *"Here I Have Lived,"* 94.
14. Douglas L. Wilson, *Honor's Voice: The Transformation of Abraham Lincoln* (New York: Alfred A. Knopf, 1998), 239.
15. Ibid., 236.
16. D. W. Cheever, "Narcotics," *North American Review* 95 (October 1862): 374–415; citation on 405.
17. Harry C. Blair, *Anson G. Henry*, Presidential Address, 14th Annual meeting of the Western Orthopedic Association, Portland, OR, October 1950, pp. 6–8.
18. N. Hirschhorn, R. G. Feldman, Ian A. Greaves, "Abraham Lincoln's Blue Pills," *Perspectives in Biology and Medicine* 44 (2001): 315–32; Joshua Wolf Shenk, *Lincoln's Melancholy* (Boston: Houghton Mifflin, 2005), chap. 3.
19. R. R. Wilson, *Intimate Memories of Lincoln* (Elmira, NY: Primavera Press, 1945), 105.
20. Hirschhorn et al., "Abraham Lincoln's Blue Pills," 315.
21. Cheever, "Narcotics," 374.
22. Abraham Lincoln to John Todd Stuart, 20 January 1841 (facsimile of letter), in Pratt, "Dr. Anson G. Henry," 13.
23. Pratt, "Dr. Anson G. Henry," 11.
24. Ibid.
25. Harry C. Blair and Rebecca Tarshis, *Colonel Edward D. Baker: Lincoln's Constant Ally* (Portland: Oregon Historical Society, 1960), 35; Pratt, "Dr. Anson G. Henry," 12.
26. Larsell, *Doctor in Oregon*, 215.
27. Pratt, "Dr. Anson G. Henry," 14.
28. Basler et al., *Collected Works*, 2:78.

29. Blair and Tarshis, *Colonel Edward D. Baker* 57.
30. Pratt, "Dr. Anson G. Henry," 15.
31. Blair, *Anson G. Henry*, 11.
32. Larsell, *Doctor in Oregon*, 257.
33. Elbert F. Floyd, "Insights into the Personal Friendship and Patronage of Abraham Lincoln and Anson Gordon Henry, M.D.: Letters for [sic] Dr. Henry to His Wife," *Journal of the Illinois State Historical Society* 98 (Winter 2005–6): 224.
34. Abraham Lincoln to A. G. Henry, 19 November 1958 (facsimile of letter), in Blair, *Anson G. Henry*, 13; Basler et al., *Collected Works*, 3:339.
35. Blair and Tarshis, *Colonel Edward D. Baker*, 92–93, 114.
36. A. G. Henry to John J. Hardin, 11 November 1843, in Pratt, "Dr. Anson G. Henry," 11.
37. Pratt, "Dr. Anson G. Henry," 32.
38. E. D. Baker to A. G. Henry, in Floyd, "Insights," 250 n.40.
39. Milton H. Shutes, *Lincoln and the Doctors* (New York: Pioneer Press, 1933), 130.
40. Floyd, "Insights," 226.
41. Ibid.
42. Undated issue of *Portland Oregonian*, 1865, quoted in Pratt, "Dr. Anson G. Henry," 34.
43. Noah Brooks, *Washington in Lincoln's Time* (New York: Century, 1896), 120.
44. Floyd, "Insights," 251 n. 50.
45. A. G. Henry to Eliza Henry, 17 February 1863, in ibid., 230.
46. Abraham Lincoln to S. P. Chase, 8 May 1863, in Basler, *Collected Works*, 6:202.
47. A. G. Henry to Eliza Henry, undated, Floyd, "Insights," 231. Hereafter all references to letters to Eliza Henry are in Floyd.
48. Brooks, *Washington in Lincoln's Time*, 58.
49. Ibid., 220.
50. To Eliza Henry, 28 December 1864, Floyd, "Insights," 233.
51. To Eliza Henry, 9 January 1865, ibid., 235.
52. Pratt, "Dr. Anson G. Henry," 37.
53. Floyd, "Insights," 236.
54. Paul M. Angle and Carl Sandburg, eds., *Mary Lincoln: Wife and Widow* (New York: Harcourt Brace, 1932), 226.
55. Floyd, "Insights," 239.
56. To Eliza Henry, 8 May 1865, in ibid., 241.
57. Mary Lincoln to A. G. Henry, 17 July 1865, in Angle and Sandburg, *Mary Lincoln*, 234.
58. Floyd, "Insights," 244.
59. Brooks, *Washington in Lincoln's Time*, 122–23.

8 ▷ The Mormon Connection:
Lincoln, the Saints, and the Crisis of Equality

Larry Schweikart

"**P**olitical liberty," wrote Alexis de Tocqueville, "bestows exalted pleasures from time to time upon a certain number of citizens. Equality every day confers a number of small enjoyments on every man. The charms of equality are every instant felt and are within the reach of all." Democratic communities, he explained, have a passion for equality that is "ardent, insatiable, incessant, invincible; they call for equality in freedom; and if they cannot obtain that, they still call for equality in slavery." Tocqueville divined what few since have; that is, the striving for equality has turned into a struggle for egalitarianism which has surpassed the quest for freedom.[1]

George Hubbard, in his article "Abraham Lincoln as Seen by the Mormons," examined an individual and a religious group which grappled with the issues of the day—slavery, polygamy, popular sovereignty, and equality. Hubbard's otherwise excellent scholarship wanes in his timid conclusion that the Mormons' intense anti-Lincoln sentiment rather miraculously shifted, simply because of Lincoln's avowed policy to "let them alone." This conclusion is at best simplistic and at worst simply false. What Hubbard failed to realize was that the true struggle facing Lincoln and the Mormons involved a solution to the antinomies of equality. The Mormons and Lincoln attempted to reconcile these antinomies in different ways. While the Mormons held an egalitarian view of equality which resembled Enlightenment concepts, Lincoln subscribed to a position which has been considered by some to be Aristotelian. In examining contacts between Lincoln and the Latter-day Saints, this work will emphasize the struggles with equality each

From *Western Humanities Review* 34 (winter 1980): 1–22.

shared. Harry Jaffa has thoroughly detailed Lincoln's views on equality; therefore the bulk of this interpretation will stress Mormon concepts of equality. Additionally, the intention here is to show that Lincoln recognized that Mormon leadership, the product of a theology devised by one man, rested solely upon the individual holding the office of church president. After some experimentation, Lincoln designed a policy which placated the leadership, thereby maintaining order in Utah. Lincoln, however, failed to recognize that his own struggle with the issues of the day resembled that of the Mormons. Mormon doctrinal inconsistencies, like Lincoln's attempts to balance notions of consent and equality, only reflected the philosophical confusion of the president and a religious group.[2]

A brief review of the concepts of equality which preceded the 1800s may be useful. The Enlightenment inverted previous teachings of Aristotle and St. Thomas Aquinas which viewed all men as equal only in their ability to choose between good and evil. Thomas Hobbes, John Locke, and Jean Jacques Rousseau contributed to a theory which held "that there exist, somehow, a state of nature and a social state with a contract between them . . . ," and also assumed, as Leo Strauss revealed, that metaphysical and ethical views were "untenable as regards their claim to be simply true."[3] The creation of the social state leveled all men by removing the moral choice. As these ideas drifted into nineteenth-century America, the leveling process, romantically called equality, became viewed as the solution to all problems.[4]

Mormons, headed by Prophet Joseph Smith, sought territory in which they could pursue their own interpretations of equality and freedom. Settling in Zion, Missouri, their dealings in local politics and their amorphous stand on slavery soon resulted in the Mormons' expulsion. Relocating in Hancock County, Illinois, the Mormons again built a settlement, Nauvoo, which soon grew to be the largest city in the state. Smith was convinced the Mormons could be an effective political force in Illinois, and his church represented a tempting bloc of voters for the party which could woo them.[5]

Lincoln first crossed paths with the Mormons in the election of 1840. Whigs and Democrats both expressed interest in the six thousand eligible Mormon voters, and as Lincoln's letter to John T. Stuart indicates, Whigs sent campaign literature to the Latter-day Saints: "Speed says he wrote you what Jo. Smith said about you as he passed here. We will procure the names of some of his people here and send them to you before long."[6]

Using votes as political leverage required the Saints to shift their support from party to party. In Missouri, Mormons tended to vote Democratic, but in Hancock County they supported the 1840 and 1841 Whig tickets.[7] Smith's friendship with Stephen A. Douglas seemed to ensure a return to the Democrats, and the prophet confirmed this by admitting the Mormons would vote as a bloc for Douglas.[8] The state polarized along Mormon/non-Mormon "party" lines, and the Whigs found themselves increasingly pictured as anti-Mormon.

Lincoln was one of the first casualties of the sliding Mormon votes when, in the November 1840 election, the Mormons removed his name as a presidential elector. As John Bennett, a Mormon spokesman, explained in a letter to the *Times and Seasons*: "We desired to show our friendship to the Democratic party by substituting the name of Ralston for some one of the Whigs."[9] Lincoln happened to be the last Whig on the ticket, but later the *Quincy Whig* indicated there was something suspicious about the move.[10]

A month later, the Nauvoo city charter came up before the Illinois legislature for incorporation. Upon its passage, Bennett recalled that Lincoln "had the magnanimity to vote for our act, and came forward after the final vote . . . and cordially congratulated me on its passage.[11] Mormon historians relate the incident with the inference that Lincoln showed favoritism to Nauvoo, but, in fact, Lincoln helped cities such as Nauvoo as a matter of course.[12]

Mormon solidarity at the polls caused some to fear the power of Joseph Smith. The prophet had not attached himself to either party, admitting to caring "not a fig for Whig or Democrat; they are both alike to us, but we shall go for our friends. . . . We are aware that 'divide and conquer' is the watchword with many, but with us it cannot be done."[13] By "going with their friends," the Saints indicated their abandonment of the Whigs, and the Democrats smashed the Whigs in the 1842 gubernatorial election in Hancock County.[14]

Within a year the Saints could outvote the rest of the county, and their power in regional politics increased so much that "every one conceded that Smith's dictum would decide the contest."[15] Another observer agreed more bluntly: "The Mormons follow Smith's wishes in politics like a sheep following the bell sheep over a wall."[16] The prophet envisioned an independent Mormon state and contemplated secession from Illinois. State laws were unconstitutional, he argued, and Nauvoo stood "in the same relation to the state as the state does to the union."[17] Convinced he could no longer trust the traditional parties, Smith announced his own candidacy for the Presidency of the United States. His campaign resulted in an increased anti-Mormon sentiment, and riots broke out in several cities.[18]

While Smith dabbled ineptly in politics, problems surfaced in the church. Amid a controversy over polygamy, Smith excommunicated fellow Mormon spokesman John Bennett. Bennett promptly set about to destroy the prophet by denouncing him in print. Others followed Bennett, most notably William Law and Sylvester Emmons, who were methodical in their written attacks and more credible in the eyes of the public. Smith retaliated by destroying the outlaw press, initiating a chain of events which resulted in his death.[19]

Lincoln, meanwhile, had kept abreast of the Mormon situation, as evidenced in a letter to Samuel D. Marshall: "Bennett's Mormon disclosiers [sic] are making some little stir here, but not very great."[20] Contact further diminished as a result of the Mormon exodus to Utah in 1846, and Lincoln heard little from the Mormons until the 1858 elections. However, events in the politics of Illinois had already given some indication of the power of the Mormon leaders.

Brigham Young, Smith's successor, led the Saints to Utah with the intention of creating an independent Mormon state there, but Congress pared off chunks of the territory until only Utah remained. Young's control, however, survived intact. As Horace Greeley noted on his 1859 visit to Utah, "Brigham Young carries the territory in his breeches' pocket without a shadow of opposition; he governs without responsibility to either law or public opinion; for there is no real power here but that of the church, and he is practically the church."[21] Clearly, from the growth of Nauvoo to the establishment of the Utah church, the Mormons rigidly adhered to a theocratic system subservient to the commands of the current leader, or president.

Lincoln again came in contact with the Mormons, this time over the issue of polygamy. By the mid-1850s, the Mormon practice of polygamy joined slavery in the political limelight. Both parties criticized polygamy in Illinois, but the Democrats found themselves in a particularly precarious position, as they had courted the Mormon votes heavily in the 1840s and now seemed to be associated with the church. By 1856, both parties tried to implicate the other with charges of supporting polygamy, as evidenced by a Republican newspaper headline proclaiming the unwelcome possibility of "Democracy-Slavery-Polygamy."[22]

Douglas, who had once been a friend of the Mormons, faced charges of being a defender of polygamy.[23] The Whig-Republican paper in Springfield used Douglas's popular sovereignty arguments to show that he favored a plurality of wives. Feeling the heat of this "friend of Mormons" label, Douglas abandoned the Saints, accusing them of subverting the United States government; and calling for the repeal of the Organic Act which made Utah a territory in 1850. Douglas, who had long insisted slavery was not a moral issue, "in order to cut down the growing criticism of his popular sovereignty concept . . . made polygamy just such an issue."[24]

Hubbard contended that Lincoln did not attack the institution of polygamy. A careful examination, however, reveals Lincoln pressed Douglas on the constitutionality of polygamy and *then* asked some important questions: "That question the Judge well knows to be this: 'If the people of Utah shall peacefully form a State Constitution tolerating polygamy, will the Democracy admit them into the Union?' There is nothing in the United States Constitution or law against polygamy; and why is it not a part of the Judge's 'sacred right of self government' for that people to have it, or rather to keep it, if they choose? These questions, so far as I know, the judge never answers. *It might involve the Democracy to answer them either way*" (italics mine).[25]

While Lincoln made no clear moral pronouncement on polygamy that day, he clearly underscored the significance of the issue and the possible ramifications of popular sovereignty. Lincoln's reply also followed the pattern he developed of requiring Douglas to attach morality to the political questions.

If, as Allan Nevins suggested, the *Illinois State Journal* spoke for Lincoln, then his feelings on polygamy were clearly expressed prior to the April 12, 1860, speech at Bloomington.[26] The March 26, 1860, issue of the *Journal* asked, "[if] Congress can abolish polygamy in Utah, why can it not forbid slavery in New Mexico? If the South grants the Power in one case, she cannot deny it in another. . . . the Democratic Party tolerates and defends all *horrible Mormon crimes connected with the beastly abomination of polygamy* (italics mine).[27]

Republicans introduced an antipolygamy bill in the House of Representatives, and the Douglas Democrats led the fight against it. In order to counter charges that he backed the Mormons and polygamy, Douglas supported a proposition that Utah be divided into two territories in such a way that non-Mormons would dominate the polls and vote polygamy out of existence, thereby vindicating the ideal of popular sovereignty.

Lincoln had his opening. "How much better," he asked, "was it to divide up the territory and attach its parts to others?" This reasoning, Lincoln added, meant, "If I cannot rightfully murder a man, I may tie him to the tail of a kicking horse, and let it kick the man to death! But why divide up the territory at all? . . . Something must be *wrong* there, or it would not be necessary to act at all. And if one mode of interference is wrong, why not the other?" (italics mine). Lincoln "supposed that the friends of popular sovereignty would say . . . that polygamy was wrong and slavery right; and therefore one might thus be put down and the other not."[28]

Even though Lincoln's election defeated popular sovereignty, Mormons had not relied exclusively on that idea to legitimize polygamy. Eight years earlier, Parley Pratt, perhaps foreseeing the constitutional questions which were now appearing, constructed a doctrine which circumvented Congress and the presidency and sought refuge in the Constitution. Pratt contended, "The Constitution gives the privilege to all the inhabitants of this country of the exercise of their religious notions, and the freedom of their faith and their practice of it. Then, if it can be proven . . . that the Latter-day Saints have actually embraced, as a part and portion of their religion, the doctrine of a plurality of wives, it is constitutional."[29] Such a view certainly fell in line with Smith's earlier pronouncement about the unconstitutionality of Illinois state laws. The Mormons ensured, in theory at least, the continued existence of polygamy through both a tacit alignment with popular sovereignty and in their vocal interpretation of the Constitution.

Cries by Republicans for the extinction of the "twin relics of barbarism," slavery and polygamy, forced Mormons into the Democratic camp. Displeased with Douglas, the Saints had a difficult choice, as they felt Lincoln's election ensured the dissolution of the Union. Despite their dissatisfaction with the federal government, Mormon theology held that the Union was created through divine inspiration; hence a vote for Lincoln was a vote to destroy that which God created.[30] While Utah residents had no voting privileges in 1860, Mormons supported the Democrats in sermon and in print. Church leaders referred to Lincoln as the "Black Republican," and one Salt Lake City newspaper ran an advertisement heralding Lincoln's election with the subheading "NIGGERS REJOICING."[31]

Lincoln's image suffered another blow in 1861 when he ordered an Indian reservation be made out of the Uintah Valley, a spot Mormons had planned for settlement. The Saints viewed this as an attempt to deprive them of land, but Lincoln, acting on advice from Superintendent of Indian Affairs Martin, thought the land unusable.[32]

Postelection animosity increased in Salt Lake City. Brigham Young publicly scoffed at "King Abraham," blaming him personally for the nation's conflict.[33] In the tabernacle, Young continued his attacks. "Our present President, what is his strength?" he asked rhetorically. "It is like a rope of sand or like a rope made of water. He is as weak as water. What can he do? Very little. Has he the power to execute the laws? No."[34] Young's remarks prefaced a series of attacks on the president. Apostle George A. Smith charged Lincoln was "put into power by that priestly influence [non-Mormon clergy and abolitionists]; and . . . should he not find his hands full by the secession of the Southern States, the spirit of priestcraft would force him, in spite of his good wishes and intentions, to put to death . . . every man that believes in the divine mission of Joseph Smith, or that bears testimony of the doctrines he preached."[35]

Feeling the government shared the responsibility for Mormon expulsions in Illinois and Missouri, Young had once seethingly labeled Washington "the most corrupt government upon the face of the earth."[36] As before, with Young setting the tempo, the band of Saints fell in line without a dissenting note.

With the outbreak of hostilities between North and South, Lincoln faced a troop shortage. Needing troops to protect mail and telegraph lines in Utah, he sent a request to the Mormon leader to raise volunteers. Young complied, "delighted with this recognition and demonstration of confidence on the part of the federal government."[37] The request, and Young's reported "delight," came only three weeks after the scathing diatribes against Lincoln noted above.

Despite the note of optimism, Lincoln's Mormon problems were just beginning. He faced, in addition to the minor matter of Robert E. Lee's Army of Northern Virginia, a multitude of political appointments. For territorial governor of Utah, Lincoln selected John Dawson of Indiana. Dawson's party loyalty, which was dubious, barely surpassed his morals and judgment, which were questionable. After Dawson's advances toward local Mormon women earned him a sound thrashing at the hands of the local Latter-day Saints, Lincoln replaced him with Acting Governor Frank Fuller over the protestations of Mormons who still preferred Brigham Young.[38] Lincoln's new appointee, Stephen S. Harding, named in March 1862, arrived the next July with a congenial attitude toward the Saints, but he soon wrote the president requesting troops to keep order among the Salt Lake City residents. On orders from Lincoln, California Volunteers marched into Utah in October.[39]

One month earlier, Lincoln's preliminary emancipation proclamation shocked the Mormon community. The *Deseret News* editorialized: "President Lincoln has swung loose from the constitutional moorings of his inaugural address . . . He is fully adrift on the current of radical fanaticism.

... He has been coerced by the insanity of radicals, by the denunciation of their presses, by the threats of their governors and senators."[40] Besides shrinking from the thought of free blacks running about loose, the Saints feared Lincoln's action might turn the individual southerner into a zealot fighting for a holy cause. The *Deseret News* predicted that southern squadrons in the field would, in effect, be doubled. As a gradual acceptance set in, the *News* referred to a Negro freedom celebration as a "display by those descendants of Ham." The celebration, it noted, "must have been a demoniacal demonstration."[41]

Mormons greeted Lincoln's federal justice appointments to Utah no more enthusiastically than they had the territorial governors. John Kinney, Thomas Drake, and Charles Waite served as justices in the three Utah districts during much of this period, although a high turnover rate characterized the positions. Low pay and constant struggles with Mormon leadership caused several judges to resign in disgust or to be replaced. Drake's predecessor, Robert Flenniken, typified the besieged Utah justices. In appeals to Lincoln, Flenniken urged the president to settle the dispute over who was the rightful appointee to Carson District, the only non-Mormon district. John Cradlebaugh also wanted the seat, and Flenniken feared that in either of the other districts, "unless I became a Mormon, I could have neither peace nor prosperity."[42]

The Saints felt Lincoln's reluctance to appoint local residents indicated his anti-Mormonism, but, in fact, he sought advice from the territorial delegates by asking them to furnish a list of names for various offices of the territory. As one observer commented, in Utah "the appointment of anyone tolerant of Mormonism was the practical equivalent of a resident appointment."[43]

A strange tug-of-war emerged between Mormons and the justices, with judges rendering anti-Mormon verdicts and Brigham Young urging his people to refuse jury duty.[44] Judge Waite brashly drew up an amendment to the Organic Act which placed sole authorization for jury selection in the hands of the U.S. marshal and allowed only the governor the power to commission militia officers.[45] When the Saints finally received a favorable ruling from Judge Kinney, who had sentenced the Morrisites to fines and prison terms, Governor Harding pardoned the entire group.[46]

Mormon tolerance had reached its peak. On March 3, 1863, several thousand of the citizenry of Salt Lake City signed a petition urging President Lincoln to remove Harding, Waite, and Drake. Kinney, who suddenly appeared acceptable, was excluded.

Lincoln's appointments to Utah could indeed be questioned. According to one student of the area, many Utah judges were "political hacks who had worn out their welcome and were appointed out West to get rid of them." He concluded, "less than half of [them] had the least understanding of the people they were appointed to serve, and less than half of them were of average competence, *even considering the time and the place*" (italics mine).[47]

The military stationed in Utah and the non-Mormon citizens found Harding, Waite, and Drake quite satisfactory. Upon hearing of the Mormon petition to dispatch the three, the local coalition drew up their own petition to Lincoln demanding the removal instead of Frank Fuller and Kinney, alleging these men to be "subservient to the will of Brigham Young."[48] Lincoln appeased both sides, recalling Harding, Fuller, and Kinney while retaining Drake and Waite. In a subtle political move, Lincoln had actually sacrificed only Fuller. By this time, Kinney had achieved popularity among Mormons, and they quickly elected him as a delegate to Congress following his removal. Harding's continued hostility to the Saints made his retention impractical. The president also knew that Mormons, aware of the high attrition rate for territorial judges, would be less likely to resist the two retentions if they thought the terms were temporary. Waite lasted only one year longer, and Drake, six.[49]

Shortly after Lincoln's response to the petition, Brigham Young sent T. B. H. Stenhouse to the White House in order to learn of Lincoln's plans for the Mormons. Lincoln characteristically replied to Stenhouse's query with a story: "Stenhouse, when I was a boy on the farms in Illinois there was a great deal of timber on the farms which we had to clear away. Occasionally we would come to a log which had fallen down. It was too hard to split, too wet to burn and too heavy to move, so we plowed around it. That's what I intend to do with the Mormons. You go back and tell Brigham Young that if he will let me alone, I will let him alone."[50]

The "three word policy," as it became known, has been frequently cited as evidence of Lincoln's tolerance, fairness, sincerity, and impartiality in his dealings with the Latter-day Saints. Indeed, there is no reason to conclude otherwise, and one might add that Lincoln's policies demonstrated remarkable political practicality. Lincoln apparently made two assumptions when dealing with the Mormons: the leader could maintain order without the help of the federal government, and Lincoln could deal directly with the leader, circumventing traditional territorial systems. Having detailed

Lincoln's direct dealings with Brigham Young, it must now be determined if Mormon leadership was sufficiently strong to maintain political order.

Saint leadership proved extremely strong. The society, theocratic in nature, reflected Mormon beliefs that an earthly society "would become the headquarters of Christ's millennial rule."[51] The church, which had been "established in a condition of apostolic purity," dominated the society; hence all secular duties took on religious significance. With no clear distinction between secular and spiritual, the church assumed a political role. Having "restored the Priesthood" through Joseph Smith, the church and the church leaders inherited the added dimension of being authoritative "as against private judgment and any spiritual illumination received by individuals."[52]

By stressing equality in this world as well as the next, the church made it easier for the congregation to comply with its rulings. The prophet's concept of progressive order in the universe contributed to notions of equality, for the lay person would eventually be as God. Fawn Brodie wrote, "The result was a pyramidal church structure resting on the broadest possible base and possessing astonishing strength. By giving each man a share in the priesthood, Joseph quickened a sense of kinship and oneness with the Church. There was a feeling of common ownership."[53]

Clearly, then, the leadership of the church, aided by the effects of equality, became monolithic. Through its "purity" and authoritativeness, internal control increased to the point that, as John D. Lee noted, "we [of the High Council] never take up anything that Pres Young lays down."[54] Additionally, Mormons associated the office of the church presidency with God, who presides over the universe. By supervising economic and community activities, Mormon leadership represented more than an ecclesiastical system, and by holding political offices, Mormons so influenced the whole political system that it "was Mormon rather than . . . American."[55] Church leaders mingled with the rank and file and encouraged lay members to attend meetings, thereby giving the appearance of popular involvement in policy making. Yet the leadership stifled dissent through social pressure. Members soon learned it was their duty to ratify decisions made by individual leaders.[56]

When viewed in this manner, Mormon actions in Illinois and their reaction to Lincoln become clearer. Several authors have concluded that Mormon turmoil in Illinois stemmed from Smith's political vacillations.[57] Unfortunately, the same commonsense approach toward the Mormons in Utah has escaped historians.

One man, the president, generally dictated ecclesiastical and political policy. More significantly, the first two leaders did not seem to have a clear picture of the policies they intended to pursue. A great deal of this indecision and confusion stemmed from the nature of Mormon teachings, which contained great inconsistencies about matters such as equality and the relation of church and state. Lincoln dealt with similar tensions, but believed he reconciled the philosophical problems in a different way. An attempt will first be made to examine the contradictions in the Mormons' doctrine and their struggles to resolve them and then investigate the same conflict, as Lincoln viewed it, and his resolution.

One important point of stress in Mormon doctrine is found in the emphasis placed on equality blended with an acceptance of slavery. Aristotelian theory holds that this is not necessarily a conflict, but the Mormon theology, having its foundation in Enlightenment assumptions discussed earlier, rejected Aristotelian and Thomistic postulates. Note, then, the importance placed on the value of "equality" in Mormon teaching. God, speaking to the Saints through the Book of Mormon, told his people, "I desire that this inequality [aristocracy] should be no more in this land, especially among this my people; but I desire that this land be a land of liberty, and every man may enjoy his rights and privileges alike."[58] Democracy blessed God's children as "they relinquished their desires for a king, and became exceedingly anxious that every man should have an *equal chance*" (italics mine).[59] Parley Pratt, one of the church fathers, wrote in the *Seer*, "the command to 'Be one' . . . embraces all other commands," and that in the ancient church, all were equal temporally. The "same order must exist [now] . . . ," Pratt continued, because "inequality in property is the root of innumerable evils . . . it is the great barrier erected by the devil to prevent that *unity and oneness* which the Gospel requires" (italics mine). He concluded, "if ye are not equal in earthly things ye cannot be equal in obtaining heavenly things."[60] Joseph Smith implanted equality in Mormon theology in *Doctrine and Covenants*: "every man was to receive portions of land equal according to his family, according to his circumstances and his wants and needs. . . . in your temporal things you shall be equal. . . . you are to have equal claims on the properties. . . . Every man should have an equal privilege to teach all the others."[61]

The prophet initially maintained apposite views on slavery, finding it wrong to interfere with a master-servant relationship. He ordered his people to avoid preaching to slaves or baptizing them contrary to their masters' wishes. This position fluctuated a great deal, however, as Smith also termed abolition of slavery and colonization of slaves "wonderful."[62] In 1843 Smith preached that Negroes "came into the world slaves, mentally and physically," but he then came to the conclusion that environment caused most of the problem, and if the Negroes could "change their situation with the whites . . . [blacks] would be like them." His solution, therefore, resembled Lincoln's early proposals: "Confine them by strict law to their own species, and put them on a national organization."[63]

The only reference to slavery in the Book of Mormon instructed that the people of Ammon should not become slaves but left the question of slave ownership open.[64] As early as 1833, though, Smith decided not only to stop "free people of color from emigrating to [Missouri], but to prevent them from being admitted as members of the Church."[65] Clearly Smith's basic teachings on slavery conflicted with his views on equality. To say those views were thoroughly inconsistent and internally contradictory would be an understatement.

When, in the 1830s, slavery became associated with the church, Mormon leaders increasingly sympathized with the South. The *Messenger and Advocate* stated, "the knowledge [that Negroes naturally were meant to be servants] should shame those who cry out against the South."[66] Orson Hyde, another church elder, added, "we do not wish to oppose the laws of the land [which recognize slavery]."[67] Smith's fluctuations only affected the official church position temporarily, for slavery existed in Utah among the Mormons in a limited fashion. Brigham Young, explaining the situation to Horace Greeley, said "slavery was of divine institution, and not to be abolished until the curse pronounced on Ham shall have been removed from his descendants." He added that "Negroes must be servants, and it was not right for them to be otherwise."[68] It appears two Negroes did hold the priesthood in the early church, but the authority of their ordination is disputed by current Mormon historians.[69] Young's speech in 1859 reminded the church members that Negroes were not to hold the priesthood, and he later warned that practicing miscegenation meant death on the spot.[70]

Some of the prosouthern sentiment among Mormons could also be traced to the feeling that the South was experiencing the same injustices the Saints had suffered. One contemporary historian of the Mormon movement felt, "with the exception of the slavery question and the policy of secession, the South stood on the same ground that Utah had stood upon just previously."[71] Congressional rejection of Utah's application for statehood caused one delegate to remark, "I tell them that we show our loyalty by trying to get in [the

Union], while others are trying to get out, notwithstanding our grievances, which are far greater than any of the seceding states!"[72]

Failure to deal with the contradictions of slavery and equality represented only one of the two major philosophical problems in the Utah church. The other—Mormons' attempts to harmonize the political and the religious—destroyed Smith, engulfed western Illinois in flaming anti-Mormon hostility, and led to Lincoln's ordering of troops into Salt Lake City. Great ambivalence existed in Mormon scripture, allowing church leaders opportunities to find precedents for or against involvement in politics.[73] Joseph Smith wrote that the church's aim "is not just to mingle the religious influence with the civil government," yet Brigham Young contended "no man can draw a dividing line between the government of God and the government of the children of men."[74] Mormon teachings held that the American government and the Founding Fathers were instruments of God, and the Declaration of Independence as well as the laws of the land "were given them by the hand of the Lord."[75]

By 1844 Smith had formulated different thoughts on government, perhaps as a result of frequent federal unwillingness to aid the Saints. The executive, he decided, should be able to extend the Bill of Rights' protection to anyone at any time. When considered in conjunction with the insistence that a plurality of wives should be regarded as an aspect of religion, and hence constitutional, the prophet had now expanded the doctrine, in effect making the chief executive responsible for protecting polygamy!

Continuing modern-day revelation, a key theological tenet of Mormon religious thought, enabled the reigning church president to change any previous doctrine. Church leaders, enjoying inspiration and revelation from God in their religious affairs, carried those aspects into their secular work. Divine inspiration therefore transferred easily to political affairs. Smith and Young's acute utilization of this inherent power resulted in the development of a mobile, maneuverable political creature. Observers, mistakenly assuming the church operated on a typical democratic foundation, believed its actions represented "the will of the people," when actually the only will expressed was that of the current leader. Consequently, conflicting and vacillating policies on such issues as polygamy and slavery alienated many Americans who assumed the Mormons had individually thought out the inevitable sum of their practices and philosophies.

With equality as a byword, using a rigid system of leadership headed by the president, the Mormons "met the challenge of a materialistic and secular world view by incorporating much of it into their own theology."[76] That the secular view they incorporated did not fit did not seem to bother the Mormons.

As desires for unity and uniformity spilled over into the Mormon intellectual and economic life, their doctrinal scope widened to international bounds. In the "Proclamation of the 12 Apostles . . . [to the] People of all Nations," the Saints forwarded the proposition that events in their nature "are calculated to reduce all nations and creeds to *one political and religious standard*" (italics mine). The proclamation advised gentiles to cast in their lot with the Saints or become their enemy. It predicted a standardization of all jarring creeds and "political wranglings" through a unification of all peoples and nations. The edict proceeded to state Mormon aims more bluntly: "We will try and convert the nations into one solid union. [We] despise the principle that divides the nation into party and faction."[77]

One must come to conclusions about Mormon interaction with Lincoln which differ from Hubbard's. Clearly the words of the leaders were law. Lincoln recognized this, as evidenced by his direct appeal to Brigham Young to raise troops in 1862 rather than acting through Governor Fuller. The population of Salt Lake City did not change its opinion of Lincoln virtually overnight. Instead, Lincoln played on the vanity of one man—Brigham Young—and emerged with an adequate policy.

Hostile anti-Lincoln comments, such as those noted earlier, more than indicating an actual distrust of Lincoln, revealed internal contradictions in Mormon doctrines. Lincoln's attack on the South struck a blow for equality, yet it assailed the states' rights and popular sovereignty theories that supported the Saints' stand on plural marriages. His desire to save the Union encompassed the central Mormon aim of total unity and egalitarianism, yet the Saints feared the disunion, which, they felt, Lincoln's election would surely bring. Mormon sympathies lay with the South, yet they found aristocracy repulsive. Functioning as a theocracy, the church actively engaged in the politics of a democracy. No wonder Lincoln said, "let them alone." "They professed," one historian wrote, "to see no inconsistency in being loyal Mormons and loyal Americans at the same time."[78] They believed a sovereign Mormon state could remain in the Union, and they "wanted nothing more than to have a government and laws of their own choosing in their own state,"[79] a view Lincoln rejected when he repudiated popular sovereignty.

Unlike the Mormons, Lincoln easily reconciled the question of religious and political harmony, or at least felt comfortable with Thomas Jefferson's framework.[80] But his resolution of the problems of equality and consent seemed to require a great deal more effort.

Lincoln worked from the "ought" to the "is," meaning he began with what a government ought to be and proceeded to determine what equality is. Harry Jaffa, whose analysis of Lincoln's political thought appears to be the most accurate, noted Lincoln did not view free government as a process, nor was it merely a government of, by, and for the people. Instead, free government meant "a government of, by, and for the people dedicated to a certain proposition."[81] The proposition Lincoln envisioned, equality, required an individual sense of obligation, or consent, which balanced the abstract absurdities of egalitarianism.

Lincoln's affinity for Aristotelianism, which Jaffa detailed, led him to reject egalitarianism. While the Negro had the right to eat the food earned by his own labor, certainly he did not have the right to eat more than he earned, and the Negro could not logically be expected to earn more than the white man. Lincoln's understanding of equality, then, was proportional, or "distributive justice."[82]

The Declaration of Independence served as the foundation for Lincoln's views on equality even more than the Constitution. He read the intentions of the authors as perspicaciously as he read the document itself. At Springfield, he said, "I think the authors of that notable instrument intended to include all men, but they did not intend to declare all men equal *in all respects*."[83] Lincoln did believe, however, that the Founding Fathers declared the *right* "so that enforcement of it might follow."[84] Jaffa contended that Lincoln transcended the original meaning of the Declaration without destroying it, thereby preserving Lockean-Jeffersonian demands. This transcendence Jaffa called an "affirmation of what [government] *ought* to be" (italics mine).[85] In the Ottawa speech, Lincoln proposed no introduction of political or social equality for blacks. He noted the black man was not his equal—"certainly not in color, *perhaps* not in moral or intellectual endowment" (italics mine).[86] By leaving this door ajar, Lincoln could admit to the Negro's moral equality at some future date, indicating a willingness to accept egalitarianism.[87] It is at this point one must part company with Jaffa; while he acknowledges Lincoln's departure from Aristotelian thinking, he later ignores this trend to a great degree.

Because Lincoln realized he was dealing not only with the equality of black men but of white men, he proceeded thoughtfully and cautiously. Yet, in spite of his pessimism about the feasibility of an interracial egalitarian society, Lincoln's plan to secure political rights for qualified Negroes indicated he was on the road to just such a society. Current court rulings indicate the extent to which this society has traveled on that road, and the discovery has been that "thoroughgoing egalitarianism does not end."[88]

Mormons continue to be plagued by their contradictions on equality. Lincoln, at least in his own mind, reconciled the antinomies of equality and consent, "thereby rescuing the egalitarianism ideal as well as the Union."[89] One could conclude, however, that equality and consent are qualities which cannot be balanced. While the Mormons could claim God as the authority for their inconsistent thought, Lincoln could only claim the Declaration. The source of the Mormons' authority was certainly sufficient, but one wonders if their claim to it was legitimate. Lincoln's claim to the Declaration was legitimate, but one wonders if the source was sufficient. It is the reconciliation of the authority of the former and the latter which troubles Americans to the present, and the possibility exists that the philosophical tools needed to properly arrange the two have long since been put in storage.

Notes

1. Alexis de Tocqueville, *Democracy in America*, 2 vols. (New York: Vintage, 1945). 2:101–2. For Tocqueville's observations on equality (which, in the context in which he uses the term, means egalitarianism), see 1:73–74, 99, 193, 264 n., 2:99, 113, 116–18, 147, 310–20. Equality, he believed, eventually would erode all bonds between individuals. Cecilia Kenyon suggested the boundlessness of such an idea could destroy all institutions, including the family. See "Alexander Hamilton: Rousseau of the Right," in Sidney Fine and Gerald S. Brown, eds., *The American Past*, 2nd ed., 2 vols. (New York: Macmillan, 1965), 1:227–40. The distinction between equality and egalitarianism is presented in Paul Eidelberg, *On the Silence of the Declaration of Independence* (Amherst: University of Massachusetts Press, 1976), 88–89.

2. George U. Hubbard, "Abraham Lincoln as Seen by the Mormons," *Utah Historical Quarterly* 31 (Spring 1963): 91–108. The antinomies of equality are discussed in Harry Jaffa, *Liberty and Equality* (New York: Oxford University Press, 1965), 128.

3. Robert J. Loewenberg, *Equality on the Oregon Frontier* (Seattle: University of Washington Press, 1976), 12; Leo Strauss, *Natural Right and History* (Chicago: University of Chicago Press, 1953), 19. For a complete discussion of natural right concepts in the ancient and modern worlds, see Strauss, *Natural Right*, 1–34 passim, and Loewenberg, chap. 3 passim. For a discussion of how the two views defined equality, see Leo Strauss, *City and Man* (Chicago: University of Chicago Press, 1953), chap. 1. Thomistic and Aristotelian concepts here are used somewhat interchangeably with the understanding the discussion refers only to their views on equality. Harry Jaffa, however, found a number of similarities in the two men and concluded Aristotle's moral doctrine served as a foundation for Thomas's natural law doctrine. See *Thomism and Aristotelianism* (Chicago: University of Chicago Press, 1952), 168.

4. Tocqueville, *Democracy in America*; see the citations in note 1. Harry Jaffa noted that in American politics "all disagreements have ultimately been disagreements concern-

ing the true import and meaning of equality." Only in America, he concluded, is the future of humanity "already committed . . . to the principle of equality" (*Liberty,* 128). Loewenberg's study details the resistance to equality by the Methodists. That resistance eventually crumbled, and the church "transposed the base of its values from theological to Enlightenment referents" (*Equality,* 232). This transposition, also made by the Mormons, results in a society that attempts "to reform itself on the model of its own doctrines" and is "condemned to oscillate perpetually between anarchism and collectivism" (Etienne Gilson, "Concerning Christian Philosophy," in *Philosophy and History,* ed. Raymond Klibansky and H. J. Paton [New York: Harper & Row, 1963], 68).

5. In Missouri, the Mormons received a county "of their own" but soon expanded into outlying districts. Proslavery elements in Missouri did not need additional northerners in the state, and Smith tried to pacify them by incorporating proslavery, antiblack doctrines in the theology. Mormon attempts to vote, as well as the rejection by Missourians of Smith's hastily conceived doctrines, led to a small war. Smith offered himself as a hostage in return for the safe departure by the Mormons from the state. Once the Saints had gone, a friendly jailer let Smith "escape." Fawn Brodie related the history of these events in *No Man Knows My History: The Life of Joseph Smith the Mormon Prophet,* 2nd ed. (New York: Alfred A. Knopf, 1970), 208–55. Nauvoo's growth is presented in Robert Flanders, *Nauvoo: Kingdom on the Mississippi* (Urbana: University of Illinois Press, 1965).

6. Roy P. Basler., ed., *The Collected Works of Abraham Lincoln,* 9 vols. (New Brunswick: Rutgers University Press, 1953), 1:206. The growth of Mormon political power is discussed in George Gayler, "The Mormons and Politics in Illinois, 1839–1844," *Journal of the Illinois State Historical Society* 69 (Spring 1956): 48–66.

7. Theodore C. Pease, ed., *Illinois Election Returns, 1814–1848* (Springfield: Illinois State History Library, 1923), 117–18; Flanders, *Nauvoo,* 217. Martin Van Buren lost Hancock County in the presidential election because of the Mormon vote. Thomas Ford suggested the Mormons reacted bitterly to their expulsion from Missouri by blaming the Democrats. See *History of Illinois from 1818 to 1847,* ed. Milo Milton Quaife (Chicago: R. R. Donnelly and Sons, 1946), cited by Gayler, "Mormons and Politics," 51 n.

8. Smith's version appears in *History of the Church,* 6 vols. (Salt Lake City: Deseret Book Co., 1964), 6:479–80.

9. *Nauvoo Times and Seasons,* January 1, 1841, quoted in Hubbard, "Abraham Lincoln," 94.

10. *Quincy Whig,* November 7, 1840, cited in Hubbard, "Abraham Lincoln," 93 n., and Gayler, "Mormons and Politics," 150 n.

11. *Nauvoo Times and Seasons,* January 1, 1841, cited in Hubbard, "Abraham Lincoln," 93–94. Democrats and Whigs unanimously approved the charter. Flanders, *Nauvoo,* 221–28; Ford, *History of Illinois,* 263.

12. Paul Simon, *Lincoln's Preparation for Greatness: The Illinois Legislative Years* (Norman: University of Oklahoma Press, 1965), 269.

13. Smith, *History of the Church,* 4:480.

14. Gayler, "Mormons and Politics," 53; Ford, *History of Illinois,* 2:67–69; Pease, *Illinois Election Returns,* 127.

15. William A. Linn, *The Story of the Mormons* (New York: Macmillan, 1902), 245.

16. Charlotte Haven, "A Girl's Letters from Nauvoo," *Overland Monthly,* December 1890, 636, quoted in Gayler, "Mormons and Politics," 56 n.

17. Smith, *History of the Church,* 5:289.

18. Linn, *Story of the Mormons,* 254–55; Brodie, *No Man,* chap. 25.

19. Joseph and his brother Hyrum Smith turned themselves in for trial. Held at Carthage jail, an angry mob of local militia shot them both to death. Brodie, *No Man*, chap. 27. Also see Dallin Oaks and Marvin Hill, *The Carthage Conspiracy* (Urbana: University of Illinois Press, 1975). Abraham Lincoln's cousin, Abram, served on the grand jury that indicted Smith's murderers. *Carthage Conspiracy*, 48. Abraham served two legislative terms with one of the indicted murderers, Mark Aldrich, ibid., 315. This was not the first time the Lincoln family had come in personal contact with Smith or his clan, as Mrs. Lincoln had been a spectator at one of the prophet's extradition hearings. Paul Angle, *Here I Have Lived* (New Brunswick, N.J.: Rutgers University Press, 1935), 126. Lincoln's secretary and biographer, John Hay, wrote an account of Smith's death for *Atlantic Monthly*, "The Mormon Prophet's Tragedy," 24 (1869): 669–789.

20. Basler, *Works of Abraham Lincoln*, 1:290–91.

21. Horace Greeley, *An Overland Journey* (Ann Arbor: Michigan University Microfilms, 1966), 228.

22. Richard D. Poll, "The Mormon Question Enters National Politics, 1850–1856," *Utah Historical Quarterly* 25 (April 1957): 2.

23. *Illinois State Journal*, Sept. 19, 1854, cited in Vern Bullough, "Polygamy and the Election of 1860," *Utah Historical Quarterly* 29 (April 1961): 119–26. Also see the *Journal* for Sept. 11, 26, 27, 29, 30, and Oct. 2, 9, 11, 16, 20, 23, 24, 27, 28, 31 illustrating the importance of polygamy as an issue.

24. On Douglas's views, see the *Illinois State Register* , April 11, 14, and 16, 1860, cited in Bullough, "Polygamy," 124–26; Brigham Roberts, *A Comprehensive History of the Church*, 6. vols. (Salt Lake City: Deseret News Press, 1930), 2:148–58

25. Basler, *Works of Abraham Lincoln*, 2:398–99.

26. Allan Nevins cited in Bullough, "Polygamy," 124.

27. *Illinois State Journal*, March 16, 1860, cited in ibid.

28. Basler, *Works of Abraham Lincoln*, 4:41–43, "Speech at Bloomington," April 10, 1860.

29. *Journal of Discourses* 1 (August 1, 1852): 54–56, Speech by Parley Pratt.

30. Smith prophesied, in one of his better efforts, the destruction of the Union. *Doctrine and Covenants* (Salt Lake City: Church of Jesus Christ of Latter-day Saints, 1958), sec. 87. One wonders how human beings could destroy that which God created and protected, as Mormons claim He created the Union.

31. John Cleland and Juanita Brooks, eds., *A Mormon Chronicle: The Diaries of John D. Lee*, 2 vols. (San Marino, Calif.: Huntington Library, 1955), 1:283.

32. William Knecht and Peter Crawley, eds., *History of Brigham Young, 1847–67* (Berkeley: Mass-Cal. Associates, 1964). The manuscript entry for October 9, 1861, reads, "Brigham Young has lost Uintah Valley—one of the most fertile in Utah, after having announced his intention to settle it with the Saints. The President, by an order dated October, has directed an Indian Reservation be made there."

33. *Deseret News*, March 6 and February 27, 1861.

34. *Journal of Discourses*, 9:4.

35. Ibid., 9:18.

36. Linn, *Story of the Mormons*, 543.

37. Hubbard, "Abraham Lincoln" 99. Lincoln's cautious message to Stanton is found in Basler, *Works of Abraham Lincoln*, 5:200, and the order to Young was reprinted in the *Deseret News*, April 20, 1862.

38. Lincoln's appointments are discussed in Harry J. Carman and Reinhard H. Luthin, *Lincoln and Patronage* (New York: Columbia University Press, 1942), 108, 108 n. Some general interpretations of the situation in the territories include Howard Lamar, "Political Patterns in New Mexico and Utah Territories, 1850–1900," *Utah Historical Quarterly* 28 (October 1960): 363–87; Earl S. Pomeroy, *The Territories and the United States, 1861–1890* (Philadelphia: University of Pennsylvania Press, 1947); Ray Colton, *The Civil War in the Western Territories* (Norman: University of Oklahoma Press, 1959) ; John P. Bloom, ed., *The American Territorial System* (Athens: Ohio University Press, 1973), 114–29. Also see Everett Cooley, "Carpetbag Rule: Territorial Government in Utah," *Utah Historical Quarterly* 26 (April 1958): 107–29; James R. Clark, "The Kingdom of God, the Council of Fifty, and the State of Deseret," *Utah Historical Quarterly* 26 (April 58): 131–51.

39. Colton, *Civil War,* 183–91. Lincoln forwarded his correspondence from Harding to Secretary of War Stanton approving the sending of some "paroled troops . . . to that territory." Basler, *Works of Abraham Lincoln,* 5:432.

40. *Deseret News,* October 22, 1862, and January 7, 1863. Lincoln did not enhance his image by signing the antibigamy bill in 1862.

41. *Deseret News,* January 14, 1863.

42. William Lee Knecht, "The Federal Judges of the Utah Territory from a Lawyer's Point of View," in Bloom, *American Territorial System,* 114–29, citation on 118 n. 39.

43. Pomeroy, *Territories and the United States,* 75. See W. H. Hooper to Lincoln, March 22, 1861, *State Appts. File Supra,* 7, cited in ibid., 75 n.

44. Knecht, "Federal Judges," 118 n. 39. One judge rendered a divorce against Young in a suit brought by one of his many wives.

45. Colton, *Civil War,* 185.

46. The Morrisites were anti-Mormons who had taken several Mormon hostages and held out in a fortified camp against territorial police in 1862. Ibid., 188–89.

47. Knecht, "Federal Judges," 117, 120.

48. Edward Tullidge, *History of Salt Lake City and Its Founders* (Salt Lake City: Star Publishing, 1886), 311.

49. Hubbard, "Abraham Lincoln," 102–3; Knecht, "Federal Judges," 127–28, Appendix.

50. Preston Nibley, *Brigham Young: The Man and His Work* (Salt Lake City: Deseret Book Co., 1960), 369.

51. Phillip A. M. Taylor, "Early Mormon Loyalty and the Leadership of Brigham Young," *Utah Historical Quarterly* 30 (Spring 1962): 103–32.

52. Ibid.

53. Brodie, *No Man,* 100.

54. *Journal of Discourses,* 12:228.

55. Taylor, "Early Mormon Loyalty," 115.

56. Ibid., 125.

57. Gayler, "Mormons and Politics," 65–66.

58. Joseph Smith, trans., *Book of Mormon* (Salt Lake City: Church of Jesus Christ of Latter-day Saints, 1961), Mosiah 29:32, 193.

59. Ibid., 29:38.

60. "Equality and Oneness of the Saints," *Seer II,* July 1854, 289–91, cited by Marvin Hill, *The Role of Christian Primitivism in the Mormon Kingdom, 1830–1844* (Chicago: University of Chicago Press, 1957), 128. Also see *Doctrine and Covenants,* sec. 78:5–6.

61. *Doctrine and Covenants* 51:3, 70:14, 82:17, 88:122. Compare this with the famous quotation from Marx, "From each according to his ability, to each according to his needs." John Bartlett, *Familiar Quotations*, ed. E. M. Beck, 14th ed. (Boston: Little, Brown & Co., 1968), 687a.

62. *Evening and Morning Star*, July 11, 1833, 218–21, cited in Brodie, *No Man*, 132.

63. Smith, *History of the Church*, 5:217.

64. *Book of Mormon*, Alma 27:8–9, 264.

65. Smith, *History of the Church*, 1:378–79.

66. *Messenger and Advocate II*, April 1836, 289, quoted in Dennis Lythgoe, "Negro Slavery and Mormon Doctrine," *Western Humanities Review* 21 (Autumn 1967): 327–38.

67. Ibid., 327, "Speech by Orson Hyde," 1851.

68. Greeley, *Overland Journey*, 211.

69. Dennis Lythgoe, "Negro Slavery in Utah," *Utah Historical Quarterly* 39 (1971): 333–35.

70. *Journal of Discourses* 7: 290–91, 10:110, 1859.

71. Linn, *Story of the Mormons*, 544.

72. Tullidge, *History of Salt Lake City*, 259.

73. *Book of Mormon*, Mosiah 29:25–32.

74. *Doctrine and Covenants* 134:4–9; Smith, *History of the Church*, 6:322.

75. *Book of Mormon*, Mosiah 29:24.

76. Hill, *Role of Christian Primitivism*, 156.

77. G. Homer Durham, "Political Interpretations of Mormon History," *Pacific Historical Review* 13 (June 1944): 136–50, 141. The proclamation apparently is kept under lock and key in Salt Lake City, with this article being the only reproduction of the statements contained therein.

78. Flanders, *Nauvoo*, 305.

79. Ibid.

80. Harry Jaffa, *Crisis of the House Divided* (New York: Doubleday, 1959), 242–45, chap. 10 passim, 331, 343, 345.

81. Ibid., 348.

82. Ibid., 307, chap. 17. Lincoln's references to egalitarianism are found in Basler, *Works of Abraham Lincoln*, 2:16, 3:255, 281–82. Other references to slavery and equality may be found in 2:408, 281–82, 500–501.

83. Jaffa, *Crisis*, 315. For Lincoln's Springfield speech, see Basler, *Works of Abraham Lincoln*, 2:405–6; for the Alton speech, ibid., 3:301.

84. Jaffa, *Crisis*, 316.

85. Ibid., 321.

86. Basler., *Collected Works*, 3:16. See Jaffa's notes on color differences, *Crisis*, 427 n. 16.

87. Jaffa, *Crisis*, 427; Loewenberg, *Equality*, 232.

88. The *Alan Bakke* case illustrates how ludicrous the "equality of opportunity" position has become. Justice Blackmun concluded, "in order to treat some persons equally, we must treat them differently," and "in order to get beyond racism, we must first take account of race." Quoted in Kenneth Tollett, "Controversy: More on the Bakke Decision," *Academe* 65 (February 1979): 53. The discussion, engaged by four distinguished scholars, reveals current academic attitudes toward equality. Consider also a lawsuit by Sears, Roebuck and Co. against the United States government in which Sears contended it could not possibly comply with Affirmative Action equal opportunity programs because they would eventually require that no one be denied a job for any reason. Steven Brill, "Sears

Suit Stumbles," *Esquire,* April 24, 1979, 13–14. Loewenberg refined Tocqueville's predictions: "In time each soul, standing totally free in a world of other totally free individuals, must turn to the state as the source of authority." Statism is what Tocqueville believed to be the promise of American life. The result is that "equality, a political principle, must ultimately create philosophical anarchy—a cosmological reduction of everything to everything else." Loewenberg, *Equality,* 231–32. Lynn Marshall noted this creeping egalitarianism present in the structural changes in the American party system, whereby rotation in office made men virtually interchangeable. "The Strange Stillbirth of the Whig Party," *American Historical Review* 72 (1967): 445–68.

89. Loewenberg, *Equality,* 230.

9 ➤ Lincoln and the Indians

David A. Nichols

The date was August 21, 1862. The news came at the worst possible moment in the war for the Union. Abraham Lincoln's armies were desperate for manpower, and it appeared that Lincoln might even have difficulty
defending Washington against Confederate attack. The telegram from the
governor of Minnesota read: "The Sioux Indians on our western border
have risen and are murdering men, women and children." Possibly five
hundred whites had died. When Gov. Alexander Ramsey demanded that
President Lincoln extend the draft deadline for Minnesota's quota of 5,360
men, Lincoln's response was harsh: "Attend to the Indians. If the draft can
not proceed, of course it *will* not proceed. Necessity knows no law. The
government cannot extend the time."[1]

Two arenas of conflict, the Indian Territory (later Oklahoma) and Minnesota, drew Lincoln directly into Indian affairs during his first two years
in office. When Lincoln entered office, he was understandably preoccupied
with the showdown with the Confederacy taking place in South Carolina.
There were those around him who argued that the Indian Territory, inhab-
ited by the "five civilized tribes," was strategically important. Held by the
North, it could be a base for attacks on Arkansas and Texas. Controlled by
the Confederacy, it could be employed to threaten Kansas.

However, Lincoln initially chose to abandon the Indian Territory, even
though his commissioner of Indian affairs, William P. Dole, dissented from
the move. Indian leaders protested to Lincoln that Confederate agents were
telling their people that "the Government represented by our Great Father at

From Gabor S. Boritt and Norman O. Furness, eds., *The Historian's Lincoln: Pseudohistory,
Psychohistory, and History* (Urbana: University of Illinois Press, 1988), 149–69.

Washington has turned against us."[2] The success of those southern agents, more than anything, probably persuaded Lincoln to reverse his decision. On November 22, 1861, the Confederacy organized the Indian Territory into a separate military department. Abandonment began to look like a blunder. On December 3, Lincoln informed the Congress, "The Indian country south of Kansas is in possession of the insurgents," and he noted press reports that the Confederates were organizing Indian troops. Lincoln communicated his new decision: "It is believed that upon repossession of the country by the federal forces the Indians will readily cease all hostile demonstrations, and resume their former relations to the government."[3]

Beyond Commissioner Dole, the man most responsible for persuading Lincoln to retake the Indian Territory was Senator James H. ("Bloody Jim") Lane of Kansas. Lane was a colorful, unscrupulous character whose tricolored brigade, composed of blacks, Indians, and drifters, was alleged to have plundered Unionist civilians as readily as they plundered Confederate civilians. Lane's great obsession was to lead an expedition designed to shorten the war by attacking the exposed flank of the Confederacy in Arkansas and Texas via the Indian Territory. But it was a flood of Indian refugees from the Indian Territory into Kansas that appears to have pushed Lincoln into approving a southern expedition. Kansans did not want hungry, dependent Indians in their midst. The refugee problem dovetailed with the need for troops to retake the Indian country from the Confederacy. In early December, the decision was made to receive 4,000 Indians into the army. They would receive pay and benefits equal to that of white troops.

Lincoln, with Dole's help, negotiated a bargain concerning the command of the so-called Lane Expedition. Lane would command the troops but be subject to the overall authority of Gen. David Hunter. Lincoln may have thought he could appease the politically popular senator, make military gains in the West, and still keep Lane's excesses under control. Hunter had no liking for Lincoln's arrangement, however. With Lane commanding the expedition, the general believed he would become a mere figurehead. Hunter angrily wrote Lincoln that he was "very deeply mortified, humiliated, insulted and disgraced." Lincoln replied that it was difficult to answer "so ugly a letter in good temper" and warned his old friend, "You are adopting the best possible way to ruin yourself."[4] However, the adjutant general confirmed Hunter's authority and that Lane would be subordinate to him: "If you deem it proper you may yourself command the expedition."[5]

Lincoln's bargain began to unravel. Commissioner Dole, on the scene, had assumed that Hunter would be content with a superior command but let Lane command the expedition. When Lane arrived in Kansas, he was shocked to read newspaper stories proclaiming that Hunter, not Lane, would command the "Lane Expedition." Accordingly, Jim Lane decided to sabotage the expedition project unless he could command it with a force of 30,000 men.

On January 31, 1862, Lincoln tried to break the Hunter-Lane deadlock and instructed the secretary of war: "It is my wish that the expedition commonly called the 'Lane Expedition' shall be as much as had been promised at the Adjutant-General's Office under the supervision of General McClellan and not any more. I have not intended and do not now intend that it shall be a great exhausting affair, but a snug, sober column of 10,000 or 15,000. General Lane has been told by me many times that he is under the command of General Hunter, and assented to it as often as told. It was the distinct agreement between him and me when I appointed him that he was to be under Hunter."[6]

Instead, the pressure increased. On February 6, the House of Representatives passed a resolution urging Lincoln to appoint Lane to head the expedition. Joseph Medill of the *Chicago Tribune* reminded Lincoln that 850,000 men in the West had voted for him in 1860, and they would not want Lane's expedition to fall through: "Mr. Lincoln, for God's sake and your country's sake rise to the realization of our awful national peril."[7] Furthermore, Lincoln's new secretary of war, Edwin Stanton, was reluctant to put Indians in the army. Secretary of the Interior Caleb Smith informed Commissioner Dole on February 6 that Lincoln was going to see Stanton "and settle it today."[8]

Weary of the whole business, on February 10 Lincoln told Hunter and Lane that he would give them one more chance to work things out: "My wish has been and is to avail the Government of the services of both General Hunter and General Lane, and, so far as possible, to personally oblige both. General Hunter is the senior officer and must command when they serve together; though in so far as he can, consistently with the public service and his own honor, oblige General Lane, he will also oblige me. If they cannot come to an amicable understanding, General Lane must report to General Hunter for duty, according to the rules, or decline the service."[9]

Lane tried again to persuade Hunter to let him command, but Hunter refused. An angry Lane left Kansas for Washington to resume his Senate seat. He is reported to have muttered all the way about the man in the White House being a "d——d liar, a demagogue, and a scoundrel." Lane believed that Lincoln was guilty of "leaving him before the public, in the light of a braggart, a fool and a humbug."[10] However, Lincoln had also decided to transfer David Hunter to the East. He ordered a reorganization that placed the Department of Mississippi, including Kansas, under Henry Halleck. The Indian expedition was canceled.

That "persistent fellow" Jim Lane then managed to convince Lincoln to restore the Department of Kansas and place Lane's man, Gen. James G. Blunt, in command. Once again, Lincoln reversed himself on the Indian expedition. One factor explaining the reversal was that Confederates demonstrated the utility of Indian troops against the Union during the Battle of Pea Ridge (Elkhorn Tavern) in Arkansas, March 6–8. A second factor was that the number of Indian refugees in Kansas had increased to 7,600 starving people.

The president ordered the commander of the Department of Mississippi to "detail two regiments to act in Indian country, with a view to open the way for friendly Indians who are not refugees in Southern Kansas to return to their homes." Five thousand Indians were to be armed and were to be "used only against Indians or in defense of their own territory and homes."[11] The new expedition was to be considerably less grand than Jim Lane's original scheme to turn the tide of the war for the Union, and he no longer wanted to command this meager force.

The expedition was launched on June 28, 1862, under the command of Col. William Weer. It included 2,000 whites and 3,000 Indians. Initially, the troops encountered little opposition. Unionist Indians, including Cherokee leader John Ross, welcomed Weer's forces. However, on July 18 white soldiers mutinied against Weer, and the expedition retreated to Kansas. A major reason for the mutiny seems to have been the resistance of white soldiers to serving with Indians. Once again the expedition was canceled. The situation of the refugees was worse than ever, and John Ross traveled to Washington in September 1862 to petition Lincoln for assistance. Two weeks after their first meeting, Lincoln wrote Ross that "a multitude of cares" had prevented him from a promised examination of the relationship of the government to the Cherokees. In October, Lincoln joined with Ross to inquire about the possibility of utilizing Indian troops already fighting the Confederacy to return the refugees to Indian country, but nothing was done.[12]

It was indeed a time of "a multitude of cares." In late 1862 Lincoln's army seemed in peril of losing the contest with the Confederacy. He had not yet identified competent military leadership for the Union army. Indian Office officials warned Lincoln that to return the Indian refugees to the Indian

Territory without military protection would only expose them to harm. For Lincoln, soldiers were scarce, and General Blunt's white troops were still reluctant to fight alongside Indians.

Lincoln eventually capitulated. John Ross went to see him again in the autumn of 1863. In May 1864, Jim Lane pushed a bill through Congress to remove the Indians from Kansas and in the process extinguished the title to lands belonging to native Kansas tribes that, the Kansas congressman openly admitted, "occupy central positions, holding large tracts of productive country in the very heart of our state." They called the removal "an act of justice to the Indians and the people of Kansas."[13]

In June 1864, 5,000 Indians were taken from Kansas to the Indian Territory where, because they arrived too late to plant crops, they endured even greater deprivation. Lincoln recognized their need as "so great and urgent" that he stretched the Constitution by authorizing $200,000 worth of clothing and food on credit and asked Congress to appropriate the money after the fact. Lincoln's indecisive policies toward the southern tribes were, by any measurement, unsuccessful. He failed to exploit any potential military advantage in the region, and the results for the Indian refugees were disastrous.

The Indian war in Minnesota broke out on August 17, 1862. Several white settlers were killed in an incident near Acton. The Sioux, fearing reprisal, launched a preventive war. This came at a time when the war with the South was going badly. Lincoln's army was short of manpower. He was discouraged with the bickering and ineptness of his generals. On August 29–30, the Union forces under Gen. John Pope were defeated at Second Bull Run. An outraged Pope was blaming his defeat on General McClellan.

In this context, the news of the Indian war had an electric effect. Governor Ramsey's insistence on delaying the draft linked together the two theaters of war. One report claimed, "Indians, from Minnesota to Pike's Peak, from Salt Lake to near Fort Kearney, [were] committing many depredations." Lincoln's own secretary, John G. Nicolay, was in Minnesota, and he reported, "We are in the midst of a most terrible exciting Indian war. Thus far the massacre of innocent white settlers has been fearful. A wild panic prevails in nearly one-half the state."[14]

Especially ominous was the possibility that the Indian attacks were part of a "deep-laid plan," a Confederate conspiracy to open a new front in the war with the Union. Interior Secretary Caleb Smith insisted months later, "I am satisfied the chief cause is to be found in the insurrection of the southern states." Lincoln himself spoke of his "suspicions" and reported to the Congress, "Information was received . . . that a simultaneous attack was to be made upon white settlements by all the tribes between the Mississippi River and the Rocky Mountains."[15]

It is in this context that Lincoln ordered Governor Ramsey to "attend to the Indians." At about that same time, Lincoln authorized the first official enlistment of blacks into the Union army. While the Indian war was not the central element in this decision, it may have influenced the timing of the orders to Gen. Rufus Saxton on August 25 to organize black soldiers. This came only three weeks after Lincoln had publicly declined to do so and two days after Senator Lane had been denied the same authority.

Governor Ramsey demanded a new military department in the Northwest. Halleck at first denied the request, but Lincoln overruled Halleck. The president intended to solve two problems with one stroke. Gen. John Pope was threatening McClellan over his failure to support Pope adequately at Second Bull Run. Lincoln needed to separate his quarrelsome generals, and the Indian war gave him some place to send Pope. Pope thought himself banished, but Stanton called the Indian war an "emergency" and assured Pope, "You cannot too highly estimate the importance of the duty now entrusted to you."[16]

By mid-September, General Pope arrived in Minnesota to join forces with Col. Henry Sibley. He immediately launched a campaign that would "utterly exterminate the Sioux." Pope claimed that 50,000 people were refugees and predicted that "the whole of Minnesota west of the Mississippi and the Territories of Dakota and Nebraska will be entirely depopulated." It would require "a large force and much time to prevent everybody leaving the country, such is the condition of things."[17]

Then in early October, General Pope informed the government that "the Sioux War may be considered at an end." The extent of the Indian war had been grossly overestimated. However, the war was not over for Lincoln. Pope's communications revealed a new problem: "We have about 1,500 prisoners—men, women, and children—and many are coming each day to deliver themselves up." Pope continued: "Many are being tried by military commission for being connected in late horrible outrages and will be executed." That phrase, "will be executed," meant that Abraham Lincoln would be confronted with a wrenching decision about whether to sanction the largest mass execution in American history.[18]

On October 14, Stanton read Pope's report aloud to Lincoln and an uncomfortable cabinet. Gideon Welles called the report "discreditable" and perceived ulterior motives: "The Winnebagoes have good land which white men want and mean to have." Lincoln moved immediately to prevent any wanton slaughter. He dispatched John P. Usher to the scene and asked Episcopal bishop Henry Whipple to assist him. On October 17, Pope informed Sibley that "the President directs that no executions be made without his sanction"[19]

On November 8, Sibley transmitted to the government a list of 303 Sioux men whom he had sentenced to death. Two days later, Lincoln wired Pope: "Please forward, as soon as possible, the full and complete record of these convictions." He instructed Pope to include any materials that might discriminate as to the most guilty and "a careful statement" concerning the verdicts. Pope's response was anything but "careful." "The only distinction between the culprits is to which of them murdered most people or violated most young girls," the general replied, and he warned Lincoln of mob action: "The people of this State . . . are exasperated to the last degree, and if the guilty are not all executed I think it nearly impossible to prevent the indiscriminate massacre of all the Indians—old men, women and children."[20]

Despite this testimony, Lincoln and his lawyers were disturbed at what they found in the trial records. The trials had become progressively shorter as they went forward, averaging only ten to fifteen minutes per case. The lack of evidence was alarming. Lawyers labored over the records for a month, trying to make distinctions. Even then, the lack of solid evidence of guilt haunted Lincoln.

Meanwhile the advocates for and against the executions crowded into the White House. Governor Ramsey offered Lincoln a way to evade responsibility: "If you prefer it turn them over to me & I will order their execution." In Lincoln's annual message, he sidestepped the issue. "The State of Minnesota has suffered great injury from this Indian War," he reported, mentioning the number killed and the alleged atrocities. Lincoln took note of the desire of Minnesotans to remove the Indians from the state, although he made no clear recommendation. Lincoln even raised "for your especial consideration" the idea of remodeling the Indian system. But he said not one word about the proposed executions.[21]

Lincoln was apparently still trying to decide what to do. On December 1, the date of his annual message, he sought advice from the judge advocate: "I wish your legal opinion whether if I should conclude to execute only a part of them, I must myself designate which or could I leave the designation to some officer on the ground." Lincoln's use of the word "designate" is significant. After a month of studying the trial records, Lincoln's lawyers apparently could not decide who merited execution. Perhaps Lincoln was tempted by Ramsey's proposal to shift the responsibility. However, Judge Joseph Holt gave him no option: "The power cannot be delegated."[22]

Lincoln, despite the lack of clear evidence, had concluded that a blood sacrifice was imperative but not on the scale sought by the Minnesotans. Welles noted in his diary: "The members of Congress from Minnesota are urging the President vehemently to give his assent to the execution of three hundred Indian captives, but they will not succeed." Lincoln had decided to execute only thirty-nine of the prisoners.[23]

The Minnesotans desperately tried to reverse the decision. Sen. Morton Wilkinson recited the details of rape and murder to the Senate. Sibley reported that citizens had attempted to attack the prisoners being held at Mankato. Lincoln was bombarded with warnings of mob action. However, once decided, Lincoln never wavered. When the Senate, at Wilkinson's instigation, demanded an explanation, Lincoln responded that he had listened to various opinions, sent for the trial records, and had them studied carefully. The president had walked a careful line between the poles of opinion: "Anxious to not act with so much clemency as to encourage another outbreak on one hand, nor with so much severity as to be real cruelty on the other, I ordered a careful examination of the records of the trials to be made, in view of first ordering the execution of such as had been proved guilty of violating females." In that statement, Lincoln tried to appease almost everyone. He had found only two Indians guilty of rape and had further attempted to distinguish those who had participated in "massacres" from those who had taken part in "battles."[24]

Lincoln remained personally involved. He had Nicolay caution General Sibley concerning one prisoner whose name was similar to another: "The President desires to guard against his being executed by mistake before his case shall be finally determined."[25] Before the year ended, thirty-eight men were hanged. A large crowd was present, but there was no violence. Evidence later indicated that, despite Lincoln's cautions, one prisoner was executed by mistake.

Lincoln's actions had a price. He reduced the execution list, but he struck a bargain with the Minnesotans that gave them much of what they wanted otherwise. Lincoln agreed to continued incarceration for the Indians not executed. The government paid the cost of the war, around $350,000, and compensated Minnesotans for damages, claims for which eventually exceeded $1.3 million. Lincoln appointed John P. Usher as his new secretary of the interior, an appointment sought by the Minnesotans because they believed that Usher sympathized with their plans for Indians. Finally, Lincoln acquiesced in the removal of both the Sioux and the Winnebagoes, the latter of which had nothing to do with the Indian war.

Lincoln traded lives for land and money. He also permitted a series of military missions during 1863–66 throughout the region. The military claimed that 8,000 to 10,000 Indians were driven out of Minnesota. Sibley boasted that "the Indians have been badly beaten, demoralized, and have sent me messages desiring peace on any terms." Lincoln, with his enormous burdens in the conflict with the South, wanted to forget the whole Minnesota affair, just as he had tended to do with the refugees in Kansas. In March 1863 Alexander Ramsey asked Lincoln about the Indian prisoners he had not hanged and reported that Lincoln "said it was a disagreeable subject but he would take it up and dispose of it."[26]

There were still 329 prisoners at Mankato, including 49 who had been acquitted in the trials but for unknown reasons had never been released. Sibley pressured Lincoln to execute 50 more, but Lincoln refused. However, he agreed to move the prisoners to Davenport, Iowa. Eventually, in response to pleas from missionaries, Lincoln pardoned 26 more men. Symptomatic of his problems with subordinates, Lincoln ordered the release of one prisoner, Big Eagle, and discovered weeks later that his order had been ignored: "Let the Indian Big Eagle be discharged. I ordered this some time ago."[27]

Lincoln never released the rest of the prisoners. The prison conditions were so unhealthy that between the executions in December 1862 and April 1864, an estimated 67 additional men died—nearly twice the number who perished on the gallows. And the prisoners were only part of the residual problem. Sibley still had 1,600 Indians, mostly women and children, in custody. Disease and starvation afflicted them. In 1863, the Sioux and Winnebagoes were removed to the Dakota Territory. Both tribes arrived too late to plant crops and found themselves in miserable conditions. Meanwhile, in Minnesota, Commissioner Dole granted Sen. Morton Wilkinson's request that the Sioux reservation be opened for settlement.

Following the 1864 election, Sen. Alexander Ramsey visited the White House and talked politics with Lincoln. The president noted that he carried Minnesota by only 7,000 votes, compared to 10,000 in 1860. Ramsey responded "that if he had hung more Indians, we should have given him his old majority." Lincoln failed to appreciate the humor of the remark. "I could not afford to hang men for votes," he said.[28]

The events in the Indian Territory and Minnesota converged in late 1862. The Indian expedition fell apart in July, and John Ross visited Lincoln in September. The Minnesota war began in late August, and by mid-October the executions were an explosive issue. Meanwhile, Lincoln had to both wrestle with the lack of success of the Union armies and find a way to emancipate the slaves.

The times pushed Lincoln more toward reformers of all kinds, both the abolitionists and those who sought to reform the "Indian system." Indeed, some of them were the same people. The reformers argued that crises like the Minnesota Indian war derived directly from the abuses of the Indian system. By the time Lincoln reached office, this structure had become a system of institutionalized corruption, deeply entrenched in the political and economic interests of ambitious men in the West. The system originated in the practice of making treaties with the tribes. Treaties were almost always negotiated as a means of removing Indians from lands that whites wished to occupy, usually following armed conflict. Removal opened valuable land for speculation and settlement.

Beyond that, the treaties usually provided government annuities for the tribes, in compensation for the land. The Indian system then revolved around the strategies that whites developed for tapping these government monies. Citizens could file claims for alleged Indian depredations. Contractors provided goods and services for newly removed, heavily dependent Indian tribes. Licensed traders on the reservations provided retail outlets for the goods, the costs of which were charged to annuities.

At the center of all this was the Indian agent. All Indian officials, including agents, were political appointees. Claims, contracts, and traders' licenses needed the agent's approval. As one Minnesotan claimed, "It is believed that the trader is, in all cases, a partner of the Agent. He is usually a near relative."[29] Agents could, through kickbacks and partnerships, become wealthy men themselves.

Corruption stories abounded. In Oregon, an 1859 report charged that one agent, on a $1,000 per year salary, retired after two years with $17,000. Another accumulated $41,000 in three years. An investigator in Minnesota charged that a superintendent had spent $100,000 to $200,000 on a $2,000 salary. Agent Walter Burleigh in Dakota Territory was accused of using government funds to transport his own goods, hiring his daughter to teach at a nonexistent school, buying farm implements that no one could locate, and hiring men to work at half the price he reported to the government. Another agent allegedly stole $870,000 in bonds out of a safe in the Interior Department.

Men like Ramsey and Sibley made the Indian system a pathway to political power. Sibley represented the traders at the Sioux treaty negotiations in 1851. That treaty granted the Santee Sioux $475,000, but Sibley put in a claim for $145,000 for *overpayments* to the Sioux for furs. That claim was approved by Indian agent Ramsey. Sibley became Minnesota's first governor in 1858. His successor was Ramsey.

Congress was central to the system. While the president appointed Indian officials, these appointments were nearly always made on the recommendation of congressmen, who themselves often got in on the spoils. Sen. Samuel C. Pomeroy of Kansas obtained 90,000 acres of Pottawatomie land after helping to negotiate a treaty with those Indians. He got 50,000 acres of Kickapoo land in similar fashion.

Sometimes the charges of corruption went high in the Lincoln administration. Commissioner Dole was frequently accused of profiting from his post. The insensitivity of the system to conflicts of interest was symbolized by the sale of Sac and Fox trust lands in 1864. Tracts of land were purchased by Commissioner Dole, Secretary of the Interior Usher, Comptroller of the Currency Hugh McCulloch, and John G. Nicolay, Lincoln's personal secretary.

The corruption reached into the presidential office in other ways, although Lincoln himself had not profited. John Hay jokingly wrote Nicolay in Minnesota, just prior to the Indian war, to steal some moccasins for him from a vulnerable Indian maiden: "The Tycoon [Lincoln] has just received a pair gorgeously quilled, from an Indian agent who is accused of stealing. He put them on and grinned. Will he remember them on the day when Caleb [Smith] proposes another to fill the peculating donor's office? I fear not, my boy, I fear not."[30]

Special Agent Augustus Wattles reported to the Indian commissioner what Clear Sky, an elderly Chippewa chief, had said about the impact of the Indian system on his people: "Dam rascal plenty here. He steal him horse. He steal him timber. He steal him every thing. He make him good business. Many agents come here. Sometimes good. Sometimes bad. Most bad. The agent say, you must not do so. The next one come, he say you do very foolish. The Government not want you to do so. Agent much dam rascal. Indian much dam fool." Bishop Henry Whipple of Minnesota described the system's impact more starkly: "It commences in discontent and ends in blood."[31]

It ended "in blood" in Minnesota in 1862. That war and the projected executions gave reformers a platform on which to push for reform of the Indian system. Lincoln's subordinates preferred the policy of concentration, which had begun in the 1850s. Commissioner Dole enthusiastically coupled his desire "to foster and protect our own settlements" with "the concentration of the Indians upon ample reservations."[32] Concentration was an updated removal policy, the logical next step when the continent no longer had uninhabited regions in the West. Concentration was really a form of racial segregation, justified to protect the Indians and make way for the advance of civilization. Concentration also, like earlier forms of removal, was the activator of the Indian system's money machine. Many reformers accepted concentration as inevitable, but they viewed it as an intermediate step toward the assimilation of the Indian into American life. Indian haters tended to view concentration as a step toward extinction.

Henry Benjamin Whipple, Episcopal bishop for Minnesota, was the man with the most coherent reform program and the reformer who most influenced Lincoln. During Lincoln's first two years in office, Whipple made several attempts to move Indian officials toward reform, all without success. On March 6, 1862, he wrote directly to Lincoln. Whipple avoided blaming Indian problems on persons with evil intent. He identified the Indian system, with its "dishonest servants, ill conceived plans, and defective instructions," as the primary cause of the degradation of the natives. Indians were degraded because the treaty system destroyed tribal governments and left their people without protection.[33]

The root of the problem was the patronage system for selecting agents and other officials. "The first thing needed is honesty," the bishop told the president. Select agents on merit and not politics. Make Indians wards of the government and help them build homes, begin farming, and adopt "civilized" life. "The Indian must have a home," the bishop contended. "He must be furnished with seed, implements of husbandry and taught to live by the sweat of his brow. The government now gives him beads, paint, blankets and scalping-knives, teaching him to idle away his time, waiting for an annuity of money he does not know how to spend." Whipple proposed paying annuities in goods, not cash, thereby cutting traders out of the money flow.

Bishop Whipple urged Lincoln to appoint a special commission to investigate and recommend further reforms. These commissioners should be "men of inflexible integrity, of large heart, of clear head, of strong will, who fear God and love man." In short, they should be "above the reach of political demagogues." Whipple's proposal to depoliticize the system was made to a lifelong politician who, in perfunctory manner, referred the bishop's letter to the "special attention of the Secretary of the Interior," one of the system's political appointees. Caleb Smith wrote Whipple a long letter, but Lincoln said nothing more.[34]

Whipple went to see Lincoln just after the Minnesota war had begun, taking his cousin, General-in-Chief Henry Halleck, along for support. Whipple made his whole case to the president—the corruption of agents and the traders, the lack of governmental protection, and examples of how corruption had led directly to bloody war. Whipple believed that Lincoln "was deeply moved." Lincoln later told a friend that Bishop Whipple "came here the other day and talked with me about the rascality of this Indian business until I felt it down to my boots."

The president's response to Whipple was one of those famous Lincoln stories: "Bishop, a man thought that monkeys could pick cotton better than negroes could because they were quicker and their fingers smaller. He turned a lot of them into his cotton field, but he found that it took two overseers to watch one monkey. It needs more than one honest man to watch one Indian agent." The story was a curious one. Did it imply agreement with Whipple, or was it a way of putting him off? Whipple obviously believed that Lincoln made a commitment, hedged with two significant "ifs." Lincoln said, "If we get through this war, and I live, *this Indian system shall be reformed.*"[35]

In his 1862 annual message, even as Lincoln struggled with the issue of the executions, he asked Congress to reform the Indian system. "Many wise and good men have impressed me with the belief that this can be profitably done," he said. Lincoln urged the Congress to give the matter its "especial consideration." It appeared that Bishop Whipple had achieved a great triumph. However, the ambiguity of Lincoln's proposal was troubling. It failed even to mention the cornerstone of Whipple's program, the depoliticization of the system. Lincoln did not risk offending the congressmen who controlled the patronage. Both Secretary Smith and Commissioner Dole joined in the reform chorus, but they, like Lincoln, said nothing about changing the mode of selecting Indian officials.[36]

While the reformers rejoiced, the omission in Lincoln's recommendation had not escaped Bishop Whipple's scrutiny. Whipple wrote the politician in the White House: "Will you not see that the commission is made up of better stuff than politicians." Whipple again enlisted Halleck's aid. "You have his ear," he wrote, referring to the president. "Do, for the sake of the poor victims of a nation's wrong, ask him to put on it something better than politicians."[37]

The euphoria did not last long. The executions were over and the Minnesota crisis faded from Lincoln's attention. Sen. Henry Rice summarized the situation: "The do nothing policy here is complete." As the months passed, Bishop Whipple's despair grew. "I tremble for my country," he wrote Commissioner Dole, "when I remember that God will compel us to reap what we sow. There is a reason why every advance of civilization is marked with blood."[38]

Lincoln maintained a verbal commitment to reform. In his 1863 annual message, he again called on Congress to reform the Indian system, proclaiming the "urgent need for immediate legislative action." Lincoln's outlook was paternalistic: "Sound policy and our imperative duty to these wards of the Government demand our anxious and constant attention to their material well-being, to their progress in the arts of civilization, and, above all, to that moral training which, under the blessing of divine Providence, will confer upon them the elevated and sanctifying influences, the hopes and consolations of the Christian faith." These words were the skeleton at the feast. More significant, Lincoln's kind words for Indians directly followed sentences expressing his pride concerning the removal of many tribes, "sundry treaties," and "extinguishing the possessory rights of the Indians to large and valuable tracts of land." Lincoln's administration had settled on an Indian policy. Commissioner Dole stated it plainly: "The plan of concentrating Indians and confining them to reservations may now be regarded as the fixed policy of the government."[39]

Bishop Whipple tried once again with Lincoln. He went to see the president in March of 1864, but Lincoln merely referred him to the chairman of the House Indian committee. John Beeson, an even more radical reformer, discussed Indian reform with Lincoln in late 1864, and the president told him "to rest assured that as soon as the pressing matters of this war is settled the Indians shall have my first care and I will not rest until Justice is done their and your Sattisfaction [sic]." Whipple could not wait. In 1864 he supported George B. McClellan for president.[40]

Meanwhile, in the wake of military success in the war against the South, Lincoln's Indian concentration policy drifted toward militarism. Secretary Usher was clear in his statement: "This department will make provision for such Indians as will submit to its authority and locate upon the reservation. Those who resist should be pursued by the military and punished." This was the harsh policy of a government at war.[41]

Abraham Lincoln was the indirect author of this policy. His determination to develop the resources of the West was linked in his mind to winning the war for the Union. Therefore, he was exultant that "the steady expansion of population, improvement, and governmental institutions over the new and unoccupied portions of the country has scarcely been checked, much less impeded or destroyed by our great civil war." Lincoln noted that "Indian hostilities" had only temporarily obstructed the formation of new governments in the West.[42]

The very order of topics in Lincoln's annual message of 1864 reflected his priorities—new territories, railroads, minerals, and finally Indians. While he spoke of "the welfare of the Indians," his first concern for the West was "to render it secure for the advancing settler." For Lincoln, that expansion was connected with the resources for winning the Civil War because "the national resources . . . are unexhausted, and as we believe, inexhaustible."[43] In this context, Indians were increasingly treated as a military problem.

Indian Office officials became increasingly uneasy about military control of the Indians. Their worst fears were realized when the operations in New Mexico and Colorado generated public scandal even as the Civil War was coming to a close. In New Mexico, Gen. James Carleton's concentration operations resulted in 7,500 starving captives and excessive costs. In Colorado, Gov. John Evans and Col. John M. Chivington launched a campaign that culminated in the Sand Creek Massacre, which killed 150 Indians, mostly women and children. The scandal over Sand Creek resulted in a congressional investigation, which produced a report in 1867 outlining a "peace policy" that was implemented in the Grant administration.

Was Lincoln's proposal in 1862 to reform the Indian system genuine or mere rhetoric? Was Lincoln a reformer? It is significant that Lincoln never directly endorsed the reformers' proposal to depoliticize the system. On the other hand, he could have chosen to say nothing about reform. His proposal gave legitimacy and exposure to reform ideas that eventually culminated in the "peace policy." As in his relationship with the abolitionists, Lincoln was more cautious than the reformers, but he was pushed in their direction by events and his own sympathies. If he was not a radical on Indian policy, he was clearly more reformist than most of the congressmen who, in reality, controlled the Indian' system through their committees. Without their help, there was little he could do.

The reform movement was doomed. The national commitment to economic development of the West, which Lincoln certainly shared, bound economic self-interest to the war effort and made Indian welfare a low priority. The war for the Union consumed too much of everyone's energies, including Lincoln's, Nevertheless, if Lincoln had lived, there is reason to believe that he would have supported the reform proposals of 1867 and tried to fulfill his pledge to Bishop Whipple: *"This Indian system shall be reformed."*

While Lincoln was a cautious reformer, that does not completely answer the question as to whether his Indian policies support his traditional image as a humanitarian. One might point to what happened to Indian people following Lincoln's interventions in both Kansas and Minnesota. While his attention was elsewhere, the Kansas refugees suffered. Lincoln's armies killed more Indians than he pardoned in Minnesota. While he pardoned a large number, he still executed thirty-eight men on superficial evidence and permitted even more to die in miserable prison conditions and under forced removal.

Nevertheless, Bishop Whipple's humanitarian pleas struck a responsive chord with Lincoln, leading to his reform proposal. The executions commanded his attention during one of the most burdensome times of his presidency. Considering his other responsibilities, it is remarkable how involved he became. Lincoln could have chosen to do nothing. There is little question that all 303 Sioux men would have died without his intervention. The remaining Indians would have fared no better. Given the circumstances, it is difficult to imagine any other president doing more.

Lincoln was clearly more humanitarian toward Indians than most of the main military and political figures of his time. He could not do it all himself. He could not reform a chaotic and brutal system without help from Congress. He could not single-handedly enforce humane treatment in Kansas or Minnesota. He could not, given the burdens of the Civil War, give these matters his full attention all of the time.

Despite his humanitarian inclinations, Lincoln's basic attitudes should be viewed in context. Most Americans of the Lincoln era, including the reformers, viewed Indians as degraded savages. Reformers blamed the degradation on the Indian system, whereas the anti-Indian forces ascribed the degradation to the Indian race itself. However, they shared many assumptions. Both believed that Indians must assimilate and learn to farm like white people or perish. Sen. James Doolittle, chairman of the Senate Indian Committee, argued that Indians were "a dying race . . . giving place to another race with a higher civilization. It is dying through natural causes growing out of its contact with a superior race inhabiting the same country. . . . And the warfare when once begun between civilized and savage life becomes an eternal and irrepressible conflict which, in the very nature of things, will only cease when the savage life ceases." This was the "irrepressible conflict" of the Indian civil war, sanctioned by God, who "in his providence is giving this continent to a hundred millions of human beings of higher civilization, of greater energies, capable of developing themselves, and doing good to themselves and the world, and leading the advance guard of human and Christian civilization."[44]

Abraham Lincoln shared most of these attitudes. In the spring of 1863, Lincoln met leaders from several tribes in the East Room of the White House. He spoke to them of the "great difference between this pale-faced people and their red brethren both as to numbers and the way in which they live. The pale-faced people are numerous and prosperous because they cultivate the earth, produce bread, and depend upon the products of the earth rather than wild game for a subsistence. This is the chief reason of the difference; but there is another. Although we are now engaged in a great war between one another, we are not, as a race, so much disposed to fight and kill one another as our red brethren."[45] In three sentences, Lincoln linked the nonfarming hunter-savage with the innately violent barbarian. Considering the bloodiness of the white Civil War in 1863, this was a remarkably ethnocentric statement. If Lincoln's prejudices were never as virulent as was common to America, he was not a social equalitarian either. He always remained a politician, forever in the middle of public opinion. Even his proposal to reform the Indian system avoided the delicate question of ending political appointments, knowing how that would upset congressmen who profited from the patronage. Lincoln managed to keep the Minnesota Republican leaders on his reelection team, despite refusing to do all they wished. If good politics is leadership toward the possible, Lincoln measures up rather well. Not much was possible, given the circumstances. Nevertheless, Lincoln recommended reform, saved lives, *and* got reelected. A man who would not "hang men for votes," he still corralled the votes he needed to govern.

Indian affairs also show up the hard side of Lincoln's nature, a side that bordered on militarism. This toughness was evident in his adamant refusal to let the South go, even if he had to use force to make his view prevail. It also surfaced in his message to Governor Ramsey in Minnesota to "attend to the Indians." The Lincoln who believed that "necessity knows no law" was the same man who, in the war with the South, threw out one general after another until he found one, in Ulysses S. Grant, willing to shed enough blood to get the job done. This Lincoln, for all his caution and political manipulations, was obsessed with a goal and would use violence to resolve problems when Indians, or anyone else, forcibly got in the way of his highest priorities.

Notes

1. Roy P. Basler, Marion Dolores Pratt, and Lloyd A. Dunlap, eds., *The Collected Works of Abraham Lincoln*, 9 vols. (New Brunswick, N.J.: Rutgers University Press, 1953–55), 5:396.

2. "Report of the Commissioner of Indian Affairs [1861]," *Senate Executive Document no. 1*, 37th Cong., 1st sess., 1861–62, ser. 1117, 651, in roll 59, microcopy 574, special file 201, Office of Indian Affairs, RG 75 , National Archives.

3. Basler et al., *Collected Works of Lincoln*, 5:46.

4. Hunter to Lincoln, Dec. 23, 1861, roll 30, Lincoln Papers, Library of Congress; Basler et al., *Collected Works of Lincoln*, 5:84–85.

5. *The War of the Rebellion: A Compilation of the Official Records of the Union and Confederate Armies* (Washington, D.C.: Government Printing Office, 1880–1901), 1 (pt. 8): 525 (hereafter cited as *Official Records*).

6. Basler et al., *Collected Works of Lincoln*, 5:115–16.

7. Resolution of the House of Representatives, Feb. 6, 1862, and Joseph Medill to Lincoln, Feb. 9, 1862, roll 32, Lincoln Papers.

8. Caleb B. Smith to Dole, Feb. 6, 1862, roll 4, microcopy 606, Letters Sent, Indian Division, Office of the Secretary of the Interior, RG 48, National Archives.

9. Basler et al., *Collected Works of Lincoln*, 5:131.

10. Albert Castel, *A Frontier State at War: Kansas, 1861–1865* (Ithaca, N.Y.: Cornell University Press, 1958), 80–81.

11. Thomas to Halleck, Mar. 19, 1862, and Halleck to J. W. Denver, Apr. 5, 1862, *Official Records*, 1(pt. 8): 624, 665.

12. Lincoln to Ross, Sept. 25, 1862, roll 42, Lincoln Papers, Library of Congress; also in Basler et al., *Collected Works of Lincoln*, 5:439.

13. *Congressional Globe*, 38th Cong., 1st sess., Mar. 3, 1864, 921.

14. *Official Records*, 1(pt. 13): 592.

15. Ibid., 590; roll 4, microcopy 606, Letters Sent, Indian Division, Office of the Secretary of the Interior, RG 48, National Archives; Basler et al., *Collected Works of Lincoln*, 5: 526.

16. *Official Records*, 1(pt. 13): 617.

17. Ibid., 648–49, 685–86.

18. Ibid., 722, 724.

19. Gideon Welles, *The Diary of Gideon Welles*, ed. Howard K. Beale, 3 vols. (New York: W. W. Norton, 1960), 1:171 (entry for Oct. 14, 1862); Pope to Sibley, Oct. 17, 1862, roll 483, microcopy 619, Letters Received, Adjutant General's Office, RG 109, National Archives.

20. Basler et al., *Collected Works of Lincoln*, 5:493; *Official Records*, 1(pt. 13): 788.

21. Ramsey to Lincoln, Nov. 28, 1862, roll 44, Lincoln Papers; Basler et al., *Collected Works of Lincoln*, 5:525–26.

22. Basler et al., *Collected Works of Lincoln*, 5:537–38; Holt to Lincoln, Dec. 1, 1862, roll 44, Lincoln Papers.

23. Welles, *Diary*, 1:186.

24. Basler et al., *Collected Works of Lincoln*, 5:550–51.

25. John G. Nicolay to Sibley, Dec. 9, 1862, roll 96, Lincoln Papers.

26. Ramsey Diary, Mar. 25, 1863, roll 39, vol. 36, Alexander Ramsey Papers, Minnesota Historical Society, St. Paul.

27. Basler et al., *Collected Works of Lincoln*, 8:116.

28. Ramsey Diary, Nov. 23, 1864, roll 39, vol. 36, Ramsey Papers.

29. John J. Porter to Alexander Ramsey, Oct. 3, 1862, roll 20, M825, Letters Received, Indian Division, Office of the Secretary of the Interior, RG 48, National Archives.

30. Hay to Nicolay, July [?], 1862, in John Hay, *Lincoln and the Civil War in the Diaries and Letters of John Hay*, ed. Tyler Dennett (New York: Dodd, Mead, 1939).

31. Report of Special Agent Augustus Wattles to Indian Commissioner William P. Dole, June 26, 1861, roll 59, microcopy 574, special file 201, Office of Indian Affairs, RG 75, National Archives; Whipple to [Dole], Nov. 2, 1863, box 40, letterbook 4, Whipple Papers, Minnesota Historical Society, St. Paul. Wattles was sent by Dole to ascertain the condition of the tribes in the Central Superintendency. While his translation of Clear Sky (the translated name) is couched in stereotypical language employed by whites in that era, Wattles was regarded by his boss, the Indian commissioner, as a reasonably reputable reporter.

32. "Report of the Commissioner of Indian Affairs [1861]," *Senate Executive Document no. 1*, 37th Cong., 1st sess., 1861–62, ser. 1117, 647.

33. Whipple to Lincoln, Mar. 6, 1862, box 39, letterbook 3, Whipple Papers; also in Henry B. Whipple, *Lights and Shadows of a Long Episcopate* (New York: Macmillan Co., 1899), 510–14.

34. Basler et al., *Collected Works of Lincoln*, 5:173.

35. Henry B. Whipple, *Lights and Shadows of a Long Episcopate* (New York: Macmillan, 1899), 136–37.

36. Basler et al., *Collected Works of Lincoln*, 5:526–27.

37. Whipple to Lincoln, and Whipple to Henry Halleck, Dec. 4, 1862, box 40, letterbook 3, Whipple Papers.

38. Henry M. Rice to Whipple, Dec. 27, 1862, box 3; Whipple to Dole, Nov. 16, 1863, box 40, letterbook 3, Whipple Papers.

39. Basler et al., *Collected Works of Lincoln*, 7:47–48; *House Executive Document no. 1*, vol. 3, ser. 1182, 129–230.

40. Basler et al., *Collected Works of Lincoln*, 7: 275; Robert Mardock, *The Reformers and the American Indian* (Columbia: University of Missouri Press, 1971), 13; Whipple to George B. McClellan, Sept. 30, 1864, box 40, letterbook 5, Whipple Papers.

41. Annual Report, Secretary of the Interior, 1864, pp. 21–22, Appendixes to Congressional Globe, 38th Congress.

42. Lincoln's Annual Message, 1864, pp. 2–4, Appendixes to Congressional Globe, 38th Congress.

43. Basler et al., *Collected Works of Lincoln,* 8:136–53.

44. *Congressional Globe,* 38th Cong., 1st sess., June 10, 1864, pt. 3, 2873.

45. Basler et al., *Collected Works of Lincoln,* 6:151–52.

➤ Lincoln and the American West:
   A Bibliographical Essay and a Bibliography

➤ Contributors

➤ Acknowledgments

➤ Index

Lincoln and the American West:
A Bibliographical Essay and a Bibliography

The more than 15,000 books published about Abraham Lincoln and his major roles in American history have covered nearly every conceivable subject, person, or event associated with the sixteenth president. But only a handful of these volumes and very few essays deal with Lincoln's important and extensive connections with the trans-Mississippi West. Even though from the late 1840s onward—for nearly two decades—Lincoln was linked with western issues and westerners, biographers and historians have been slow to treat those ties. That means a significant part of Lincoln's manifold influences has been largely overlooked. This book is a modest attempt to remedy some of that oversight.

A few scholars have discussed Lincoln's western linkages, however. Their writings are discussed in this brief bibliographical essay, which has two purposes: to note the major books and essays treating Lincoln and the West; and to chart a few noticeable trends in this scholarship. I include full citations at the end of this essay for the sources discussed as well as other essays and books that touch on Lincoln and the West.

In the seventy years following Lincoln's nomination and election to the presidency in 1860–61, campaign biographers, memoirists, journalists, and popular historians rarely said much about Lincoln's connections with the West. Although nearly all full-length books dealt with the Mexican War, the Kansas-Nebraska controversies, the possible expansion of slavery into the territories, and congressional legislation impinging on the country beyond the Mississippi, most of the discussions were at best glancing and usually had a national rather than a regional focus. That meant readers encountered very little written about the connection between Lincoln and the West before the late 1920s.

Surprisingly, the most extensive biography to date of Lincoln, appearing at the end of the nineteenth century, contained limited information on his ties to the West. Written by two men who served as Lincoln's personal secretaries during his presidency, John G. Nicolay and John Hay, the ten-volume *Abraham Lincoln: A History* (1886, 1890) devotes well more than half of its gargantuan length to the military history of the Civil War. Although the first and second volumes provide a good deal of information on Bleeding Kansas, these and subsequent volumes contain very limited discussion of the Mexican War, nothing on Lincoln's western patronage appointments, and little on Lincoln's dealings with Indians or the Mormons. Only the president's ongoing political and military dilemmas in Missouri receive more than passing attention. This neglect of western topics is all the more inexplicable because Nicolay spent several weeks in the West during Lincoln's presidency examining western subjects the president asked him to review.

The nineteenth-century writer and journalist Noah Brooks of California dealt with western topics more than other authors. Perhaps Brooks's position as a Sacramento newspaperman and his friendship with the Lincoln family helped him to gather more on Lincoln's links with the West, especially for his book *Abraham Lincoln and the Downfall of American Slavery* (1888, 1894, 1904). Brooks not only dealt with pioneer influences on the young Lincoln but also discussed Lincoln's Illinois connections with Edward D. Baker and Anson G. Henry, who later sent him so much useful political information from California and the Oregon Country. Brooks's discussions of Lincoln's rejection of the Oregon governorship, California's role in the election of 1860, and the president's troubled relationships with Missouri are more extensive than those in other early accounts.

From the 1890s to the late 1920s, the emergence of the frontier school of American historians obviously influenced interpretations of Lincoln. The leader of the school, Frederick Jackson Turner, viewed Lincoln as the country's "greatest frontiersman," "the greatest American," who "represented more fully than any other American the ideals and achievements of the pioneer stock" (Jacobs, *Frederick Jackson Turner's Legacy*, 163, 141, 111). The West had thoroughly and positively shaped the character of Lincoln, "the very flower of frontier training and ideals" (Turner, *Frontier in American History*, 217). The leading U.S. historian of the early twentieth century, Turner put his mark on American historical writing from the 1890s onward, calling the historical profession as well as other lay historians and biographers to comprehend the shaping force of the West on American "traits." Turner was convinced that Lincoln stood out as the prime example of the molding power of the frontier West.

This optimistic view of Lincoln's frontier experiences surfaced in the writings of some of Turner's contemporaries. Perhaps the most popular writer about Lincoln of this era was Ida Tarbell, the noted muckraking journalist, biographer, and historian. Lincoln, she asserted, did not grow up a crude backwoodsman. Despite all the drawbacks in his social refinements, formal education, and cultural opportunities, she wrote in *The Life of Abraham Lincoln* (1900), he "developed a determination to make something out of himself, and a desire to know, which led him to neglect no opportunity to learn" (1:40). "There was nothing ignoble or mean in this Indiana pioneer life," Tarbell added. "If their lives lacked culture and refinements, they were rich in independence and self-reliance" (47). Here was a stimulating frontier West out of which a man like Abraham Lincoln could emerge.

Although they owed little to the Turnerian school of historiography, the Lincoln biographies by Carl Sandburg probably did more than the writings of any other author before 1940 to popularize the life and times of Abraham Lincoln. In the preface to his two-volume *Abraham Lincoln: The Prairie Years* (1926), Sandburg told readers that for thirty years he had been planning to "sketch the country lawyer and prairie politician who was intimate with the settlers of the Knox County neighborhood where I grew up as a boy" (1:viii). Sandburg chose to portray a folksy, human Lincoln attractive to general readers but less so to footnote-and-bibliography addicts. More questionable for some of his critics, Sandburg also created "conversational utterances . . . based word for word on sources [he] deemed authentic" (1:16). Poems, stories, and vignettes overflow on numerous pages. But not much appears on the trans-Mississippi West, although the discussion of the Mexican War extends beyond a few pages.

Nor does Sandburg provide much western information in his later four-volume study of Lincoln's presidency, *Abraham Lincoln: The War Years* (1936–37). In the more than 2,500 pages, we get a few paragraphs of Lincoln's support for congressional legislation influencing the West and his dealings with a conflicted Missouri, but almost nothing on Lincoln's western patronage. Sandburg does provide a capsule discussion of the president's controversial actions concerning the New Almaden mine in California and mentions the research of Milton H. Shutes as important for this discussion. Overall, though Sandburg's poetic, dramatic, and literary treatment of Lincoln revealed much of his own talents at depicting an epochal president, he did not use Lincoln's ties with the West to paint that portrait.

At the same time Sandburg was publishing his two-volume history of Lincoln's journey to the White House, former senator Albert J. Beveridge was also at work on an extensive biography of Lincoln. His four-volume *Abraham Lincoln, 1809–1858* (1928), which also appeared in a two-volume edition, carried Lincoln's life through November 1858 and provided the most thorough account of that period to date. Beveridge was an indefatigable researcher, a tireless reviser of his text, and an energetic pursuer of Lincoln scholars and collectors for new sources and obscure information. Although he was unable to gain access to the huge Lincoln collection in the hands of Robert Todd Lincoln, he made thorough use of the valuable William Herndon archive of oral histories and interviews, letters of reminiscence, and other important manuscript materials. Especially thorough was Beveridge's coverage of Lincoln's career in the U.S. Congress, including his opposition to the Mexican War. Beveridge was mistaken, however, in asserting that the Oregon governorship was "never offered" to Lincoln (2:196) in 1849 because he failed to locate that letter. The sections on the Kansas-Nebraska Act and the Kansas controversies that followed were equally extensive. Some critics thought Beveridge was too supportive of

Lincoln's rival Stephen A. Douglas and less enthusiastic about Lincoln than earlier biographers. Perhaps, but no scholar had published such a full portrait of the early Lincoln by 1930 as Beveridge had.

At the other end of the historiographical spectrum from Sandburg, and more akin to the work of Beveridge, was the scholarly, four-volume biography by James G. Randall, a longtime professor at the University of Illinois. Touted as the first well-researched, academic study of Lincoln's administration, Randall's *Lincoln the President* (1945–55) remains one of the towering achievements in the field—but it tells us little about Lincoln's links with the West. Early on, Randall's writing suggested that he might be attuned to the notion of Lincoln as a westerner: "If one takes a cue from Frederick Jackson Turner, Lincoln embodied the West when the West was the most characteristically American of the sections. From the great prairie environment he had drawn his strength" (1:49). Unhappily, that western emphasis rarely appeared again in Randall's numerous pages. He furnished background for the Oregon, Texas, Mexican War, and Bleeding Kansas subjects, but not much more. The same was true for Lincoln's involvements in congressional legislation dealing with the West in 1862. One subject that received thorough attention was Lincoln's clashes with the Radicals—or "Vindictives," as Randall termed them—which meant that muddled Missouri and its conflicts over slavery and Reconstruction were extensively discussed. But the ways in which these controversies played out in the rest of the West were not covered.

At the same time that Sandburg, Beveridge, and Randall were publishing their multivolume biographies, the first books devoted to Lincoln and his involvement in a single topic were appearing. On the whole, they were disappointing. Even though John W. Starr's *Lincoln and the Railroads* (1927) included coverage of Lincoln's dealings with railroads in the West and is still the only book on that topic, the volume was narrowly conceived and superficially researched. Sandburg, Beveridge, and Randall had proved how much a diligent researcher could turn up on a wide range of Lincoln topics, but Starr, less energetic in his searches, produced an inadequately researched volume. A decade and half later, Milton H. Shutes's *Lincoln and California* (1943) was similarly flawed. The subject was worthwhile—we still need a strong book on this subject—but Shutes seemed satisfied, primarily, to cobble together several of his previously published essays, add a bit of new information, and publish the resultant collection. When Shutes wrote early on that, despite going east to become president, Lincoln "remained a Westerner at heart and a Far Westerner in deep personal interest" (viii), one could hope for a searching, thorough study of those Lincoln-West connections. It did not come.

From the 1960s onward, several essays and a few books have been published with important findings about Lincoln's ties to the trans-Mississippi West. In addition, nearly all recent general overviews of Lincoln contain discussions of his opposition to the Mexican War and to Stephen A. Douglas's concept of popular sovereignty. In writings covering the presidential period of Lincoln's life, most treat his patronage appointments and his other political friends in the West. Other scholars discuss his involvements with the Pacific Railroad Act, the Homestead Act, and the Morrill Land Grant College Act. Still others comment on Lincoln's dealings with Indians, military affairs, slavery, and Reconstruction. Taken together, these publications of the past half-century have begun to fill in a few of the larger dimensions of Lincoln's western links. Much additional work remains to be done, however.

Historians early in the first decades of the twentieth century, following the lead of Albert J. Beveridge and others, concluded that Lincoln's criticism of President James K. Polk and the origins of the Mexican-American War greatly damaged his Whig political prospects in Illinois. But key essays by Gabor S. Boritt and Mark E. Neely Jr. in the 1970s have convincingly revised the previously negative interpretations, showing that most Whig newspapers and returning veterans did not roundly criticize Lincoln or leave the Whig Party because of his antiwar stance. Conversely, Donald W. Riddle, in *Congressman Abraham Lincoln* (1957), followed the earlier, less friendly view of Lincoln's stance on the Mexican-American War and was generally critical of what he considered the limitations of the Illinois congressman. Paul Findley, in his book *Lincoln: The Crucible of Congress* (1979), a less thorough work than Riddle's, is also much more sympathetic to Lincoln's views.

Meanwhile, research on the crucial decade of the 1850s has expanded notably in recent decades. Don E. Fehrenbacher's *Prelude to Greatness* (1962) remains the best overview of this period, but William C. Harris is particularly thorough and helpful on Lincoln's prepresidential years in *Lincoln's Rise to the Presidency* (2007), including strong sections on the controversies in Kansas and the Lincoln-Douglas debates. Allen C. Guelzo's *Lincoln and Douglas: The Debates That Defined America* (2008) is now the best overview of that subject. Also very helpful is the introduction in Harold Holzer's edited volume, *The Lincoln-Douglas Debates* (1993). For the Douglas side of the debates, as well as his pioneering efforts at developing the West (well before Lincoln began to look west), consult the definitive biography of Lincoln's competitor in Robert W. Johannsen's *Stephen A. Douglas* (1973).

No author has done much with Lincoln's short trips into the country west of the Mississippi, although Waldo W. Braden's brief essay "Lincoln's Western Travel, 1859" provides an introduction. One should also consult the abbreviated discussion in Harris's *Lincoln's Rise to the Presidency*. Unfortunately, Carol Dark Ayres's book *Lincoln and Kansas: Partnership for Freedom* (2001), although furnishing much essential information, is too uncritical and too inclined to quote without analyzing to be of large help.

Only one brief essay evaluates the findings of books and essays written about Lincoln's connections with the West during his presidency. In "The Pragmatic Lincoln: A Historiographical Assessment of His Western Policy" (1984), Samuel

E. Bell and James M. Smallwood, after examining publications dealing with Lincoln's western policies, conclude that he pursued a "pragmatic policy" that encouraged loyalty to the Union, adherence to the Republican Party, and acceptance of the Thirteenth Amendment. The authors reviewed publications published up through the 1970s.

A few collections of essays also deal with Lincoln's presidential links to the West. The most useful of these is Ralph Y. McGinnis and Calvin N. Smith's edited volume *Abraham Lincoln and the Western Territories* (1994). This collection of fifteen essays by eleven different authors, all nonspecialists in Lincoln studies, focus primarily on Lincoln's political dealings with western territories during his presidency. Most of the essays, regrettably, are narrowly and sometimes superficially researched, but the essays on Nebraska, Idaho, Dakota, and Indian Territory are worthy of further attention. Two other collections, edited by LeRoy H. Fischer, appeared first as special theme issues of the *Journal of the West*. "The Western States in the Civil War" (1975) and "The Western Territories in the Civil War" (1977), gathering essays written by graduate students, provide useful information on these two topics but not a great deal on Abraham Lincoln.

Several historians have discussed Lincoln's support for the congressional legislation that expanded railroads, homesteads, and agricultural education in the West. Leonard P. Curry in *Blueprint for Modern America* (1968) and Heather Cox Richardson in *The Greatest Nation on Earth* (1997) furnish particularly helpful treatments of these topics. Briefer in coverage but nonetheless sure guides are the discussions of these important subjects in Phillip Shaw Paludan's two books: *"A People's Contest": The Union and the Civil War, 1861–1865* (1988) and *The Presidency of Abraham Lincoln* (1994). Another volume, Gabor S. Boritt's *Lincoln and the Economics of the American Dream* (1978), comments provocatively on this legislation in light of Lincoln's economic ideas. Louis B. Schmidt also deals with these topics in a series of four brief and general essays in the spring, summer, fall, and winter 1962 issues of *Arizoniana*.

Not surprisingly, given its central importance to his presidency, Lincoln's patronage and political connections in the West have received fuller coverage than any other western topic among historians and biographers. The beginning place for careful study of Lincoln's political appointments in the West—indeed for all his patronage selections—is Harry J. Carman and Reinhard H. Luthin's *Lincoln and the Patronage* (1943). Exhaustively researched and broad-reaching in its coverage, this hefty volume remains an indispensable guide for studying Lincoln's most important connections with the American West. It provides national coverage of Lincoln's patronage, but it also makes clear the regional patterns as well of the president's political appointments.

The best of the book-length overviews of western territories and their political organization is Earl Pomeroy's gem-of-a-book, *The Territories and the United States, 1861–1890* (1947), which deals with interior (western) as well as exterior (eastern) administration of western territories. Also of major importance are two volumes by Howard R. Lamar: *Dakota Territory, 1861–1889* (1956) and *The Far Southwest, 1846–1912* (1966). All three books discuss Lincoln's important administrative connections with the western territories. Dozens of other books treat western territories during Lincoln's presidency, and nearly all at least mention his influence on these areas. Of note in this regard are Ronald H. Limbaugh's study of Idaho territorial governors, *Rocky Mountain Carpetbaggers* (1982), Deren Earl Kellogg's doctoral dissertation, "The Lincoln Administration and the Southwestern Territories" (1998), and E. B. Long's *The Saints and the Union: Utah Territory during the Civil War* (1981).

For discussions of Lincoln and western states in the early 1860s, one might well begin with two books on Missouri. William E. Parrish's *Turbulent Partnership: Missouri and the Union, 1861–1865* (1965) provides a useful overview, and Michael Fellman's *Inside War: The Guerilla Conflict in Missouri during the American Civil War* (1989), a model monograph, clarifies why Lincoln had so much difficulty with the competing factions and ever-present violence in Missouri. Also helpful for understanding three other territories and states is David Alan Johnson's *Founding the Far West: California, Oregon, and Nevada, 1840–1890* (1992). On another new state, see Albert Castel, *Civil War Kansas* (1958, 1997). Much other useful information on connections between Lincoln and western territories and states, as well as on dozens of other subjects, appears in an invaluable source, Mark E. Neely Jr.'s *The Abraham Lincoln Encyclopedia* (1982).

Several of the essays on Lincoln's political appointments in the West remain useful. Earl Pomeroy's "Lincoln, the Thirteenth Amendment, and the Admission of Nevada" (1943; reprinted in this volume) cautioned against a too-neat calculus in viewing Lincoln's connections with Nevada as entirely pragmatic and politically driven; and John Denton Carter's brief piece "Abraham Lincoln and California Patronage" (1943) remains the best available discussion of that subject. Casting a wider net, Vincent G. Tegeder in his essay "Lincoln and the Territorial Patronage: The Ascendancy of the Radicals in the West" (1948; reprinted in this volume) shows how influential the Radical Republicans were in determining the western patronage appointments during the Lincoln administration.

More recently, Robert W. Johannsen provides a less friendly view of Lincoln's patronage appointments in the Pacific Northwest in his essay "The Tribe of Abraham: Lincoln and the Washington Territory" (1992; reprinted in this volume). Gerry L. Alexander in "Abe Lincoln and the Pacific Northwest" (2002–3) and David H. Leroy in "Lincoln and Idaho: A Rocky Mountains Legacy" (1994) are less inclined to accept those negative conclusions. On other subregions of the West, one should consult Deren Earl Kellogg's "Lincoln's New Mexico Patronage: Saving the Far Southwest for the Union" (2000; reprinted in this volume), George U. Hubbard's "Abraham Lincoln as Seen by the Mormons" (1963), Larry Schweikart's "The Mormon Connection: Lincoln, the Saints, and the Crisis of Equality" (1980; reprinted in this volume), Walter B. Stevens's

"Lincoln and Missouri" (1916), and the collected essays in "Abraham Lincoln," the special issue of *Palimpsest* on Lincoln and Iowa (February 1960).

Alongside Lincoln's patronage connections in the West were his influential political friendships. On his notable acquaintance Edward D. Baker, one should begin with the very positive treatment in Harry C. Blair and Rebecca Tarshis's *Colonel Edward D. Baker: Lincoln's Constant Ally* (1960), and Robert W. Johannsen's illuminating discussions of Baker in *Frontier Politics and the Sectional Conflict* (1955). Another longtime Illinois friend who also moved to Oregon, Anson G. Henry, is profiled in Harry Edward Pratt's two-part essay "Dr. Anson G. Henry, Lincoln's Physician and Friend" (1943) and in Harry C. Blair's booklet *Dr. Anson Henry* (1950). Simeon Francis and David Logan, two other members of Lincoln's quartet of political acquaintances in Oregon, receive brief treatment in Johannsen's book. Logan and Baker are also discussed in David Alan Johnson's *Founding the Far West: California, Oregon, and Nevada, 1840–1890* (1992). The erratic friendship of Senator James Lane of Kansas with Lincoln is detailed in Albert Castel's *Civil War Kansas* (1958, 1997). Lincoln's acquaintance with the Cherokee principal chief John Ross is treated in Gary E. Moulton's *John Ross: Cherokee Chief* (1978).

Social and cultural shifts in the United States from the 1960s onward encouraged a raft of new studies of race and ethnicity, slavery, and race relations. In turn these trends influenced the publication of a freshet of essays and books on Lincoln's relationships with minority groups and his stances on slavery. These sociocultural transformations helped spawn the only book and a clutch of essays on Lincoln's dealings with Indians. David A. Nichols's *Lincoln and the Indians* (1978), diligently researched and the best study we have on this subject, is rather unsympathetic to Lincoln. Nichols depicts the sixteenth president as unwilling to push ahead with his promised reform of the nefarious Indian System and too culture-bound to understand the rights and needs of the Native Americans. Nichols summarizes these findings in essays before and after the publication of his valuable book. But other scholars, especially Harry Kelsey and Gary Moulton, have been less critical in their essays on Lincoln, Commissioner of Indian Affairs William Dole, and their Indian policies.

Several books have appeared on one topic involving Lincoln and Indians, the Sioux uprising in Minnesota in 1862. Some of the best of these studies are Charles M. Oehler's *The Great Sioux Uprising* (1959), Gary Clayton Anderson's *Little Crow: Spokesman for the Sioux* (1986), and Duane Schultz's *Over the Earth I Come: The Great Sioux Uprising of 1862* (1992). Gradually, too, discussions of Lincoln's dealings with Native Americans have been appearing in general overviews of the president. See, for example, such treatments in William C. Harris's *Lincoln's Last Months* (2004) and William Lee Miller's *President Lincoln* (2008).

But on slavery and the general topic of race, not many historians have ventured west. For example, the superb recent books by Allen C. Guelzo, *Lincoln's Emancipation Proclamation* (2004), Richard Striner, *Father Abraham: Lincoln's*

Relentless Struggle to End Slavery (2006), and George M. Fredrickson, *Big Enough to Be Inconsistent: Abraham Lincoln Confronts Slavery and Race* (2008) contribute valuable accounts of Lincoln's struggles to deal with slavery and race, but none does much with the western ramifications of those topics, save with the controversies surrounding the Kansas-Nebraska Act and subsequent troubles in Kansas during the 1850s. Thankfully, one book does focus on slavery in the West: Eugene H. Berwanger's *The Frontier against Slavery: Western Anti-Negro Prejudice and the Slavery Extension Controversy* (1967). The author of this helpful volume devotes separate chapters to slavery and racial controversies in California, Oregon, and Kansas, whereas other chapters deal with these topics generally in the trans-Mississippi West.

On the topic of Reconstruction in the West, scholars have been more extensive in their coverage. The beginning place for the study of Reconstruction is *Reconstruction: America's Unfinished Revolution, 1863–1877* (1988), Eric Foner's mammoth and brilliantly conceived overview. The author includes extensive sections on Reconstruction in Louisiana and Arkansas, as well as helpful discussions of Missouri and Texas, and makes clear Lincoln's connections with these areas. Two other volumes contain thorough information on Reconstruction in western states: William B. Hesseltine's *Lincoln's Plan of Reconstruction* (1960) and Peyton McCrary's *Abraham Lincoln and Reconstruction: The Louisiana Experiment* (1978). Still other helpful sources are Conrad Berry III's doctoral dissertation "Arkansas and Abraham Lincoln: Wartime Reconstruction and the President's Plan for the State" (1992), Don E. Fehrenbacher's essay "From War to Reconstruction in Arkansas" (1987), and appropriate sections of William C. Harris's *With Charity for All: Lincoln and the Restoration of the Union* (1997). For an innovative study that deals with post-Lincoln Reconstruction with a focus on the West, see Heather Cox Richardson's *West from Appomattox: The Reconstruction of America after the Civil War* (2007).

Finally, probably more books have been written about the military history of the Civil War than on any other war-related topic, but not many deal with the trans-Mississippi West and almost none at all with Abraham Lincoln's involvement in the western theaters of the Civil War. Fortunately Alvin M. Josephy Jr. provides a sweeping overview in his stirringly written account, *The Civil War in the American West* (1991). Covering less of the West, Ray C. Colton focuses on the Southwest and southern Rockies in his fact-filled volume, *The Civil War in the Western Territories: Arizona, Colorado, New Mexico, and Utah* (1959). G. Thomas Edwards furnishes a very helpful account of another western subregion often overlooked in Civil War accounts in his dissertation, "The Department of the Pacific in the Civil War Years" (1963).

This survey of publications leads to two observations: first, that increasing numbers of scholars are discovering Lincoln's ties to the trans-Mississippi American West; and second, on nearly every major Lincoln–West connection, more research remains to be done. Consider the prepresidential period. We still know little or nothing about Lincoln's attitudes toward the Oregon Country and Texas, and our understanding of Lincoln's stance on the Mexican War and the impact of that controversial position is limited. We could also use a full examination of Lincoln's support for the so-called Wilmot Proviso from 1847 to congressional legislation ending slavery in the territories in 1862. How obvious, too, that the Kansas-Nebraska, Bleeding Kansas, and Lincoln-Douglas debates focused in large part on the no-extension principle, but we still have no careful, extensive examination of the western implications of these measures and other events of the 1850s.

Similar lacunae are evident in the presidential years. The largest need for the 1861–65 period is a book-length treatment of Lincoln's numerous patronage appointments in the West. Similarly, a volume on Lincoln's western political and nonpolitical acquaintances would be in order. Edward D. Baker and David Logan of Oregon, James H. Lane and Mark W. Delahay of Kansas, Noah Brooks of California, and John S. Watts of New Mexico are among the many persons worthy of treatment in such a book. (Paul M. Zall has in preparation a book on some of these Lincoln friends in the Far West.) A complementary volume could draw together the personal correspondence of these appointees or friends; their letters, few of which have been published, give voice to the West that so intrigued Lincoln. There is room, too, for a brief monograph about Lincoln's support for congressional legislation such as the Pacific Railroad Act, the Homestead Act, the Morrill Land Grant College Act, as well as other bills such as that ending slavery in the territories.

Other projects present themselves. We should have a new book on Lincoln and Native Americans, one drawing on the new ethnographical insights of scholars dealing with Indians and Indian policies. Likewise, we do not have a complete study of Lincoln's involvements in the planning and implementation of military policies in the West. That needed volume could draw together information on Lincoln's decisions about the Sioux uprising in 1862, Indian relations in Indian Territory, and his reactions to several other incidents scattered across the West. Lincoln's strong connections with western states, territories, and subregions such as Missouri, California, Kansas, and the Pacific Northwest also merit separate books.

Quite clearly, Abraham Lincoln's connection with the trans-Mississippi West is a scholarly field still undercultivated. The research opportunities outnumber the workers. And if much of this necessary research and publication is accomplished, we shall be closer to fulfilling the most pressing need of all: a full-scale study of Lincoln and the American West, covering the twenty years of his important and expanding ties with the region.

In addition to the books and essays cited in the foregoing bibliographical essay, the following bibliography includes other publications that focus on Abraham Lincoln's links with the trans-Mississippi American West.

Books, Dissertations, and Theses

Anderson, Gary Clayton. *Little Crow: Spokesman for the Sioux*. St. Paul: Minnesota Historical Society Press, 1986.

Ayres, Carol Dark. *Lincoln and Kansas: Partnership for Freedom*. Manhattan, KS: Sunflower University Press, 2001.

Berry, Conrad C., III. "Arkansas and Abraham Lincoln: Wartime Reconstruction and the President's Plan for the State." Ph.D. diss., University of Mississippi, 1992.

Berwanger, Eugene H. *The Frontier against Slavery: Western Anti-Negro Prejudice and the Slavery Extension Controversy*. Urbana: University of Illinois Press, 1967.

Beveridge, Albert J. *Abraham Lincoln, 1809–1858*. 4 vols. Boston: Houghton Mifflin, 1928.

Bigglestone, William. "Lincoln and the Northern California Press, 1860–1865." Master's thesis, Stanford University, 1951.

Blair, Harry C. *Dr. Anson Henry: Physician, Politician, Friend of Abraham Lincoln*. Portland: Binfords and Mort, 1950.

Blair, Harry C., and Rebecca Tarshis. *Colonel Edward D. Baker: Lincoln's Constant Ally*. Portland: Oregon Historical Society, 1960.

Boritt, Gabor S. *Lincoln and the Economics of the American Dream*. 1978; Urbana: University of Illinois Press, 1994.

Brooks, Noah. *Abraham Lincoln and the Downfall of American Slavery*. New York: G. P. Putnam's Sons, 1888, 1994.

Burlingame, Michael. *Abraham Lincoln: A Life*. 2 vols. Baltimore: Johns Hopkins University Press, 2008.

Carman, Harry J., and Reinhard H. Luthin. *Lincoln and the Patronage*. New York: Columbia University Press, 1943.

Castel, Albert. *Civil War Kansas: Reaping the Whirlwind*. 1958; Lawrence: University Press of Kansas, 1997.

Colton, Ray C. *The Civil War in the Western Territories: Arizona, Colorado, New Mexico, and Utah*. Norman: University of Oklahoma Press, 1959.

Cox, Hank H. *Lincoln and the Sioux Uprising of 1862*. Nashville, TN: Cumberland House, 2005.

Curry, Leonard P. *Blueprint for Modern America: Non-Military Legislation of the First Civil War Congress*. Nashville, TN: Vanderbilt University Press, 1968.

Donald, David. *Lincoln*. New York: Simon and Schuster, 1995.

Edwards, G. Thomas. "The Department of the Pacific in the Civil War Years." Ph.D. diss., University of Oregon, 1963.

Emery, Richard L. *Abraham Lincoln and the Latter-day Saints*. Bloomington, IN: Author-House, 2005.

Fehrenbacher, Don E. *Prelude to Greatness: Lincoln in the 1850s*. 1962; New York: McGraw-Hill, 1964.

Fellman, Michael. *Inside War: The Guerilla Conflict in Missouri during the American Civil War*. New York: Oxford University Press, 1989.

Findley, Paul. *A. Lincoln: The Crucible of Congress*. New York: Crown, 1979.

Fischer, LeRoy H., ed. *The Western States in the Civil War*. Manhattan, KS: Journal of the West, January 1975.

———, ed. *The Western Territories in the Civil War*. Manhattan, KS: Journal of the West, April 1977.

Foner, Eric. *Free Soil, Free Labor, Free Men: The Ideology of the Republican Party before the Civil War.* New York: Oxford University Press, 1970.

———. *Reconstruction: America's Unfinished Revolution, 1863–1877.* New York: Harper and Row, 1988.

Fredrickson, George M. *Big Enough to Be Inconsistent: Abraham Lincoln Confronts Slavery and Race.* Cambridge, MA: Harvard University Press, 2008.

Guelzo, Allen C. *Lincoln and Douglas: The Debates That Defined America.* New York: Simon and Schuster, 2008.

———. *Lincoln's Emancipation Proclamation: The End of Slavery in America.* New York: Simon and Schuster, 2004.

Hageman, Todd. "Lincoln and Oregon." Master's thesis, Eastern Illinois University, 1988.

Harris, William C. *Lincoln's Last Months.* Cambridge, MA: Harvard University Press, 2004.

———. *Lincoln's Rise to the Presidency.* Lawrence: University Press of Kansas, 2007.

———. *With Charity for All: Lincoln and the Restoration of the Union.* Lexington: University Press of Kentucky, 1997.

Hazen, David Wheeler. *Mr. Lincoln.* Portland, OR: University of Portland, 1941.

Herriott, F. I. *Iowa and Abraham Lincoln.* Des Moines: N.p., 1911.

Hesseltine, William B. *Lincoln's Plan of Reconstruction.* 1960; Chicago: Quadrangle Books, 1967.

Holzer, Harold, ed. Introduction. *The Lincoln-Douglas Debates: The First Complete Unexpurgated Text.* New York: HarperPerennial, 1994.

Jacobs, Wilbur R., ed. *Frederick Jackson Turner's Legacy: Unpublished Writings in American History.* San Marino, CA: Huntington Library, 1965.

Johannsen, Robert W. *Frontier Politics and the Sectional Conflict: The Pacific Northwest on the Eve of the Civil War.* Seattle: University of Washington Press, 1955.

———. *Stephen A. Douglas.* New York: Oxford University Press, 1973.

Johnson, David Alan. *Founding the Far West: California, Oregon, and Nevada, 1840–1890.* Berkeley: University of California Press, 1992.

Josephy, Alvin M., Jr. *The Civil War in the American West.* New York: Alfred A. Knopf, 1991.

Kellogg, Deren Earl. "The Lincoln Administration and the Southwestern Territories." Ph.D. diss., University of Illinois, 1998.

Lamar, Howard R. *Dakota Territory, 1861–1889: A Study in Frontier Politics.* New Haven, CT: Yale University Press, 1956.

———. *The Far Southwest, 1846–1912: A Territorial History.* New Haven, CT: Yale University Press, 1966.

Limbaugh, Ronald H. *Rocky Mountain Carpetbaggers: Idaho's Territorial Governors, 1863–1890.* Moscow: University of Idaho Press, 1982.

Long, E. B. *The Saints and the Union: Utah Territory during the Civil War.* Urbana: University of Illinois Press, 1981.

McCrary, Peyton. *Abraham Lincoln and Reconstruction: The Louisiana Experiment.* Princeton, NJ: Princeton University Press, 1978.

McGinnis, Ralph Y., and Calvin N. Smith, eds. *Abraham Lincoln and the Western Territories.* Chicago: Nelson-Hall, 1994.

Miller, William Lee. *President Lincoln: The Duty of a Statesman.* New York: Alfred A. Knopf, 2008.

Moulton, Gary E. *John Ross: Cherokee Chief.* Athens: University of Georgia Press, 1985.

Neely, Mark E., Jr. *The Abraham Lincoln Encyclopedia.* New York: McGraw-Hill, 1982.

Neil, William MacFarlane. "The Territorial Governor in the Rocky Mountain West, 1861–89." Ph.D. diss., University of Chicago, 1952.

Nichols, David A. *Lincoln and the Indians: Civil War Policy and Politics.* Columbia: University of Missouri Press, 1978.

Nicolay, John G., and John Hay. *Abraham Lincoln: A History.* 10 vols. New York: Century, 1886, 1917.

Norby, Charles H. "The West in the Civil War Decade." Ph.D. diss., University of Iowa, 1935.

Oehler, Charles M. *The Great Sioux Uprising.* New York: Oxford University Press, 1959.

Owens, Kenneth Nelson. "Frontier Governors: A Study of the Territorial Executives in the History of Washington, Idaho, Montana, Wyoming and Dakota Territories." Ph.D. diss., University of Minnesota, 1959.

Packard, Roy D. *The Lincoln of the Thirtieth Congress.* Boston: Christopher Publishing House, 1930.

Paludan, Phillip Shaw. *"A People's Contest": The Union and the Civil War, 1861–1865.* New York: Harper & Row, 1988.

———. *The Presidency of Abraham Lincoln.* Lawrence: University Press of Kansas, 1994.

Parrish, William E. *Turbulent Partnership: Missouri and the Union, 1861–1865.* Columbia: University of Missouri Press, 1965.

Pomeroy, Earl S. *The Territories and the United States, 1861–1890: Studies in Colonial Administration.* Philadelphia: University of Pennsylvania Press, 1947.

Randall, James G. *Lincoln the President.* 4 vols. New York: Dodd, Mead, 1945–55.

Reck, W. Emerson. *A. Lincoln: His Last 24 Hours.* 1987; Columbia: University of South Carolina Press, 1994.

Richardson, Heather Cox. *The Greatest Nation on Earth: Republican Economic Policies during the Civil War.* Cambridge, MA: Harvard University Press, 1997.

———. *West from Appomattox: The Reconstruction of America after the Civil War.* New Haven: Yale University Press, 2007.

Riddle, Donald W. *Congressman Abraham Lincoln.* Urbana: University of Illinois Press, 1957.

Robertson, John Bruce. "Lincoln and Congress." Ph.D. diss., University of Wisconsin, 1966.

Sandburg, Carl. *Abraham Lincoln: The Prairie Years.* 2 vols. New York: Charles Scribner's Sons, 1926.

———. *Abraham Lincoln: The War Years.* 4 vols. New York: Harcourt, Brace, 1936–37.

Schultz, Duane. *Over the Earth I Come: The Great Sioux Uprising of 1862.* New York: St Martin's Press, 1992.

Shutes, Milton H. *Lincoln and California.* Stanford, CA: Stanford University Press, 1943.

Starr, John William. *Lincoln and the Railroads: A Biographical Study.* New York: Dodd, Mead, 1927.

Striner, Richard. *Father Abraham: Lincoln's Relentless Struggle to End Slavery.* New York: Oxford University Press, 2006.

Tarbell, Ida. *The Life of Abraham Lincoln.* 2 vols. 1900; New York: Macmillan, 1917.

Turner, Frederick Jackson. *The Frontier in American History.* New York: Henry Holt, 1920.

White, Ronald, Jr. *A. Lincoln: A Biography.* New York: Random House, 2009.

Wiel, Samuel C. *Lincoln's Crisis in the Far West.* San Francisco: Privately printed, 1949.

Essays and Periodicals

"Abraham Lincoln." Special issue (on Lincoln and Iowa), *Palimpsest* 41 (February 1960).

"Abraham Lincoln and Colorado." *Denver* [Chamber of Commerce], February 10, 1929, 8–9.

Alexander, Gerry L. "Abe Lincoln and the Pacific Northwest." *Columbia: The Magazine of Northwest History* 16 (Winter 2002–3): 3–6.

Angle, Paul. "Lincoln's Land Holdings and Investments." *Abraham Lincoln Association Bulletin* 16 (September 1929).

Ascher, Leonard W. "Lincoln's Administration and the New Almaden Scandal." *Pacific Historical Review* 5 (March 1936): 38–51.

Barker, Malcolm E. "When Sam Brannan Stumped for Abraham Lincoln." In *California and the Civil War, 1861–1865.* San Francisco: Book Club of California, 1992.

Barr, John M. "If Lincoln Had Lived: Texans Reconsider Lincoln's Assassination." *Lincoln Herald* 91 (Winter 1989): 151–55.

———. "The Tyrannicide's Reception: Responses in Texas to Lincoln's Assassination." *Lincoln Herald* 91 (Summer 1989): 58–64.

Bell, Samuel E., and James M. Smallwood. "The Pragmatic Lincoln: A Historiographical Assessment of His Western Policy." *Lincoln Herald* 86 (Fall 1984): 134–42.

Boritt, G. S. "A Question of Political Suicide? Lincoln's Opposition to the Mexican War." *Journal of the Illinois State Historical Society* 67 (February 1974): 79–100.

Braden, Waldo W. "Lincoln's Western Travel, 1859." *Lincoln Herald* 90 (Summer 1988): 38–43.

Brinkerhoff, Fred W. "Address of the President: The Kansas Tour of Lincoln the Candidate." *Kansas Historical Quarterly* 13 (February 1945): 294–307.

Buck, Solon J. "Lincoln and Minnesota." *Minnesota History* 6 (December 1925): 355–61.

Bullard, F. Lauriston. "Abraham Lincoln and the Statehood of Nevada." Pts. 1 and 2. *American Bar Association Journal* 26 (March 1940): 210–13, 236; 26 (April 1940): 313–17.

Carter, John Denton. "Abraham Lincoln and the California Patronage." *American Historical Review* 48 (April 1943): 495–506.

Chandler, Robert J. "Crushing Dissent: The Pacific Coast Tests Lincoln's Policy of Suppression, 1862." *Civil War History* 30 (September 1984): 235–54.

———. "The Release of the *Chapman* Pirates: A California Sidelight on Lincoln's Amnesty Policy." *Civil War History* 23 (June 1977): 129–43.

Chomsky, Carol. "The United States–Dakota War Trials: A Study of Military Injustice." *Stanford Law Review* 43 (November 1990): 13–98.

Davis, Jane S. "Two Sioux War Orders: A Mystery Unraveled." *Minnesota History* 41(Fall 1968): 117–25.

Dickson, Edward A. "Lincoln and Baker: The Story of a Great Friendship." *Historical Society of Southern California Quarterly* 34 (September 1952): 229–42.

Etulain, Richard W. "Abraham Lincoln: Political Founding Father of the American West." *Montana: The Magazine of Western History* 59 (Summer 2009): 3–22.

———. "Lincoln Looks West." *Wild West* 21 (April 2009): 26–35.

Fenton, William D. "Edward Dickinson Baker." *Quarterly of the Oregon Historical Society* 9 (1908): 1–23.

Fehrenbacher, Don E. "From War to Reconstruction in Arkansas." In *Lincoln in Text and Context*. Stanford, CA: Stanford University Press, 1987. 143–56.

Fischer, LeRoy H., ed. "The Western States in the Civil War." Special issue, *Journal of the West*, January 1975.

———, ed. "The Western Territories in the Civil War." Special issue, *Journal of the West*, April 1977.

Floyd, Elbert F. "Insights into the Personal Friendship and Patronage of Abraham Lincoln and Anson Gordon Henry, M.D.: Letters for [*sic*] Dr. Henry to His Wife, Eliza." *Journal of the Illinois State Historical Society* 98 (Winter 2005–6): 218–53.

Graham, Burdett. "A Lost Lincoln Letter: An Episode in the History of the First Iowa Cavalry." *Annals of Iowa* 33 (July 1955): 47–50.

Harbison, Winfred A. "President Lincoln and the Faribault Fire-eater." *Minnesota History* 29 (September 1939): 269–86.

Harlan, E. R. "Lincoln's Iowa Lands." *Annals of Iowa* 15 (April 1927): 621–23.

Hawley, Charles Arthur. "Lincoln in Kansas." *Journal of the Illinois State Historical Society* 42 (June 1949): 179–92.

Hazen, David Wheeler. "Lincoln and Old Oregon." Chap. 4 in *Mr. Lincoln*. Portland, OR: University of Portland, 1941.

Herriott, Frank I. "Iowa and the First Nomination of Abraham Lincoln." Pts. 1, 2, and 3. *Annals of Iowa* 8 (1907): 81–115, 186–220, 444–66; 9 (April 1909): 45–64; 9 (October 1909): 186–228.

Hoeflich, M. H., and Virgil W. Dean, eds. "'Went at Night to Hear Hon. Abe Lincoln Make a Speech': Daniel Mulford Valentine's 1859 Diary." *Kansas History* 29 (Summer 2006): 100–115.

Hofsommer, Donovan L. "William Palmer Doyle, Commissioner of Indian Affairs, 1861–1865." *Lincoln Herald* 75 (Fall 1973): 97–114.

Hubbard, George U. "Abraham Lincoln as Seen by the Mormons." *Utah Historical Quarterly* 31 (Spring 1963): 91–108.

Johannsen, Robert W. "The Tribe of Abraham: Lincoln and the Washington Territory." In David H. Stratton, ed., *Washington Comes of Age: The State in the National Experience*. Pullman: Washington State University Press, 1992. 73–93.

Kellogg, Deren Earl. "Lincoln's New Mexico Patronage: Saving the Far Southwest for the Union." *New Mexico Historical Review* 75 (October 2000): 511–33.

———. "'Slavery Must Die': Radical Republicans and the Creation of the Arizona Territory." *Journal of Arizona History* 41 (Autumn 2000): 267–88.

Kelsey, Harry. "Abraham Lincoln and American Indian Policy." *Lincoln Herald* 77 (Fall 1975): 139–48.

———. "William P. Dole and Mr. Lincoln's Indian Policy." *Journal of the West* 10 (July 1971): 484–92.

King, Jeffrey S. "'Do Not Execute Chief Pocatello': President Lincoln Acts to Save the Shoshoni Chief." *Utah Historical Quarterly* 53 (Summer 1985): 237–47.

———. "A Memorable Spectacle: Lincoln's Meeting with Plains Indians on March 27, 1863." *Lincoln Herald* 81 (Spring 1979): 20–27.

Kubicek, Earl C. "Lincoln's Friend: Kirby Benedict." *Lincoln Herald* 81 (Spring 1979): 9–20.

Leroy, David H. "Lincoln and Idaho: A Rocky Mountains Legacy." In Frank J. Williams et al., eds., *Abraham Lincoln: Sources and Style of Leadership.* Westport, CT: Greenwood Press, 1994. 143–62.

"Lincoln in Kansas." *Transactions of the Kansas Historical Society* 7 (1901–2): 536–45.

"Lincoln's Sioux War Order." *Minnesota History* 33 (Summer 1952): 77–79.

Linkugel, Wil A. "Lincoln, Kansas, and Cooper Union." *Speech Monographs* 37 (August 1970): 172–79.

McDonnell, Anne, ed. "Edgerton and Lincoln." *Montana: The Magazine of Western History* 1 (October 1950): 42–45.

McFarland, Carl. "Abraham Lincoln and Montana Territory." *Montana: The Magazine of Western History* 5 (October 1955): 42–47.

Miller, David. "Lincoln and the Sioux Outbreak." In Allan Nevins and Irving Stone, eds., *Lincoln: A Contemporary Portrait.* Garden City, NY: Doubleday, 1962. 111–30.

Miller, Paul I., ed. "Lincoln and the Governorship of Oregon." *Mississippi Valley Historical Review* 23 (December 1936): 391–94.

Miner, Craig. "Lane and Lincoln: A Mysterious Connection." *Kansas History* 24 (Autumn 2001): 186–99.

Moulton, Gary E. "John Ross and W. P. Dole: A Case Study of Lincoln's Indian Policy." *Journal of the West* 12 (July 1973): 414–23.

Murphy, William G. "Lincoln and the Union Pacific." *Lincoln Herald* 46 (June 1944): 40.

Neely, Mark E., Jr. "Lincoln and the Mexican War: An Argument by Analogy." *Civil War History* 24 (March 1978): 5–24.

———. "President Lincoln, Polygamy, and the Civil War: The Case of Dawson and Deseret." Pts. 1 and 2. *Lincoln Lore* 1644 (February 1975): 1–4; 1645 (March 1975): 1–4.

Nichols, David A. "Lincoln and the Indians." In Gabor S. Boritt and Norman O. Furness, eds., *The Historian's Lincoln: Pseudohistory, Psychohistory, and History.* Urbana: University of Illinois Press, 1988. 149–69.

———. "The Other Civil War: Lincoln and the Indians." *Minnesota History* 44 (Spring 1974): 2–15.

Owens, Patricia Ann. "Wyoming and Montana during the Lincoln Administration." *Lincoln Herald* 91 (Summer 1989): 49–57.

Peterson, William J. "Lincoln and Iowa." *Palimpsest* 41 (February 1960): 81–103.

Pomeroy, Earl S. "Lincoln, the Thirteenth Amendment, and the Admission of Nevada." *Pacific Historical Review* 12 (December 1943): 362–68.

Pratt, Harry Edward. "Dr. Anson G. Henry, Lincoln's Physician and Friend." Pts. 1 and 2. *Lincoln Herald* 45 (October 1943): 3–17; 45 (December 1943): 31–40.

———, ed. "22 Letters of David Logan, Pioneer Oregon Lawyer." *Oregon Historical Quarterly* 44 (September 1943): 254–85.

Ray, Murray. "Iowa Remembers Lincoln." *Palimpsest* 41 (February 1960): 122–29.

Ross, Earle D. "Lincoln and Agriculture." *Agricultural History* 3 (April 1929): 51–66.

Rutledge, William, III. "Lincoln's Last Message." *True West* 9 (March/April 1962): 11, 68–69.

Schapsmeier, Edward L., and Frederick H. Schapsmeier. "Lincoln and Douglas: Their Versions of the West." *Journal of the West* 7 (October 1968): 542–52.

Schmidt, Louis B. "Abraham Lincoln's New Deal for Agriculture." *Arizoniana* 3 (Summer 1962): 9–16.

———. "Abraham Lincoln's New Deal for Industrial Education." *Arizoniana* 3 (Spring 1962): 10–15.

———. "Abraham Lincoln's New Deal for the Argonauts." *Arizoniana* 3 (Winter 1962): 25–35.

———. "Abraham Lincoln's New Deal for the Pioneer." *Arizoniana* 3 (Fall 1962): 34–43.

Schweikart, Larry. "The Mormon Connection: Lincoln, the Saints, and the Crisis of Equality." *Western Humanities Review* 34 (Winter 1980): 1–22.

Scott, Leslie M. "Oregon's Nomination of Lincoln." *Oregon Historical Quarterly* 17 (September 1916): 201–14.

Shiras, Frances. "Major Wolf and Abraham Lincoln: An Episode of the Civil War." *Arkansas History* 2 (1943): 353–58.

Shutes, Milton H. "Abraham Lincoln and the New Alamaden Mine." *California Historical Society Quarterly* 15 (March 1936): 3–20.

———. "Colonel E. D. Baker." *Historical Society of Southern California Quarterly* 17 (December 1938): 303–24.

Simon, John Y. "Lincoln, Douglas, and Popular Sovereignty: The Mormon Dimension." In John Y. Simon et al., eds., *Lincoln Revisited: New Insights from the Lincoln Forum* (New York: Fordham University Press, 2007). 45–56, 336–37.

Splitter, Henry Winfred. "Lincoln Rails in the California Presidential Campaign of 1860." *Pacific Historical Review* 19 (November 1950): 351–55.

Steen, Ralph W. "Texas Newspapers and Lincoln." *Southwestern Historical Quarterly* 51 (January 1948): 199–212.

Stevens, Walter B. "Lincoln and Missouri." *Missouri Historical Review* 10 (January 1916): 63–119.

Taft, Robert A. "A Century of Kansas History: Abraham Lincoln in Kansas." *Kansas Teacher* 63, no. 6 (1955).

Tegeder, Vincent G. "Lincoln and the Territorial Patronage: The Ascendancy of the Radicals in the West." *Mississippi Valley Historical Review* 35 (June 1948): 77–90.

Temple, Wayne C. "Dr. Anson G. Henry: Personal Physician to the Lincolns." Lincoln Fellowship of Wisconsin, *Historical Bulletin No. 43* (1988): 1–15.

Van Winden, Kathy. "The Assassination of Abraham Lincoln: Its Effect on California." *Journal of the West* 4 (April 1965): 211–30.

Welch, Frank W. "Lincoln and American Higher Education." *Lincoln Herald* 75 (Summer 1973): 65.

Wells, Merle. "Idaho and the Civil War." *Rendezvous* 11 (Fall 1976): 9–26.

———. "Idaho's Centennial: How Idaho Was Created in 1863." *Idaho Yesterdays* 7 (Spring 1963): 44–58.

Westwood, Howard C. "President Lincoln's Overture to Sam Houston." *Southwestern Historical Quarterly* 88 (October 1984): 125–44.

Wood, Harry. "How Both Abraham Lincolns Helped Found Arizona." *Lincoln Herald* 78 (Fall 1976): 109–16.

Wynne, Patricia Hochwalt. "Lincoln's Western Image in the 1860 Campaign." *Maryland Historical Magazine* 59 (June 1964): 165–81.

Zornow, William Frank. "The Kansas Senators and the Re-election of Lincoln." *Kansas Historical Quarterly* 19 (May 1951): 133–44.

Contributors

Michael S. Green is professor of history at the College of Southern Nevada. He is the editor of the *Nevada Historical Society Quarterly* and author of numerous articles and books on western history, including *Freedom, Union, and Power: Lincoln and His Party during the Civil War* (2004) and the forthcoming *Politics and America in Crisis: The Coming of the Civil War* and *Lincoln and the Election of 1860*.

Robert W. Johannsen, professor emeritus of history at the University of Illinois, Urbana-Champaign, is the country's leading authority on Stephen A. Douglas. His books include *Frontier Politics on the Eve of the Civil War* (1955), which dealt with Douglas's influence on the Pacific Northwest, *The Letters of Stephen Douglas* (1961), and the definitive biography *Stephen A. Douglas* (1973).

Deren Earl Kellogg is a doctoral graduate in history at the University of Illinois, Urbana-Champaign, where he studied with Robert W. Johannsen. A native of Illinois, he currently resides in Jackson, Mississippi, where he serves as the operations director of a nonprofit organization.

Mark E. Neely Jr. is McCabe Greer Professor of Civil War History at Pennsylvania State University. His books include *The Abraham Lincoln Encyclopedia* (1981); *The Fate of Liberty: Abraham Lincoln and Civil Liberties* (1991), winner of the Pulitzer prize; *The Last Best Hope of Earth: Abraham Lincoln and the Promise of America* (1993); and *The Boundaries of American Political Culture in the Civil War Era* (2005).

David A. Nichols is a former professor and academic dean at Southwestern College in Kansas. His books include *Lincoln and the Indians: Civil War Policy and Politics* (1978) and *A Matter of Justice: Eisenhower and the Beginning of the Civil Rights Revolution* (2007).

Earl S. Pomeroy was one of the country's premier western historians. A longtime professor of history at the University of Oregon and the University of California, San Diego, he authored numerous articles and books, including *The Territories and the United States, 1861–1890* (1947), *The Pacific Slope* (1965), and *The American Far West in the Twentieth Century* (2008).

Larry Schweikart is professor of history at the University of Dayton, where he teaches courses in business, economic, and military history. He is the author or coauthor of more than a dozen books, including *Banking in the American South* (1987) and *A Patriot's History of the United States* (coauthored with Michael Allen, 2004).

Vincent G. Tegeder was a longtime professor and archivist at St. Johns University (Minnesota) and a specialist in the Civil War era. He received his doctorate from the University of Wisconsin in 1949.

Paul M. Zall, with degrees from Swarthmore and Harvard, taught at Cornell, University of Oregon, and California State University, Los Angeles, for forty years before joining the Huntington Library in 1987 as a research scholar, where he is the resident authority on Lincoln stories. His most recent book is *Lincoln's Legacy of Laughter* (2008), and he is completing a group biography of Lincoln's friends who helped him win the West.

Acknowledgments

I wish to thank the following journals, publishers, and authors for allowing me to reprint the following essays in this collection.

Mark E. Neely Jr. "Lincoln and the Mexican War: An Argument by Analogy." *Civil War History* 24 (March 1978): 5–24. Reprinted with permission of The Kent State University Press.

Earl S. Pomeroy. "Lincoln, the Thirteenth Amendment, and the Admission of Nevada." *Pacific Historical Review* 12 (December 1943): 362–68. Copyright © 1943 by the Pacific Coast Branch, American Historical Association. Reprinted with permission of the University of California Press.

Vincent G. Tegeder. "Lincoln and the Territorial Patronage: The Ascendancy of the Radicals in the West." *Mississippi Valley Historical Review* 35 (June 1948): 77–90. Copyright © Organization of American Historians <http://www.oah. org>. Reprinted with permission.

Deren Earl Kellogg. "Lincoln's New Mexico Patronage: Saving the Far Southwest for the Union." *New Mexico Historical Review* 75 (October 2000): 511–33. Copyright © University of New Mexico Board of Regents. All rights reserved. Published by permission.

Robert W. Johannsen. "The Tribe of Abraham: Lincoln and the Washington Territory," in David H. Stratton, ed., *Washington Comes of Age: The State in the National Experience.* Pullman: Washington State University, 1992, 73–93. Reprinted with permission from Washington State University Press. All rights reserved.

Larry Schweikart. "The Mormon Connection: Lincoln, the Saints, and the Crisis of Equality." *Western Humanities Review* 34 (winter 1980): 1–22. Reprinted by permission of *Western Humanities Review* and the author.

David A. Nichols. "Lincoln and the Indians," in Gabor S. Boritt and Norman O. Furness, eds., *The Historian's Lincoln: Pseudohistory, Psychohistory, and History.* Urbana: University of Illinois Press, 1988, 149–69. Copyright 1988 by the Board of Trustees of the University of Illinois. Used with permission of the University of Illinois Press and the author.

Index

abolition and abolitionists,10, 13–14, 16, 18, 93, 168; Lincoln's attitudes toward, 13–14, 16, 224–25, 236

Abraham Lincoln: A History (Nicolay and Hay, 1886, 1890), 233–34

Abraham Lincoln and Reconstruction (McCrary, 1978), 241

Abraham Lincoln and the Downfall of American Slavery (Brooks, 1888, 1894, 1904), 234

Abraham Lincoln and the Western Territories (McGinnis and Smith, 1994), 238

Abraham Lincoln, 1809–1858 (Beveridge, 1928), 9, 68, 235–36

Abraham Lincoln Encyclopedia, The (Neely Jr., 1982), 239

Abraham Lincoln: The Prairie Years (Sandburg, 1926), 235

Abraham Lincoln: The War Years (Sandburg, 1936–37), 235

Adams, James, 176–77

agriculture, 24. 27–29; Lincoln's attitudes toward, 27

American System, 26, 94; Lincoln's support for, 5–6

American West. *See* trans-Mississippi American West

Anderson, Gary Clayton, 240

anti-expansionism, 6–8; Lincoln's views of, 6–8. *See also* Wilmot proviso

anti-Nebraska movement, 16; Lincoln's role in, 16, 57–58

Aristotelianism, 189–90, 203

Arizona, 47, 48, 54, 142; Lincoln's political appointees in, 48

Arkansas, 48, 55–56; and Reconstruction, 55–56

"Arkansas and Abraham Lincoln: Wartime Reconstruction and the President's Plan for the State" (Berry, 1992), 241

Arnold, Isaac N., 5

Arny, William F. M., 125, 126, 127, 149

Ashley, James M., 115, 117

Ashmun, George, 69

Ashmun Amendment, 69, 75

Ayres, Carol Dark, 237

Baker, Edward D., 11, 37, 45–46, 70, 82, 84; and Anson Henry, 179–80, 181; and Lincoln, 162–63, 181; and Mexican-American War, 159, 179; in Oregon, 38–39, 160, 181, 242

Bancroft, Hubert Howe, 140

Bates, Edward, 36, 52, 114–15, 127, 155

Baylor, John R., 54

Beeson, John, 32, 223

Benedict, Kirby, 47, 126–27, 138, 149

Bennett, John, 191, 192

Berry, Conrad, III, 241

Berwanger, Eugene H., 241

Beveridge, Albert J., 9, 14, 68–69, 235–36, 237

Big Enough to Be Inconsistent: Abraham Lincoln Confronts Slavery and Race (Fredrickson, 2008), 241

blacks, 50, 56, 104, 196, 203–4, 215. *See also* Negroes

Blair, Harry C., 240

Blair, Montgomery, 36, 52, 147

Blair family, 147–48

Bledsoe, Albert Taylor, 68

"Bleeding Kansas," 15–16; Lincoln's comments on, 15–16, 20, 242

Blueprint for Modern America (Curry, 1968), 238

Blunt, James G., 213–14

Boritt, Gabor S., 9, 68–69, 237, 238

Brooks, Noah, 1, 234, 242

Brother Jonathan, 174, 186

Brown, John, 15, 20; Lincoln's comments about, 20–21

Brown, William, 82

Bryant, William Cullen, 90

Buchanan, James, 15, 100, 103–4, 138

Butler, Benjamin, 56

Butterfield, Justin, 11, 158, 179

Calhoun, John C., 79, 80–81

California, 1, 26, 45–46, 99, 100, 160; Edward Baker and patronage in, 162–63; Lincoln's interests in, 45; political clashes in, 45–46, 162–63

California Gold Rush, 3, 45, 46

Carleton, James H., 54, 126, 127, 138, 224

Carman, Harry J., 135, 238

Cass, Lewis, 95

Chandler, Zachariah, 121, 123

Chase, Salmon P., 130, 167, 168, 183

Cherokee Indians, 31–32, 213

cholera and treatment, 176, 177, 179, 180

Church of Jesus Christ of Latter-day Saints. *See* Mormons

Civil War, 34–35, 51, 134, 224; impact on West, 51–54, 224

Civil War in the American West, The (Josephy, 1991), 241

Civil War in the Western Territories, The: Arizona, Colorado, New Mexico, and Utah (Colton, 1959), 241

Clay, Henry, 7, 8, 12, 85, 93; Lincoln's admiration for, 8, 13, 95–96

Clemens, Orion M., 44, 127

Cole, George E., 169

Colfax, Schuyler, 1, 125, 128

Colonel Edward D. Baker: Lincoln's Constant Ally (Blair and Tarshis, 1960), 240

colonization plans, 50; Lincoln's support for, 50

Colorado, 41, 115, 117, 124–25; territorial governors in, 42–43, 124–25, 146–47

Colorado militia, 43, 54. *See also* Sand Creek Massacre (1864)

Colton, Ray, 241

Committee on Territories, 156

Compromise of 1850, 12, 99

Confederacy, 22–23, 31–32, 49, 51–52, 211; and New Mexico, 141–42, 148–49. *See also* South

Congress, 44, 51, 83; legislation in, 24–29, 242. *See also specific enactments*

Congressman Abraham Lincoln (Riddle, 1957), 237

Connelly, Henry, 47, 49, 127, 137, 138–39, 143–44, 148

Constitution, 22, 194; Lincoln's comments on, 23, 25, 203

Cooper, James Fenimore, 3

Cooper Union speech (1860), 20–21, 90–91, 97

Corwin, Thomas, 72, 75

Council Bluffs, Iowa, 20, 25

Cox, "Sunset," 115–16

Curry, Leonard P., 238

Curtis, Samuel R., 52–53

Dakota Territory, 41, 123–24; Lincoln's political appointees in, 41, 123–24

Dakota Territory, 1861–1889 (Lamar, 1956), 239

Dana, Charles Anderson, 113–17

Davis, David, 87

Davis, Jefferson, 141–42

Dawson, John W., 128, 136, 195

Declaration of Independence, 14, 201; Lincoln's admiration for, 203–4

Delahay, Mark W., 20, 124, 242

Delaware, 147

Democratic Party, 8–9, 36; in Illinois, 80; in Indiana, 75; in New Mexico, 143; in West, 36, 39, 47; Lincoln's criticism of, 78

Denny, John, 163–64

Department of Agriculture, 27–28

"Department of the Pacific in the Civil War Years, The" (Edwards, 1963), 241

Dodge, Grenville M., 20; and railroads, 20, 25

Dole, William P., 31–32, 210–11, 220; and Lincoln, 31–32, 211

Donald, David, 24, 135

Doolittle, James R., 138, 167, 226

Douglas, Stephen A., 6, 7, 12–14, 96, 156; competitions with Lincoln, 17–20, 101–2, 104–7, 154; and Mormons, 192–93

Doty, James D., 130

Drake, Thomas, 128, 129, 196

Dr. Anson G. Henry (Blair, 1950), 240

"Dr. Anson G. Henry (1804–65): Lincoln's Junkyard Dog" (Zall), 174–88

Dred Scott decision, 17, 18–19; Lincoln's opposition to, 17, 19, 103

drugs, 176, 177–78, 179; and Lincoln, 177–78

Dunn, George G., 74, 75–76, 80, 81

Edgerton, Sidney, 40, 41

Edmunds, James M., 123, 124

Edmunds, Newton, 41, 124

Edwards, Cyrus, 179

Edwards, G. Thomas, xi, 241

election of 1860, 4, 22–23, 153

election of 1864, 184

Emancipation Proclamation, 50, 51

Embree, Elisha, 73, 74–75, 80, 81

Etulain, Richard W., 233–50, 263

Evans, John, 43, 125

Evanston, Illinois, 43

farmers, 27–28; Lincoln's attitudes toward, 27

Far Southwest 1846–1912, The: A Territorial History (Lamar, 1966), 239

Father Abraham: Lincoln's Relentless Struggle to End Slavery (Striner, 2006), 240–41

Fehrenbacher, Don E., 105, 237

Fillmore, Millard, 143

Findley, Paul, 237

Fischer, LeRoy H., 238

Five Civilized Tribes, 31–32. *See also* Ross, John

Flenniken, Robert, 128, 196

Foner, Eric, 50, 241

Ford's Theater, 1, 57

Founding Fathers, 15, 90, 98, 201; Lincoln's comments on, 21, 90, 98

Founding the Far West: California, Oregon, and Nevada, 1840–1890 (David Johnson, 1992), 239, 240

Francis, Simeon, 38, 39, 159, 162–63; in Oregon, 38

Fredrickson, George M., 241

Frémont, Jesse Benton, 35; Lincoln's conflict with, 35

Frémont, John C., 16, 52, 148; and Lincoln, 35, 103, 148; competitions and conflicts with, 35

Freeport, Illinois, 18

Freeport Doctrine, 18. *See also* Lincoln-Douglas debates

Free Soil Party, 94, 95

Frontier against Slavery, The: Western Anti-Negro Prejudice and the Slavery Extension Controversy (Berwanger, 1967), 241

Frontier Politics and the Sectional Conflict (Johannsen, 1955), 240

Fuller, Frank, 197, 202

Gadsden Purchase, 142

Gamble, Hamilton R., 36, 52

Ganaway, Loomis Morton, 135

General Land Office, commissioner of, 11, 158; Lincoln's quest for, 11, 158, 179

Gilpin, William, 42–43, 49, 124–25, 136, 146–47

Glorieta Pass, battle of, 54

Goodwin, Doris Kearns, 22

Goodwin, John N., 48

governors, 104. *See also* territorial governors; *names of individual governors*

Grant, U. S., 53, 227

Great Britain, 6–7

Greatest Nation on Earth, The (Richardson, 1997), 238

Great Sioux Uprising, The (Oehler, 1959), 240

Greeley, Horace, 105, 125–26, 136, 139–40, 141; and Lincoln, 4; on New Mexico, 141

Green, Michael S., x, 90–112, 251
Guelzo, Allen C., 237, 240
Gurley, John A., 48

Halleck, Henry, 213, 222, 223
Hanks, John, 4
Harding, Stephen S., 128–29, 195
Harris, William C., 237, 240, 241
Hay, John, 233–34
Henry, Dr. Anson G., 11, 37, 159, 174–88; and Lincoln, 171, 177–78, 179, 182–83; and Edward Baker, 181–82; in Pacific Northwest, 37–38, 39–40, 163–66, 170
Henry, Eliza, 175
Henry, John, 82–83
Herndon, William, 8, 11, 68–70, 81; and Mexican-American War, 8, 68–70, 81
Hesseltine, William B., 241
Hill, George D., 123, 124
Hispanos, in New Mexico, 140, 148
Holmes, James H., 126, 144–46, 149
Holzer, Harold, 21, 90
Homestead Act (1862), 27–28, 29, 242
House Divided speech, 17, 105–6
Houston, Sam, 49
Hubbard, George, 189, 193, 202
Hunter, David, 211–13

Idaho, 1, 40–41, 182; Lincoln's political appointees in, 1, 40–41, 170
Illinois, 5, 17–20, 21–22; Republicans in, 22
Illinois legislature, 5, 14, 82
Illinois State Register, 85, 86
Indiana, 71–75, 80, 122, 128, 143
Indian Office, 224
Indian policy, 29–33, 54, 219–27; Lincoln's attitudes about, 32–33, 223–27, 242. *See also* Dole, William P.
Indians, 24, 29–33, 43, 210–29; Lincoln's attitudes toward, 29–30, 223–27, 242. *See also names of individual tribes*
Indian Territory, 31–32, 136, 210–11, 213–14, 242
internal improvements, 5, 13; Lincoln's support for, 2, 5–7, 13. *See also* American System
Iowa, 20; Lincoln's travels in, 20

Jackson, Andrew, 154
Jaffa, Harry, 190, 203
Jayne, William, 41, 123, 136
Jefferson, Thomas, 49, 202–3
Johannsen, Robert W., x, 7, 40, 153–73, 237, 140, 251
John Ross: Cherokee Chief (Moulton, 1978), 240
Johnson, Andrew, 117, 174
Johnson, David Alan, 239, 240
Josephy, Alvin M., Jr., 241
judges. *See* territorial judges
Julian, George W., 121, 124, 128

Kansas, 15–16, 214, 225; Lincoln's trip to, 20–21
Kansas-Nebraska bill and act, 13–14, 96–97, 102; Lincoln's opposition to, 13–14, 97–100, 242
Kellogg, Deren Earl, x, 48, 134–52, 239, 251
Kellogg, William Pitt, 1
Kentucky, 3, 134, 147, 148
Kinney, John, 129–30
Knapp, Joseph G., 138
Know-Nothing movement, 16, 102–3

Lafayette, Oregon, 180
Lamar, Howard Roberts, 135, 239
land grant legislation, 25–26, 28. *See also* Morrill Land-Grant College Act; railroads
Land Office, commissioner of. *See* General Land Office, commissioner of
Lane, James H., 125, 144, 211–13, 242
Lane, Joseph, 153
Lane Expedition, 211–13
Latter-day Saints. *See* Mormons
Leavenworth, Kansas, 20
Lecompton Constitution, 15, 100
Liberty Party, 76
Life of Abraham Lincoln, The (Tarbell, 1900), 234
Limbaugh, Ronald H., 239
Lincoln, Abraham: attitudes toward slavery and its extension, 9, 10–11, 14, 21, 23, 97–99, 108; backgrounds of, 2–5, 156; and colonization, 50; as Congressman,

2, 8–11, 68–87; as Man of the West, 3–5, 58, 91, 155–56, 236; speech by, at Cooper Union, 20–21, 90–91; —, House Divided, 17, 105–6, —, at Peoria, 14; —, at Young Men's Lyceum, 92; and Wilmot Proviso, 2, 9, 16, 103, 242

Lincoln, Abraham, attitudes toward West, 13, 23, 49, 242; and Indians, 29–33, 54, 57, 58, 194, 210–27, 240, 242; military policy of, 51–54, 242; and Mormons, 41–43, 128–30, 189–204, 239; political patronage of, 33–49. *See also* names of western states and territories

Lincoln, Edward (Eddie, son), 12

Lincoln, Mary Todd (wife), 1, 11, 83, 183, 184–86

Lincoln, Robert Todd (son), 183

Lincoln, Thomas (father), 30, 92

Lincoln, William Wallace (Willie, son), 12

Lincoln and California (Shutes, 1943), 236

Lincoln and Douglas: The Debates That Defined America (Guelzo, 2008), 237

Lincoln and Kansas: Partnership for Freedom (Ayres, 2001), 237

"Lincoln and the American West: A Bibliographical Essay and Bibliography" (Etulain), 233–50

Lincoln and the Economics of the American Dream (Boritt, 1978), 238

"Lincoln and the Indians" (Nichols), 210–29

Lincoln and the Indians (Nichols, 1978), 240

"Lincoln and the Mexican War: An Argument by Analogy" (Neely), 68–89

Lincoln and the Patronage (Carman and Luthin, 1944), 238

Lincoln and the Railroads (Starr, 1927), 236

"Lincoln and the Territorial Patronage: The Ascendancy of the Radicals in the West" (Tegeder), 121–33

Lincoln-Douglas debates, 5, 17–20, 105–7, 242

Lincoln's Emancipation Proclamation (Guelzo, 2004), 240

Lincoln's Last Months (Harris, 2004), 240

"Lincoln's New Mexico Patronage: Saving the Far Southwest for the Union," (Kellogg), 134–52

Lincoln's Plan of Reconstruction (Hesseltine, 1960), 241

Lincoln's Rise to the Presidency (Harris, 2007), 237

Lincoln: The Crucible of Congress (Findley, 1979), 237

Lincoln the President (Randall, 1945–55), 236

"Lincoln, the Thirteenth Amendment, and the Admission of Nevada" (Pomeroy), 113–20

"Lincoln, the West, and the Antislavery Politics of the 1950s" (Green), 90–112

Little Crow: Spokesman for the Sioux (Anderson, 1986), 240

Logan, David, 37, 38; in Oregon, 37, 242

Logan, Stephen, 9, 37, 70, 85

Long, E. B., 239

Louisiana, 48; Reconstruction in, 56–57

Lovejoy, Owen, 16, 103

Luthin, Reinhard H., 135, 238

Lyon, Caleb, 40, 49

Lyon, Nathaniel, 52

Manifest Destiny, 7, 58, 78, 93, 157

Mankato, Minnesota, 218

Man of the West (Lincoln), ix, 3–5, 58

McBride, John R., 170, 182

McClellan, George, 212, 214, 215, 223

McCrary, Peyton, 241

McGaughey, Edward, 73

McGinnis, Ralph Y., 135, 238

Methodists, 43

Mexican-American War, 2, 7–9, 11, 68–69; Lincoln's opposition to, 8–10, 68–71

Mexico, 7, 74, 79

Miller, William Lee, 240

miners and mining, 1, 44, 46, 48; in California, 1, 46. *See also* California Gold Rush

Minnesota, 29–33, 210, 217, 218–19, 225; Sioux uprising in, 29–33, 54, 210, 214–19

Mississippi River, 6, 51–52

Missouri, 34–37, 140; military conflicts in, 52–53; political squabbles in, 34–37, 52–53

Missouri Compromise, 10, 100; Lincoln's support for, 100

Missouri River, 25

Montana, 40–41

"Mormon Connection, The: Lincoln, the Saints, and the Crisis of Equality" (Schweikart), 189–209

Mormons, x, 104, 189–209; in Illinois, 190–92, 198; Lincoln's attitudes toward, 104, 190–91, 202–4; and slavery, 199–201; in Utah, 192–201. *See also* Young, Brigham

Morrill, Justin, 28

Morrill Land-Grant College Act (1862), 27–28, 242

Moulton, Gary, 240

Murphy, Isaac, 55–56

Native Americans. *See* Indians

Nauvoo, Illinois, 190, 191

Nebraska, 1, 102, 124. *See also* Kansas-Nebraska bill and act

Need, William, 138, 139, 142

Neely, Mark E., Jr., x, 9, 68–69, 237, 239, 251

Negroes, 196, 203–4; Lincoln's attitudes toward, 14, 104, 203–4; and Mormons, 200. *See also* blacks; racism

Nevada, 43–45, 113–17, 127–28; Lincoln's political appointments in, 44, 127–28

New Mexico, 47–48, 54, 98, 99, 125, 134–50; Lincoln's political patronage in, 47–48, 125, 134–50

New Salem, Illinois, 3

Newton, Isaac, 28

New York City, 20, 22

New York Tribune, 105, 125–26, 139–40, 142

Nichols, David A., x, 210–29, 240, 251

Nicolay, John G., 36–37, 214, 217, 220, 233–34

Northwest Ordinance of 1787, 10, 21

Nullification, 96

Nye, James William, 44, 49, 116, 127, 128

Oehler, Charles M., 240

Oregon, 2, 6–7, 9–12, 34, 157; Lincoln as possible secretary and governor in, 10–12, 95, 158–59; Lincoln's friends in, 37–39, 242

Oregon Question, 6, 9

Oregon Statesman, 181, 182, 184

Oregon territory, 9–10, 95, 158, 159

Otero, Miguel A., 47–48, 125–26, 137–38, 139–40, 144

Over the Earth I Come: The Great Sioux Uprising of 1862 (Schultz, 1992), 240

Owen, Robert Dale, 74

Pacific Coast, 162–63, 166

Pacific Railroad Act (1862), 25–26, 122, 242

"Pacific Republic," 45–46, 52, 138

Paludan, Philip Shaw, 50, 135, 238

"Pardon and Amnesty Proclamation," 32

Partch, Adam Scofield, v, xi

patronage, 33–49, 121–31, 134–50, 238; Lincoln's role in, 33–49, 121–31, 134–50, 242. *See also names of individual territories and states*

"People's Contest, A": The Union and the Civil War, 1861–1865 (Paludan, 1988), 238

Peoria speech, 14

"Perpetuation of Our Political Institutions, The," 92

Pickering, William, 40, 130, 167

Pierce, Franklin, 170

Poe, A. M., 182

Polk, James K., 7–9, 49, 77, 93

polygamy, 104, 129, 192–94

Pomeroy, Earl S., x, 113–20, 238, 251

Pomeroy, Samuel C., 117, 125, 146, 220

Pope, John, 30–31, 54, 214–16

popular sovereignty, 15, 97–98, 160; Stephen A. Douglas's support for, 15, 97–98; Lincoln's criticism of, 97–102, 105–6; and Mormons, 192–94

Portland *Oregonian*, 38

Pratt, Parley, 194, 199

Prelude to Greatness (Fehrenbacher, 1962), 237

Presidency of Abraham Lincoln, The (Paludan, 1994), 238
President Lincoln (Miller, 2008), 240
Proclamation of Amnesty and Reconstruction, 55

racism, 203–4; Lincoln's attitudes about, 106, 203–4
Radical Republicans, 35–37, 47, 52, 55–57, 121–31, 236; and New Mexico, 136, 143–46
railroads, 24–26, 125. *See also* Pacific Railroad Act (1862)
"Railsplitter," 4, 22
Ramsey, Alexander 29, 210, 214–19, 220, 227
Randall, James G., 135, 236
Reconstruction, 54–57; Lincoln's plans for, 54–57
Reconstruction: America's Unfinished Revolution 1863–1877 (Foner, 1988), 241
Reed, James, 130
Rencher, Abraham, 141
Republican Party, 4–5, 21–23; divisions in 35–37, 52, 121–22; in California, 45–46; in Oregon, 160; in Washington Territory, 154–55, 161–63, 165; in West, 34, 35–37, 37–39, 50, 116; Lincoln's role in, 16, 96–97
Richardson, Heather Cox, 238, 241
Riddle, Donald W., 237
Rio Grande, 74, 80
"Robber Barons," 29
Rodrigue, Sylvia Frank, xi
Ross, John, 30, 31–32, 213–14

Salt Lake City, 202
Sandburg, Carl, 116, 235
Sand Creek Massacre (1864), 33, 43, 224
Sangamo Journal, 5, 7, 82, 176–77
Santa Fe, New Mexico, 142, 148
Saunders, Alvin, 124
Schmidt, Louis B., 237
Schultz, Duane, 240
Schweikart, Larry, x, 189–209, 251
Second Confiscation Act, 50–51
secretaries, 104. *See also* territorial secretaries

Seward, William H., 90, 127, 130, 136, 154–55
Shutes, Milton H., 235, 236
Sibley, Henry Hastings, 215, 217, 220
Sibley, Henry Hopkins, 54, 126, 148
Simonton, James W., 46
Sioux uprising (1862), 30–31, 54, 210, 214–19, 242
slave code, in New Mexico, 125, 139, 141
slavery, 7, 12, 49–51; in West, 49–51; Lincoln's opposition to, 49–51, 97–99, 108. *See also* abolition and abolitionists
Smith, Caleb Blood, 32, 122, 212, 214–15, 220, 222; in Indiana, 72, 80
Smith, Calvin, 238
Smith, Henry Nash, 3
Smith, Joseph, 41, 190–92, 199–201
Smith, Victor, 130, 167–68, 183, 184, 186
South, 22–23, 202
Speed, Joshua, 15–16, 101, 103
"Spot Resolutions," 8–9, 94
Springfield, Illinois, 123, 175–78, 180
Stanton, Edwin M., 212
Starr, John W., 236
Steck, Michael, 144
Steele, Frederick, 55
Stenhouse, T. B. H., 42, 197–98
Stephen A. Douglas (Johannsen, 1973), 237
Stevens, Isaac I., 153–54
Stevens, Thaddeus, 121, 130
Stewart, William M., 1
Stone, Dan, 93
Striner, Richard, 240–41
Stuart, John Todd, 11, 82
Sumner, Charles, 144, 146
Szasz, Ferenc M., xi

Taney, Roger, 103
Tarbell, Ida, 234–35
Tarshis, Rebecca, 240
Taylor, Zachary, 10, 12, 69, 74, 79, 85, 94. 95; Lincoln's reactions to, 157–58
"Team of Rivals" (Goodwin), 22
Tegeder, Vincent G., x, 121–33, 135, 251
"10 percent plan," 55
territorial governors, 135. *See also* names of individual appointees

territorial judges, 127–28, 135, 196

territorial secretaries, 135. *See also names of individual appointees*

Territories of the United States, 1861–1890, The (Earl S. Pomeroy, 1947), 238

Test, Charles, 72

Texas, annexation of, 7–8, 76–77

Texas and Texans, 6, 48, 49, 53, 157, 242; and New Mexico, 142, 148–49

Thirteenth Amendment, 45, 51, 113, 115–16, 125, 127

Thirtieth Congress, 70, 81, 85

Thompson, Richard W., 72–74, 80, 84–85

Tocqueville, Alexis de, 189, 204 n.1

Todd, John Blair Smith, 41, 123

transcontinental railroad, 24, 25, 26. *See also* Pacific Railroad Act (1862)

trans-Mississippi American West, x, 20–21, 242; map of , xiv. *See also* Lincoln, Abraham, attitudes toward the West; *names of individual states, territories, and regions*

"Tribe of Abraham, The," 39, 159, 165, 167

"Tribe of Abraham, The: Lincoln and the Washington Territory" (Johannsen), 153–73

Trumbull, Lyman, 16, 105

Turner, Frederick Jackson, 91–92, 234, 236

Turney, Leander, 164, 167

Twitchell, Ralph Emerson, 140

Union Pacific Railroad, 25, 122, 124

U. S. House of Representatives, 83, 135; Lincoln's role in, 8–11, 69, 71–72, 83–85, 86–87

U. S. Senate, 140, 181

U. S. Supreme Court, 106. See also *Dred Scott* decision

Usher, John P., 122, 216, 218, 220

Utah, 41–42, 103–4, 128–30; Lincoln's appointees in, 42, 128–30; Lincoln's conflict with Mormons in, 42, 129–30, 189, 194–97, 202–4

Vicksburg, battle of, 53

Virgin Land: The American West as Symbol and Myth (Smith, 1950), 3

Wade, Benjamin, 121, 124, 127, 136

Wade-Davis Bill, 57

Waite, Charles, 128, 129, 196

Wallace, William Henson, 30, 130, 136, 163–64, 166–67; in Idaho 40–41, 49

Washington, George, 49

Washington Territory, 39–40, 130–31, 153–73; Lincoln's political appointees in, 39–40, 164–71; political clashes in, 39–40, 163–71

Watts, John S., 47–48, 143–44, 146, 242

Webster, Daniel, 84

Weer, William, 213

West, x, 3, 50. *See also* Lincoln, Abraham, attitudes toward the West; trans-Mississippi American West

West Coast, 1, 2, 25, 26, 183

"Western States in the Civil War, The" (Fischer, 1975), 238

"Western Territories in the Civil War, The" (Fischer, 1977), 238

West from Appomattox: The Reconstruction of America after the Civil War (Richardson, 2007), 241

"Whig in the White House," 24–25

Whig Party, 5–7, 9, 16; in Illinois, 5–7, 9, 13; in Indiana, 72–75; in West, 77, 80, 81, 83–84, 91–93

Whipple, Henry Benjamin, 31, 32, 216, 221–23, 225

Wilmot, David, 9, 94

Wilmot Proviso, ix, 2, 9, 23,103, 242. *See also under* Lincoln, Abraham

Winnebago Indians, 216, 218

Wisconsin, 27, 167

With Charity for All: Lincoln and the Restoration of the Union (Harris, 1997), 241

Young, Brigham, 42, 102–3, 192, 200; Lincoln's conflicts with, 42, 194–95, 197–98

Zall, Paul M., x, xi, 38, 174–88, 242, 25

Richard W. Etulain is a professor emeritus of history at the University of New Mexico. A specialist in the history and literature of the American West, he has authored or edited more than forty-five books on U.S., and particularly western U.S., culture. His books include *Conversations with Wallace Stegner on Western History and Literature* (1983, 1996), *The American West: A Twentieth-Century History* (coauthored with Michael P. Malone, 1989, 2007), *Re-imagining the Modern American West: A Century of Fiction, History, and Art* (1996), and *Beyond the Missouri: The Story of the American West* (2006). His writings have won several awards, and he has served as president of both the Western Literature and Western History Associations.